HYMNS AND THE CHRISTIAN "MYTH"

HYMNS
and the
CHRISTIAN
"MYTH"

LIONEL ADEY

University of British Columbia Press
Vancouver
1986

HYMNS AND THE CHRISTIAN "MYTH"

© The University of British Columbia Press 1986

This book has been published with the help of a grant from the Canadian Federation for the Humanities, using funds provided by the Social Sciences and Humanities Research Council of Canada.

Canadian Cataloguing in Publication Data

Adey, Lionel.
    Hymns and the Christian "myth"

    Bibliography: p. 239
    Includes index.

    1. Hymns — History and criticism.
2. Myth in the Bible. I. Title.
BV310.A34 1986   264'.2   C86-091263-9

INTERNATIONAL STANDARD BOOK NUMBER 0-7748-0257-X
Printed in Canada

To my wife

CONTENTS

PREFACE

> . . . those first affections
> Those shadowy recollections,
> Which, be they what they may,
> Are yet the fountain light of all our day,
> Are yet a master light of all our seeing.
>
> Wordsworth, ODE: INTIMATIONS OF IMMORTALITY

Among my first recollections of life in the English Black Country are the Victoriana at my grandparents' former public house: aspidistras in Grandma's window, her horsehair sofa, candleholders on her piano, Millais's picture, *Bubbles,* on her wall, and beneath it mahogany furniture. Past the front window came hospital carnivals and Sunday school anniversary parades of complacent girls in white and sniggering boys in grey. One image that remains unaccountably permanent is Great-Aunt Tilly's black dress, so long and voluminous that to my infant eyes her legs appeared to fold in sections, in the manner of an accordion, as she sat down, swept the cat from her lap (for she could not abide cats), and recalled in tones of wistful reprehension the long defunct family prayers and Sunday evening performances of what she described as "beautiful 'ymns."

My mother would often recollect from her childhood a curious Sunday evening observance at the pub, then owned by my grandfather's elder brother. After Evensong the gentlemen choristers would process from the parish church to the "Duke of Wellington," seat themselves around the specially polished mahogany table in His Grace's front parlour, lay down their top-hats, and, for the edification of the erring sheep in the public bar, sing a hymn. They would then drink a half-pint of ale provided by my pious great-uncle in return for this assurance of divine mercy upon publicans and sinners. Their mission and nocturnal office concluded, the ministers of grace would rise, resume their top-hats, and recess from that secular outpost of Holy Church into this world's dark night.

Whereas Great-Aunt Tilly's family prayed and sang hymns at home during the 1870's, it is safe to assume that during the 1890's many of the customers in the "Duke of Wellington" prayed only to the barman, that to request and hear a hymn was their only form of Sunday observance.

Few if any Black Country working people had heard of Matthew Arnold, let alone read his prophecy in 1880 that "More and more mankind will discover that we have to turn to poetry to interpret life for us . . . console us . . . sustain us," that "most of what now passes with us for religion and philosophy will be replaced by poetry."[1]Arnold took little account of folk songs, so whether he would have agreed that the hymn-singing ritual confirmed his forecast seems doubtful. Once you admit that some folk songs are poems, you have but to marry to the hymn the Victorian love ballad, beget of them that heavenly half-breed or earthly miscegenate the sacred song, ponder the implications of a Sunday census in 1851 that discovered at best ten million adults in church out of eighteen million,[2] and you might convict Arnold of forecasting after the event.

The cutting loose of hymns from their liturgical moorings to become independent expressions of mass emotion or sources of musical entertainment shares with many similar processes the ill-sounding name "secularization." A further recollection may clarify its meaning. Each Remembrance Day during the 1930's, the boys of my and no doubt other grammar schools lined up in the school hall before the gilded lists of Old Boys killed in the First World War, sang "For all the saints," then stood in silence between the Last Post and Reveille, sounded by a trumpeter from the school cadet corps. No boy ever remarked in my hearing that junior officers and soldiers did not *ipso facto* become Christian martyrs by dying in battle or that Bishop How had composed the hymn for a Christian feast day of which few boys had heard. The solemn ritual and Vaughan Williams's splendid tune, admiration and pity for our "elder brethren," and sometimes parental reminiscences of dead or maimed relatives compelled respectful assent to this diversion of religious imagery and emotion to a secular object. For that day, at least, "the supreme sacrifice" had meant "death in battle" rather than "Crucifixion," and the victims were young men stumbling through the mud of "Passion-dale" rather than the Figure on the Cross.

This transference of religious emotion and ritual was but one form of a secularization that has continued in increasing measure for two centuries or more. Many who have described its various facets in relation to the arts, literature, and learning in the West, and the majority of social or economic historians, think secularization a great benefit. In this and a subsequent book, *Class and Idol in the English Hymn,* I shall consider how secular concerns have intruded upon the sacred domain of hymnody, how words and images in those Christian folk songs we call "hymns" have changed their meaning according to the circumstances and education of those who have sung them, and what impressions of the Christian religion they have imparted to those who have used them as the principal expression of devotion. The Two books were conceived as one, under the title *Myth, Class, and Idol in the English Hymn,* until the introductory study of early and medieval hymns outgrew its proposed dimensions.

If any hymns perverted Christian teaching and devotion, what was it they perverted? The answer to this deceptively simple question demands a somewhat lengthy search for the origins of modern religious attitudes in ancient and medieval hymnody. To many verses quoted from Latin hymns I supply translations intended solely to give the literal meaning.

The conclusions will, I hope, provoke further reflection upon the present and future direction of what our ancestors called "Christendom," that civilization enfolding multitudes who now live without God and expect no future beyond the crematorium.

This book is not a history of hymnody. Indeed, it owes much to earlier historians like Louis F. Benson, whose *English Hymn: Its Development and Use* (1915, 1962) remains unrivalled, and John Julian, whose *Dictionary of Hymnology* (1892, 1907, 1957, 1985) remains indispensable. No less does it owe to the *English-Speaking Hymnal Guide, Panorama of Christian Hymnody* (1979), and earlier works of Erik Routley, the true successor of Benson and Julian. Its other main sources were some volumes of the *Analecta Hymnica Medii Aevi*. Its aim, finally, is not to explain the circumstances under which hymns were written, the subject of numerous books, but what they must have conveyed within the contexts in which they were sung. To my knowledge, no one has attempted such explanation before. Because of the immense number of hymns composed since the Reformation, those originating in Germany, the United States, and other countries, and those written during the present revival of hymnography can only be incidentally considered, my inferences being drawn essentially from medieval Latin or standard English hymns. While the following reflections will at times lend support to each of the value systems — Marxist, Freudian, Christian — within which historians and critics have considered hymns, they are intended to interest any open-minded student not only of religion but of related disciplines: literature, psychology, history, or sociology. The past and future direction of Christianity in English-speaking countries and the effects upon the individual or collective psyche of Christian folk poems ceaselessly reiterated, especially in childhood, are matters too important to be confined to in-groups or fenced into a corner labelled "theology." They will, I hope, repay the attention of all who have not arrived at unchangeable certainties concerning the human condition, and even more, perhaps, of those who have.

ACKNOWLEDGEMENTS

To the Victorian Studies Association of Western Canada for my first opportunity to pursue this topic; to the Hymn Society of Great Britain and Ireland and the Northwest Conference on Christianity and Literature for further chances to develop it in conference papers.

To the late Dr. Erik Routley, to whose scholarship this and every modern hymnologist is indebted, for advice on sources and assistance in securing grants; also to the late George Whalley and the happily surviving George Tennyson for the latter service.

To the University of Victoria for funding short-term research and providing typing and word-processing services carried out with inexhaustible patience by Tracy Czop, Colleen Donnelly and Sue Meisler, and for funding the word-count by Sharon Parker recorded in the Appendix.

To the Social Sciences and Humanities Research Council of Canada for funding research in Britain, the indispensable services of my research assistants John Duder and Maria Abbott, and a long leave for the writing of this book and its sequel.

To the librarians of University of Victoria, University of British Columbia and University of Washington, Vancouver School of Theology, Princeton Seminary, the British Library, the Evangelical Library, New College, Edinburgh, St. Cross College, Oxford, Westminster College, Cambridge and Dr. William's Library.

To my departmental colleague Patrick Grant for first reading the manuscript and contributing to the opening chapter; to Gerald Hobbs and Elizabeth Hannon, both of Vancouver School of Theology, for advice on otherwise undetected biblical allusions in the manuscript and on recent biblical scholarship; to James Butrica, John Fitch, Herbert Huxley, and Michael Hadley, all of University of Victoria, for reading and advising on my translations from Latin and German texts; to Gabriele Winkler, of St. John's University for first suggesting the *Odes of Solomon* and to J.H. Charlesworth, then of Duke University, for advice and permission to quote from his translation. To Roger Beehler, Bryan Gooch, Gordon Kinder, Henry Summerfield, David Thatcher and countless other colleagues and friends consulted on details.

To Dr. J.W. Grant for permisssion to quote from his translations of two Latin hymns. To Maria Abbott for permission to quote her literal translations of German hymns adapted by John Wesley; Curtis, Brown, Ltd. and Oxford University Press for permission to quote from C.L. Lewis's "Summae" and from *Early English Carols*. Sincere apologies are offered to copyright-holders who could not be contacted or whose rights I may inadvertently have infringed.

To Jean Wilson, who made invaluable suggestions and to Jane Fredeman, Senior Editor of University of British Columbia Press, for much encouragement and wise advice. Finally, to Dennis Clarke, who read the galley proofs.

FOREST GREEN. (D.C.M. Words irreg.)

In moderate time ♩ = 60.

English Traditional Melody.

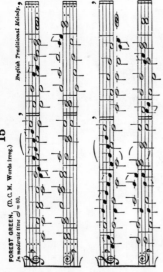

Suitable till Candlemas.

O LITTLE town of Bethlehem,
How still we see thee lie!
Above thy deep and dreamless sleep
The silent stars go by.
Yet in thy dark streets shineth
The everlasting light;
The hopes and fears of all the years
Are met in thee to-night.

2 O morning stars, together
Proclaim the holy birth,
And praises sing to God the King,
And peace to men on earth;
For Christ is born of Mary,
And gathered all above,
While mortals sleep, the angels keep
Their watch of wondering love.

3 How silently, how silently,
The wondrous gift is given!
So God imparts to human hearts
The blessings of his heaven.
No ear may hear his coming;
But in this world of sin,
Where meek souls will receive him, [still
The dear Christ enters in.

4 Where children pure and happy
Pray to the blessed Child,
Where misery cries out to thee,
Son of the mother mild;
Where charity stands watching
And faith holds wide the door,
The dark night wakes, the glory breaks,
And Christmas comes once more.

By. Phillips Brooks, 1835–93.

Org.

CHRISTMAS EVE

5. O holy Child of Bethlehem,
Descend to us, we pray;
Cast out our sin, and enter in,
Be born in us to-day.
We hear the Christmas Angels
The great glad tidings tell:
O come to us, abide with us,
Our Lord Emmanuel.

A - men.

Easter.

Hymn 125.

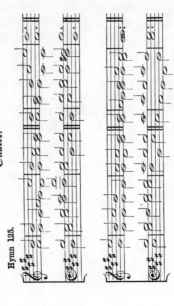

"O death, where is thy sting? O grave, where is thy victory?"

YE choirs of new Jerusalem,
Your sweetest notes employ,
The Paschal victory to hymn
In strains of holy joy.

For Judah's Lion bursts His chains,
Crushing the serpent's head;
And cries aloud through death's domains
To wake the imprisoned dead.

Devouring depths of hell their prey
At His command restore;
His ransomed hosts pursue their way
Where Jesus goes before.

mf To Him in one communion bow
All saints in earth and heaven.

ff Triumphant in His glory now
To Him all power is given;

While we, His soldiers, praise our King,
dim His mercy we implore,
cr Within His palace bright to bring
And keep us evermore.

f All glory to the FATHER be,
All glory to the SON,
All glory, HOLY GHOST, to Thee,
While endless ages run.

Al - le - lu - ia! A - men.

THE CHRISTIAN YEAR

122

arr. J. H. A.

Mode iii.

A - men.

OFFICE HYMN. *Saturday evenings:*
i.e. 1st E. of Sundays after Easter.

Chorus novae Jerusalem.

St. Fulbert of Chartres, c. 1000.
Tr. J. M. Neale.

YE choirs of new Jerusalem,
  To sweet new strains attune your theme;
The while we keep, from care released,
  With sober joy our Paschal feast:

EASTERTIDE

122 (MODERN TUNE)

JOHN LAW.

MONTESANO. (L.M.)
In moderate time ♩ = 108.

A - men.

NOTE.—*This hymn may also be sung to* BROCKHAM (*No. 220*).

2 When Christ, unconquer'd Lion, first
    The dragon's chains by rising burst:
  And while with living voice he cries,
    The dead of other ages rise.

3 Engorged in former years, their prey
    Must death and hell restore to-day:
  And many a captive soul, set free,
    With Jesus leaves captivity.

4 Right gloriously he triumphs now,
    Worthy to whom should all things bow;
  And joining heaven and earth again,
    Links in one commonweal the twain.

5 And we, as these his deeds we sing,
    His suppliant soldiers, pray our King,
  That in his palace, bright and vast,
    We may keep watch and ward at last.

6. Long as unending ages run,
    To God the Father, laud be done:
  To God the Son, our equal praise,
    And God the Holy Ghost, we raise. **Amen.**

139

ST. FULBERT. (C. M.)
Moderately slow ♩ = 66.

H. J. Gauntlett, 1805-76.

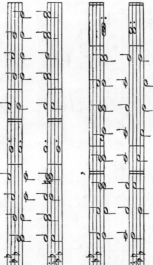

Al - le - lu - ya! A - men.

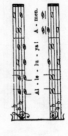

Chorus novae Jerusalem.

YE choirs of new Jerusalem,
Your sweetest notes employ,
The Paschal victory to hymn
In strains of holy joy.

2 How Judah's Lion burst his chains,
And crushed the serpent's head;
And brought with him, from death's domains,
The long-imprisoned dead.

St. Fulbert of Chartres, c. 1000.
Tr. R. Campbell.

3 From hell's devouring jaws the prey
Alone our Leader bore;
His ransomed hosts pursue their way
Where he hath gone before.

4 Triumphant in his glory now
His sceptre ruleth all,
Earth, heaven, and hell before him bow,
And at his footstool fall.

5 While joyful thus his praise we sing,
His mercy we implore,
Into his palace bright to bring
And keep us evermore.

6. All glory to the Father be,
All glory to the Son,
All glory, Holy Ghost, to thee,
While endless ages run. Alleluya! Amen.

The following are also suitable:

93 The God of love my Shepherd is.
319 Lord, enthroned in heavenly splendour.
380 Come, ye faithful, raise the anthem.
451 O praise our great and gracious Lord.
490 The King of love my Shepherd is.
491 The Lord my pasture shall prepare.
494 The strain upraise of joy and praise.
534 Praise the Lord of heaven.
535 Praise the Lord! ye heavens, adore him.
536 Praise to the Lord.

The Hymn: Beginnings and Forms

1

WHAT HYMNS ARE

"Tell me, Joxer, what is the stars?"
Sean O'Casey, JUNO AND THE PAYCOCK

A distinguished listener to the conference paper for which my researches began confessed to having taken in little of its argument because of the flood of memories brought back by the hymn titles. The frequency of phrases unsung for generations — "rich man in his castle," "pearly gates," and the like — in the conversation of quite areligious people shows how deeply even obsolete hymn verses lie embedded in the collective unconscious. Such allusions can well up in defiance of logic. In a train, a newly widowed young woman disclaimed all religious belief while consoling herself with the reflection that life is "portioned out" for us.[1] Perhaps this quotation from a defunct Sunday school hymn showed more faith than she realized.

While the religious historian L.E. Elliott-Binns avows that "hymn singers take but little notice of the words they are using,"[2] some Victorian divines thought their congregations more than subliminally affected. R.W. Dale, introducing his hymnal for his vast congregations at Carr's Lane, Birmingham, said: "Let me write the hymns and I care not who writes the theology." John Mason Neale, whose translations brought into use so many Latin and Greek hymns, complained that "The hymn-book has almost usurped the place of the Bible," and Archbishop Benson that "The habit of hymn-singing has weakened the sense of truth."[3] (For such reasons, the Orthodox and Reformed churches forbade the singing of non-scriptural verse.) Even recently, David Martin, instancing the use of "Jerusalem" and "Abide with me," has called the hymn "the most central item in the religion of Britain," and in 1951 Erik Routley compiled a list of some fifty "national anthems" from services for private and public occasions.[4] More recently, Jonathan

Gathorne-Hardy attributed the tribal bond between alumni of different boarding schools to a common core of "simple, stirring" Anglican hymns.[5]

It is not too much to claim that in England, between the mid-eighteenth century and the rise of the popular press in the late nineteenth, the child or semi-literate adult formed both his explicit convictions and to a large extent his inner world from the the Bible and the hymn-book. People who had attended village schools or Primitive Methodist chapels formed impressions of the Christian faith and the Christian life radically at variance with those their contemporaries had formed at "public" schools or fashionable churches.

It is easy enough to see how such epithets as "subjective" and "objective," "explicit" and "implicit," "perennial" and "historically-conditioned" could apply to a study of the influence of hymns upon Anglophone cultures. Such epithets, with a new one, "reflexive," shortly to be introduced, also indicate the complexity of the question. The history of hymns, after all, is as long as that of Christianity itself, and as deeply rooted in it as it is in us. So, although my main focus in this book will be the English hymn of the eighteenth and nineteenth centuries, I must first indicate something of its complex interplay of elements by pinning some flags upon the chart of the Christian hymn's 2,000-year voyage.

THEIR "MYTH"

What St. Paul named as "psalms, hymns and spiritual songs" (Ephesians 5.19) together transmitted a common belief and ethic not yet separated out as "Christian." In time, Christian poets related critical episodes of man's spiritual history from his Creation and Fall to his Redemption and Last Judgment. What Northrop Frye calls the Mythos, or sacred story, I shall, like Martha England, call the "Myth."[6] This implies no judgment concerning the historical truth of those incidents. Readers who believe them a projection of the human psyche would doubtless agree with Frye that the Bible supplies the only evidence we have that the Exodus took place or that Jesus ever existed.[7] Others would agree with C.S. Lewis in his essay "Myth Became Fact":

> The old myth of the Dying God, without ceasing to be myth, comes down from the heavens of legend and imagination to the earth of history. It *happens* — at a particular time and place, followed by . . . historical consequences. We pass from a Balder or Osiris, dying nobody knows when or where, to a historical Person crucified under Pontius Pilate.[8]

In either case, only the portion concerning the life and death of Christ and the subsequent growth of the Church is capable of historical proof or disproof. While the Old Testament records many historical events, the implied meaning of these, the spiritual and moral evolution of the chosen people, is a matter of interpretation. Likewise, the Christian perception of Christ as the Messiah fulfilling all prophecies conditions the record and to a large extent the teaching of the Gospels, Acts, Epistles, and Revelation. The Myth that supplies the subject-matter of far more hymns than does the teaching or natural life of Jesus consists of: the Fall of the rebel Angels, the Creation, and the Fall of Man; the Messiah's Advent, Incarnation, Passion, Harrowing of Hell, Resurrection, Ascension, and sending of the Holy Spirit; and His Second Coming, Judgment, and sentence of human beings to Hell or Heaven.

Awesome as may be the task of tracing an evolution of the Christian Myth in the hymnody of two millenia (and however imperfectly performed here), it will give deeper meaning to my account in a subsequent volume of class-conditioning and, alas, idolatry in the English hymn. Of necessity, the present book must be confined to those elements of the Myth common to all major English denominations, to the exclusion of hymns on the Blessed Virgin, purgatory, baptism, and other subjects of special interest to particular churches. These elements have been defined briefly as God (Father, Son, Holy Spirit) and the human expectation of Four Last Things (Death, Judgment, Hell, or Heaven). With rare exceptions, the following explorations must be confined to hymns, originally in Latin or English, that were anthologized before the Second World War, any attempt to describe or evaluate the innumerable hymns composed during the past two decades being premature.

Among the finest complete retellings is Prudentius' "Corde natus ex Parentis,"[9] never intended as a hymn but still sung at Christmas to a haunting plainsong melody. Among the greatest accounts of any single event is the "Vexilla regis" of Venantius Fortunatus, discussed in a later chapter on Passion hymns. From this processional it is only a step to medieval iconography, the Stations of the Cross, and religious drama.

After the Council of Laodicea (A.D. 361), because the attractive hymns of the Arians threatened to swamp those of the orthodox, nearly all hymns concluded with a trinitarian[10] formula and objectively recounted the Myth in whole or in part or else offered praise appropriate to their liturgical occasions. During the ensuing five centuries, systems of objective hymnody were evolved to fit the Benedictine daily offices or, in the Byzantine Empire, to celebrate triumphal events of the Old and New Testaments.[11]

Such objective hymns as the "Vexilla regis" focused entirely upon the divine Victim. Where present at all, the human race appeared collectively. Down the ages, however, the human viewpoint, and analogies drawn from human society, became more evident in even the most austere liturgical hymns.

THEIR FUNCTIONS

The medieval Church taught the Myth and instilled devotion in the common man through its visual and aural media — icons, architectural motifs, ritual, drama, and vernacular homilies — since none of these required him to read his own tongue, let alone Latin. As Ruth Messenger shows, the Latin office hymns sung as appropriate during the liturgical year not only narrated the Myth and commemorated the saints, but also trained a spiritual élite in the cardinal and theological virtues.[12] By this double standard of education, the Church provided an apostolic conditioning for monks and nuns who had renounced the world and for the laity a simplified ethical training or none at all, depending on rank and education. This distinguished the educated from the uneducated even more sharply than was the case in the eighteenth century, when the Wesleys produced what are by common consent some of the finest English hymns.

For the hymnody of the Evangelical revival, John Wesley's Preface to his *Collection of Hymns for People Called Methodists* (1780) is a manifesto as fundamental as the instructions of St. Paul for that of the early Christians. To allude briefly to a document later expounded in detail, Wesley declared his intent to perform through the hymnal the devotional and to some extent the teaching function for which the medieval Church had employed its battery of aids listed above.[13] (His other teaching instrument, needless to say, was the Methodist class meeting.) Intending his *Collection* for use by the poverty-stricken majority of Methodists, Wesley arranged its items according to the experience of guilt, conversion, and acceptance of salvation rather than the liturgical calendar in the *Book of Common Prayer*. Its hymns, therefore, are in principle (though often not in practice) subjective, rather than objective.

Just where Wesley's emphasis upon subjective experience might lead can be seen from the preface to *Hymns of Praise and Prayer* (1874), compiled by the great Unitarian divine James Martineau, who takes a giant step towards secularization. Criticizing the hymnals of the Oxford Movement for having revived the "Christian mythology" evident in the Creeds, he complains that these "objective and mythological elements" which had "crept into the faith of Christendom" frustrated "simple and natural piety" that would "fly to the immediate communion with God" but was "flung back on some superfluous mediation of intercession or sacrament." Claiming that supernatural incidents, if unhistorical, could "retain their significance for the inward life," Martineau expresses a view remarkably like that of Matthew Arnold discussed above: "More and more of the modern Christian hymns do but touch for a moment the ground of historical incident and pass on at once to some spiritual counterpart which is the real theme of the poet's inspiration." This he calls "the natural method of evolving the future from the past."

Between the fourth and the nineteenth centuries, then, hymnody had evolved from objective representation of God's creative and redemptive action, through human response and inward realization, to ideas and feelings of mid-Victorians, prompted by mythical or historical incidents long ago and far away. On Martineau's premise, Christianity must follow the Graeco-Roman myths into the poet's compost box. If his contention (too radical for later Unitarian compilers)[14] has any validity, Victorian and later hymnists were bound to treat secular themes in Christian guise. Until after the First World War, this was precisely what many of them did. Martineau was, as he said, describing a process already under way.

Martineau condemns the ancient and medieval hymns so ably translated during the Oxford Movement and Catholic revival as irrelevant to the inner lives of nineteenth-century worshippers. If, as Arnold alleged, Christianity "has materialized itself in the fact, and now the fact is failing it," the fact also fails the translator.[15] Although these objective hymns continue to please many worshippers who find hymns of the Evangelical revivals self-centred and guilt-haunted, they appeal primarily to the educated. The barely literate seem to prefer subjective devotional hymns, however "bloody" or sentimental. To realize this is to realize also that until long after the Wesleys, the barriers of education and of class were one and the same. Those whose parents could afford to send them to school and perhaps university or dissenting academy usually worshipped in Anglican or in Congregational churches or else in Presbyterian conventicles that increasingly became Unitarian during the eighteenth century. The poor and ill-educated mostly attended Methodist meetings, then during the nineteenth century Primitive Methodist or Baptist "tin tabernacles." Because the classes practised radically different forms of Christian piety and ethics, they were prone to different heresies and idolatries. The essence of upper class religion lay in its suitability for order-givers, who could choose their paths in life; that of lower class religion in its suitability for order-receivers, who took what work they could find, preferably close to home. A major theme of Victorian novels and hymns alike is the search of the disinherited for "home" in this world or the next.[16]

The complexities of the English class structure, the shifts of religious alignment during the nineteenth century, and the difficulties of categorizing hymn-book religion must await discussion in the sequel to this book.[17] Allowing for all kinds of exceptions and reservations there specified, it remains true that hymnals encouraged order-givers to undertake personal, social, and national responsibility, with Heaven as reward for a life of service, while those used by order-receivers laid emphasis upon domestic love and the life hereafter, work being "toil" intrinsically meaningless that they must endure during their voyage through the "wilderness" or "tempestuous sea" of this life.

THEIR KINDS

From the beginning, Christian hymnody fulfilled each of its present functions — praise, adoration, recital of the Myth, and celebration of the foundation and worship of the Church. While the descent of the Holy Spirit upon the demoralized disciples, its mighty wind and tongues of flame, their glossolalia and preaching of Christ Crucified and Risen, certainly form part of the Myth, hymns on worship and the worshipping community form an additional category, that I will call "reflexive."

For example, the oldest Christian hymn widely known today /Φῶς ἱλαρόν, "Phos Hilaron" ("Hail gladdening light") is the evening hymn sung about the worship offered as candles were lit at sunset.

> Now we are come to the sun's hour of rest,
> The lights of evening round us shine,
> We hymn the Father, Son and Holy Spirit divine.

That Keble's translation should have so many recent rivals seems best explained in terms of the impulse to recover the fundamentals of Christian worship that has been responsible for the many new liturgies.[18] The oldest surviving hymnbook, the first-century *Odes of Solomon,* includes reflexive hymns, while earlier, the 150th Psalm is at least as much about the act of worship as the God to be acclaimed.

Upon reading any important denominational hymnal, we might naturally equate the ruling class, or "Learned," tradition with objective hymns of praise and the lower class, or "Popular," tradition with subjective hymns of devotion, assuming from their usual dates that the former gave place to the latter. Even the ensuing bird's-eye survey of early Christian and medieval hymns will show these assumptions to be at best half-truths. They founder at once, for example, upon "Rock of Ages," that most egocentric of lyrics, which was for nearly two centuries beloved by Protestants of all classes. While St. Augustine's famous definition of hymns as "singing in praise of God"[19] would fit most of the Psalms, not a few voice typically Hebraic longings and experiences through a representative "I." In modern times, paraphrases of or hymns based on psalms have expressed not only praise, as in "O worship the King," but personal devotion, as in "As pants the hart for cooling streams" or "The King of love my Shepherd is."

While lower class believers predictably preferred subjective hymns soused in blood and tears to the more restrained objective hymns, "Rock of Ages" and "Jesu, Lover of my soul" appeared in almost every major hymnal and ranked high in every survey of taste, regardless of social class.[20] Moreover, the distinction that William James drew in his *Varieties of Religious Experience* (1902) between "healthy-minded" and "morbid" religion does not suffice to identify the first with objective hymns and the second with subjective.[21] Scrupulously as James states the case for the guilt, fear, or dependence characteristic of "morbid" religion, we tend even in our dark age to prefer the optimism and extroversion of "healthy-minded" religion. Yet it by no means follows that all subjective lyrics are morbid, while some reflexive ones appeal to those unhealthily obsessed with ecclesiastical ritual. The majority of objective texts, certainly almost all the Psalms, were composed in times that few would prefer to the present. To establish valid links between the texts and their circumstances of composition or use, we need finer distinctions.

Although in my subsequent book as many as fifteen categories of hymn will be proposed, suffice it for now to suggest some as subdivisions of the objective, subjective, and reflexive kinds. When, as in Byzantium or Calvinist England, hymnographers were limited to scriptural material, they would imitate a biblical ode or paraphrase a psalm. Early Byzantine poets composed two forms of objective hymn, the song of praise and the seasonally appropriate mythic narrative. In the latter category, we should include the credal hymn, such as Mrs. C.F. Alexander's version of the Atonement, "There is a green hill far away." We owe our oldest metrical psalm of praise still in use, "All people that on earth do dwell" ("Old Hundredth"), to a Calvinist poet of the Reformation. Closely related is the providence-hymn, "God moves in a mysterious way," "We plough the fields and scatter" ("Wir pflügen"), or "Eternal Father, strong to save." The objective hymn offers praise or beseeches mercy for all (or a large segment of) mankind, or else conveys events or teachings common to all recognized believers. Where didactic, it has a firm basis in scriptural teaching, as in "Blest are the pure in heart."

Lyrics of unquestionable objectivity can nevertheless have a subjective application. Most congregations sing "Nun danket" ("Now thank we all our God") to mark an occasion celebrated by the nation, local community or family, victory, a deliverance from peril, or a wedding. "Praise, my soul, the King of Heaven," though couched in the first person, permits each singer to apply it to his own case. The same holds good for "Fight the good fight," for within the same congregation "Lay hold on life, and it shall be / Thy joy and crown eternally" might embolden one singer to take some drastic step like going abroad and another to put up with some trying situation at home.

Whether, celebratory, narrative, or didactic, the objective hymn invites all sorts and conditions of mankind to shed in adoration all worldly distinctions and concerns. At worst dull or irrelevant, it can at best instil peace, security, or joy, a sense of reposing on the bedrock of the timeless. English hymnody can supply lyrics more fervent than "Our God, our help in ages past," but none more likely to imbue the singer with unshakeable assurance.

At its best, the subjective devotional hymn contains a core of objective assertion. Thus, "Love Divine, all loves excelling," on Christ reincarnate in the hearts of believers, ends in a prayer so collective that we should probably regard the whole piece as objective. "Christ, whose glory fills the skies," however, and still more "Come down, O Love divine" have an unmistakably personal tenor. In Watts's great passion hymn "When I survey the wondrous Cross," the lines

"All the vain things that charm me most / I sacrifice them . . ." have a meaning personal to each singer, one that might require either action or renunciation.

In "Rock of Ages," despite the echoes of prophecy, psalm, and Crucifixion narrative, the nature of the dependence has changed since the day of Toplady, a Calvinist fanatic who maintains against the Arminian John Wesley that no human act of faith can assure salvation for those not chosen of God:

> Not the labours of my hands
> Can fulfil thy law's commands;
> Could my soul no respite know,
> Could my tears for ever flow,
> All for sin could not atone;
> Thou must save, and thou alone.

The soldiers who sang this in France, or the dying officer who begged his chaplain to recite "Jesu, Lover of my soul," depended upon an earlier Sacrifice to assure them of life beyond their early graves.[22] That long-exploded legend of its composition in a cave during a storm cloaks yet in a way expresses its existential meaning, that in the womb we all depended on a "fountain" of life, that we brought nothing here and can take nothing hence. Upon the fact of the Atonement all Christians agree, but a post-Freudian reader sees all too readily the birth images in the "cleft," "riven side" and "naked" figure in need of cleansing. If the author sought shelter from sin and death, the modern singer can hardly miss the connotation of hiding from life.[23]

Because Charles Wesley limited such physical images, "Jesu, Lover of my soul," that most erotic and regressive of Wesleyan hymns, has outlasted "Rock of Ages." It has even outlived "Lead, kindly Light," which appealed to perplexed Victorians by its image of light beyond darkness (a different kind of birth image) but has since lost ground, perhaps on account of its regressive lines on "angel-faces" known in childhood but "lost awhile."[24]

Most of us would probably call both "Jesus shall reign where'er the sun" and "Guide me, O thou great Jehovah" objective hymns. They display two faces of the eighteenth-century revival, beginnings of missionary expansion within this world and the worshipper's pilgrimage to the Promised Land beyond. Watts can scarcely have intended "The prisoner leaps to lose his chains" literally, yet even as a metaphor for ex-pagans liberated by missionaries from idolatry and super-stition it seems to contradict Watts's own account of the Christian community as a "garden walled around."[25] Few today would take it in the sense of purely inward liberation that is compatible with the enclosed garden figure. Although Williams adheres more closely than Watts to his biblical source, innumerable poor worshippers must nevertheless have projected their own meaning into his image of the desert crossing.

After these typological applications of biblical passages, we should notice the large and important class of hymns concerned with the final segment of the Myth, the Four Last Things (Death, Judgment, Hell, Heaven). As the ensuing account will show, these became either more subjective or else more unreal. While the majority allude to the Gospels or the Apocalypse with dread or yearning, there is a world of difference between the collective fear for mankind in "Dies irae, dies illa" and Addison's personal fear in "When rising from the bed of death, / O how shall I appear?"; between "Hora novissima" (or "Jerusalem the golden") and "There's a beautiful land where the rain never beats" or "Palms of glory, raiment bright."

The reflexive hymn most lends itself to idolatry. "The Church's one foundation" adheres closely to its Pauline source texts on the "church of God" purchased with Christ's blood and loved as His bride (Acts 20.28; Ephesians 5.25), yet, like them, it hovers on the edge of ecclesiolatry. Even texts that make an idol of the Church, being contingent on the central Myth, outlast those that deify home, school, or nation. Reflexive lyrics concerned with the act of worship, though present from the early centuries, observe the rule that the more detached they are from immediate circumstances, the longer they live. Thus Watts's "Come, let us join our cheerful songs," with its apocalyptic refrain,

> "Worthy the Lamb that died," they cry
> "To be exalted thus";
> "Worthy the Lamb," our lips reply,
> "For he was slain for us"

and the ageless "Te Deum laudamus" have outlasted Ellerton's vesper hymn for peace "Saviour again to thy dear name we raise" and one aspect of "The day thou gavest, Lord, is ended," the allusion to the empire on which the sun never set.[26] Hymns on the Bible that concern the Myth of the divine Word outlast more combative lyrics written in response to some contemporary challenge. The eighteenth-century "Father of mercies, in thy Word" and "How firm a foundation" or the Victorian "Lord, thy Word abideth" proved more durable than any counterblasts to the Darwinians or the biblical critics save "The Church's one foundation," in which only the instructed could recognize a response to Bishop Colenso's argument for the multiple authorship of the Pentateuch. What saved this lyric was its typological image of the divinely sustained Church.[27]

Exception may be taken to my use of the term "Myth" for what has always been regarded as the core of the Christian faith: that the God who created us in His image took flesh for our redemption, was crucified, rose, and will return to be our Judge. "Faith," however, also has another sense: belief in and response to the divine. It will be contended in this book that down the ages the focus of hymns has shifted from the objective events constituting the "Myth" to the human response, a development essential for the fulfilment of the commandment to love each other as ourselves, hence to the Christianization of society.

My treatment of objective and mythic hymn texts, in particular, will probably not satisfy the specialist. When tracing lines of development over so many ages I must often visit a text briefly to extract what is relevant rather than subject it to either the thematic or the stylistic analysis it deserves. The medievalist familiar with all fifty-five volumes of the *Analecta Hymnica* may wish for more, the Orthodox scholar for quotation of Byzantine texts in Greek, the Methodist for thorough discussion of "Wrestling Jacob" or even the famous epigram on God "contracted to a span, / Incomprehensibly made man." To each I can but plead my wish to treat a broader range of Christian hymnody on the Myth, for a wider readership than hymnologists normally attempt, and my consequent preference for texts likely to have been sung in their day and known in ours. When did any of us last hear "Come, O thou Traveller unknown" or "Let earth and heaven combine" sung in church? Why illustrate Wesley on the Incarnation from a profound but unsingable instance of metaphysical wit when "Love Divine" or "Hark! the herald angels sing" will make the point?

THEIR CULTURAL SIGNIFICANCE

As the central Myth of Creation, Redemption, and the Last Judgment became internalized and in part fell into disuse, idols domestic, natural, or tribal filled the vacuum. In some hymns and secular poems, faith became faith-in-a-faith, adoration of altar and service. Conversely, Arnold's "Dover Beach" and Nietzsche's *Thus Spake Zarathustra* assert the decline of belief rather than disproving any creed. As C.S. Lewis would have said, late Victorians came to "contemplate" a faith their ancestors had enjoyed."[28] Internalization of myth and more self-conscious worship by no means connote total loss, for the social gospel that had lain dormant for a millennium or more during the "ages of faith" was awakened by Dissenting hymnists and came of age in the hymnody of the Broad Church. In ensuing chapters I hope to demonstrate from Latin hymns a similar but more subtle balance between the Myth and the cult of nature, so preparing the ground for my central assertion in the subsequent book that during the nineteenth century the transcendent deity became more and more immanent within nature and society.

The family became sacred in hymnody for the lower classes, the nation, church, and empire in the hymnody favoured by the order-giving classes. In the generation before the First World War, hymnals for pupils of all save, ironically, the great public schools (most of which observed the Anglican Church calendar) inculcated an idolatrous nationalism that in this century has sacrificed countless multitudes upon heathen altars, as have communism and corporate fascism, the corresponding idolatries in the social sphere.

To a great extent, the cults of family and nation represent a reaction against the egocentric, world-denying pietism of the Evangelical era, itself intensified by the impact of the early industrial revolution and its laissez-faire economics.[29] In quieter times, Christianity, like its parent Judaism, has always consecrated the life and structure of the family and realm. Judaeo-Christian attitudes to the nation, however, illustrate a special characteristic that largely explains how hymns could supersede psalms and canticles in the affections of Protestants.

More than any other kind of poem, a hymn can change its meaning according to how it is edited and by whom it is sung. The image of the holy nation lies embedded in the historical, prophetic, and poetic books of the Old Testament. In Christian mythology, the Church replaces Israel as the people of God. But in post-Reformation hymnody, because of this flexibility of meaning, the focus shifted back towards the nation, as in one famous example, Watts's "Our God, our help in ages past." Based on a psalm and arguably composed when the sudden death of Queen Anne removed a threat of further discrimination against Dissenters, this was changed to "O God . . . " by John Wesley, who had in mind a broader community than any Calvinist "gathered church" of the elect. The community broadened further once the editors of *Hymns Ancient and Modern* (1861) added its sturdy old tune. By the late nineteenth century, it became the tribal lay of the English, sung on national occasions.[30] At the same time, however, it consoled the mourning family by its assurance of immortality. To the nation, it offered that peculiarly British sense, derived in part from the 1,000-year monarchy, that the tribe would survive present troubles. With good reason, Watts and his fellow-Dissenters professed loyalty to the Hanoverian kings and portrayed Britain as a "second Israel," favoured and chastened of the Lord. Watts intensified this intuition when he fathered forth the English hymn by Christianizing the psalms. Inevitably, Dissenters saw the armed forces of Protestant powers as God's bulwark against the "anti-Christ" of Rome. In the Victorian age of national and missionary expansion, the Calvinist sense of election readily transferred to their membership of God's most favoured nation, or, in the United States, to "God's own country."

Blatantly idolatrous lyrics rarely outlast their generation, but an insidious danger lies in the tendency for hymns to change their meaning. Though no more guilty than Roman Catholic clergy who gave tribute to Caesar by blessing the young who fought fellow-Catholics of other nations, pastors fostered German nationalism by reinterpreting Lutheran hymns.

As should by now be clear, "idolatry" here means the treatment as an end of what God has intended as a means of life: the Church, the nation, the family, or (as was once generally assumed) nature. The nature hymns that abounded in the late nineteenth century owed much to the Romantic movement, which itself tended to substitute an immanent for a transcendent deity.

The children's hymn "All things bright and beautiful" celebrates divine creation with unimpeachable orthodoxy but for its notorious verse:

> The rich man in his castle,
> The poor man at his gate,
> God made them, high or lowly,
> And ordered their estate.

According to one story, Mrs. Alexander had in mind her father's gatekeeper in Norfolk, who lived very happily in the cottage provided on a small income eked out with produce from the estate. To singers, who usually disregarded the punctuation in the third line, she sanctified the feudal hierarchy that lingered on in rural areas. By the early twentieth century, these lines had faded out with their idol, a system that had served its turn.[31]

In what sense can the English class hierarchy be deemed an idol? The royal metaphor for Christ goes back at least to his trial, and if "Lord" be scorned as a hangover from the feudal system, any English term for the Hebrew word *Yahweh* or the Latin *Dominus* must have meant something similar. Idolatry comes in when a system that reflects the economic and power structure of a given time and place is treated as divinely ordained and immutable. For long periods before the scientific and industrial revolutions, the divine will and the social structure were easily confounded. Even after the decline of belief in the imminent Second Advent, St. Paul's advice, "be subject to the higher powers," lent itself to the consecration of the *status quo*. How far a clergyman could justifiably teach his flock to remain content in their present station, ignoring the future tense in the Anglican catechism ("to which God *shall* be pleased to call me"), varied according to the case.[32] The clerical compiler of any hymnal for an eighteenth-century charity school or orphanage could only prepare children to do their duty as labourers or domestic servants. The same lyrics in a late Victorian council school hymnal, when talent and energy could reap their reward, would deserve far harsher judgment. We must distinguish between hymns or collections intended to train Christians to function in their probable circumstances, those intended to manipulate their feelings in the interests of the ruling classes, and those reflecting the sensibilities of authors or compilers.

To cite three examples of the final category, Charles Wesley's description of work as an "easy yoke" (in "Forth in thy name, O Lord, I go") is that of a university-educated clergyman steeped in his New Testament and obsessed with redemption and the future state; Ebenezer Elliott's secular hymn "When wilt thou save the people" is the product of a Christian radical absorbed in the social ferment that engendered the Chartist movement; and "Great God, what do I see and hear? / I see the end of things appear" represents the belief of its author and translator in an imminent Apocalypse during a time of social upheaval. We cannot fairly accuse Wesley of manipulative conditioning, Elliott of disbelief in Christianity, or Collyer of harbouring delusions.[33] Each represents a Christian doctrine or saying according to the sensibility of his time. Because of the great gulf fixed between the literate and the illiterate, virtually no hymnist had experienced the life of a miner, mill hand, or scullery maid. It is the compiler or editor who conditions, rather than the poet.

After tracing here the evolution of the Myth in hymns over many centuries, its changing representation of God and the human prospect, its internalization and astonishingly swift transformation concerning death and the future state during the eighteenth and nineteenth centuries, I hope in the subsequent volume to show how the Learned and Popular traditions of English hymnody bifurcated and eventually converged, to observe the idolatries that compensated for the erosion of classical Christianity, and finally to face some questions crucial for the future of Christianity and Western civilization alike. Were "man-made" as distinct from divinely inspired lyrics bound to turn into secularized expressions of mass emotion? Does the tendency of modern hymns to focus on human action or consciousness represent a loss or a gain? Was there, after all, as a Victorian divine thought, more knowledge of God in the ancient world?[34] Or does our humanistic and socially conscious religion represent an upward evolution of consciousness? Finally, and most important, what remains of Christ, indeed of God, after we have allowed for the projection in hymns of the current social and economic conditions? Are God and the Christian Myth but figments of the collective imagination that conform to the likeness of the time, baleful and threatening in the iron time after the Napoleonic Wars, benign and brotherly in the prosperous late Victorian era? Or does some transcendent reality underlie and bind together the devotion of all ages, some eternal light of the human spirit?

2

HYMNS AND THE BIBLE

*Let the word of Christ dwell in you richly in all wisdom; teaching
and admonishing one another in psalms and hymns and spiritual
songs, singing with grace in your hearts to the Lord.*
COLOSSIANS 3:16

be filled with the Spirit;
Speaking to yourselves in psalms and hymns and spiritual songs,
singing and making melody in your hearts to the Lord.
EPHESIANS 5:19

Had other New Testament injunctions been obeyed like these, the world might
be in a happier state, but what distinction St. Paul had in mind between psalms,
hymns, and spiritual songs remains in dispute. C.F.D. Moule and, more recently,
Geoffrey Wainwright, consider that he may have had none since, as Moule says,
psalmoi referred to "Christian improvisations" and "singing with melody in your
hearts" to "secret recollections of corporate praise."[1] At the other extreme, Egon
Wellesz, the historian of Byzantine hymnody, draws a precise distinction, observing that patristic authors confused the three kinds after Christians had ceased
attending Jewish services. In his view, *psalmoi, hymnoi,* and *odai pneumatikai*
had always the special sense of ecstatic songs accompanied by instruments,
which from the age of Samuel had infused singers and listeners alike with the
Spirit and so conferred the gift of prophecy.

Serious doubt has recently been cast by J.A. Smith upon Wellesz's view that
Christian psalmody originated in Jewish public observances, either in Temple or
synagogue. In Smith's view, the earliest Christians, like other Jews, sang the
Hallel (Psalms 113-18) at domestic services centred on a meal, and fathers sang
psalms to their children as part of religious instruction. Jesus and the Apostles
sang a hymn at the Last Supper, and hymns of some kind formed part of the
eucharistic services held in household assemblies until "well into the third century." About A.D. 112, however, Pliny records antiphonal chanting of verses in
honour of Christ "as if to a God" *(quasi deo).*[2]

Byzantine hymnody consisted mainly of the "Nine Odes," some of which
western Christians know as their Canticles, such as the "Magnificat." To this
day the Anglican liturgy specifies these rather than hymns, which could not be

used legally until 1822. The Canticles, with the "Gloria in excelsis" and hymn fragments in the Apocalypse, are regarded by R.P. Martin as evidence for the singing of "messianic psalms" by Jewish Christians.[3]

Hymns were, however, sung in both Temple and synagogue to melodies ranging from chants to hymn tunes requiring a different note for each syllable. The custom of freely paraphrasing rather than exactly quoting the Scriptures led to an orthodox reaction and, by the fourth century, the attempted suppression of hymns not amounting to exact quotations. Very few of the earliest hymns remained in use as such.[4]

What St. Paul called *odai pneumatikai*, or spiritual songs were, according to Wellesz, "songs of jubilation" set to a melismatic chant, such as the Alleluia. As St. Augustine said centuries later, "He who jubilates, speaks no words."[5] Such songs of joy without words were sung ages before Christ and flourish still in present-day charismatic worship.

Although Psalms and Canticles still retain their distinct liturgical functions, they have inspired many of our greatest hymns, both native and translated. So, too have the *odai pneumatikai*, for the Eastern Church employed alleluias and songs of praise, while the Latin church developed from the Alleluia the distinctive form of hymn known as the Sequence. The "Te Deum" and "Gloria in excelsis," hymns not entirely scriptural, have become part of most eucharistic liturgies.

To list the other scriptural passages that have inspired poets would require a separate book, but it is safe to adduce the following as the chief sources of modern hymns: biblical poems and songs, such as the Psalms, Song of Songs, and triumphal songs from that of Moses after the Red Sea crossing to that of Mary at the Visitation; passages understood as prophecies or announcements of the Messiah's Advent; and visions, especially the Apocalypse, or dream-revelation, concerning the Redeemer's Second Advent and final reign. Like the New Testament writers themselves, poets, preachers, and theologians practised typology, interpreting every conceivable incident, image, prophetic utterance, or devotion in the Old Testament in terms of the Christian schema of Creation, Fall, and Redemption. Inevitably, therefore, the image of the Lord as Shepherd in Psalm 23 was transferred to and used by Christ, and the Song of Moses was applied to the Resurrection by a practice endorsed in the Apocalypse.[6]

To do justice to post-Reformation psalmody would require full discussion of metrical psalters by Sternhold and Hopkins (the "Old Version," 16th century), Tate and Brady ("New Version," 1698), Genevan and French Calvinists, and Presbyterians (the "Scottish Paraphrases," 18th century). Suffice it here to mention the more obvious examples of hymns fashioned from psalms. Taking some examples in order, there are many variants of Psalms 23 and 24, together with many figures and phrases, for example, "For we have no help but Thee" in "Lead us, heavenly Father, lead us" (Ps. 3.2),[7] and Charles Wesley's curious plea for King George II to be given his enemies' necks (Ps. 18.40, "Thou hast given me also the necks of mine enemies").[8] Then come "As pants the hart for cooling streams" (Ps. 42), "Ein feste Burg" (Ps. 46), and "Glorious things of Thee are spoken," the first verse of the latter being taken verbatim from Psalm 87.3. Psalm 90 (vv. 1-5) has given us "Our God, our help in ages past," and Psalm 97 another hymn of Watts no less popular in its day, "The Lord Jehovah reigns." Milton might have taken the refrain "For his mercy aye endures" from at least three psalms, but he actually based "Let us with a gladsome mind" on Psalm 136. Of the numerous hymns made from Psalm 148, probably the best known is "O praise ye the Lord."

In a more general sense, the Psalmist bequeathed to the English hymnographers a pattern of introduction, body, and conclusion, a tone of public rejoicing at once in the royal and the divine power (as in "O worship the King"), and a radical theme, the Lord's perennial care for the needy and the downtrodden. Thus "For He shall deliver the needy when he crieth; the poor also, and him that hath no helper" and the following verse, which became a famous stanza of "Jesus shall reign where'er the sun," were taken from Psalm 72 (vv. 12-13), quarried also by James Montgomery for "Hail to the Lord's Anointed." At the time when hymns meant most to the English-speaking public, psalms primarily conveyed a personal trust and commitment, as in a once-beloved hymn (based on Psalm 34), "Through all the changing scenes of life." The psalm of public thanksgiving has for obvious reasons tended to appeal more to the usually Anglican (or in Scotland the Presbyterian) ruling class. Thus in 1945 Parliament celebrated victory by singing the Scottish paraphrase of Psalm 124, "Now Israel may say, and that truly," which would have meant little to the public at large.

For upwards of a thousand years, recitation of the Psalter among orthodox Christians had in any case been confined to users of the Breviary, that is to say, monks, nuns, and clergy.[9] By prescribing its recitation entire each month during Morning and Evening Prayer, the compilers of the *Book of Common Prayer* made it available to the English laity (as it was to their continental brethren). In Scotland, all worshippers knew their Psalter, but in England it was the future élite educated in "public" schools who were most likely to have swallowed and digested the psalms. Of the biblical odes incorporated by the Eastern church into its fixed canon of hymns, those best known to singers in English have entered the hymnal by way of the Eastern Resurrection Kanon, the German chorale, or, of course, the Canticles. Thus, the Song of Moses, applied to the Resurrection, was translated in the mid-nineteenth century as "The Day of Resurrection" and the Watchtower prophecy (Habakkuk 2) as "Wake, O wake" (from "Wachet auf").

If the Song of Songs has directly inspired the passion-poet rather than the hymnist,[10] its typological figures of the bride and groom, applied to the Church and its Founder, and of the enclosed garden (*hortus conclusus*) applied to the Church or the elect, have indirectly inspired a number of famous hymns.[11]

The dream-vision of the Apocalypse, or Revelation, has given rise to more

major hymns than any other book in the New Testament. It has virtually created the Christian myth of the future state. To trace all incidental references would be a labour of years, but we shall have occasion to notice the following allusions.
—(1) "I am Alpha and Omega, the beginning and the ending . . . the first and the last" (Rev. 1.8, 11; 21.6; 22.13) in "Corde natus ex Parentis," the great hymn on the Incarnation formed out of a poem by Prudentius (4th century).[12]
—(2) "And before the throne there was a sea of glass like unto crystal . . . (and the four beasts . . . rest not day and night saying) 'Holy, holy, holy, Lord God Almighty, which was, and is, and is to come.' " (4.6, 8) in Bishop Heber's famous hymn on the Trinity.[13]
—(3) "Behold, he cometh with clouds, and every eye shall see him, and they also which pierced him: and all kindreds of the earth shall wail because of him." (1.7), which reappears verbatim in various lines of Charles Wesley's hymn on the Second Coming, "Lo! he comes, with clouds descending," usually sung in Advent.[14]
—(4) Many verses combine to supply the leading motifs of the "Dies irae," incorporated into the Requiem Mass as the quintessential expression of fear and trembling before the Judgment: the *day of wrath* (11.18, 16.1); *the Judge's descent* from heaven (ibid); the *trumpet* (4.1, 8.2, 6); the *book* (5 *passim*, 10.2, 8-11; 13.8, especially 20.12ff.); and, of course, the undying *fire* to receive the unworthy (20.15).[15]
—(5) "And the city has no need of the sun, neither of the moon, to shine in it, for the glory of God did lighten it" (21.23), in the final stanza of the Epiphany hymn "As with gladness, men of old," and, needless to say, numerous verses in hymns on the heavenly city.[16]
—(6) "Blessed are the dead, which die in the Lord . . . . that they may rest from their labours" (16.13) in what is probably the best-known hymn on Heaven, "For all the saints, who from their labours rest."
Finally, for two centuries annual performances of Handel's *Messiah* have fixed many verses of the Apocalypse in the minds of millions.

Apart from certain psalms, biblical versions recognizable as hymns are unmistakably objective, rather than subjective or reflexive. Events in the Jewish scriptures, prophecies of the Messiah, His deeds, and posthumous sayings about them all became part of the objective record in, for example, St. Paul's hymn, composed long before any creeds: "And without controversy great is the mystery of godliness: God was manifest in the flesh, justified in the Spirit, seen of angels, preached unto by the Gentiles, believed in the world, received up into glory" (1 Timothy 3.16). Here the Apostle epitomizes the whole Christ-myth.[17]

Again, a Pauline passage that became a well-known hymn is now generally regarded as being itself a "Christological hymn," its key verses being:

Wherefore God also hath highly exalted him, and given him a name which is above every name.

That at the name of Jesus every knee should bow, of things in heaven, and things on earth, and things under the earth.

And that every tongue should confess that Jesus Christ is Lord, to the glory of God the Father. (Philippians 2.9-11)[18]

The ninth verse, which concludes an account of the Incarnation, makes an objective assertion authorizing the predictive imperative that follows, so leaving no room for any qualifier such as "I hope" or "I believe."

Similarly, St. Paul presents as fact an experience that a modern author would treat as subjective, in: "Wherefore he saith, 'Awake, thou that sleepest, and arise from the dead, and Christ shall give thee light'" (Ephesians 5.14). The verse, as Moule points out, could refer to life after death, or to personal enlightenment, or even to baptism.[19] Read literally, it alludes to St. Peter's deliverance from prison; read metaphorically, it can be applied to the individual believer's conversion, as in hymns of the Evangelical revival. The mutual dependence of a minority, however, encouraged collective awareness in early as it increasingly does in modern Christians. Thus even the Canticles of thanksgiving for so personal a blessing as childbirth, the "Magnificat" and Song of Elizabeth, associate the event with divine favour to the poor,[20] while the most subjective, the "Nunc dimittis," ends in praise for the offer of salvation to the people of Israel.

In what may be a baptismal hymn, Colossians 1.13-20, St. Paul extends the meaning of *religio*, or binding-back to the divine. Describing Christ as "image of the invisible God" and agent of both Creation and Redemption, the Apostle addresses himself to those that "have redemption" in the Saviour's blood and so draws together the Creation myth, the ministry and Crucifixion of Christ, and the believers thereby reconciled to Him.

In another possibly baptismal hymn, St. Peter exhorts the faithful to endure their trials and temptations "for a season," forasmuch as God has "begotten" them again by the Resurrection to a "lively hope" of an "inheritance incorruptible and undefiled and that fadeth not away" (1 Pet. 1.3-9). In his ringing message, he too prophesies the final consummation with the same certitude he shows in relating the divine sacrifice and present sufferings.[21]

While various psalms (e.g., Pss. 48, 50, 122, 132) might be regarded as reflexive, neither St. Luke's account of the angelic chorus at the Nativity nor St. John the Divine's of the celestial praise at the end of time (Rev. 9.1-7) constitutes a reflexive hymn, for the praise of worship itself came into being after the Christian community had evolved into a Church independent of the synagogue or Temple. The former, nevertheless, inspired hymns, anthems, oratorio-choruses, and the "Gloria in excelsis" said or sung in most forms of the Eucharist. To notice an essential feature not only of hymnody but of religion itself, let us assume that the event took place as recorded. On a hillside at night some shepherds heard voices from on high singing in their own tongue "Glory to God in the highest, and on earth, peace, goodwill" (Luke 2.14). Whether, as in the Authorized Version, peace would descend upon all or whether, as in the Vulgate, upon men of goodwill *(bonae voluntatis,* ἐν ἀνθρώποις εὐδοκίας), would seem theological quibbles to rustics overwhelmed by the sense of divine glory and ineffable peace. Visionary experiences in all ages are essentially wordless. It is afterwards that mystics record them and theologians transpose them into propositions. The encounters themselves consist essentially of "knowing" rather than "knowing about" God.

Still entranced, the shepherds find in the village below a mother and new-born child. Especially before childbirth became safe, what father would not warm to the mother's radiant gaze upon the child, after her ordeal? Birth itself had a visionary aspect, the more so when observed by unlettered peasants amid the squalor of the stable. Under the spell that would bind them after their encounter with the divine glory, they were impelled by their sense of peace and goodwill to kneel and worship. How would we ever tell that the babe before whom they knelt was he whom later generations crucified or worshipped as Jesus?

What we call faith is a propensity to link spiritual experiences with the external world when no rational grounds exist for connecting them. No historical investigation can prove that these blessedly common experiences, the nocturnal vision and the joy of childbirth, once pertained to a child both human and divine. That of all things must remain a matter of faith.

Every myth or legend has its roots in some experience, and every human experience involves some form of encounter or interplay between a person, as subject, and an environment, as object. Our separation of these two may well be of comparatively recent attainment. In ancient literature, characters are recorded as literally hearing voices and seeing faces that we hear and see in imagination.[22] The essence of *religio* lies in its linking of such experiences and of diverse people not only to the ground of their being but also to each other. Historical and scientific analysis require events or phenomena to be examined in isolation and traced to their immediate rather than universal causes. Religion and poetry are by nature unitive; science and prose by nature analytic. So far as the most sensitive among our ancestors experienced whatever portion of the world they did know as a living unity, they knew its divinities better than we who may be better informed about Him, or them. Poetry, as Wainwright insists, can "'speak' transhistorically, transculturally and transpersonally."[23]

3

THE *ODES OF SOLOMON*
AND THE EARLY CHRISTIANS

The Odes of Solomon *is ... the first Christian hymn-book.*
J.H. Charlesworth[1]

The most recent translator justifies his awe-inspiring claim by arguing that the forty-one odes[2] on a long-lost scroll rediscovered in 1909 by J.R. Harris were composed by a Jewish convert for singing by his congregation in Palestine. If correctly dated by Charlesworth, they were composed at the very latest no further from the Crucifixion than this book from the First World War.[3]

To the hymnologist and literary historian alike they should come as a second revelation, for they demonstrate not only each kind of hymn — objective, subjective, and reflexive — in use from the dawn of Christianity, but organic metaphors, polarity, and dramatic monologue, usually thought peculiar to Romantic and Victorian poetry. Moreover, the poet who employs the pseudonym "Solomon" presents a version of the Christian Myth in some ways more attractive than that spread by St. Paul.

As Charlesworth has argued earlier, that alternative faith is not Gnostic but Christian.[4] To judge from the events he relates or assumes, "Solomon" drew upon the Gospels or their sources, yet he could have been writing before the composition of the Apocalypse. As Charlesworth also shows, the poet draws extensively upon the Old Testament. Several tendencies and motifs concern us here. First of all, he draws typological parallels between Old Testament images or events and the mission of the Messiah, the Rock of Salvation who has touched his lips and caused truth to gush forth as from a fountain.[5] The Messiah leads him to a Promised Land beyond the river of death. That paradise is no city with gates of pearl and golden streets, but a well-watered orchard, with trees rooted there but spreading into our world. The underworld that the Messiah visited to set free the captives of the Evil One was not the Christian Hell but the Jewish

Sheol. Its locked doors[6] and iron shackles signify not only their bondage but the Jewish tendency to associate manufactured or inorganic images with the demonic[7] and organic images with the divine. The living poet enjoys the same ecstasy of liberation not from the flesh but from death, the River that he will ford in the Messiah's footsteps. He expects the new faith to overspread the earth like the Flood that sweeps aside all in its path.

This leads us to a difficult and important question, whether the oncoming war that "Solomon" expects the Christians to survive can be the final Armageddon preceding the millenium. Did he and his congregation practise the doomsday morality that Albert Schweitzer called an *interimsethik*?[8] Had they, like modern Christians of the lunatic fringe, walled themselves up to await the Second Coming? Our translator having rolled back the film of history, shall we recognize not the church-goers we know but ancient Jehovah's Witnesses or Plymouth Brethren? Evidently they sang much better verses than modern hot-gospellers, but was their faith one the "mainstream" Christian of today can respect, if not exactly share?

Sometimes "Solomon" does write as if the end is near. He trusts that, being united with "Him who is immortal," he will be "immortal" and thus survive the war (Ode 4). He provides no hymns to accompany the great occasions of life, the natural seasons, or the times of day. He urges a fellow Christian to love and clothe the naked in acknowledgement of the love shown him by Christ. Forbidding him to purchase as slave "a stranger, because he is like thyself" (Ode 20, stanza 6), he acknowledges the bond of Jews with Gentiles, on whose countenances Christ has set traces of light (10.5)[9]. Likewise, his elaborate symbol of the river overspreading the earth and assuaging the thirst of all who drink implies successful missionary work rather than final catastrophe (6 *passim*). Christ, moreover, forms a bond between the generations (12.8) and His followers will be found uncorrupted in all ages (8.22). This clearly implies the continuance of life on earth. In this spirit must we therefore interpret "Solomon"'s prophecy that peace shall succeed the impending war, false prophets die away, and "gentle voices" praise the "majestic beauty" of the Most High (7.23).

The Odes comprise paeans of praise to the Most High;[10] missionary or didactic exhortations;[11] brief, ecstatic lyrics;[12] and monologues, first by the Blessed Virgin, then by Christ, introduced by brief reflections or lyrics.[13] The former two classes recall psalms or hymns as we know them, the latter Romantic and Victorian poems. Some apparent nature images are really typological. When the Virgin sings that the Most High "like a crown ... of truth" caused His "branches to bloom" in her (1.1-2), she alludes to the prophecy of Isaiah concerning the root of Jesse.[14] The unfading light and ever fruitful trees towards which Christ leads the unshackled dead likewise recall the original Paradise now regained. The land of Palestine, nevertheless, pervades these lovely poems: a land of deep chasms, valleys watered from mountain springs, rocks and adjoining sea, flaming sun and black shadow. This thirsty, toilsome land of prophets and psalmists, conducive to fantasies of showers and fountains, milk and honey, and to dreams of eternal rest, is "Solomon"'s source, not his subject, for he mentions no flocks or shepherds. His realistic images of rocks, mountains, and sea, however, suggest that he writes of the land he knows. His subject-matter throughout is the spiritual life and events within the heart.

It is less clear whether the antitheses within the Odes imply the dualistic religion common to Zoroastrians and Gnostics or some form of polarity. The association of daylight, sun and sky with Christ and of night and the subterranean region with Satan could denote either dualism or what Goethe called the *Ur-Polarität*,[15] or primal polarity of light and dark. Christ's defeat of the Dragon (almost the only image to suggest familiarity with the Apocalypse) resembles an allegorical episode by Spenser or Bunyan, but the symbols of the Wheel and the Letter (23 *passim*) clearly imply polarity. Without presuming to interpret in detail two symbols that even orientalists find obscure, we can safely infer that together they represent the benign and destructive aspects of God. Upon the Wheel that crosses any river and uproots any forest in its path revolves Christ, His head now above and now beneath His feet. His Letter that commanded the faithful from all regions to assemble becomes a huge volume penned by God, from which their persecutors are "extinct and ... blotted out" (23.21). That letter bears the seal or sign of the Cross, signified in the image of Christ bound upon the Wheel and mimed in the poet's cruciform posture of prayer.[16] It resembles both the arrow and the thought of the Most High, and many hands vainly rush to open it. The Wheel that overrides all obstacles and adversaries (23.11-16) bears the sign of God's "kingdom and providence." Clearly these symbols represent God's dual nature, loving and dreadful. Similarly, the stream that turns into a river no human skill can dam will quench the thirst and invigorate the torpid wills of those who drink therefrom. The symbolism expresses a sense of inevitable triumph now found chiefly among Marxists, attributing to the divine will the beneficent but unsparing power that Marx discerned in the historical process. The strongest link between the Odes and modern poetry, sacred or secular, is their unique double sequence that on first sight differentiates them from any modern hymns. Unlike the Wesleyan hymns, or the Psalms, or Shakespeare's sonnets, or the Song of Songs, they follow an inner and outer sequence. In the inner core of monologues, the Virgin, then Christ, reflects upon episodes found in our Gospels, from her first awareness of being with child to His final deliverance of souls from Sheol. In the outer and roughly parallel sequence, the Odist describes his deepening commitment as a disciple called to compose sacred poems and the deepening of any Christian's faith from baptism to death. The inner sequence, by recounting major incidents in the life and ministry of Christ from His viewpoint, serves the purpose of an objective hymn cycle such as that of the Roman Breviary. The outer sequence reflects the stages of a Christian's experience, like the Wesleyan hymn-book. Some Odes therefore convey objective data, some subjective insights, but some are "reflexive" hymns since they dwell upon the act of composing the never silent "Odes of His rest." The latter in no wise hinder devotion, for beyond any other world religion Christianity has incorporated the singing of "psalms, hymns and spiritual songs" into its vision of worship here and in eternity.

Although "Solomon" writes before the New Testament canon was established, and avoids identifying his "persecutors" as either Jewish or Roman, he assigns to Christ monologues meaningful only to worshippers familiar with events related in the Gospels. After the Virgin has announced the redemptive purpose of her pregnancy ("Thy fruits are full ... of Thy salvation": 1.5), Christ urges those upon whom He set his seal before they became individuals (8.13) to "hear the word of truth / And receive knowledge of the Most High," which mystery "Flesh may not understand" (8.8-9). This gives a gnostic twist to Christ's choosing of the Apostles and His self-announcement in the Synagogue.

Soon afterwards, Christ begins an account of the redemption: "I took courage and became strong and captured the world ... for the glory of the Most High" (10.4-5), a version of "I have overcome the world"[17] in which some might discern the Adoptionist heresy. The minor miracles of healing and walking on water form part of the poet's outer sequence, but Christ himself relates the supreme miracle of raising the dead (22.8-9). Otherwise, Christ conveys His motives rather than events normally described from an external viewpoint. Thus, He tells of being persecuted because He "continually did good" to all by foes who surrounded Him "like mad dogs" that "attack their masters" and who vainly sought His death (28.13-14, 18). Calling the afflicted to "receive joy," he relates how He "endured and held my peace and was silent, / But I stood undisturbed like a solid rock / Which is continually pounded by columns of waves and endures" (31.10-11). This humiliation He bore "to redeem my nation and instruct it" (31.12).

Externally perceived events, the dove fluttering overhead at the Baptism in the Jordan (24.1) and the Crucifixion, alluded to in the Wheel symbol (23) rather than described, occur in the poet's own monologues. Again, it is the poet who with apparently intentional irony introduces Christ's account of the Trial by declaring, "Chasms vanished ... and darkness dissipated before His appearance" (31.1). Christ throughout is presented as the light-bringer, the Sun that knows not his going down.[18]

Before recounting His descent into Sheol, Christ asserts His divine origin "from another race," possessed "from the beginning" by "the Father of Truth" (cf. the Devil as the "Father of lies"): "For his riches begat me, / And the thought of His heart" (41.8-10). His account of bringing "vinegar and bitterness" (42.12) to Sheol would have a touch of ironic reversal for a congregation familiar with any of the Crucifixion narratives. Among the dead, Christ has made a "congregation" of "the living," who run to Him crying: "Son of God, have pity on us

... bring us out of the bonds of death ... open for us the door / By which we may come out with Thee," for they perceive that death "does not touch Thee" (42.15-17).

While neither Christ nor "Solomon" in his own persona describes the Resurrection, the Ascension is clearly implicit in Christ's final declaration of intent to hide Himself from "Those who possessed me not" and to throw over those who love Him the "yoke" of His love, "Like the arm of the bridegroom over the bride" (42.7-8). The bridal image from the Song of Songs seems here to apply to responsive souls rather than the institutional Church but in any case implies the assumption of "all power in heaven and earth."[19]

In the outer sequence of monologues in his own persona, "Solomon" develops the theme of discipleship, likening his course mainly to that of Christ, but sometimes to that of the Virgin. Thus, at the outset he declares, like the Virgin, that he could not have loved God had not God "continuously loved me." He identifies with Christ, trusting because he loves "the Son" to become "a Son" (3.3, 7). When he recollects his baptism and calls on God to open the "bountiful springs" of milk and honey then administered as part of the rite (4.10),[20] God descends upon his head as formerly though "all things visible perish," for Christ "is with me / And I with Him" (5.13-15).

As the Most High ordained Christ to preach, so the Spirit moves the Odist to utter verses "As the wind glides through a harp" (6.1), a biblical and Romantic metaphor for poetic inspiration.[21] The Spirit will likewise in the Christian community overspread the earth like a river (6.8-11) and refresh those athirst for divine knowledge and grace. The Syriac verb *yd'*, "to know," refers to cognition rather than acquaintance,[22] but if "Solomon" appears in gnostic fashion to equate this with grace, his blessing upon "ministers" who, having drunk of the river, bring others to refresh parched lips implies grace rather than esoteric knowledge. A product of the synagogue rather than the Temple, he never refers more specifically to church or sacrament, but concerns himself with prayer, preaching, and the love of Christ, all of which imply intimate acquaintance and shared knowledge.

This personal devotion reaches a climax in the beautiful Eleventh Ode. Having introduced the messianic claim to have overcome the world, the Odist declares his heart opened by the Light and claims the unforbidden fruit of inward peace. Announcing his consecration as poet of a universal rather than national religion, he proclaims himself "circumcised" by the Holy Spirit, which has caused the flower of grace to spring in his "pruned" heart. He employs three typological metaphors that in Christian hymnody keep recurring down the centuries.[23]

> I was established upon the *rock* of truth
> And speaking waters touched my lips
> From the *fountain*[24] of the Lord, generously,

And so I drank and became intoxicated
From the living water that does not die. (11.5-7)

Having plucked off vanity and folly, he is clad in the garment of renewal and possessed by the divine light of the Most High, who confers the gift of "immortal rest."[25] Transported in vision to the heavenly Eden, the poet beheld there "blossoming and fruitbearing trees." "Rest" to the poet means more than the stasis of the Platonic ideal state, for having passed from "darkness to light" he beholds himself as a "crown" with "branches sprouting" and roots spreading from an "immortal land," irrigated by a "river of gladness" (11.11-16). Viewed as the cause of fertility and growth, the heavenly rest resembles poetic inspiration rather than the exhausted sleep of so many feeble Victorian hymns on heaven.[26] Again, as always in the *Odes,* the fountain image refers not to the blood of Christ but to the spring of inspiration.

This similitude between religious and poetic inspiration, between the Old and the New Creation, renders his vision more attractive, to the lover of nature and art at least, than St. Paul's brief account of being "caught up into the third heaven."[27] No doubt "vanity and folly" mean much the same as the human condition of "sin" that the Apostle describes in such detail, but the vitally metaphorical language sheds over the whole episode a lightness and freshness wanting in most verses of the Epistles.

The Eleventh Ode marks the high point of "Solomon"'s enthusiasm. Subsequently, the focus shifts back and forth between renewal (never called rebirth) and the vocation to preach. The former Christ requires of all who would enter His Kingdom; the latter he has transmitted by ordaining "Solomon." After avowing that since he is so ordained, truth gushes from his mouth "like the flowing of waters" (12.1-3), the Odist himself calls upon his congregation to examine their faces in their "mirror," the Most High, to "wipe the paint" therefrom, love Him and put on "His holiness," and so appear "unblemished" before Him (13.1-3).

In similarly organic metaphors, "Solomon" calls Christ his "Sun" whose rays have "dismissed all darkness" from his face (15.1-3), the Word who has "destroyed death" and "vanquished Sheol" before him. Of his poetic vocation, he says that as the ploughman must guide the plough, the helmsman steer the ship, so the poet must praise the Lord, for "My art and my service are his His hymns / Because His love has nourished my heart / And His fruits he poured unto my lips" (16.1-2). As Christ liberated His disciples among the dead, so "My chains were cut off by His hands; / I received the face and likeness / Of a new person ... walked in Him and was saved" (17.4-5). As "priest," the Odist urges a convert to offer the sacrifice of righteousness in lips and heart, "thy inward being" (20.1-5), before instructing him in his duty to his neighbour. As poet, he urges the convert to make and wear a "garland" from the paradisal tree as pledge of joy.

In his latter monologues, the redeemed poet's course more and more resembles that of Christ. When "Solomon," too, was "despised and rejected" by the many (25.1-3), God set a guiding lamp on each side and clothed him with the Spirit, so enabling him to dispense with his "garments of skin" (25.7-8). He resolves to recite God's "holy Ode / Because my heart is with Him" and "His harp is in my hand" (26.1-3).

Where the paths diverge, they do so as cause and effect. While introducing Christ's account of being hunted down by His enemies, "Solomon" likens the Spirit's watch over his heart to that of a dove upon its nestlings. As the babe leaps in the womb, so his heart "continually refreshes itself and leaps for joy" (28.1-2). Since Christ met persecution by sweetness, his suffering has brought joy and the madness of his persecutors evoked divine wisdom. To confirm the antithesis between Christ and His foes, the Odist depicts grace as an uncorrupted virgin (33.1.5), false religion as the imitation by a corrupt bride and groom (38.9-12) of the wedding feast of the true Beloved. In these symbols he hints at the Temple and the Eucharist only to contrast the elaborate display of a false religion with the childlike trust of a "simple heart," a trust already enjoined in his plea, "Believe and be saved" (34.1, 6). He thus pares down his teaching to bare trust and obedience before, in the final eight Odes, presenting Christ's death and preparing for his own. Sprinkled by the Most High, he is "tranquil" in God's "legion," carried like a child by its mother.

As in many modern hymns, the river symbol now refers to death.[28] The power of God, like a raging river, will "send headlong" all who despise it (39.1-3). Those who "cross in faith" bearing the "sign" of Christ follow Him across the bridge His word has formed (39.7-9). Thus, the poet brings together the miracles of the Red Sea and the Messiah walking on water to signify the final overcoming of death that salvation clearly means to him. The "way" is "appointed" for all who cross after Christ, keeping to the "path of faith" and adoring His name (39.13). In a last exhortation before Christ recounts how He delivered the dead, the Odist calls on the Lord's "babies" to sing of His love in the "great day" that has dawned upon them: "Let our faces shine in His light ... our hearts meditate" day and night "upon his love" (42.1-6).

Since the Council of Laodicea (A.D. 360) forbade the use of any non-scriptural hymns, its ban proves only that the *Odes* were still extant. As regards their doctrinal soundness, a layman can merely relate what they say about the nature of God and the destiny of man.

"Solomon," as we have seen, presents God as bipolar, that is, at once loving and terrifying. In the Old Testament, these aspects alternate, love tending more and more to predominate. In the *Odes*, the polarity is presented by means of a primitive perception of the Trinity, for the gentleness of Christ mitigates the dreadfulness of the Most High. In a metaphor rather than a doctrinal assertion, the poet presents the deity as not only bipolar but also bisexual. In the Incarnation, the Holy Spirit drew from the breasts of the Most High the milk of the Word, mixed that with its own, then poured it into a cup, the Son, who conveyed it to mankind.[29]

This endearing anthropomorphism suggests a psychological basis for that most inexplicable of dogmas, the Trinity. The incarnate Son bears the abstraction secreted by the Most High but rendered acceptable to the human mind and heart by the same Spirit that renews and thus transfigures them. Untold centuries later Coleridge was to conceive of the poetic imagination as "two forces of one power, the one infinite, the other struggling to apprehend or find itself," that is, to identify itself, within this infinitude.[30] Since he draws a parallel between the human and divine acts of creation, he finds in the imagination an abstract or universal and a concrete or incarnational aspect.

In some myths and legends, in visionary experiences of the kind Wordsworth called "spots of time," or even when in crisis acting as members of a larger entity, we seem to experience the fusion of the particular with the universal, of the concrete with the abstract, that is implied by this symbolism of the Word as food from on high.

A poet rather than logician, the Odist falls short of explicitly or consistently presenting Christ as a person of the Trinity, a dogma never defined until the Arian heresy threatened to take over the Church in the fourth century.

While the *Odes* do not provide for sacramental rites, from their recurring images of rivers and fountains, of renewal and reclothing, we could reasonably infer a belief in baptismal regeneration, and from the wedding feast symbol, a belief in the Eucharist.

It is otherwise with the verses on the human prospect, which astonish no less by their intensity of conviction than by their omissions. In his ecstasy at the conquest of death, the poet scarcely completes a verse without offering thanks for the assurances of immortality. Of his account of being liberated by Christ, it would be an understatement to say that like Isaac Watts he finds that "the prospect of heaven makes death easy."[31] For to him heaven is more than a prospect. As a visionary poet who has already travelled there, he represents heaven in terms not heretical but increasingly unfamiliar, as the unpeopled paradise of Genesis rather than the celestial city of the Apocalypse. Upon angelic as upon ecclesiastical hierarchies, he remains silent. He envisages no shouts of praise, no adoring figures round the Throne, only fountains and ever-bearing trees. Like Wordsworth, he envisages a natural paradise, as Blake views vision and reality as indivisible.

Nowhere does the Odist expect a Second Coming or depict any Judgment or eternal punishment. The Sheol from which Christ delivers the willing dead is the Jewish or Greek underworld, a place of sad resignation rather than terror or torment. It has locks and chains, but no fires.[32] If his complex symbol of the Letter cum Volume could imply belief in the dread Scroll of the Apocalypse, the poet betrays no fear of any grand assize, no images of the courtroom. It was, I believe, Kierkegaard who remarked that in the ancient world men chiefly feared death, in the medieval world judgment, and in the modern world insignificance.[33]

Above all, "Solomon" appears devoid of any sense of sin. Like Puritans and Romantics long afterward, he has turned his back on the vanities of this world, but he engages in no self-examination, shows no sign of penitence. While in this sense most theologians would find him heretical by omission, his silence on personal guilt raises the intriguing and doubtless unanswerable question of whether in the *Odes,* rather than in the Epistles of St. Paul, we behold the essence of early Christianity. Did the faith confer upon the typical believer an ecstatic sense of deliverance from death, rather than of sins forgiven and punishment remitted?

Whether the earliest Christian hymnal is heretical, in treating the faith as revealed only to those Christ has marked with His seal, depends upon whether "seal" denotes simply baptism or some further mark of election. In any case, it cannot be called Gnostic, for it accords love a higher priority than esoteric knowledge and depicts only Christ as supernatural. Its pun on the name of Peter, the Rock on whom Christ builds His Kingdom, is a model of orthodoxy.[34]

For other than doctrinal reasons, no denominational hymn lover would feel quite at home with the *Odes of Solomon.* The Methodist or Evangelical would find them disconcerting because they dwell on the Cross but never on the Blood. The Catholic would find them lacking in dogmatic, sacramental, and eschatological precision. The Lutheran would find them Calvinistic inasmuch as Christ seals His holy ones before birth (7.13) and hides Himself from the unbeliever (42.3). The Calvinist would find them lacking in logical rigour and exclusiveness. No hymn lover could feel at ease with a hermaphrodite Creator whose milk, transmitted by the Spirit, enabled the Virgin to bear Christ without pain.[35] Even the Moravian would find their eroticism disconcertingly directed to the Saviour's birth rather than His bleeding wounds.

Although by special pleading the *Odes* could be seen as following the liturgical year from Advent to Easter, and the Christian's experience minus sense of sin, most hymnologists would find their scriptural reference too inexplicit, their symbolism too elaborate. In St. Augustine's definition, "Singing in praise of God," they nevertheless count as hymns. If their imagery be repetitive, their poetic richness, their Christian spirit of joy, thankfulness, and, above all, love suggest that they may have been among the beautiful hymns for which early Christian services were renowned.[36] Their serene assurance of their faith's eventual triumph could not nowadays be matched outside Communist states; yet because the figure of Christus Victor is offset by that of Christus Sponsus, they remain singularly free from the vulgar triumphalism found in not a few well-known hymns.

Their tone thus resembles the enthusiasm of Methodist hymns or charismatic chants rather than the austere objectivity of Latin hymns, the decorous exuberance of Byzantine *kanons*, or the grave measure of Calvinist psalmody. Their wide variations in length (from three to twenty-odd verses) and requirement for soloists or antiphonal choirs to sing the introductions and monologues suggest that the *Odes of Solomon* combined the functions of antiphonary, anthem-book, hymnal, psalter, and even oratorio.[37] It was a first step towards a service book, for a Christian church still in the making.

Lest the foregoing comparison appear unfair to the Apostle Paul, who in the last analysis composed the most moving of all odes to Christian love and who was chiefly responsible for the rapid spread of the faith among the Gentiles, a recent translation of hymns and psalms in use among the community of Qumran (in the Dead Sea Scrolls) reveals a far more punitive and world-denying faith. Sheol is consistently envisaged as "the Pit," the world outside as full of enemies "mighty" and "ruthless." It is the "rivers of Belial," however, that overflow their banks and, like consuming fires, destroy trees and houses. God, who has elected and delivered the worshippers, "thunders" and His "army of heaven" will conquer the whole earth, and His followers become as nurseling children.[38]

In short, the Qumran faith appears more dualistic than the Christian, whether of the Odes or of the Epistles. It appears to distinguish more sharply between the circumcised and the uncircumcised. The former live more separately from and in fiercer conflict with the latter than does the church of St. Paul or the Odist. What distinguishes the Odes and the Epistles from the Qumran hymns is that their authors know and follow Christ.

4

A NOTE ON THE BYZANTINE HYMN

Two Romes have now fallen, and the third one, our Moscow, yet standeth; and a fourth one there shall never be. ... In all the world thou alone art the Christian Tsar.

Philotheos, 16th-century monk[1]

Before launching upon a study of the Myth in Latin hymnody, there is much to be said for a brief sojourn in Byzantium, where nearly all the issues that have divided English theologians and hymnists arose almost a millennium before the Reformation: the role of the state in regulating worship, ritual, and use of images, puritan attacks upon hymns, and their defence by churchmen. In every direction save that of legalistic definition, the Christianity centred upon Constantinople went to greater extremes than that of Jerusalem or Rome: in its asceticism, its otherworldly mysticism, its elaboration of ritual and architecture, in its dogmatic and philosophical abstraction, and particularly in its paying of tribute to Caesar.[2] Its hymnody also transcended that of Rome both in dramatic realism and liturgical formalism.

A Kontakion, or chanted homily, by the great sixth-century hymnographer Romanos, also a Jewish convert,[3] recalls the *Odes of Solomon* in its distribution of roles among singers or choirs, and anticipates the oratorio or Bach passion setting in its blend of biblical typology with dramatic verisimilitude. In his Kontakion on the Passion, Peter, Christ, Pilate, and the Crowd sing paraphrases of their words in the Gospels. In that on the raising of Lazarus, even Death and Hades have singing roles.[4]

As if to illustrate a "sacred bridge"[5] linking the Hebraic with the Latin culture, via the Syriac and Byzantine, the Kontakion of Romanos on the Entry into Jerusalem harks back to the Hebraic *midrash*, or chanted scriptural exegesis,[6] yet nevertheless anticipates the medieval mystery or modern passion play. Like the *midrashim*, it expounds the Old Testament myths yet in the Christological interpretation called "typology." Like the *Odes of Solomon*, it allows the dramatis personae of the Passion story to speak for themselves, yet like the great Latin hymns of the Middle Ages, it represents the human viewpoint collectively. Like the Franciscan *laude* or the mystery plays, it abounds in dramatic realism, depicting the sun rising as Christ mounts the ass and emphasizing His nudity when he is scourged.[7] Yet, just as the rising sun commonly typifies the coming of the Messiah, so the deliverance of Jonah typifies the Resurrection. Strangely enough, the pillar of cloud that led the Israelites through the desert typifies the pillar at which the Victim was beaten. "Weary" and "defeated," mankind begs Christ to "tear up the written decree" of its doom by undergoing His Crucifixion.[8] The typological use of Old Testament myths and natural phenomena was the prevailing wind in ecclesiastical hymnody for a thousand years.

Even two centuries later, the Resurrection Kanon of St. John Damascene resembles the Syriac *Odes* in its liberation motif and the Kontakia in dramatic immediacy. "But yesterday" entombed with Christ, the poet-cantor today drinks at the fount of immortality that gushes from the Empty Tomb, hailing Christ as Liberator of Jonah and the children in the Furnace.[9] As this and other portions indicate, within these two centuries the hymn has become even more explicitly typological. Nevertheless, as Werner shows, its Nine Odes, each treating a scriptural passage typologically, from Habbakuk's prophecy of the Incarnation to the "Magnificat" as a foreshadowing of the New Jerusalem, were derived from the Hebrew hymnody.[10] By this time the nature images — sea, river, mountain, or valley — that link the Kontakion with the *Odes of Solomon* have vanished.

The collective viewpoint and requirement upon the sacred poet to restrict his subject-matter to the Nine Odes[11] drove out not only nature images but those allusions to the social teaching of Jesus that give the *Odes of Solomon* a modern ring. Even Romanos confined himself to miracles, from the turning of water into wine to the casting out of devils and raising of Lazarus.

The subject-matter of the Byzantine Kontakion, still more of the later Kanon, resembles the Anglican Canticle rather than the metrical hymn in English or Latin. The brief portions of the Golden Kanon translated as Victorian resurrection hymns can mislead us in this regard. Since the form of the Mass did not vary as in the West, the Byzantine hymnographers instead wrote for the morning and evening offices. They began from the Psalms, by inserting *troparia,* or brief credal or scriptural paraphrases, between the psalm verses. They then linked a group of *troparia* into a *Hirmos,* or verse-paragraph, such as the Emperor Justinian's version of the Creed. The Kontakion consisted of a *Hirmos* followed by twenty or thirty *troparia,* making it comparable in length with the Anglican Litany or sermon. The Kanon could consist of the Nine Odes in full and thus have the effect of an oratorio rather than a homily. Wellesz describes its performance as that of "hymns of praise in exultant or eschatalogical mood, expressing dogmatic ideas" by varied repetition so as to evoke a corresponding "mystical mood" intensified by the solemn procession of icons.[12] The chanting was intended as a human counterpart to the heavenly hymn-singing by the nine angelic choirs.[13] If the singing of a Kanon before the non-participating congregation exceeded in splendour any form of service to be found in a modern English cathedral, that of the final kind of Byzantine hymn, the Stichera, anticipated the Western nativity or passion play.

Although able to observe the action at the Eucharist until quite late in the Byzantine period,[14] the congregation had not for centuries participated actively. The rite derived its numinous solemnity and remoteness less from the echoing space and dominant choir of an Anglican cathedral than from the sense of heavenly and ecclesiastical hierarchy latent in its verbal formulae, music, and visual symbolism. Despite the highly scriptural, and therefore Hebraic, flavour of the hymns, Byzantine theology was neoplatonic in its "super-essential" deity reigning above and beyond the material world, and in its parallel hierarchies, celestial and terrestrial.[15] In his remoteness, the supreme God resembled the heavenly Father of the Puritans, but nothing in Protestant verse after *Paradise Lost* would prepare us for the nine orders of angels that sang his praise or for choirs and courtiers that sang acclamations to the Emperor, a practice followed in tsarist Russia.

In the East, the Church was at once more otherworldly and more subservient to the monarchy than in the West.[16] Based upon the Eusebian doctrine that the Emperor represented God upon earth, it became, beyond even the Anglican or Lutheran churches, an organ of state, consecrating a static social order and according the Emperor a veneration reserved in the West for the Pope.[17] At the Great Entrance, the choir sang a "Cherubic Hymn," supposedly composed by Justinian, in which they resolved to "lay aside worldly cares" so as to "receive the King of the Universe invisible / Attended by the angelic orders."[18] The sense of the rite as an initiation into a mystery, the ethereal beauty of the chant, and the solemn splendour of the ritual must have aroused a numinous awe that conditioned the attitudes of the people to both church and state.[19]

Not only in its "Caesaro-papism" but also in its conflict between church and state, Byzantium anticipated England under the Tudors.[20] Almost from the beginning, monks of the *lavras,* or desert communities of ascetics, had inveighed against hymns and indeed all liturgical singing. An abbot's furious retort to an account of charismatic singing and dancing, that monks had not emigrated into the desert "to perform before God" but to pray "with tears and sighs…in reverence and contrition,"[21] betokens a conflict older than Christianity itself, between Apollonian and Dionysian religion.

During the Iconoclastic movement of the eighth and ninth centuries, however, it was the regular or Basilian monastic communities that led the popular resistance to the endeavours of emperors and soldiers to purge the church of wealth and superstition.[22] If the looting of monasteries did not occur on the same scale as in Henry VIII's time, the image-breaking rivalled that during the Puritan Commonwealth.

The greatest Byzantine hymnist, St. John Damascene, defends the icon as meaning to the "uneducated and uncivilised what the book means to those who can read," a rationale resembling that of Wesley for the Methodist hymn.[23] The protests of St. John and other monks against the civil intrusion into the spiritual domain recall those of Newman, Keble, or Pusey. The Oxford Movement, moreover, led to the reintroduction of ritual and iconography.

Had the Iconoclasts not destroyed irreplaceable manuscripts, our first-hand knowledge of Byzantine hymnody would be more extensive. We can remark not only the parallel between Iconoclastic and Calvinistic intolerance of images and "man-made" hymns but also that between the arguments propounded for hymn-singing, which the very founder of the Orthodox liturgy, St. John Chrysostom, had justified in the late fourth century on grounds similar to those of Protestant hymn lovers from Luther to General Booth of the Salvation Army. Contrasting the "wanton" songs of pagan drinking parties with spiritual chants at Christian meals, he bade his hearers teach their wives and children to offer praise after meals in "sacred hymns" and psalms, lest the Devil make use of "drunkenness, gluttony, laughter, disorder and dissipation.",[24] It is a rationale resembling that offered many centuries later for prayer, psalmody, or hymn-singing in Puritan, Methodist, or Evangelical households.[25]

If no more content to leave the best tunes to the Devil, the Byzantine hymnographer attended much less than his Evangelical counterparts to the desert across which Moses led the Israelites and Christ the human race. Although St. Joseph of the Studios rejoices that "Slaves are set free, and captives ransomed" by Christ,[26] his allusions to this place of our exile have nothing like the force of Bunyan's "wilderness of this world" or "Guide me, O thou great Jehovah." In their stylized raptures concerning the victory Christ had won for mankind, the Byzantine poets simply ignored this material and natural world.

But their belief in the divine sanction of the political and ecclesiastical hierarchies, and supremely the law-giving office of Emperor, proved more deep-seated and enduring than that of the most rabidly Tory Anglican hymnist in the divine sanction of the English nation and class system.

The Myth in Medieval Christendom

5

"CREATOR OF ALL THINGS": GOD THE FATHER

A good hymn is like a good prayer — real, earnest and relevant."
Bishop W.W. How[1]

No one who thumbs through the "Ancient Office Hymns" in *Hymns Ancient and Modern* can fail to note their preoccupation with time, temptation, and the Trinity, accountable to their use by early Benedictines and their composition by poet-theologians locked in deadly combat with Arianism. The renowned hymns of the Arians had won so many hearts that early Latin hymns tend to address the Trinity rather than the Father.[2] We owe their preservation to Benedictine compilers between the sixth and tenth centuries.[3] In addition, two prose hymns prescribed by St. Benedict himself, the "Te Deum" and "Gloria in excelsis," were eventually absorbed into the Offices and the Mass.

Little can be made of the fact that so few medieval hymns concern the Father, for all monastic liturgies prescribed regular singing or recitation of the Psalms. As Werner remarks, "From the magnificently illuminated 'Books of the Hours' in the possession of rich princes, down to the simply-improvised *Laude* of Francis of Assisi's followers, one supreme path is followed ... psalmody in all its varying forms."[4] The same authority, nevertheless, admits that by reason of elaborate musical performance in monasteries and singing schools, psalm-singing became less and less a means of popular devotion in the West.[5]

As one effect of trinitarian teaching, hymns tended to praise Christ for man's creation and treat the Father as remote, even abstract. As early as the "Te Deum," Christ assumed the role of Judge, as in virtually all medieval judgment hymns, while the personal devotion addressed in psalms to God was in hymns addressed mainly to the Virgin.[6] Undoubtedly, this influenced Anglicans and Puritans, following Calvin, to banish hymns in favour of Psalms.

In the early Latin hymns, however, God the Father performed the functions later assigned to Christ and the Virgin. In "Deus creator omnium" by St. Ambrose (4th century), He sends the blessing of sleep to comfort and renew the weary and ease the troubled soul of its sorrow. As to Him clings chaste affection (*castus amor*), so faith in Him must cool the bodily heat of the sleeper that begets lust (*castis fides refrigerans / somni vaporem temperet*).[7] In similar vein, the poet trusts that the light of faith may keep the sleeper free of fears and delusions, by possessing his heart with dreams of God. To console and strengthen the worshipper and to substitute a holier love for the body's lust have for centuries been the burden of prayers to the Virgin and to Christ.

As in the East, the Myth drove out that awareness of nature evident in Prudentius' "Corde natus ex Parentis" (4th century) and even Fortunatus' "Tempora florigero rutilant" (6th century).[8] In the "Te Deum," it is the angels, cherubim, and seraphim that praise their Creator rather than the birds or beasts. This great chorus rises to a wholly supernatural deity, worshipped by a hierarchy of spirits, rather than to the source of the visible universe. The opening of "Splendor paternae gloriae," one of the oldest and grandest Latin hymns, implies an image of the Father as hidden sun and invisible source of the light manifest in Christ:

Splendor paternae gloriae,	Splendour of the Father's glory
de luce lucem proferens,	Bringing light from light,
lux lucis et fons luminis,	Light of light and source of light,
diem dierum illuminans.	Illuminating the day of days.[9]

These original hymns of the Learned tradition might, in Nietzschean phrase, be called Apollonian, having displaced those to the sun.[10] In "Rector potens, verax Deus," it is the Father who gives day and night, health and peace, and who quenches strife and passion.[11] In "Rerum Deus tenax vigor," the Father, the binding force of all creation, guides the sun in its course and at life's evening lights his faithful through a holy death to eternal glory.[12] In a morning hymn, "Lux ecce surgit aurea," the Father watches over the brethren:

Speculator adstat desuper,	A watchman stands by on high
qui nos diebus omnibus	Who each day watches
actusque nostros prospicit	Us and our actions
a luce prima in vesperum.	From first light to evening.[13]

This image of God as all-seeing eye, apparently originating in 2 Chronicles, 16.9 (*Oculi enim Domini contemplantur universam terram, et praebent fortitudinem his, qui corde perfecto credunt in eum*) or in the prophetic image of the Messiah as "sun of righteousness" (Malachi 4.2), was to haunt the sensitive child once transferred from the monastic service-book to the puritan "good, godly" children's book and thence to the Evangelical school hymnal.[14]

In post-Empire hymns, what had changed was the poetic method rather than the doctrinal emphasis. "Immense caeli Conditor," prescribed for Monday Vespers, describes the Creator's work on the second day, in dividing the waters of heaven and earth. After begging for the waters to temper the sun's heat, the poet shifts key to the inner world, by beseeching God to inject his gift of unfailing grace (*infunde ... donum perennis gratiae*) that new sins may not supplant the old.[15] His method of analogy, which governs the structure of innumerable medieval hymns, relates a quasi-historical episode to some need of the aspiring soul.

Less frequently, the poet will by analogy relate the divine to the natural. In "Aeterna caeli gloria," Christ is addressed as son of Him who "thunders on high" (*Celsitonantis*).[16] Nature concerns the sacred poets chiefly as a means of explaining the supernatural. The long history of analogy stretches through Spenser and Milton down to the poetry of the Romantic and Oxford movements. While the Oxford reformers and their poetic progeny, even at times Gerald Manley Hopkins, employ analogy in the medieval manner,[17] most nineteenth-century poets focus primarily on the natural environment and the inner world of the psyche. This shift of the poet's gaze from the supernatural and monastic to the natural and lay worlds has occasioned a deliberate retouching by Percy Dearmer of "Nocte surgentes vigilemus omnes," attributed to St. Gregory (6th century). The subject of this Sunday nocturnal hymn is the act of rising by night to meditate in psalms and sing hymns of praise. Its second stanza,

> Ut pio regi pariter canentes
> cum suis sanctis mereamur aulam
> ingredi coeli, simul et beatam
> ducere vitam

("That singing together to the holy king we may deserve to enter the court of heaven with his saints and to lead the blessed life"),

says little to correspond with Dearmer's second verse:

> Monarch of all things, fit us for thy mansions;
> Banish our weakness, health and wholeness sending;
> Bring us to heaven, where thy saints united
> Joy without ending.[18]

For modern congregations, Dearmer naturally turns this into a morning hymn and introduces his modern sense of the religious life as a condition of health. Originally "salvation," from the same root as "salve" and "salvage" alike, referred to the soul's health, a state unattainable in this world. Dearmer gets rid of the whole notion of salvation earned by good works, for "health and wholeness" come as divine gifts. While monastic hymns certainly involve some measure of determinism,[19] without the doctrine of salvation by works as well as faith few could have endured the rigours of early monastic life.

For that very reason, monastic devotion and ethics inevitably became self-conscious, as in the still famous "Iam lucis orto sidere" ("Now that the daylight fills the sky") and "Te lucis ante terminum" ("Before the ending of the day"). In the former, the singers plead for God to restrain their tongues and tempers and to screen their eyes from vanities. Praying for inward purity (*pura cordis intima*) and the grace to crush the pride of flesh (*carnis ... superbiam*), they trust again to sing praise at evening, unspotted by the world. In this partially reflexive hymn, virtue is rewarded by the power to sing in good conscience.[20] The latter hymn has so endeared itself to Roman Catholics and Anglicans that to point out its drift seems a blasphemy. It begs the Creator to ward off ill dreams and nocturnal fantasies (*noctium phantasmata*) that our bodies be not stained or polluted (*polluantur corpora*). Without doubt, the Latin poet had in mind sexual dreams as well as nightmares.[21]

For all their sober magnificence and exalted conception of the Creator, these Latin hymns of the first millennium exalt the ascetic life itself. The natural environment they tend to ignore, for notwithstanding that monks raised crops in the fields, monastic poets derived their nature imagery from the Psalms and Genesis and used it by way of analogy to the Myth. Certain psalms and canticles seem likely to have mitigated this introversion.[22] Psalm 148, for example, recited daily, praises God for creating not only the heavens but all creatures of sea and earth.

6

THE COMING OF CHRIST

As the sceptic and the fundamentalist will agree, the Gospels reflect the preoccupations of their authors: Matthew's with prophecy, Mark's with fact, Luke's with social relationships, healing, and ethics, John's with ideas. Carefully as the authors have set the events within an actual time and place, the accounts by Matthew and Luke of the Messiah's coming and by all save Mark of His departure have the formal structure of myth. His coming has three phases: advent, nativity, and epiphany; Christ expected, born, and beheld. Likewise, His departure consists of passion, resurrection, and ascension; he undergoes three temptations and hangs on one of three crosses after being thrice denied. In addition to shaping His life in triads, the Evangelists, and still more the early theologians, are forever drawing typological parallels between prophecy in the old and event in the new dispensation, contrasting the Virgin with Eve, Christ with Adam, the Redemption with the Fall.

Theologians and poets love to couple the first with the second coming of Christ. Advent hymns often exhort us to repent in preparation for the second coming, as John the Baptist preached repentance before the first. The attempt to treat them chronologically is full of pitfalls. One still used in translation, "Conditor alme siderum" ("Creator of the stars of night") may not have been composed for Advent.[1] The sixth-century hymn "Vox clara ecce intonat" ("Hark a thrilling voice is sounding") underwent rewriting in classical metre during the 1632 revision of the Breviary.[2] Do we therefore consider it as ancient or modern? Two more composed in Latin, "Jordanis oras praevia" and "Veni, veni Emmanuel," date only from the age of Watts and Wesley, and a much used Victorian translation, "O come, O come, Emmanuel," differs significantly from the original.[3]

Even the earliest extant hymn for Advent, "The great Creator of the worlds" (dated A.D. 150), represents Christ, the "immortal truth" or "word" of God, as the Creator's Son and King in his own right.[4] Byh the seventh or eighth centuries, all the principal images for the Saviour have entered the monastic hymnal: the sacrificial Lamb (a parallel between the Passover and the Passion) in "Vox clara ecce intonat"; the Bridegroom of the Wise Virgins, in the Eastern hymn Ἰδοῦ ὁ Νύμφιος ἔρχεται Idou ho Nymphios erchetai" (8th century);[5] the light and "true sun" (versus sol), in St. Ambrose's "Splendor paternae gloriae";[6] the divine healer, in the Mozarabic hymn "Gaudete flores martyrum."[7] If these primary images resound through the Advent hymnody of a thousand years, it by no means follows that poets fail to express the moods or interests of their times. Those of the second and even the fourth centuries know nothing of the pessimism that informs "Conditor alme siderum" (6th-7th centuries), where Christ is the Eternal Light (*aeterna lux*) and the world is drawing towards nightfall (*vergente mundi vespere*).[8] In its 1632 revision, this majestic poem acquired dogmatic detail in additions hailing Christ as sinless victim issued from the sacred womb (*sacrario*) to die for our sins and thereby prevent a world from sickening unto death because of the devil's wiles (*demonis ne fraudibus / Periret orbis*), whereas the original poet had assumed the end must come soon. So far has the sense of the impending *Parousia* weakened that even amid the troubles of the Counter-Reformation, the revisers view the divine act of love as having preserved the world.

In the fourth-century eucharistic prayer now widely sung as "Let all mortal flesh keep silence," history's central event, the coming of Christ the King of kings, fills the singer with fear and awe in this very moment.[9] As Christ gives himself for "heavenly food," the communicant's eye sweeps upward to the angels singing "Alleluia" as the "Light of light" descends to overcome the powers of darkness in the cosmos and therefore the soul.

The substitution of Judaeo-Christian for heathen mythology in late Roman verse has been amply documented by F.J.E. Raby, who has also shown that the first great Christian poet in Latin, Prudentius, finds in the splendid new basilicas evidence not of the decay but of the renewal of Rome through the triumph of the true faith over the pagan mystery cults.[10] We can too easily read back our historical awareness of the barbarian invasions into the late Roman era when for Christians myth and history are one. As a former judge, the poet knew the secular world better than his successors, yet he saw Roman history as relevant to man's creation, fall, and redemption in a way that British and American history can never be. He knew of no such external reality as our geological and biological data on evolution. Nature to him symbolized the Myth: like the Messiah, the cock summoned man to new life; the twittering of sparrows at eventide evoked the image of Christ as Judge; sleep represented death, darkness the night of sin. Myth and reality were one.

If the Ambrosian hymns were to drive Christian doctrine into the hearts of

Latin worshippers, the great hymn "Corde natus ex Parentis," excerpted from Prudentius' long poem *Cathemerinon*, represents the earliest and most complete account still in use of the Christian myth, that enfolds history:

Corde natus ex parentis	Of the Father's heart begotten,
ante mundi exordium	ere the world from chaos rose,
A et O cognominatus,	he is Alpha: from that Fountain
ipse fons et clausula	all that is and hath been flows;
Omnium quae sunt, fuerunt,	He is Omega, of all things
quaeque post futura sunt	yet to come the mystic close,
saeculorum saeculis.	evermore and evermore.[11]

With even more typological detail in the complete poem, Prudentius etches in the celestial hierarchies, the creation of earth, heavens, and ocean, the creation and fall of man, types and prophecies of the Saviour, before ever reaching the Gospel narrative. Only then does he burst into rejoicing:

O beatus ortus ille,	O how blest that wondrous birthday,
virgo cum puerpera	when the Maid the curse retrieved,
edidit nostram salutem	brought to birth mankind's salvation;
foeta sancto Spiritu,	by the Holy Ghost conceived;
et puer Redemptor orbis	and the Babe, the world's Redeemer
os sacratum protulit. ...	in her loving arms received. ...
ecce, quem vates vetustis	This is he, whom seer and sybil
concinebant saeculis.	sang in ages long gone by.

The Edwardian translation obscures one vital detail, that "the Babe, the Redeemer of the world, revealed His hallowed face."

Having set in its cosmic context this central fact of the virgin birth, having sketched in Christ's healing, resuscitative, and feeding miracles, His death, descent into Hades, and ascension, the poet calls on all creation, from archangels to children, to praise Father, Son, and Holy Ghost, *saeculorum saeculis*.

Ironically, we moderns, who know the Western church to have appropriated the birthday of Mithras, celebrate not the central mystery of the Incarnation, the Word made flesh, but the attendant circumstances that few New Testament scholars would confirm upon oath: the stable, the announcement to the Shepherds, the visit of the Magi (three kings only from the third century).[12] Did our ancestors dwell so lovingly on the details of the Nativity and so neglect its meaning? From "Corde natus ex Parentis," at all events, we know that Christians of the late Roman empire celebrated it not as a holiday from reality but as the incursion of the supreme reality into human life.

A century or more afterwards, Sedulius, in his acrostic hymn "A solis ortus cardine," gives more narrative detail, yet he also sets the Nativity within its scriptural context.[13] He too defines the purpose of the holy birth, that what God had created should not perish, for he leaps from the Annunciation to the Crucifixion, defeat of Satan, and Resurrection before dwelling upon the homely details:

Faeno iacere pertulit,	He endured to lie in the hay
praesepe non abhorruit,	and did not abhor the manger,
parvoque lacte pastus est,	and was fed with a little milk,
per quem nec ales esurit.	[he] through whom not even a bird
	hungers.

Though his verses limp, Sedulius affirms the paradox of the Omnipotent lying helpless that has haunted the poetic imagination almost through the Christian era. As in a folk tale, in a real time and place the angels reveal to a poor maiden and shepherds the coming of the child whom a king fears and wise men adore, the Creator born amid the beasts. The sceptic can trace the whole Christian *mythos* to imagination reversing in fantasy the conditions of human society, the liberal theologian treat as fantasy the Nativity, that inversion of man's dependence on God. Even the Roman Catholic Raymond Brown observes in successive layers of narrative the Messiah being disclosed at progressively earlier moments. The "classical Christian" and fundamentalist, however, will insist upon the historical accuracy of SS. Matthew and Luke. Given the Incarnation, why quibble over a star?[14]

The pre-eminence of doctrine over narrative may be seen from early nativity hymns that with one notable exception convey the wonder and mystery of Christ's coming in terms of pagan sun myths yet leave its earthly details to the gospel reader. In his masterpiece "Splendor paternae gloriae," St. Ambrose calls Christ *lux lucis et fons luminis* ("Light and fount of light") and "true sun" (*verusque sol*) by implied contrast with Apollo and Phoebus. In his "Intende, qui regis Israel," he refers to one aspect that fascinated ancient and, still more, medieval poets:

non ex virili semine	Not from male seed but by the
sed mystico spiramine	Spirit's mystic action the Word
Verbum Dei factum est caro	of God was made flesh, and the
fructusque ventris floruit.	fruit of the womb blossomed.[15]

In the seventh-century Greek hymn "Μέγα καὶ παραδόξου Θαῦμα," "Mega kai paradoxon thauma" ("A great and mighty wonder") the "Divine Paradox" is that the Virgin gives birth yet remains *intacta*; the Word becomes flesh while remaining on high.[16]

Otherwise, to judge from surviving texts, early and medieval hymnists neither dwelt sentimentally upon nor drew social implications from the Nativity. Instead, they averted their eyes from the natural and social order to the spiritual drama: the Messiah's descent to restore eternal day.

In "Gloriam Deo in excelsis hodie," Paulinus of Aquileia, a poet and theologian elevated to the episcopate by Charlemagne, invests his lengthy narrative of the Nativity, Epiphany, flight into Egypt, slaughter of the Innocents, and Crucifixion with both wonder and a symbolic dimension.[17] The angels announce the birth *sub noctis silentio* ("under the silence of night"). The gifts *demonstrant mysterium*, the gold showing the *regis* ... *excellentia* (royal pre-eminence) of Christ, the incense his *summum sacerdotem* (high priesthood), and the myrrh his future interment. Paulinus adds one touch of an early medieval legend drawn on by Shakespeare for some beautiful lines in *Hamlet*, that on the holy night even the sea lay at peace.

The only Roman and early medieval hymns we have come from men steeped like Prudentius in the classical poets or else, like Paulinus, in the Christian Fathers. Until the high Middle Ages it is impossible, therefore, to compare monastic hymns on the Nativity with popular carols. The former are all we have.

Any comprehensive account of medieval nativity hymns and carols would require a separate book. A single volume (XX) of the *Analecta Hymnica* devoted to anonymous texts has 179 on the Christ child, mostly from the thirteenth century, followed by 123 on the Virgin. Of the latter, one-third are from thirteenth-century and a quarter from fourteenth-century manuscripts. In each case, the twelfth-century manuscripts come mainly from France, those of the thirteenth century, mainly from Germany.[18] So far as this evidence goes, it suggests not only an increasing concentration on the Virgin but a decline of poetic compilation in France that was no doubt hastened by the Hundred Years War. Here we can but illustrate major trends in nativity hymns and in English popular lyrics.

Inevitably, hymns for liturgical use lack the tenderness towards Virgin and Child of carols and dramatic lyrics. By the same token, the cult of the Virgin evinces a matriarchal trend in medieval religion as compared with the patriarchal cast of the Puritan culture, but one too universal to have arisen from the suppressed sexuality of celibates. Nor do the charming lyrics still anthologized, "The Friendly Beasts," "Maiden in the moor lay," or "The Christ child shivering with cold," imply that our ancestors all enjoyed a child-like faith, for in passion and subtlety those of Abelard or Adam of St. Victor as far transcend them as Mozart arias the folk songs of the eighteenth century.

In general, nevertheless, the finest monastic hymns express joy or wonder in the mystery of the Incarnation, and folk lyrics compassion for the Mother and Child. So far as any distinction can be drawn between Learned and Popular devotion in the Middle Ages, it lies between awed contemplation of the inexplicable fact embedded in a dogma, *Verbum caro factum est* ("The Word was made flesh") and the tenderness evoked in every heart by the image of a young mother and child lying in the manger. Even in voicing the latter, a monastic poet conceals within his apparent artlessness a kernel of dogma and typology:

Rutilat hodie	The day glows red [dawns]
Dies laetitiae,	The day of gladness;
Dat sol justitiae,	the Sun of Justice
Radios gratiae,	gives beams of grace,
Adest in specie	present in our guise is [this day]
Nostra rex gloriae.	the King of glory.[19]
(13th century)	

In the very act of imitating the great hymns, "A solis ortus cardine" or "Conditor alme siderum," condemned by Raby as "mediocre" because considered apart from their musical and liturgical settings,[20] monastic poets reveal a highly allusive art. Yet, beneath even their most pointless ingenuity runs a current of life. Medieval hymnists are always bursting to acclaim the "new" era Christ has ushered in a thousand years since. Victorians, by contrast, often treat the birth narrative as one handed down from "long ago."[21]

Nevertheless the narrative hymn "Lumen clarum rite fulget," ascribed to the sternly evangelical Raban Maur (9th century),[22] combines wonder at the divine descent and the profound transcendence of early Latin hymns with the social concern of later English hymns in the Learned tradition in its prayer for Christ to protect widows and virgins, parents and children.

Perhaps because scriptural readings in the Mass and Offices rendered narration superfluous, hymns mostly became meditations. As early as the ninth century, "Gloriam nato cecinere Christo," attributed to the Carolingian poet Walafrid Strabo, turns quickly from the coming of the Magi to its moral implication, the peace and joy that Christ's love brings mankind.[23]

In "Salus mundi, sator universi," Othloh (d. 1072) meditates on Christ, who by taking human flesh has renewed the world.[24] In his stanza *Natus est nobis novus / Auctor orbis* ("The creator of the world is newborn to us"), Othloh avers that faith in the new birth, though beyond human reason, perpetually renews the world and so robs grief of its power. Here, like the modern Evangelical, he shifts his attention from the divine object to the worshipping subject, but in the collective sense usual in medieval hymnody. This note of renewal resounds in poets from the Carolingians down at least to Adam of St. Victor, in the twelfth century. In the fourteenth and fifteenth, it is heard less.

Devotional meditation and the sense of renewal characterize Nativity hymns of the high Middle Ages. In "Verbum aeternaliter," the skilful poet Gottschalk of Limburg (d.1098) forsakes history for antiphonal devotions to the Good Shepherd.[25] Similarly, in his Epiphany hymn "Laus tibi, Christe," he focuses on the symbolic gifts and on the rebirth of the newly baptized to a life of inner obedience.[26]

Peter Abelard (1079-1142), the most gifted of all these meditative poets, reflects in his office hymns for the convent of Heloïse upon the Virgin's conception of the Word by the Word. In "Verbo verum"[27] he expounds the idea that the *claritas* of truth spreads amid surrounding darkness. The supreme exponent of the Christian paradox, Abelard contrasts the Saviour's lowliness here with his celestial power above, yet suggests that Christ and his stainless mother needed no bath, literal or baptismal. In "Dei patris" his love of paradox and wonder finds expression in dramatic contrasts: between Christ's mean hovel and heavenly mansion (*vili tugurio* and *caeli palatio*); between his crying in the manger and thunderclaps of heaven (*caelum tonitribus*); between the fodder of beasts here and refection of angels above. (Notably, in post-Reformation psalmody thunder pertains to the Father.) In "Quam beatam" Abelard pictures the Virgin's humble bed of straw and poor diet only to point the contrast between this world's neglect and the angels' adoration of Christ.

The Christmas sequences of Adam of St. Victor, Abelard's only rival in poetic skill, deserve attention for their harmonies and rhythms rather than for their ideas. While most of his ideas and symbols are drawn from the common stock of medieval hymnists, Adam astonishes by his sense of wonder and joyous renewal. His imagery, when original, tends towards allegory rather than paradox, as in developing the conceit of Christ within the Virgin as a nut within its hull.[28]

In the dismal fifteenth century, a long poem on the Incarnation attributed to Thomas à Kempis, whose *Imitatio Christi* distils the sweetest essence of late medieval spirituality, bears a quite different stamp. Throughout the twenty-three quatrains of "Apparuit benignitas," the author insists upon the human needs that out of his boundless love Christ came to supply.[29] In our hymn "O amor quam ecstaticus" ("O love how ecstatic, how overflowing") he recounts the birth of Christ, poor and in exile yet King of Glory, then for three or four stanzas returns in every line to *nobis* or *nos,* as though to insist upon our central place in God's affections.[30] Before his concluding doxology, he enjoins us like any modern hymnist to visit Bethlehem and adore with the Shepherds. If his verse be prolix and overheated, it manifests a radical change from the otherworldly and impersonal splendour of the earliest Latin hymns on the Incarnation.

As a leader in the brotherhood of the Common Life, the blessed Thomas stood near the end of a tradition that had begun with the Franciscans in the early thirteenth century. By processional rites and drama, but above all, by carols supplied predominantly by friars, the Church endeavoured with much success to turn to devotional use energies formerly employed in the pagan entertainments that its councils had failed to suppress. The history of the English carol, like that of the French and Italian *lauda,* has been thoroughly quarried during the past half century. Whether the term "carol" be used, as by R.L. Greene, solely to denote the song, sacred or secular, consisting of burden sung by all and stanzas sung by a leader, or whether in the common meaning of the popular song for a religious or seasonal celebration, it clearly lies between the folk song and the hymn or courtly lyric. The pagan and by the same token pre-feudal elements in popular carols — Yule, ring-dancing, the contention of male holly with female ivy — were well suited to the matriarchal aspect of medieval devotion. During the twelve days from Christmas to Epiphany, with their cluster of holy days, not only religious but social distinctions were to an extent set aside by customs like the enthronement of the Boy Bishop and the invitation for tenants to participate in the feasting at manor house or castle.[31] Carol collections, nevertheless, afford an insight into both social conditions and the devotion to the Holy Family that was inculcated by these songs, in Greene's phrase "popular by destination" rather than "by origin."[32]

Direct allusions to social conditions are few and obvious. In "Farewel, Advent, Christemas is cum," tentatively ascribed to the fifteenth century Franciscan James Ryman, lack of meat during the Advent fast has sent the singers hungry to bed, unable to eat "stynking fisshe" or afford "Salt fisshes" and "samon."[33] Consigning Advent to monks and friars, the carolist laments that "Thou maist not dwell with labouring man, / For on thy fare no skille he can, / For he must ete both now and than." Another Advent carol, "O clavis David inclita," hails Christ as liberator from the prison of sin and pictures Heaven as "joyfull halle" where forever "ys lyff withowten desstresse."[34] Though the Nativity carol "Now syng we, syng we/ Gloria tibi, Domine," being from a sixteenth century manuscript, cannot for certain be regarded as medieval, its conclusion represents the clearest identification of Christ with the poor:

> Between an ox and an asse
> *Enixa est puerpera;*
> In pore clothyng clothed he was
> *Qui regnat super ethera.*[35]

More often, social allusions come indirectly, in the many carols on the Shepherds and beasts. This preoccupation with the humble circumstances in which the Son of God was born distinguishes carols for the peasantry both from those for the gentry and from hymns for monks and nuns. A minority of carols, however, stand out as unmistakably upper class. Thus "Make we mery bothe more and lasse" begins with the injunction:

> Lett no man cum into this hall,
> Grome, page, nor yet marshall,

> But that sum sport he brying withall,
> For now ys the tyme of Crystmas.[36]

Another, "Proface, welcom, wellcome," hails Christ as "kynges sone and emperoure" and welcomes all on behalf of "The gode lord of this place."[37] Both, again, exist in early sixteenth-century manuscripts and may therefore have been written in a time of increasing awareness of social rank.

We may with more confidence distinguish those carols copied between the thirteenth and sixteenth centuries that encouraged tenderness towards the Child and his Virgin Mother from those that explored the meaning of his Incarnation. Of ninety-two "Carols of the Nativity" collected by Greene, twenty-one recount the Child's birth amid the beasts or allude to His poverty. A further nine (four by Ryman) prominently feature the Shepherds.[38] We may say, then, that one-third stress the poverty of the birth and its attendants. By contrast, of fifty-seven "Carols to the Virgin" and a further twenty-five on the Annunciation, only one alludes to the Virgin's lowly social status.[39] The overwhelming majority call her "Lady," "Queen," or even "Empress" or else develop a typological image, the root of Jesse or rose of Sharon.[40] A few call her meek and mild (terms used in the eighteenth and nineteenth centuries for Christ), but far more treat her as a model of womanly chastity and maternal tenderness.[41] As regards her rank, the lowly maiden had been appropriated by the ruling class.

To what extent does the language of Nativity and Epiphany carols bespeak the social consciousness of the nobility or the doctrinal preoccupations of the clergy? How far do we find in them the inescapable condescension of the privileged addressing the lower orders or the clerical concern with the Christian Myth and its meaning? How far, also, do secular concerns impinge upon sacred?

The last question should be put in reverse, for as Greene and other authorities insist, the tradition of dancing in a circle while singing a burden in response to verses sung by a leader dates from before the conversion of the Franks. In the medieval carol, unlike the modern hymn, the sacred intruded upon the secular.[42] This adaptation of the dance song represents the last phase in the Christianization of northern Europe.

As regards the themes and social implications of ninety "Carols of the Nativity" in Greene's collection, we may distinguish the following groups:

(1A) Birth narrative: Nos. 21, 24, 27C, 32, 34, 35, 41, 45, 50, 58, 75, 77, 78, 79, 80, 81, 89, 91
(1B) Birth narrative (including visit of Wise Men): 27, 37, 38, 44, 47, 51, 74, 76, 82, 87. These two groups together amount to 28, or 31.1 per cent.
(2) Nativity and also Crucifixion: Nos. 12, 19, 25, 48, 53, 60.1, 87 in all 7, or 7.8 per cent.

(3) Whole Myth (Fall, Redemption, etc.): Nos. 16, 18, 31, 46, 61, 62, 93, 95 in all 8, or 8.9 per cent.

(4) Blessed Virgin (mainly): Nos. 22, 26, 29, 30, 49, 54, 57, 59, 60 in all 9, or 10 per cent.

(5A) Prophecies of Messiah: Nos. 40, 43, 63, 66, 67, 68, 69, 70, 72, 73.

(5B) Typological images: Nos. 41, 60.1, 65. These together amount to 14, or 15.5 per cent.

(6) Incarnation, its theology or meaning: Nos. 12, 14, 20, 23B, C; 33, 34, 36, 39, 42, 50, 55, 56, 64, 71, 84, 92, 93, 96. These amount to 19, or 21.1 per cent.

(7) Its moral or social implications: Nos. 13, 25, 30, 50, 52, 64, 85, 86 i.e., 10, or 11.1 per cent.

(8) Feasts of Twelve Days (including SS. Stephen, John, Holy Innocents, New Year, Circumcision) Nos. 7, 8, 9, 23, 28, i.e., 5, or 5.5 per cent.

(9) Merriment Nos. 10, 11, 15, 17, i.e., 4, or 4.4 per cent.

(10) Upper-Class celebration, Nos. 11 and 13 or 2.2 per cent.

Even this rough grouping presents difficulties. Analysis of a single example will indicate why some appear in more than one group. No. 50, in a sixteenth-century manuscript, has the burden

> I pray you, be mery and synge with me
> In worship of Christys nativite.

Its first stanza announces the birth:

> Into this world this day dide com
> Jhesu Criste, bothe God and man
> Lorde and servant in on person,
> Born of the blessid virgin Mary.

The second stanza (paraphrasing 2 Cor. 8: 9) presents the divine descent as well as a social descent:

> He that was riche withowt any nede
> Appered in this world in right pore wede
> To mak us that were pore indede
> Riche withowt any nede trewly.

The third dwells upon the poverty of his surroundings:

> A stabill was his chambre; a crach was his bed;
> He had not a pylow to lay under his head;

With maydyns mylk that babe was fedde;
In pore clothis was lappid the Lord Almyty.

and the fourth upon moral and theological implications:

A noble lesson here is us tawght:
To set all worldly riches at nawght,
But pray that we may be theder browght
Wher riches ys everlastyngly.

This pedestrian but comprehensive carol thus appears in groups 1A, 9, and 10. If poetically inferior to some carols discussed by Routley, it goes far to explain the universal appeal of the Nativity. With Christ as "lord and servant," rich beyond human compare yet poorer than the poorest, fed by the divinely consecrated virgin, people of each rank, sex, or occupation can identify. With the Marxist mythology one would expect only the underprivileged to identify. In the educated who espouse their cause, world or rather class denial takes the form of social displacement, a secular descent.

The Marxist can reasonably accuse some Evangelical hymnists of preaching world-and-life denial to the poor while overcompensating them with images of future bliss. With regard to Nativity carols at least, he cannot fairly level this charge against the medieval Church. Certainly, as No. 50 shows, the world-denying ethic inseparable from monastic life and office hymns predominated in Franciscan preaching to the laity, but medieval Catholicism no less profoundly sanctified the more innocent forms of mirth and love. As Routley remarks in his superb study of "Tomorrow shall be my dancing-day," that ballad-carol consecrates the eros of man and woman in representing Christ as Lover; and thus it reveals a fundamental paradox in medieval religion:

Then I was born of a virgin pure,
Of her I took fleshy substance;
Thus was I knit to man's nature,
To call my true love to my dance.

This carol, in which Christ recounts his whole life, has a burden suited for dance steps: "Sing, O my love, O my love, my love, my love: / This have I done for my true love."[43] The more familiar Coventry Carol likewise sanctifies the universal tenderness of mother for child, as do the many lullaby-carols collected by Greene. This instinctively human, life-affirming joy and love, transcending tribe and class, Marxism seems to exclude.

To discuss comparable features of medieval religion — its open air processions, mystery plays, feasts, and carnivals — would take us beyond the confines of this book, but two distinctions must be remarked between medieval and post-Reformation verse for Christmas hymnody, and one between medieval and modern religion in general.

First, medieval carols draw no sharp line between sacred and secular rejoicing. They enjoin feasting, dancing, sports and games, along with holy joy in the Infant and Madonna. Few run to the extremes of this, whose singers would evidently join in the fooling of Malvolio:

> Yiff he say he can not syng,
> Sum oder sport then lett hymn bryng,
> ...
> Yiff he say he can nowght do,
> The for my love aske hym no mo,
> But to the stokkes then lett hym go,
> For now ys the tyme of Crystmas.[44]

But monk and layman, knight and peasant alike could sing the burden of another: "Man, be glad in halle and bour; / This tyme was born our Sauyour."[45]

Second, medieval carols and hymns did not split off Christmas from the rest of the Christian year. The author of No. 16 devotes a stanza each to Good Friday, Easter Day, and Ascension Day. As the table above will show, a considerable proportion of carols extend forward to the Passion or back to the prophecies. The concentration of the Evangelical revival on the Atonement and of our post-Christian culture on the Nativity are two facets of the post-Reformation separation of church and life. The Puritans would have been no less scandalized by the indecorous behaviour of medieval Christians within a church than by their idolatries without.

Because religious and secular behaviour were less clearly demarcated, a less clear line was drawn between the inner and the outer life. Some carols, though not many, enjoin a religion of the heart. One revealing monastic influence celebrates the place in which "The sunne of grace" has shone and a holy birth that "to the herte stongyn."[46] Another bids man beware how he treat Christ, born for his sake.[47] Since medieval Nativity carols usually call for collective celebration of the Birth rather than inward rebirth, they involve all classes. If world-and-life-denial predominates in hymns for religious houses, in popular carols there remained, even in the late middle ages, a strong element of joy in life. By contrast, Evangelical hymns that were "popular by destination" tended towards world-and-life-denial. While biblical narrative, prophecy, and the feudal system supplied images for poets of the Nativity, the practice of doubling inspired a distinctive strain of imagery in hymns on the Epiphany. Two of the Epiphany hymns that compared the Messiah's manifestation to the Gentiles with that to the Jews at His baptism, "Jesus refulsit omnium" and "A patre unigenitus," were included in the Anglo-Saxon *Hymnarium*.[48] The earliest in this strain, "Inluminans altis-simus," attributed to St. Ambrose, relates the birth to the baptism, changing of water into wine, and feeding of the five thousand.[49] These miracles of Christ are never-failing courses of springs (*meatus fontium*) for they multiply in the deeds of his disciples. A text in the Mozarabic hymnal, "Agni genitur Domine," describes the child as fount of life (*fons vitae*) sent to refashion light to the blind (*lumen caecis reformare*).[50] This imagery of the renewing fountain recurs in later hymns that relate the Epiphany to the Baptism, as it does in countless modern hymns not specifically linked with either.

Two famous hymns on the Gifts of the Magi, however, expose a simple and enormous gulf between ancient and modern devotion. Caswall's translation of "O sola magnarum urbium," a cento from the *Cathemerinon* of Prudentius, as "Bethlehem, of noblest cities" does not materially change the sense of its beautiful but difficult original and so will serve for illustration.[51]

After apostrophizing Bethlehem as pre-eminent among cities, Prudentius shifts into the past tense to describe the Star that announced God's descent in earthly form as fairer than the morning sun. Like numberless succeeding hymnists, he then interprets the gold, incense, and myrrh as symbols of the child's royalty, divinity, and "future tomb." The Magi proffer them in an eternal present. We behold but in no way participate in the rite.

In the one Victorian Epiphany hymn everyone knows, "As with gladness men of old" (W.C. Dix, 1860), the narrative, set in the distant past, is followed at each stage by an application that involves us in the present.[52] As the "men of old" were led to the cradle, so may we be led to God. As they bent the knee before "Him whom heaven and earth adore," so may we "ever seek the mercy-seat." As they offered "gifts most rare," no longer specified, so may we "our costliest treasures bring." Finally, Dix forsakes narration to beg guidance for our "ransomed souls", to the land where they need no "guiding star," where "no clouds Thy glory hide." Whereas Prudentius compared the Star to the rising sun, Dix presents Christ as the unsetting sun visible "in the heavenly country," as the King to whom we shall sing alleluias.

Dix draws on an age-old repertoire of images and turns of phrase.[53] What is new is his method, one that largely confirms the dictum of Martineau, that modern hymnists "do but touch upon" the biblical scene to apply it to the spiritual lives of the present worshippers. Dix's very vagueness, by comparison with the precision of Prudentius, can be excused on the ground that by his time the merest allusion to the Gifts would suffice. In his conclusion, moreover, he implicitly compares the present worship with the eternal, alluding no longer to that of the Magi.

Between the ages of Watts and of Dix, few hymns require more of us than to participate imaginatively in the biblical episode. The ancient hymn arouses awe and admiration without requiring any conscious effort to imitate Christ or

implement His teaching. Although the dangers of egocentric and idolatrous application appear in well-nigh every hymnal compiled between the time of Watts
and the First World War, personal involvement is surely a prerequisite for the
Christianizing of both the individual and the social organism. That the monks
and nuns who sang the Latin hymns imitated Christ in their very calling does
not invalidate the contention that in contrast to the ancient poet versifying Christian history and mythology, the late Victorian or twentieth-century hymnist,
though rarely so accomplished a poet, seeks to engage the worshipper actively
in the transformation of the inner and social worlds into the divine likeness.
Numinous awe radiates from the objective hymns of a millennium or more; mirth
resounds from countless lyrics and carols composed in worse times than our
own; but only hymns of recent centuries require their singers not to abandon this
world, but to participate in its transformation. Participation is inseparable from
suffering.

7

THE HEART OF THE MYTH:
CHRIST CRUCIFIED AND RISEN

Christ has died. Christ is risen.
Christ will come again.

These Memorial Acclamations enshrine the Christian history and myth re-enacted in the Eucharist. Unmistakably, Jesus was crucified outside Jerusalem c. A.D. 29. His Incarnation is a matter of faith, the accounts of his birth partly or wholly legendary, his Resurrection a physical event to some, a symbolic or psychological truth to others, and to some a fiction. But that he was crucified believers and unbelievers for the most part agree. When Christians turned persecutors, the whitewashing of Pilate and heaping of blame upon the Jews in the Gospel narratives were to cause immense and tragic suffering. Nevertheless, the Crucifixion happened.

The disciples having melted into the crowd, this cruel but routine punishment of a young preacher adjudged a danger to public order should have ended the matter. Governments have executed dangerous young men since the dawn of history. But the claim that Jesus lives confers upon this execution a meaning no other judicial slaying ever had. Eighteen centuries later, John Henry Newman sent a shiver of awe through his university congregation by bidding them remember that this thing was done to Almighty God.[1]

How the faithless disciples came to preach Christ crucified and resurrected remains a mystery, an incomprehensible fact. His parables, even his miracles, do not explain the cult but for which they would remain unrecorded. Only the belief in his divinity and resurrection, by those who deserted him, can account for that first, most astounding revival. The Gospels did not create that faith; it created them.

Only Christians make the sign of defeat. Communists raise the clenched fist and Fascists, like ancient Romans, raise the right arm in token of conquest. None but the Christians have so long and so fervently hymned their founder's execution. Some of their songs achieve tragic nobility, others a morbidity that offends the critical sense in believer and sceptic alike. Even when text and melody rival those of the grandest canticle or tenderest love song, beauty can never be their end. Unbelievers who cheerfully sing Christmas carols do not sing passion lyrics. The Cross moves or offends, but rarely entertains. Even in the film *Jesus Christ, Superstar* its meaning transcends entertainment.

More fully than the Acclamations, the so-called "Apostles' Creed" recounts the Myth: "born of the Virgin Mary, suffered under Pontius Pilate, was crucified, dead and buried ... descended into Hell ... rose again ... ascended into Heaven ... sitteth on the right hand of the Father ... shall come again to judge the quick and the dead. ..." The Harrowing of Hell, Resurrection, and Ascension took precedence in hymnody of the Roman and Byzantine eras, the suffering and death in Western hymnody during the high and declining middle ages.

THE KING ON THE CROSS

The earliest Latin hymns on the Passion and Resurrection still in use are the "Vexilla Regis" and "Pange lingua" (and "Salve festa dies") by Venantius Fortunatus, Bishop of Poitiers in the late sixth century.[2] These and a few attributed to Prudentius, St. Ambrose, and the great Byzantine hymnist Romanos show what Christ and his Cross signified to the Church before and after the collapse of the Western Empire.

The Roman and Byzantine hymnists envisaged Christ as victorious King and liberator. Not only did the Cross appear in Constantine's dream as a sign of victory, but also an Ambrosian Easter hymn represents Christ as climbing upon it.[3] The Kontakion of Romanos on the Entry into Jerusalem presents Him as redeemer of helpless mankind. Christ the "Modeller" of man assures his "clay" that

> It is for me alone to free you from your debt ...
> I am to be sold in exchange for you, and I shall free you,
> I am to be crucified for you, and you will not die.[4]

Even more than the legal metaphors, the dramatic tone brings out the triumphal activism of Christ as envisaged during the Byzantine autocracy. Even when scourged He appears the victor rather than the victim. The bleeding head and sorrowful eyes belong to the Christ of medieval and later Western art and poetry.[5] The Christ of Byzantium and Imperial Rome wears the victor's crown rather than the crown of thorns.

Latin poets treat Christ Crucified and Risen as a monarch foretold by David and Solomon, though Prudentius, like T.S. Eliot in this century, regards the water and the blood as signs of cleansing and martyrdom.[6]

In the "Vexilla regis," composed for a procession bearing a fragment of the True Cross, Bishop Fortunatus imitates the triumphal entry into Jerusalem.[7] Like Abelard seven centuries later, this last Roman and first medieval poet loves the paradox or ironic contrast. His royal banners herald not the crowned monarch but the cross, Y-shaped like a tree, with its victim hanging as on a Roman balance.[8] Round his images of banners, cross, and victim the poet weaves classical, Hebraic, and Christian associations: the tree reverses the doom wrought by the paradisal tree; the divine blood stains it in the purple of Roman royalty; as David prophesied, God here declares himself among the Gentiles; above all, kingly radiance streams from the Cross. The images confront us unscreened, for the poet nowhere enters the poem, nor does he establish a viewpoint, since *ut nos lavaret* (that he might cleanse us) refers to the entire race.

Vexilla regis prodeunt,	The banners of the King go forward
fulget crucis mysterium,	The mystery of the Cross shines
quo carne carnis conditor	by which in the flesh the Creator of flesh
suspensus est patibulo.	was suspended on the yoke.
confixa clavis viscera	His body pierced by nails
tendens manus, vestigia,	stretching out his hands, his feet,
redemptionis gratia	here for [our] redemption
hic inmolata est hostia.	the victim was sacrificed.
quo vulneratus insuper	Whereon wounded beside
mucrone dirae lanceae,	from the sharp point of the cruel spear
ut nos lavaret crimine	that he might cleanse us from sin
manavit unda, sanguine.	he shed forth water and blood.
inpleta sunt quae concinit	fulfilled is what sang
David fideli carmine,	David in his song, faithful to the truth,
dicendo nationibus:	saying to the nations:
"regnavit a ligno Deus."	"God reigns from the tree."
arbor decora et fulgida,	[O] beautiful and glowing tree
ornata regis purpura. ...	adorned with purple [the blood] of the King. ...

In ascribing prophecy of the Messiah to David, Fortunatus seems to have in mind 1 Chron. 16.31, in the Vulgate, *Laetentur caeli, et exultet terra: et dicant in nationibus, Dominus regnavit,* to which he adds "a ligno" (from the tree).

Nowhere does he mention the crown of thorns, yet his image of royalty has a double irony, in that the "king" the Roman soldiers mocked did indeed triumph by his death, to reign over their descendants.[9]

Down the ages the "Vexilla regis" has been rearranged and added to by the compilers of the Roman Breviary, translated by an Anglo-Saxon poet, by the Franciscan William Heribert, by poets such as Lydgate and Crashaw, by the Anglican hymnologists Neale and Dearmer and the Catholic Caswall, and in our day painted and paraphrased by David Jones.[10] While, as Routley remarks, it has "defeated every known translator," being for that reason omitted from the recent *New Catholic Hymnal,*[11] it has inspired strokes of genius such as the anonymous seventeenth-century version of *tulitque praedam tartari*, "spoiled the spoiler of his prey."[12] The Christ of a translation tends to resemble the hero figure of the translator's own culture.

So, to an extent, did the Christ of Fortunatus. If J.A.W. Bennett exaggerates in calling this, rather than the "Pange lingua," the "most martial of all Latin hymns,"[13] the Christ of the "Vexilla regis" far more resembles a Roman or Frankish monarch than a carpenter's son.

At the high noon of British imperial glory two Anglican versions illuminate this portrayal of Christ in the image of the translator's own time. For *dicendo nationibus,* Neale translated "Amidst the nations ... saith he (David)," which the editors of *Hymns Ancient and Modern* (1861) retouched to "How God the heathen's King should be, / For God is reigning from the tree."[14] Their rendering is legitimate insofar as *nationes* had an old meaning "Gentiles," but to mid-Victorians "heathen" signified Africans, Asians, and Polynesians.

In an adaptation so free as to amount to variations on a theme, Percy Dearmer, about 1933, retouched this again to "and unfold / Love's crowning power, that all see / He reigns and triumphs from a tree." For *tulitque praedam tartari,* an image ironically reversing a Roman war custom by making Christ bear away Satan's prey, the human race, Neale follows the brilliant seventeenth-century version. Dearmer, however, says: "priceless treasure, freely spent / To pay for man's enfranchisement." By adding to this his earlier couplet "There was he slain in noble youth, / There suffered to maintain the truth" we see that in the original hymn of the sixth-century God reversed the Fall by fulfilling David's prophecy; in the 1861 version he manifested his power to the heathen, and in the one composed after the First World War youth was slain to liberate mankind and thereby show love triumphant. The compilers of *Hymns Ancient and Modern* treat Christ as an English missionary; the compiler of *Songs of Praise* treats him as a young hero sacrificed for freedom's sake.

J.W. Grant's version in the Canadian *Hymn Book* (1971)[15] constitutes an even freer paraphrase, but one much closer to the spirit of the original. "The flaming banners of our King / advance through his self-offering," designed to fit an arrangement of the Sarum Plainsong tune (7th century), incorporates both St. Paul's dictum that the Resurrection robbed death of its sting and a modern reflection on the ethical inspiration of the sacrifice: "The best are shamed before that wood; / the worst gain power to be good." These assertions, naturally enough, appeal less than the images taken directly from the original ("Messiah reigning from a tree") or else adapted to fit the Canadian environment ("With what strange light the rough trunk shone, / its purple limbs a royal throne.") Despite some prosaic lines and an objectivity comparable with that of the original, this, the most recent version of the "Vexilla regis" known to me, testifies to the poetic evolution of the Myth over fourteen centuries, in its movement from the defeat of death and cleansing sacrifice to moral transformation and human participation in the final lines "O grant, most blessed trinity, / that all may share the victory."

Turning to early images of the Cross, we find a greater emphasis upon typology than royalty, for though Prudentius treats the Cross as a royal standard or emblem, Fortunatus in "Pange lingua" develops the Pauline and Augustinian image of the Cross as the tree reversing the Fall. In the metre of the Roman marching song, he celebrates the victory won upon the Cross, then turns to the fatal fruit. After recounting the effects of the Fall, Nativity, and Passion, he hails the *crux fidelis,* the *dulce lignum* that bore so sweet a weight:

> flecte ramos, arbor alta, tensa laxa viscera,
> et rigor lentescat ille quem dedit nativitas,
> ut superni membra regis mite tendas stipite....

> Bend, O lofty Tree, thy branches,
> Thy too rigid sinews bend;
> And awhile the [stubborn] hardness,
> Which thy birth bestow'd, suspend;
> And the limbs of [heaven's] high Monarch
> Gently on thine arms extend.[16]

In this as in other ancient hymns, poet and worshippers remain passive, indeed absent from the picture, their salvation provisionally assured by the Cross as sign or talisman.

During the Middle Ages, the Cross acquired a range of meanings. For the gentry during the eighth century, jewel-encrusted crosses became valued ornaments.[17] Prudentius has allegorized its four arms as typifying virtues.[18] In "Vexillum regis" Fulbert of Chartres (d. 1028) treats the Cross glittering above all stars of heaven as evidence that Christ's love will fortify those who sign themselves therewith against the Seven Deadly Sins.[19] Similarly, in "Salve, crux sancta," attributed to Heribert of Rothenburg (d. 1042), the sign of the Cross protects from evils that beset the body and soul:

Protege, salva, benedic, sanctifica	Protect, save, bless, sanctify
Populum cunctum crucis per	All people through the seal of [Thy]
signaculum,	cross,
Morbos averte corporis et animae,	Avert diseases of body and soul.
Hoc contra signum nullum stet	Let no peril stand against this sign.[20]
periculum.	

While the Augustinian Reginald of Canterbury (d. 1109) devotes most of "O decus, o clavi suaves in stipite suavi" (O beauty, O sweet nails on sweet branch")[21] to the triumphal deliverance from Satan, he addresses the Cross and Blood like any Franciscan or Evangelical, devotes more attention to our triumphal deliverance from Satan, and in "O crux, vivificum quae pondus sustinuisti," addresses the Cross itself as our ransom.[22]

CHRIST RISEN

If Bennett distinguishes too sharply between the Jesus of passion hymns and the Christ of Easter hymns,[23] the latter certainly stress the mythical and typological aspect of the Resurrection. Already, in "Corde natus ex Parentis," Prudentius had triumphantly recounted the Harrowing, Resurrection, and Ascension to the neglect of the biblical narratives. In "Salve, festa dies," culled from his long poem *Tempora florigero rutilant distincta sereno* and still in use as an Easter processional, Fortunatus hails the spring day's brightness that befits the resurrection of the Victor whose death and burial have ensured that man shall not lie forever in the grave.[24] The poet does describe in some detail the graveclothes Christ threw off, before calling on him to free the dead and fashion the newly baptized into pure children of Heaven, but finally (like the Odist) prays that Christians may cause a floral crown to bloom for the Redeemer who has won them a heavenly crown. Thus, after his celebrated description of the lengthening days, meadow flowers and bird songs, Fortunatus brings together springtime, the Resurrection, baptismal renewal, and the wreath or crown of victor and martyr. In treating spring as a symbol of the Resurrection, he foreshadows the medieval way of perceiving the natural world as an emblem of the spiritual.

In "Aurora lucis rutilat" ("Light's glittering morn bedecks the sky"), a contemporary or earlier poet likewise associates the morning sun with Easter. While this hymn dwells more than "Salve, festa dies" upon the events of the first Easter, it chiefly interests us in associating Christ with the "Sun of righteousness" in the prophecy of Malachi 4.2: *Et orientur vobis timentibus nomen meum Sol justitiae et sanitas in pennis ejus (AV:* "And for you that fear my name, shall the Sun of righteousness arise with healing in his wings"):

Claro paschali gaudio	In this our bright paschal joy
sol mundo nitet radio	the sun shines with pure ray;
cum Christum iam apostoli	the apostles now Christ
visu cernunt corporeo.	with corporeal vision behold.[25]

Here, as in Fortunatus' praise of spring, the Roman poet anticipates his medieval successors, for whom Christianity had saturated earth and cosmos with its symbolism.

In another sense hymns of the Resurrection and Ascension form a bridge between the ancient and the medieval world. In one text of the Venerable Bede's "Hymnum canamus gloriae," the first known hymn composed in England, Christ clears out Avernus and mounts to Olympus:

> Omnes Averni faucibus
> Salvavit a ferocibus.
>
> Victor petit quo fulgidi
> Jesus Olympus [*sic*] ianuas.
>
> Cum rege regum lucidi
> Portis Olympi adproximant.[26]

As this example suggests, Western hymns on the Risen Christ involved the singers more than did the early passion hymns. Beginning with the invocation "let us sing" (*canamus*), Bede prays Christ to grant the monks ("us") by devotion (*sedula devotione*) to tend heavenwards. His Victorian translator adapts the text for use by rendering *Sicque venturum asserunt / quaemodum hunc viderunt* as "Again shall *ye* behold him — so as *ye* to-day have seen him go." (By that time, the classical allusions have long since disappeared.) Although Bede sought aid in the works of prayer and fasting that pertained to salvation, his final stanza called for the worshippers to be filled with the Spirit and so implied inward response.[27]

Even the poet of "Aurora lucis rutilat" begs Christ to possess "our" hearts (*corda nostra posside*) that "we" may for all time return due praise (*ut tibi laudes debitas / reddamus omni tempore*), and to defend His people from every onslaught of death (*ab omni mortis impetu*), presumably violent.[28] The poet of "Tibi laus, perennis auctor," Fortunatus or a contemporary, describes the candidates baptized in white robes on Holy Saturday in Pauline phrase as buried with Christ (*consepulti*) and reborn (*renati*) in the faith. St. Paul enunciates the doctrine (Romans 6.4, Colossians 2.12), though not the symbolism.[29]

Although Neale fashioned two famous hymns from the Golden Kanon, his prose version more accurately renders this most joyous of Byzantine hymn cycles. A representative cantor ("I") exhorts the congregation to rejoice in the Passover of Christ "from death to life, and from earth to heaven" (Ode 1) by drinking the "new drink," from the fountain of immortality gushing from no barren rock but from the Empty Tomb. "Yesterday, I was buried and crucified together with Thee," but "today, with Thee ... I arise" (3). In each Ode (with brief choral responses between), the poet works from a biblical episode to the triumph of Christ: from the watch-tower prophecy of Habakkuk to His Incarnation and shining from the tomb as "beautiful Sun of Righteousness" (4). Inviting worshippers to visit the tomb with the women (5) he hails Christ as liberator of Jonah from the whale (6) and the children from the furnace (7), before celebrating His destruction of hell (7), proclaims Easter the "lady and queen of feasts" (8), lauds the inception of the New Jerusalem (9), and shares the Virgin's joy in the Resurrection: "O Wisdom and Word and Power of God! grant us expressly to partake of Thee, in the day of Thy kingdom that hath no evening" (9).[30]

The Golden Kanon shares with the *Odes of Solomon* the theme of liberation, but from earth and sin rather than from death or the Law. It employs already ancient images, the fountain, rock, and rising sun, for biblical typology, orthodox doctrine, and verbal and metrical skill, not originality, were expected of the Byzantine poet.[31] The collective narrator, though "crucified" with Christ, never identifies with the Good Thief as did Cowper in "There is a fountain filled with blood."[32] This bodiless co-sufferer neither acts, depends, nor apparently feels; still less does he inwardly replay the Gospel events like a Wesley.

Taken as a whole, the Kanon relates the *mythos* with an otherworldly rapture scarcely paralleled in Christian hymnody. This numinous radiance comes through the Greek chant of the first Ode, 'Αναστάσεως ἡμέρα "Anastaseos hemera," beside which the swinging German march tune "Ellacombe," sung at Easter celebrations in English churches, has a brassy triumphalism quite foreign even to Neale's "Day of Resurrection," let alone its sublime original.[33] Neale's prose version brings out the keynote of the Byzantine Christ:

On the day of the Resurrection let us, O people, be clothed with gladness; it is the *Pascha* [Passover] ... of the Lord: for from death to life, and from earth to heaven, hath Christ our Lord caused us to pass over, singing the Hymn of Victory.

Cleanse we our souls, and we shall behold Christ, glittering in the unapproachable light of the Resurrection, and we shall clearly hear Him exclaiming, "Hail!" and singing the Hymn of Victory.

Let the Heavens, as it is meet, rejoice, and let the earth exult: and let the whole universe, visible and invisible, keep festival. For Christ hath arisen, and there is eternal joy.

But for the concluding generalities, farewell the natural springtime lauded by Fortunatus. The Byzantine hymnist and singers abode completely within the Myth.

Because the glut of the eleventh century led the Eastern bishops to fix the canon of liturgical hymns, we cannot trace an evolution during the long decline of Byzantium, as during that of Britain.[34] The question whether or not the poets of an ascendant empire represent Christ as conqueror, poets of one in decline as victim, must await our study of late Victorian hymns on the Myth.

TRIUMPH AND PARTICIPATION

As Bennett has shown, the Christ of Anglo-Saxon poems on the Passion conforms to the contemporary ideal of the "warrior-prince."[35] In liturgical hymns this could hardly be expected, but in "Gloria, laus et honor" ("All glory, laud and honour"), the image of Christ as triumphant King acclaimed while entering his city in procession takes its origin as much from the Palm Sunday rite in Orleans as from the Gospel narrative. After the blessing and distribution of palms, a particularly magnificent procession of clergy bearing Gospels and banners, followed by the congregation carrying palm branches and singing hosannas, would halt at the city gates, where after the Gospel and prayers for the city a children's choir would sing from the city walls.[36] The text, partially included in the mass for Palm Sunday, shows Theodulf not only steeped in the biblical genealogy and narrative but conscious of the time that has elapsed since the original event:

> 2 Israel es tu rex, Davidis
>   et inclyta proles,
>   nomine qui in Domini
>   rex benedicte *venis* ...
>
> 4 plebs Hebraea tibi
>   cum palmis obvia *venit*:
>   cum prece, voto, hymnis
>   *adsumus* ecce tibi.
>
> 5 hi tibi passuro
>   *solvebant* munia laudis;
>   nos tibi regnanti
>   *pangimus*, ecce, melos.
>
> 7 hi placuere tibi;
>   placeat devotio nostra ....[37]

Theodulf uses past tenses for the original acclamation but the present for the Palm Sunday rite and the angelic praises and so links earthly with celestial worship.

The fifth stanza treats the Crucifixion as the climax of a procession. It was for the sequences and passion lyrics of the later Middle Ages to dwell upon the sufferings with that morbid particularity so rewarding to the Freudian athirst for sado-masochistic imagery. Of Carolingian as of Byzantine hymns on the Entry and Passion, the keynote is that spirit of martial triumph more natural in texts on the Risen Christ.

When sung in procession the Kontakion of Romanos upon the Entry into Jerusalem, blending dramatic immediacy with typology when the sun rises as Christ mounts the ass, may have drawn as eager a response as a Western pageant, yet its verse homily does not involve the worshippers as does "Gloria, laus et honor." In the Eastern rite, the poet's eye remains fixed on the heavenly triumph rather than earthly suffering or worship. From "Let all mortal flesh keep silence" (4th century)[38] to the "Golden Kanon" of St. John Damascene (c. 750), the sublime figure of Christ the Victor leads Christians to the promised land as Moses did the Israelites.[39] Byzantine poets ignore the world through which Christ leads them.[40]

NATURE AND THE MYTH

Though bound to start and finish with praise of Christ, composers of the Sequences that extended the Alleluia at High Mass had more freedom than earlier hymnists to depart from the biblical texts. Notker Balbulus (10th century) Christianized the Benedicite in describing the praise of the Risen Christ by nature baptized and reborn. His "Alleluia sequence" "Cantemus cuncti melodum nunc" has a universality comparable to that of "Corde natus ex Parentis." The heavenly choirs (*caelestes chori*) and the saints in their paradisal fields (*prata paradisiaca*) echo the ransomed people's praise. Responsive alleluias ring out from stars, clouds, thunder, and lightning above, to be taken up by ocean, rain, wind, frost, snow, and cloudless day beneath. Thus the poet skilfully modulates from the supernal to the earthly realm, calling on forests, mountains, valleys, birds, and beasts to join in singing alleluias to their Creator, before returning to the heavenly song to command young and old to join in the alleluias to the Trinity. Yet Notker chooses to adapt the generalized nature imagery of the Benedicite rather than, like Fortunatus, draw upon first-hand experience of spring flora.[41]

Earlier Western hymns had evinced both a delight in springtime and a dawning human response to the divine initiative. Paulinus of Aquileia (8th century), in "Refulget omnis luce mundus area," had called upon stars, scented air, earth, and ocean to rejoice, before turning to the Harrowing of Hell and Resurrection, but had also drawn upon the Benedicite and Psalms for his nature imagery.[42] in "Haec est alma dies" Sedulius Scottus (d. 874), however, had fused classical and Judaeo-Christian myth with first-hand images of reddening sun and moon, stars, and flowering bulbs.[43]

Signs of human response appear in "Ad coenam Agni providi," sorely mangled in the 1632 revision.[44] While the main emphasis of this well-known Easter hymn, as of its Byzantine counterparts, is on typology and ritual, human application appears in the endings, notably of the second verse:

Ad coenam Agni providi,	Awaiting the banquet of the Lamb
et stolis albis candidi,	and brilliant in white robes,
post transitum Maris Rubri	after the crossing of the Red Sea
Christo canamus Principi;	let us sing to Christ our Prince;
cuius corpus sanctissimum	whose most holy body [lay as if]
in ara Crucis torridum:	burnt-up on the altar of the Cross:
cruore eius roseo	tasting of his rose-coloured blood
gustando, vivimus Deo.	we live to God.

Later, like St. John Damascene, the poet celebrates Christ's liberation of his "captive people" (*plebs captivata*) from the "tyrant" Satan.[45]

In "Cantemus Domino Deoque nostro," attributed to Raban Maur, however, Christ has redeemed "us" from the infernal regions (*nos ... infernalibus*)[46] by his Passion, treated in more detail than his Resurrection. If the poet shows a lamentable pleasure in the agonies of the damned, he also shows a new interest in the reactions of the Apostles, Mary Magdalene, and the Jews.

In his sequence "Paschalis festi gaudium"[47] Peter Damiani (11th century), begins with a call for heavens, earth, and sea to join in the alleluias. His imagination plays around rather than on the events, for a cry of desolation rings from an empty hell after a battle linked to those of the Red Sea and Jericho by broken chariots and fallen ramparts. The Victim on the Cross having tipped the scale against the Prince of this world, the Empty Tomb challenges the sceptic to produce the body or believe. Those who rejoice in their deliverance metaphorically daub their doorposts with the Lamb's blood to expunge Roman corruption. Though briefly addressing the natural world, this gifted poet-monk seems as encapsulated as his Byzantine counterparts within the Judaeo-Christian cosmic myth.

The same is true of his contemporary St. Fulbert of Chartres, author of "Chorus novae Jerusalem" ("Ye choirs of new Jerusalem"), the only medieval resurrection hymn still widely sung.[48] This owes its popularity less to its original text than to the sweet cheerfulness of its modern tune "St. Fulbert" and the innovations of Robert Campbell's translation. Neale's version, however unsingable, adheres so closely to the original sense that it can safely be used to show the extent to which the hymn by Campbell is a Victorian creation.

In Neale's first stanza, the "choirs" attune their theme to "sweet new strains" as "from care released" they keep "with sober joy" the "Paschal feast." In Campbell's, the joy becomes a conscious yet unrestrained shout of victory: "Your

sweetest notes employ, / The paschal victory to hymn / In strains of holy joy."
For "Christ, unconquer'd Lion" and "The dragon's chains by rising burst,"
Campbell gives us the now familiar "Judah's lion burst his chains / Crushing the
serpent's head." His "wake the imprisoned dead" has far more gusto than Neale's
more accurate rendering "the dead of other ages rise." Then the Catholic convert
Campbell renders *Soli polique patriam / Unam fecit rempublicam* as "in one
communion bow / All saints in heaven and earth" where the Anglican Neale has
"And joining heaven and earth again / Links in one *commonweal* the twain."
Finally, Neale's version of the fifth stanza (Fulbert's application of the Ascension),
if Victorian in its final line, adopts the viewpoint of monastic "soldiers" of Christ:

> And we, as these his deeds we sing,
> His suppliant soldiers, pray our King,
> That in his palace, bright and vast,
> We may keep watch and ward at last.

Campbell's as retouched in the familiar verse from *Hymns Ancient and Modern*
applies to the whole worshipping community:

> While we, his soldiers, praise our King,
> His mercy we implore,
> Within his palace bright to bring
> And keep us evermore.[49]

A recent Canadian hymnal[50] updates the text still further by omitting the "soldier"
verse, while in the *New Catholic Hymnal,* Anthony Petti, likewise omitting
"palace" and "soldiers," gives Campbell's version a more democratic flavour in
"The gates were opened, free the way / To life and liberty" and "His glory shines
on all."[51]

THE SACRIFICE AND ITS MEANING

Except for some sequence writers, then, by the twelfth century Eastern and
Western poets of the Passion and Resurrection saw human life, history, and
destiny entirely in terms of Creation-Fall, Redemption, and final Judgment. The
spiritual upsurge begun by St. Francis led to three developments that have affected
Christian hymnody and spirituality to this day: the return of nature, albeit
spiritualized; the simplification of popular piety to love of the Virgin and Child
and of the Crucified; and a distinction between such popular devotion and the
intellectual spirituality of the Dominican and older religious orders. The first two
developments prefigured both the "natural piety" of Romantic poets and Broad

Church hymnists and the "Crosstianity" of the Evangelical hymnists, the third the class division between the Learned and Popular traditions of modern Protestant hymnody.

Any addition to recent accounts of the Franciscan lyric by David Jeffrey and others would extend this inquiry beyond its scope.[52] Suffice it to record the distinction between the natural world of the Franciscan lyric and that of the *Carmina burana* and other quasi-pagan lyrics. In the former tradition, as in the poems of Chaucer and Langland, sun, moon, stars, birds, beasts, flowers, and trees subsist by virtue of divine power and love, within a providential order centred upon the relationship of God and man.[53] Of the latter, the central determinants are the rhythms of the seasons, the human life cycle, and sexual passion. As any lover of Chaucer must know, this distinction cannot be rigidly enforced, yet in the most sensual of the *Canterbury Tales* the adultery of Nicholas and Alison proceeds while the bell summons the nearby friars to Lauds.[54] Again, the famous Epilogue to *Troilus and Criseyde* contrasts the enduring love of Christ with the fickle passion of the pagan Criseyde.[55] In the same poem, with incomparable majesty, Chaucer portrays the providential order sustained by the divine love, that "hooly bond of thynges."[56]

The Franciscans developed, but did not invent, the dialogue rhythm. Already, in the great "Victimae Paschali" sequence attributed to the Burgundian Wipo (d. 1050), antiphonal cantors or choirs record Mary's discovery of the Empty Tomb, command sinners to praise the sinless Christ for reconciling them to His Father, and invite Mary to attest the Resurrection and respond with her account.[57] Nor did the Franciscans alone invite mankind to identify with the Crucified Christ, for the Bonaventuran tradition of meditation upon the Passion extended beyond that Order.[58] Even the spiritualized natural world of their lyrics can be paralleled in the bestiaries read more by children of the nobility rather than of the common people to whom the friars preached. For our purposes, the most important features of the Franciscan lyric were its scope and its tone.

Its scope may be defined as tenderness towards the Virgin and Child, devotion to the Crucified and his sorrowing Mother, and invocation of both at the coming Judgment. The consecration of the poor family in Franciscan carols has already been remarked. The absorption with the Passion may be realized from the fact that no medieval hymn on the resurrection composed after "Victimae Paschali" and "Chorus novae Jerusalem" remains in common use. Even the spare but thought-provoking resurrection lyrics of Peter Abelard have become museum pieces, and not merely because of their difficulties.[59] Remembering the many distinguished hymns on the Passion, we must admit the truth of the Orthodox criticism that the Western church became obsessed with suffering and death. In his *Panorama*, Routley included only three medieval hymns on the Resurrection: the Sequences of Balbulus and Wipo and one text of the fifteenth century.[60] Whether the cause of this preoccupation with the Passion lies in the Franciscan movement alone, or also in the Crusades or socio-economic conditions, is a matter for the medieval historian.

The contrast of tone and emphasis between monastic and Dominican, and therefore "learned" passion hymns, and Franciscan hence "popular" lyrics, may be illustrated from three medieval classics: the "Pange lingua" of Aquinas, "Solus ad victimam" of Abelard, and "Stabat mater" of Jacopone da Todi (1230-1306).

The "Pange lingua" hymn being, in Routley's words, "the densest and most difficult ... ever written," I shall illustrate Aquinas' treatment of the Last Supper from the Breviary gloss.[61] Adopting the viewpoint of any participant in the new rite for Corpus Christi,[62] he links the Passion with Christ's Nativity and earthly reign: "Praise, [my] tongue, the mystery of the glorious Body and ... precious Blood which the king of the nations, fruit of a noble [royal] womb, poured out as the world's ransom." After recounting the Redeemer's birth, social intercourse, and spreading of His word and wondrous close of His ministry on earth, Aquinas, consciously alluding to Fortunatus, reaches the heart of the Eucharist:

As He is reclining with His brethren on the night of the supreme banquet, He complies with the Law in regard to legal [Passover] foods and then gives Himself with His own hands as food to the group of twelve.

The Word made flesh by a word changes true bread into His flesh, and wine becomes His blood. If a man cannot perceive this change, faith itself is enough to convince the well-disposed.

While setting the Supper within the context of Christ's life and death, Aquinas has passed from narration to symbolism. From the ransom and transubstantiation theories of the Atonement and Eucharist, he justifies the Passion and Last Supper as culminating and superseding the Jewish animal sacrifices and as the means by which later disciples may know and adore Christ. His hymn requires nothing beyond adoration, no partaking of the Sacrament, nor continuance of redemptive work in the world. Raby well describes the "Pange lingua," nevertheless, as among the "most sublime productions of sacred poetry."[63]

The Sequence St. Thomas composed for Corpus Christi, "Lauda, Sion Salvatorem," in Raby's words the "supreme dogmatic poem of the Middle Ages,"[64] has a grandeur scarcely paralleled in liturgical verse. An exact exposition of his doctrine of transubstantiation in his *Summa theologica,* it and the "Pange lingua" belong supremely to the Learned tradition. Ironically they have won the hearts of untold millions whether philosophers or peasants, for the Roman church set them in a ritual context. Walking backward, strewing flowers before the symbols of the King of kings, or watching the glittering monstrance form the Sign of the Cross above, the worshipper at Corpus Christi or Benediction hails the entry of Christ into his heart, and bows his head before the divine suffering that gives meaning to his own. So, decade by decade, the mystery heard, seen, and adored reforms itself within the psyche. As according to William Empson understanding a poem is reconstructing it in one's own mind, what the senses fail to grasp is by the senses imprinted upon the heart.

> Verbum caro panem verum
> verbo carnem efficit,
> fitque sanguis Christi merum,
> et, si sensus deficit;
> ad firmandum cor sincerum
> sola fides sufficit.[65]

In his hymn cycle, Peter Abelard treats the events of Passion week with no less objectivity but with more dramatic realism, relating each event to its commemorative Office. In that for Compline, Christ is interred, and in that for Sext, "Solus ad victimam" ("Alone to sacrifice, O Lord, thou goest"),[66] Christ, ironically, offers himself to the very death He has come to remit. Paradox or no, the poet dramatically represents the human figure of Christ, jeered, scourged, and crowned with thorns, and the darkness that fell at this sixth hour as He ascended the Cross.

Without doubt the "Stabat mater," attributed to the supreme Franciscan lyrist Jacopone da Todi (1230-1306) was "popular by destination." As commentator, the poet-narrator laments the suffering of both Christ and his Mother, who stands by the Cross, gazing on the forsaken Victim and hearing his Last Words.[67] As representative of all for whom Christ died, the narrator prays to share her sorrowful love, that she may defend him at the Judgment. Only then does he beseech of Christ himself a place in Paradise.

Because the stanzas to the Virgin, sometimes changed or even omitted in translation, mark an important stage in the evolution of the Myth, the following paraphrase is offered:

Ah Mother! fount of love, make me feel the force of your sorrow, that I may grieve with you. Make my heart burn in loving Christ my God, that I may please him with you. Holy Mother, fix the wounds of the Crucified deeply in my heart.

Share with me the torments of your wounded Son, who deigned to suffer so much for me, as long as I shall live. I long to stand with you by the Cross, and share with you in lamenting.

Most noble virgin of virgins, let me grieve with you, be not now vexed with me; make me share in the Passion and recall the blows.

Let me be wounded with his wound; make me drunk with the Cross and the Blood of your Son.

Through you, Virgin, let me not burn alight with flames; be my defence
on the Day of Judgment.

Christ, when I must go hence, confer through your Mother upon me the
palm of victory. When my body dies, make the glory of Paradise be granted
to my soul.[68]

The Virgin is to mediate between the speaker (or by implication anyone to whom
Franciscan and other clergy ministered) and Christ the Judge. (Christ Himself
mediates for Protestants.) The speaker turns to Christ only after using her as
intermediary. As in Moravian and Evangelical passion hymns, he longs to experience the suffering inwardly. As in modern hymns to the Precious Blood and
Sacred Heart, the "Stabat mater" reveals an erotic fascination with the Blood
and the Cross, coupled with fear of the Judgment. These naturally commended
it to the Flagellant friars, who after the Black Death sang it in procession all
over Western Europe, smiting each other's bare backs until the blood flowed. In
themselves, however, these beautiful lines attribute to God a maternal tenderness
and compassion countering His paternal sternness and evoking that most unconditional of loves, the mother's for her suffering child. Indeed, by excluding St.
John, the soldiers, and the thieves, the poet limits our vision to the mother and
son, as nativity carols often focus on the mother and child. It was the supreme
achievement of the Franciscan poets to represent the divine compassion in these
elemental tableaux of a love understood by the meanest intelligence and felt by
the most hardened heart. Nowadays, ironically, the "Stabat mater" is better known
in the elaborate settings of Palestrina and innumerable later composers than in
the simple reiterative chant that by the fifteenth century resounded throughout
Latin Christendom.

A thirteenth-century hymn attributed to St. Bonaventura, "O crux frutex sal-
vificus," which adheres closely to the biblical narrative from Nativity to Passion,
concludes in a prayer for Christ to embolden the fearful and inspire the pious,
for, as the hymnist has implied by his long recital, Christ has known every ill
His servants must endure.[69] Both the Bonaventuran meditation suitable for con-
templatives or the leisured class and the Franciscan sermon or lyric intended for
the populace taught the worshipper to share in the suffering of Christ and bewail
those sins that were its cause.

This relentless insistence on the bloody stripes and crown of thorns and this
self-accusation impart a morbidity to late medieval art and poetry of the Passion
in keeping with the sense of doom consequent upon the Black Death, the Hundred
Years War, and other disasters.

This morbidity was by no means universal, for the Scottish poet Dunbar[70]
and a hymnist thought to be Thomas à Kempis internalized the Passion while
avoiding sado-masochism. A verse of "Tota vita Jesus Christi"[71] breathes the
spirit of a Watts or Wesley:

Passio tua, Domine,	Your suffering, Lord,
Facta est amara valde;	was made very bitter;
O quantum me dilexisti,	O how much you loved me
Cum pro me mortem subisti.	when you died for me.

Cross, nails, and spear being fixed in his heart not by erotic pleasure but by gratitude, the poet (such as he is) thus anticipates the personal devotion of Evangelical hymnists. His identity must remain in doubt, for the better-known lyric also ascribed to Thomas, "O amor quam ecstaticus," acknowledges the Sacrifice collectively, *pro nobis.*

THE MEANING OF CHRIST

While not even the finest devotional hymns of the Latin Middle Ages quite match the *Imitatio Christi,* several convey an image of Christ's personality. Considering the thousands of hymns to Jesus from the first century to the Reformation, and the exhortations, prayers, and meditations beyond computation, it is equally astounding that so few poets say what manner of man they conceive Him to have been or distil His teaching.

From the beginning, the Odist and others hailed Christ as Victor and Liberator from death and persecution. The early Christians, no doubt, saw in His freeing of the righteous dead the final defeat of the living demons who howled "Christians to the lions." Ascetics, Egyptian or Benedictine, found in His forty-day fast the ultimate assurance that, as Prudentius declared, fasting would cleanse the debauched heart and subdue the intemperate flesh.[72] While eschewing the anti-intellectual fanaticism that caused the destruction of the library at Alexandria, the Benedictines imitated Christ in their faith.[73] The earliest known Compline hymn bids Christ, as new day and morning star, assist them against treacherous foes that assault their souls by night, leaving us to infer sexual or depressive dreams.[74] That hymn introduces another image common to hymns of all periods from the *Odes of Solomon* to the Victorian gospel song, Christ as the soul's rest.

As early as the fourth century, Synesius of Cyrene wrote a hymn that, to judge from a Victorian translation, contains every major image of Christ. In "Lord Jesus, think on me" (Μνώεο Χριστέ)[75] Christ will "purge away" sin, set free from "earthborn passions," inwardly purify and give rest to his "loving servant," sustain him amid "battle's strife," be "Health and life to the sick," and in darkness or doubt point the "heavenly way," "That, when the flood is past / I may the eternal brightness see / And share thy joy at last." From all these images emerges one that gives meaning to them all: Christ as the source and satisfaction of every longing. Of this the most profound expression comes in two hymns culled from *De contemptu mundi,* by the twelfth-century poet Bernard of Morlas, often confused with St. Bernard of Clairvaux.[76] In this far from cheerful, at times bitingly satirical account of corruption in church and state, "Dulcis Jesu memoria" and "Jesu, dulcedo cordium" convey a supreme insight that may well outlast the images of Christ as Victor, King, and even Victim: Jesus as true source and object of what C.S. Lewis called *Sehnsucht,* literally a "yearning,"[77] appeasable only by his presence.

Dulcis Jesu memoria	Sweet is the remembrance of Jesus,
dans vera cordis gaudia	bringing man his heart's true joy, but
sed super mel et omnia	sweet beyond honey and all created things,
dulcis eius praesentia.	is His presence.

The Breviary gloss, slightly adapted, enables us to ponder these lines undistracted by the cloying tune "St. Agnes" associated with Caswall's mellifluous but wilfully inaccurate translation.[78] The poet defines the love of Jesus by negatives; nothing sweeter can be sung, or contemplated, or heard, than Jesus, Son of God. How kind is Jesus to those that seek him. But no skill of tongue or pen can convey what it means to find Him. Like George Herbert long afterward, Bernard counterbalances triumphal images of Christ as King and Conqueror, and even the erotic image of Christ as the Lover prefigured in the Song of Songs, by his sense of our Lord's ineffable sweetness:[79]

Jesu, rex admirabilis,	O Jesus, King most wonderful
et triumphator nobilis,	and Conqueror most glorious,
dulcedo ineffabilis,	our consolation beyond all telling,
totus desiderabilis.	"Nothing in You but awakes desire."

When Jesus visits the heart, declares the poet, in the same vein as the early Christian Odist, truth shines thereon, the world's vanity becomes worthless (*vilescit vanitas*), and charity glows within (*intus fervet caritas*). In "Jesu, dulcedo cordium," he develops his insight, hailing Jesus as fount of life (*fons vitae*) and light of minds (*lumen mentium*) to whom, whatever their lot, all that know Him turn in longing from any lesser joy.

Bernard thus describes both the longing for the divine and, as evidence of its fleeting attainment, what can only be called "heavenliness," that irresistible blend of love, cheerfulness, and inward peace in the countenance and bearing of, alas, a tiny minority. St. Paul and the composer of "Veni, sancte Spiritus," to be considered in the ensuing chapter, understand heavenliness as do Bernard and mystics of every faith. Its passing, should religion die out, would be a loss no survey could measure.

8

THE TESTAMENT OF THE SPIRIT

The First Age of the world . . . began with Adam . . . and was consummated in Christ.
The Second began with Oziah . . . and will receive its consummation in these times.
The Third Age, taking its beginning from St. Benedict ... is itself to be consummated
in the consummation of the world. The First Age . . . is ascribed to the Father . . .
the Second . . . to the Son; the Third . . . to the Holy Spirit.
Joachim of Fiore[1]

No doctrine, myth or fact of experience better repays study than that of the Holy Spirit. Lest the literal minded cavil at the term "myth," applied to the Creation in Genesis and to the spirit's descent in Acts of the Apostles, let me define it as referring to a supernatural intrusion narrated in symbolic events, whether or not historical. That gas and water cooled into the form of our round earth we know, that they did so under divine direction any faith in a transcendent deity obliges us to believe. In consequence, "the Spirit of God moved upon the face of the waters" (Gen. 1.2) must mean that the Spirit "in-formed" matter previously without form. That God formed man from the dust, "and breathed into his nostrils the breath of life" so that man "became a living soul" (Gen. 2.7) must again signify that God caused formless matter to take a distinctive form. The breath symbol, however, has deeper implications shortly to be explored. Conversely, elements not so in-forming would have remained formless, without meaning.[2]

Whether or not the inception of the Church took place literally as described in Acts 2.6-13, it is a fact no less historical than the Crucifixion that the adherents of Jesus turned into an evangelizing community the like of which the world had not seen, propagating a faith impervious to proscription, torture, and execution. The symbols of "rushing, mighty wind," "tongues like as of fire," and speaking in other languages (glossolalia) denote in-forming by the Spirit. While Peter's ensuing sermon refers the symbolic events to an apocalyptic prophecy[3] it is the preceding inspiration (or "breathing-in'" that explains his urge to preach.

According to Owen Barfield, who points out that the Greek word *pneuma* (πνεῦμα) connoted "wind," "breath," and "spirit," our ancestors perceived the wind on their faces and the breath of their nostrils and the Spirits within their bodies as one and the same. Likewise, the Hebrew word *ru'ah* connotes "wind" and "spirit." Conversely, as the unbreathing body lay inert, so the being without spirit (Latin *spiritus*, "breath") remained without meaning beyond the mere effort to survive.[4]

Again, the tongue of fire settling upon each apostle symbolizes the inner light and warmth that transformed him from a dispirited former devotee to one afire with faith. In the biblical account, the glossolalia signify not as nowadays a meaningless babble in words unknown to the enthusiast ("god within") but, as the polyglot assembly notes with wonder, a God-given capacity to address each spectator in his native tongue, the prerequisite for spreading the Gospel.

It took the genius of St. Paul to apply the creative and enlivening aspects of the Spirit in his contrast between the letter that kills and the spirit that gives life (2 Cor. 3.6); in his antithesis between the flesh and the spirit (Gal. 5.16-23); in his account of the gifts conferred by the Spirit (1 Cor. 12); above all in his Ode to Love (1 Cor. 13). The poets followed the preachers in identifying this, *Agapē*, as the Spirit's inward fire glowing in a heart that loves not in order to possess but to serve.

Finally, the prediction in the Fourth Gospel (John 16.3) that the Spirit would abide forever in the Apostles and lead them into all truth has been interpreted in both an individual and a collective sense, as the Inner Light of the Quaker or the guidance of the Church in making doctrinal or practical decisions.

All these and other aspects figure in ancient, medieval, or modern hymns on the Holy Spirit. Between the ancient and the medieval periods, the balance tilts from the pentecostal events to their moral and theological significance. Early poets, however, were also given to reflection. The Ambrosian hymn for the third hour, when the Spirit possessed the Apostles, promises that tongue, mind, and body shall proclaim God and urges the Spirit to inflame the heart with love that its ardour may kindle other souls. "Nunc sancte nobis Spiritus" thus articulates a belief, as early as the fourth century, in the indwelling of the Spirit with *Agapē* as its witness.[5] A later hymn, "Iam Christus ascenderat", sung at Lauds on the feast of Pentecost, opens with an account of the tongues of flame and glossolalia so literal as to include the crowd taunting the Apostles with being drunk (as in Acts 2.13). The hymnist nevertheless interprets the flame as love and alludes to the gifts of the Spirit before bringing in a new aspect, the Spirit as a talisman ensuring peaceful times (*quieta tempora*).[6]

This quasi-magical invocation of the Spirit brings us to its magic number seven. In hymn after hymn the Spirit's gifts are "sevenfold" (*septemplex*). The magical significance of "seven" as "wholeness" no doubt led Isaiah to list seven virtues[7] and early Christians to rejoice in the Spirit's visitation seven weeks (seven times seven days) after the Resurrection. The seven virtues protected the devotee against the seven devils of the parable,[8] and, once the medieval code of ethics had been developed, against the seven deadly sins.[9] Abelard, in "Adventu sancti spiritus," finds the sevenfold gifts efficacious against the seven devils (*Contra septem / illa daemonia*), while trusting also that the Spirit, by its anointings (*charismatibus*), will confirm those it has regenerated.[10]

The balance, then, tilts from retelling the myths to invoking the spirit or describing its operations within the soul or Church. With conscious symbolism, "Beata nobis gaudia," sung at Lauds on the feast of Pentecost, describes the Spirit's original descent upon the Apostles before beseeching its gifts for the present singers. As in days of old it filled their hearts with grace, so let it now pardon our sins (*nostra crimina*) and grant us peaceful times.[11] "Emitte, Christe, spiritus," attributed to Bede, relates the pentecostal tongues of flame to light and grace in the heart, marvelling at the unity of all thus inspired.[12] In "Organum mentis tibi", Fulbert, content with oblique historical allusion, speaks of the Spirit's creative work of love, of its victory over error and witness to truth, its cleansing of heart from guilt and rekindling of inward life.[13] In his sequence "Assit iam nobis clementia spiritus almi," Othloh takes a further step towards psychological application, for after cleansing our hearts of sin and darkness the Spirit confers interior sight, enabling us to discern the heavens. He turns then to the Spirit's role in Creation.[14]

Internalization never became total, however, for later in his hymn Othloh deals with the Spirit's aid against schism and idolatry. Gottschalk pursues the theme of the Spirit's gifts to heroes and prophets of the Old Testament,[15] and Hildegard (d. 1179) that of the gifts to New Testament figures.[16] Even Abelard, for all his inventiveness, harks back from the flame of love to the biblical tongue of flame, reflects upon the glossolalia, and quotes from St. Peter's sermon on the prophecy fulfilled in the Pentecostal events.[17]

Only the two greatest Latin hymns on the Spirit, "Veni Creator Spiritus" and "Veni sancte Spiritus," do not refer directly to the first Pentecost. Knowledge of the "Veni Creator" (9th century), uncertainly attributed to Raban Maur, extended far beyond the religious orders, as witness Joinville's account of its performance in 1248 when Louis IX departed on a Crusade. "Then all, with a loud voice, sang the beautiful hymn of *Veni Creator* from the beginning to the end: and while they were singing, the mariners set their sails in the name of God."[18]

Most Anglophones know the "Veni Creator" only in Cosin's somewhat wooden translation of 1627, used at Anglican ordinations and sometimes at confirmations. The Latin original enshrines virtually every doctrine and symbol of the Spirit, which visits and fills the souls of its dependents with supernatural grace. It is at once living fountain, fire, love (*caritas*), and spiritual unction ("anointment"), conferring sevenfold gifts and speaking through the preacher. What probably endeared the hymn to warriors was the Spirit's power to fortify and protect:

accende lumen sensibus,   Your light kindle in our senses,

infunde amorem, cordibus	pour your love into our hearts;
infirma nostri corporis	the infirmity of our body
virtute firmans perpeti.	strengthening with power to endure.
hostem repellas longius	Drive our enemy far off
pacemque dones protinus;	and grant us peace forthwith;
ductore sic te praevio	you being our guide before us
vitemus omne noxium.	may we avoid every harm.[19]

Obviously the Crusaders believed themselves fighting in God's name. With purer motives than many Crusaders, those fighting under the visionary Maid invoked divine help in ridding France of the English, who had all but destroyed its civilization. Whether like Shaw's St. Joan they could have thought their nation as such under divine protection may be doubted.[20]

Since *amor* denotes *Eros* rather than *Agapē*, its use indicates a warmer tone in the Latin than in Cosin's translation. To equate the love besought by the monastic poet with sexual passion would be to exaggerate, for *amor* appears side by side with *caritas* in a charming hymn for Maundy Thursday used from the time of Charlemagne:

> Congregavit nos in unum Christi *amor*,
> exultemus et in ipso iucundemur,
> timeamus et *amemus* deum vivum
> et ex corde diligamus nos sincero.
> ubi *caritas* est vera, deus ibi est.[21]

Disguised sexuality appears rather in the finest late medieval lyric on the Spirit, "Discendi, amor santo" ("Come down, O Love divine").

None of the many translations of "Veni Creator" quite conveys this warmth. That in the 1549 Prayer Book comes nearest, in "Kindle our hearts with fervent zeal to serve," but "zeal" has since acquired the overtone of fanaticism.[22] Dryden's famous "Creator Spirit, by whose aid" brings together the two senses of love, charity and passion, in "Thrice-holy fount, thrice-holy fire. / Our hearts with heavenly love inspire." Dryden, however, inserts a note typifying the era of Locke and Newton, for the sevenfold gifts become "rich in sevenfold energy" and the Spirit the "strength" of God whose power "does heaven and earth command." His rationalization of the gift of tongues as "eloquence" completes his translation of a medieval masterpiece into the tongue of a burgeoning scientific and imperial culture.

In his imitation "Come, Holy Spirit, Heavenly Dove," Watts catches the note of God-possessedness ("enthusiasm") in the title "Breathing after the Holy Spirit" and the lines: "With all thy quick'ning powers: / Kindle a flame of sacred love/

In these cold hearts of ours."[23] This note was to become more explicit in the hymnody of Methodism.

In "Come, O Creator Spirit, come," Robert Bridges interchanged the two kinds of love, for *fons vivus, ignis, caritas* became "The well of life, the fire of love" and *infunde amorem cordibus* "our hearts to heavenly love reclaim." The rhyme word "reclaim," like the earlier "sevenfold *dower*" and "making *rich* / with saving truth, our earthly speech" imparts a modern bourgeois flavour to what is otherwise the most faithful extant translation.[24]

An adaptation by J.W. Grant, in the Canadian hymnal cited earlier, fits the soaring plainsong melody but again introduces modern ideas. For the convenience of non-Canadian readers, it is given in full:

1. O holy Spirit, by whose breath
   life rises vibrant out of death:
   come to create, renew, inspire;
   come, kindle in our hearts your fire.

2. You are the seeker's sure resource,
   of burning love the living source,
   protector in the midst of strife,
   the giver and the Lord of life.

3. In you God's energy is shown,
   to us your varied gifts made known.
   Teach us to speak; teach us to hear;
   yours is the tongue and yours the ear.

4. Flood our dull senses with your light;
   in mutual love our hearts unite.
   Your power the whole creation fills;
   confirm our weak, uncertain wills.

5. From inner strife grant us release;
   turn nations to the ways of peace.
   To fuller life your people bring
   that as one body we may sing:
   praise to the Father, Christ his Word,
   and to the Spirit: God the Lord.[25]

Grant transposes the two senses of love by turning *ignis, caritas* into "burning love" and *amor* into the ambiguous "mutual love." He extends this sense of amity by calling on the Spirit to convert nations to non-violence. His most interesting importation combines allusions to the Spirit's role in the Creation and to the Resurrection. Out of context, it could be read in a secular sense, as recounting, like Wallace Stevens's line "Death is the mother of beauty," how new life springs out of decayed flesh and vegetation.[26] It is followed up by "God's energy," in the third stanza. After an allusion to St. Paul's teaching on vocations ("varied gifts"), the ambiguous phrase "inner strife" superimposes the modern theme of inward conflict resolved by the Spirit's guidance upon the primary theme, in the Latin text, of internecine strife.

Of the three supposed authors of the "Veni sancte Spiritus", King Robert I of France has dropped out and Archbishop Stephen Langton been preferred to Pope Innocent III, who appointed him to the primacy of England and whose commendation of the "Golden Sequence," in Raby's view, caused him to be credited with its authorship.[27] Distinction, whether of rank or scholarship, befits a poet of such wisdom and discernment.

Fortunate as this loveliest of medieval hymns has been in its translators, the nuances of its terse Latin phrases will not go into English verse.[28] Because, beyond any hymn of the high Middle Ages, it speaks both to its own age and to ours, it repays study in the original. Its structure and meaning are more readily grasped from the original three-line stanzas suited by the plainsong than from the six-line stanzas of Neale or Caswall. Palestrina, incidentally, composed a "through-setting" from the three-line stanzas. By way of compromise, the text is given below in continuous form, with the original stanzas numbered, and with my parallel gloss:

1   Veni, sancte Spiritus
     et emitte caelitus
      lucis tuae radium;

Come holy Spirit,
and send out from Heaven
the ray of your light.

2   veni pater pauperum;
     veni, dator munerum;
      veni, lumen cordium.

Come, father of the poor;
come, giver of gifts;
come, light of hearts.

3   consolator optime,
     dulcis hospes animae,
      dulce refrigerium,

Best comforter,
sweet guest of the soul,
sweet refreshment,

4   in labore requies,
     in aestu temperies,
      in fletu solacium.

in labour rest,
in heat coolness,
in crying, solace.

5   o lux beatissima,
     reple cordis intima
      tuorum fidelium:

O most blessed light
fill the heart's innermost [recess]
of your faithful:

6 sine tuo numine

without your divine power

nihil est in homine,	there is nothing in mankind
nihil est innoxium.	nothing free from evil.

7	lava quod est sordidum,	Wash what is stained,
	riga quod est aridum,	water what is dry,
	sana quod est saucium.	heal what is wounded.

8	flecte quod est rigidum,	Bend what is rigid,
	fove quod est languidum,	strengthen what is weak,
	rege quod est devium,	govern what is wandering.

9	da tuis fidelibus	Give to your faithful
	in te confidentibus	trustful in you
	sacrum septenarium;	your sevenfold mystery.

10	da virtutis meritum;	Grant the reward of virtue;
	da salutis exitum,	grant the end of salvation,
	da perenne gaudium.	grant eternal joy.[29]

Considering first the structure of verse and thought, we notice that identical rhyme links the concluding lines (indented above), so marking a sequence of effects of the Spirit: light, cooling or refreshment, comfort or solace, healing, government or straightening, "mystery" (applicable to sacred acts and symbols), and joy. Next, we note in the Latin resonances often lost in translation. *Lucis . . . radium* becoming *lumen cordium* survives translation as the divine light in the hearts of the faithful. Likewise, the English "of the poor" embraces the lower and the religious orders, the humble of heart and the spiritually barren, but "gifts" does not quite extend from bounty and vocation to spiritual reward and enlightenment. Again, neither "coolness" nor "refreshment" quite fits *temperies*, the moderating effect of the Spirit amid both inner and external agitation. But the greatest loss in translation is the ambiguity of *hospes*, which denotes both the guest and the host, and thus implies a loving reciprocity between the human and the divine spirit: not fanaticism, babble, or obsession but inner freedom. Again, *beatissima*, as superlative of *beatus*, connotes the heavenliness of *beati*, the saints, a nuance lost in English. *Numen*, finally, eludes the translator, who cannot in context refer it to "numinous," but clearly means something subtler than "divine power": that divine instress and interior radiance without which the human heart becomes subject to corruption. *Innoxium* (root word of "innocent") specifically denotes freedom from sinfulness, but in context implies that without the Spirit we become, as T.S. Eliot said, "hollow men."

Finally, after invoking the calming and preventative powers of the Holy Spirit, the poet with masterly compression invokes it as cure for almost every ill that afflicts the human psyche: guilt, barrenness, hurt or shock, the opposed extremes of rigidity and softness, waywardness, heresy, and perhaps perversion. The gifts that accrue to those who put their trust in the Holy Spirit necessarily precede the attainment of virtue requisite for salvation. In the final lines, the key words speak of a dimension unknown to classical or to secular modern poets. In English, "reward of virtue" sounds altogether more prim than the Latin poet's idea of "merit" as a moral power of the Spirit within the heart, while "joy" has almost faded out of common parlance, with the state it here connotes.

Both Stephen Langton and Innocent III, in whose reign the medieval papacy attained its peak of political and moral influence, were men of practical as well as intellectual distinction. In order to secure Langton's election, the Pope did not shrink from placing King John and his realm under an interdict, nor Langton, once in England, from throwing himself into the movement leading to Magna Carta. Yet the Golden Sequence, clearly founded upon St. Paul's teaching concerning the fruits of the Spirit (love, joy, peace, temperance, meekness, etc.),[30] remains among the definitive assertions of the Christian ethic in hymnody of all ages. In no way conflicting with "Veni Creator Spiritus," it works out the moral theology of the Spirit in more detail, focusing on psychological operation and moral qualities rather than upon traditional images of fire and fountain. In contrast to the oversweet tune "Veni Sancte Spiritus" (Webbe, 1782), set to the Neale and Caswall translations, the Sarum plainsong chant has the proper air of cheerful detachment.

For a reason shortly to be suggested, between the thirteenth and fifteenth centuries the moral theology of the Spirit proved less popular but no less meaningful. Themes from the "Veni sancte" crop up in medieval and later hymns.[31] This metrical prayer composed for the Mass of Pentecost, one of the few Sequences still in use, caught on immediately in France and Germany, but took a century to do so in England.

Two years before Innocent ascended the throne (1198), his predecessor Lucius III had officially blessed a monastery founded in Calabria five years earlier by the Cistercian Joachim of Fiore (c. 1130-1202).[32] In his *Introductorium in evangelium aeternum*, Joachim had propounded a theology of three Dispensations, those of the Father, Son, and Spirit. In that of the Old Testament, man lived under the law; in that of the New, he lived under grace; in that to be inaugurated in 1260 (a date arrived at by the most complex of all numerologies), he would live in love and liberty, by what Joachim called a *spiritualis intellectus* proceeding from the Old and New Testaments. Joachim is sometimes thought to have said that a testament of the Spirit remained to be written.[33] Since Innocent, who to his eternal discredit led the Fourth Lateran Council that founded the Inquisition (1215), was about to pronounce judgment on this doctrine as tritheistic and therefore heretical when Joachim died, it was undoubtedly familiar to him as it was, no doubt, to Langton. So far as the *spiritualis intellectus* ever became manifest, it did so, in my view, in the psychology of the "Veni Creator," the

"Veni sancte," and their derivatives between the thirteenth and the fifteenth centuries.

The last of these appears to have been the Italian *lauda* "Discendi, amor santo" by Bianco of Siena (d. 1434), of which R.F. Littledale's beautiful translation (1867) in Vaughan William's setting has become one of the few classics of modern hymnody.[34] This exquisite lyric combines a central symbol from the "Veni Creator," the fire of love, with the self-denying ardour of Joachim and the ethic of the "Veni sancte." With a passion expressed far more intensely than in Langton's sequence, the Italian poet bids the Spirit visit his soul. His *m'infiammi* and repeated invocations of *amor ardente* bespeak a passion more ardent than is conveyed by "visit it with thine own ardour glowing." In *Arda si fortamente / che tutto mi consumi* he utters a wish to be consumed by this ardour rather than, as in the translation, inviting the Spirit to turn "earthly passions" into dust and ashes. Cooler and more impersonal though the High Church version may be, it has made this lyric one that, with the possible exception of "weeps with loathing" (over "shortcomings"), English-speaking congregations can sing in all sincerity.

In the event, the year 1260 was to usher in not the age of the Spirit but that of the *memento mori*, the Dance of Death, and the "Dies irae." Nor has either the demythologizing or, by the time of writing, the charismatic renewal of our time led to an outpouring of hymns to the Spirit. In the late twentieth century, at least, the Testament of the Spirit remains to be written.

Joachim had in mind a millennial era to be ushered in at the date (1260) commonly worked out by calculations based on the book of Revelation. Nothing better exposes the great gulf fixed between the minds of Christians in his day and in ours than the respect then accorded an exercise now perceived as a symptom of religious mania. While some form of belief in the prophecies of Revelation remains widespread, it is not the kind of belief we accord the predictions of astronomers or geophysicists, but one we might accord inferences of a philosophical historian such as the late Arnold Toynbee, or the insights of a Blake or Dante. Probably most present-day Christians think of Revelation as they would of poetic symbolism or allegory. Precision and authority pertain to the testable calculations and predictions of the physical sciences.

Even the poet of "Veni, sancte Spiritus," who was beyond question sane and civilized, believed the Spirit capable of safeguarding the believer from doctrinal error (*quod est devium*), in the light of the dominical prediction that it would guide the disciples "into all truth" (John 16.13). Today those who regard an accurate understanding of Christian dogmatics as essential for salvation are, to say the least, very much in the minority. What did somehow survive the Reformation was an assumption that the Spirit would in some way direct the deliberations of clergy or elders so as to ensure the continuing spread of the faith.

At times since Joachim's day mystical sects such as the first Quakers, or even the early Methodists, have believed themselves led and possessed by the Spirit. Some eighteenth-century Moravians, apparently even their leader Count Zinzendorf, believed themselves thereby exempt from obedience to law or commandment. Within the past twenty years, not only Pentecostalists but worshippers at charismatic services within the mainstream churches have believed themselves impelled by the Spirit to sing sometimes wordless songs of jubilation as in St. Augustine's time, to fling their arms into the cruciform posture of the early Christians and likewise practise healing by laying on of hands.

The greatest medieval hymns on the Spirit sanction none of these things save, regrettably, intellectual authoritarianism. They show the power of the Spirit to form a heavenly disposition and character, to guide the believer's heart and conscience. If no longer able to accept that insistence upon "correct" or "true" belief which from that day to this has brought immeasurable and undeserved suffering upon the countless victims of spiritual or secular totalitarianism, we can in these great medieval hymns to the Holy Spirit, as the classic hymns of all ages, observe a deep comprehension of what it is to live as a citizen of heaven.

9

THE FOUR LAST THINGS

Do not speak like a death's head; no not bid me remember mine end.
2 HENRY IV 4.235

Until recently, the Church reminded the Christian of his end like no institution since the empire of the Pharaohs. Sarcophagi portrayed the illustrious dead, flaming west windows the Judgment, doorways and niches the martyrs, east windows Christ and the saints in glory, paintings over chancel arches the dead arising and the damned being thrust into Hell. Epic poems tend to leave their readers with an image of bliss rather than torment: the *Divine Comedy* with Heaven; *Paradise Lost* with the world, rather than hellfire, before the exiled Adam and Eve. Nor does this difference between the medieval and the puritan epics denote a shift of imagination from heaven to earth, for as the *Pilgrim's Progress* ends, Christian enters the Celestial City, having passed the final side-turning to Hell. What J.R.R. Tolkien called "Eucatastrophe," or joyous upturn, is congenital in Christian art.[1] There can be no Christian tragedy save damnation. The reader's imagination nevertheless seizes upon the circles of Dante's Hell, the flaming infinitudes of Milton's, rather than upon the gardens and palaces of Paradise, into which it rarely passes from the gates of pearl and golden streets. For early and medieval Christians, sculptor, painter, and poet displayed the Christian Myth not merely in its horror — but in its triumph and final glory. In their unending procession of corpses across our screens, our secular image-makers display only the doom. Between the purgation and final bliss of the *Divine Comedy*, the exile and prospective redemption of *Paradise Lost*, the flight and spiritual homecoming of the *Pilgrim's Progress*, between these and the astringent pessimism of a Bertrand Russell or a George Orwell, let alone of journalists and photographers who fashion their unceasing dance of death, have intervened three centuries of secularized pilgrimage. On the one hand, in novels by such as Fielding and Dickens — devout if undogmatic Christians — the outcast found his rightful but earthly mansion and (a significant cliché), "wedded bliss." On the other, the image of this life as exile and return lived on, and not merely in hymns, for it inspired the utopian visions of Marx, Morris, and Wells, not to mention the aspirations of the ecological and the black American movements.

DEATH

In the hymnody of man's future state, the balance shifts towards imminent apocalypse near the end of the first millennium, towards death and judgment in the declining Middle Ages, towards individual rather than collective judgment after the Reformation. To trace an evolution parallel to that demonstrated by Philippe Ariès in his monumental study of funerary art and customs *In The Hour of Our Death*, from a long sleep with refreshment (*refrigerium*) of body and soul to an instant passage before the Judge would be to oversimplify.[2] The pilgrimage of "Solomon" the Odist concludes like Bunyan's, at the river of death, the Jordan to the Promised Land. As the Israelites had crossed the Jordan to the Promised Land, and John baptized the Messiah therein, so the early Christian died to sin when symbolically baptized in the Jordan — often on Easter Eve — and at death would cross to Paradise. The analogy between death and baptism was to resurface so late as the fantasy of George MacDonald and the satire of Samuel Butler,[3] but by the fourth century the instant passage had been superseded by the long sleep. As will be seen later, the reverse took place during the eighteenth and nineteenth centuries. As both conceptions find support in the Scriptures, so in poetry and art each remains a vestigial presence in the ascendancy of the other.

In two funeral poems, Prudentius displays complementary aspects of the long sleep image. In "Deus ignee fons animarum," God has combined the principles of body and soul. By natural dissolution, dry earth will claim the body, the atmosphere the *liquorem* of the soul. The redeemed will likewise triumph over "black death" (*atra morte*), for by enslaving himself to death, Christ has opened their way to Paradise.[4] In "Iam maesta quiesce querella," a favourite of the early Lutherans,[5] Prudentius bids the bereaved parent weep no more, for the vacant body but sleeps out a brief interlude until it rejoins the soul on high, given new life like a planted seed. Meantime, let earth embrace it in her soft lap, for God who fashioned man in his own image will in his own time restore it to life. As Raby remarks, the resurrection of flesh and bones had become a dogma so entrenched that the Church had to reassure those whose relatives had perished by fire.[6]

JUDGMENT AND HELL

"Apparebit repentina dies magna Domini", an acrostic paraphrase of the Second
Coming (Matt. 25.30-46), composed by the seventh century, again implies the
long sleep.[7] It describes stars falling, flames engulfing earth and sea, the elect
assembling to the right of Christ the Judge, to his left the trembling sinners He
will despatch to the flames. Some ambiguity appears in the conditions of admis-
sion to Heaven, for Christ praises those who have sustained his poor yet the
hymn ends in an exhortation to chastity and watchfulness. Salvation is attained
at once by social good works and the keeping of monastic vows.

The long sleep, though established by the fourth century, does not preclude
a residual consciousness, as in "Rerum Deus fons omnium."[8] In the main,
however, hymns treat of the Apocalypse itself, of timely repentance, and of
social levelling at the Judgment. Thus in the lyric poem "Hymnus de die judicii,"
Bede sits under a tree meditating on his sins, to be repented before the Judgment.[9]
The poet of "Rerum Deus" enjoins a similar repentance upon the faithful that
amid the final terror they may enjoy peace. The insistence in "Aeterne Rex
altissime" that only grace, not works, may then avail recalls that time when the
Church still needed to frighten the barbarians into submission.[10]

Terror, repentance, and radicalism conjoin with paradisal longing in the Judgment Kanon by Theodore of the Studios (759-826), modelled upon the dramatization by Romanos to be considered in connection with the "Dies irae." Of the
two poets, Theodore shows more social and self-concern, as if articulating every
worshipper's anxiety.

> I shudder to foresee,
> O God! what then shall be!
> When Thou shalt come, angelic legions round,
> With thousand thousands, and with trumpet sound;
> Christ, grant me in the air
> With saints to meet Thee there!

He bids his soul lament its sins that of the "strict judgment" it may be free,
before contrasting the portions of the damned and the saved:

> The terror! — hell-fire fierce and unsufficed:
> The bitter worm: the gnashing teeth: — O Christ,
> Forgive, remit, protect;
> And set me with the elect!

> That I may hear the blessed voice that calls

> The righteous to the joy of heavenly halls:
> And, King of Heaven, may reach
> The realm that passeth speech.

At the judgment,

> . . .rich and poor the same tribunal own;
> And every thought and deed
> Shall find its righteous meed . . . .
>
> Master and slave one doom shall undergo;
> Widow and maiden one tribunal know.[11]

In the final ode, "fires of deep damnation roar and glitter," while the bitter cup and undying worm of conscience gall the representative figure who implores mercy. Theodore's Kanon stops short of the morbid particularity of Western judgment hymns, but for all its grandeur it lacks the personal devotion and tenderness of the "Dies irae." The Greek poets portray no vengeful judge with frowning face, but voice anxiety the keener for the infinitude of their envisaged loss or gain.

Angst, at least in the cloister, intensified as A.D. 1000, the millennium of Revelation 21.5-7, drew near. Whether it affected the illiterate we cannot know, for poets tell us only how kings, heroes, and monks viewed death, funerary artists only how the spiritual or social élite interred in churches were commemorated.[12]

Two lyrics by the same tenth-century poet confirm evidence from sermons that many expected Christ to return in A.D. 1000. The first, "Adpropinquat finis saeculi," proclaims that as the end draws nigh all peoples become agitated, trembling at Judgment. "That great day will be, as it were, a thousand years, when the ancient foes come to the battle" to devour souls. The other, "Quique de morte redempti," contrasts the anticipation of those liberated by the "precious blood of the Son of God," with the state of the wicked, who must dread the impending return of "Christ, Emperor of Heaven," to judge the world.[13] As lightening flashes across the wide arch of sky, the trumpet shall sound, the Redeemer appear, the dead rise at His voice, the heavens roll up, and stars fall. What terror will seize the unrighteous on that "day of wrath . . . of trumpets and clangour, of mourning and trembling, when the weight of darkness will fall upon sinners," and the "angry King" comes, and Hell opens to torment them with sulphur, flames, and dragons! What refuge shall they find, when saints themselves tremble at God's majesty? Two centuries before the mighty "Dies irae," terror of the Judgment has swallowed up the ancient fear of death.

That the manuscript came from Verona does not prove its gloom occasioned by the troubles of northern Italy, beset by Magyar invaders.[14] The perils besetting not only the land but the Church unquestionably influenced the religious revival of the eleventh century, when the hermit and unwilling cardinal St. Peter Damiani (1007-82) composed what are surely the most lurid of all verse meditations on the Last Things.[15]

He exploits three conventions of the medieval apocalypse vision: the detail of celestial calamity derived from biblical and classical omens and prodigies, perhaps enriched from known earthquakes and eruptions; the sinner's abject terror of an angry God [16] and that consecrated nightmare, the disclosure of all secrets. Nowhere in this poem does Damiani invoke or suggest divine forgiveness.

In "De Die Mortis," Damiani describes the dying body in graphic images: kidneys dissolve, stomach and bowels quiver as the mind represents the body's terrifying appearance. As the soul wrests itself free, the tongue moistens, the eyes are relaxed (in death), the heart palpitates, the mouth pales, the members grow still, and the body's beauty departs. Before the dying man's unwilling eyes assemble his thoughts, words, deeds, and course of life. Though every sin stings his conscience, time for amendment has passed. How bitter now each brief delight of flesh when endless torment must ensue. In his fearful recollection, the dying man implores Christ to lead him to his homeland.

While this *memento mori* can scarcely have been sung, it deserves consideration on account not merely of its artistic power but of its being the nearest thing in Latin hymnody to a Calvinist sermon on total depravity. Unlike the hero of Everyman, the dying figure cannot depend upon his good deeds, if any, but on Christ alone. The poet employs his gifts to express a hatred of life often found among religious fanatics.

The flames and phantasms that haunt the imagination in the hour of death pale beside the terrors he describes in "De Extremo Judicio" and "De Poenis Inferni." In the former poem, safe as may be the sons of Gehenna under a mortal king, they will not escape Christ when darkness envelops sun and moon, stars torn from the sky seek the low-lying earth, and a ball of seething flame blows through the vast air. Discerning God's terrible countenance, they will pray for the mountains to cover them. Soon shall the secrets of each heart lie open, each word and deed be seen as plain as the solid body.

His imagination in no wise fails him in the latter poem: "O quam dira, quam horrenda, / voce iudex intonat." His image of flames flowing from mouths, nostrils, and eyes conceivably recalls an actual fire, but the seven plagues that torment the damned, their tears and gnashing of teeth, the hissing serpents, roaring lions, and wide-throated dragons clearly derive from biblical and apocryphal myth.[17] Let the *insani* but hold this vision before their eyes to free themselves from the chains of sin. Only in this concluding praise of the "holy King" does the poet mention God, let alone offer hope.

In effect Damiani denies the reality of death and the privacy of the heart.

Branded before heaven, the condemned yearn for the prospect of extinction that would have terrified their pagan forebears, as it does their post-Christian descendants. No chimera with which the human mind has tormented itself has so imperilled its sanity as that of hell's undying fire, burlesqued by James Joyce[18] but in medieval poems and sermons conjured up with horrific sincerity.

The "Dies irae" appears to have been composed as a meditation on the model of "Apparebit repentina," then adapted as a sequence,[19] but the Judgment Kontakion of Romanos was undoubtedly intended for public performance. Werner has demonstrated a number of parallels between both poems and a post-biblical Jewish *piyyut* extant in the time of Romanos, a converted Jew.[20] These consist of the trumpet, the trembling of the angels as the book is opened, the metaphor of sheep-counting, and the confession that none merits acquittal. What do the differences reveal about the evolution of the Myth over some 500 years? In the Kontakion, when God comes in glory, "A river of fire flows in front of the judgment seat, / Books are opened up and secrets are made public." The images of famine and drought, of refugees from ruined cities, and of opening graves, evidently drawn from the books of Revelation and Daniel, have a scriptural yet ominously modern ring. Despite the first person viewpoint ("rescue me from the inextinguishable fire"), the fear is collective:

> When we, both sinners and righteous before the judgment seat of
>   Christ
> Undergo a just examination,
> Then the righteous will stand to the right,
>   like gleaming light:
> And the sinners will take the left
>   with mourning and lamentation;
> For no chance for defence will be given them,
> Since all the deeds done by each have been discussed.[21]

The Jewish parallels to the Day of Judgment were the New Year (the "day of writing") and the day of Atonement ("sealing" God's Judgment). The *piyyut*, or chanted prayer, *unethane toqef*, had as central a place in the appropriate liturgies as the "Dies irae" eventually attained in the Requiem Mass. It was in use while Romanos held office in the Byzantine civil service, which then ruled Palestine.[22] Leaving aside obviously Christian motifs, the Jewish, Greek, and Latin hymns differ mainly in the conditions for pardon. In the *piyyut*, "penitence, prayer and charity can avert the evil decree," even on the day of death. In the Kontakion, a verse homily, "Penitence and prayer will save *you*," and the "injury of the sin *we* may heal" by remorse. In the "Dies irae," *preces meae non sunt dignae* (my prayers are not worthy) for only the pity of Jesus can save "me" (mankind) from the undying fire.

The differences between the Christian hymns in structure and viewpoint derive from their functions as liturgical homily and Franciscan meditation. In the "Dies irae" the poet confines himself to the human field of vision, setting the apocalyptic scene in a single line, *solvet saeclum in favilla* ([that day] will crumble the world into ashes) before moving into the hearts that tremble as the judge descends and the trumpet call echoes through the sepulchres. By adopting the personal yet universal stance of an "I" who is Everyman, he can combine strictest objectivity with tenderest pleading. With matchless economy, he records the wakening of creation to answer the Judge and the scroll that tells all, then turns to the human predicament: *quid sum miser tunc dicturus* (what am I, wretched, then to say?). He can but entreat God in general, as *rex tremendae majestatis* yet *fons pietatis* (King of tremendous majesty . . . fount of pity), and *pie* (kind) Jesus in particular. After pleading *salva me*, he enforces his plea by reminding Jesus *quod sum causa tuae viae* (that I am the cause of your journey), alluding not only to the Via Dolorosa but to the Incarnation itself. In Franciscan style, he adduces more specifically the Savior's person mission and suffering:

Quaerens me sedisti lassus	You have sat weary seeking me;
redemisti crucem passus,	You have redeemed me by enduring the Cross;
tantus labor non sit cassus.	lot not such labour be vain.

Having first, as Everyman, made his plea, the poet shifts to God as *juste judex*, and to the universal prayer for absolution before the day of reckoning, citing the mercy of Jesus to the Magdalene and the Good Thief. His simple entreaty *ne perenni cremer igne* (let me not burn in eternal fire) and plea to be numbered among the sheep, achieves an intensity more moving than all Damiani's horrific catalogue.

As the poet shifts into the viewpoint of the blessed, he modulates from the explosive consonants of *cuncta stricte discussurus* (who will scrupulously examine all things) and the ominous reverberations of *tuba mirum spargens sonum* (the trumpet will spread forth a wondrous sound) via the soft consonants of *recordare* (remember), *Jesu pie*, and the spat-out syllables of *confutatis maledictis* (the wicked confounded) to the gentle sounds of *voca me cum benedictis* (call me with the blessed). In his original ending (before the six-line addition to adapt the poem for liturgical use) he alludes with exquisite aptness to his opening, in *cor contritum quasi cinis* (my contrite heart is as if ground to ashes).[23]

What distinguishes the medieval Latin poem on the Judgment from the early Byzantine is not its dramatic power but its shift of emphasis and viewpoint. Although in both a representative figure pleads for mercy, the focus of the Kontakion is upon the Grand Assize itself, that of the "Dies irae" upon the sinner's loving dependence on his Redeemer and Judge.

In the iron times of the Black Death and Hundred Years War, the "Dies irae" spread far and wide to become part of the common culture.[24] In modern times, neither of the most successful translations, by W.J. Irons and Sir Walter Scott,[25] could in the end make its sombre vision of collective judgment part of the common heritage from Latin hymnody. By the nineteenth century, there had been a radical shift of what Newman called "real" as distinct from "notional" assent, a shift not only from the long sleep to the instant passage before the Judge (notably in Newman's own *Dream of Gerontius*), but from collective to individual consciousness.[26] The evidence of Ariès on individualistic funerary inscriptions interlocks with that of Barfield on post-Reformation compounds from "self."[27]

Waves of hysterical millenarianism recur in times of crisis as in the seventeenth and early nineteenth centuries, but by now apocalyptic numerology has become confined to the lunatic fringe. Before 1260, arrived at by multiplying thirty years (i.e., a generation) by seven and then by six,[28] the basis of expectation would be either numerological (especially before A.D. 1000), or liturgical, in that the whole Myth was enacted in the liturgy. So far as it was based upon calamitous events, the barbarian invasions in St. Augustine's time or Moslem ones later, millenarianism did not find its way into the hymnal. While in every age a Damiani or an Edward Irving is predisposed towards apocalyptic visions, the collective chiliasm of Muggletonians in the seventeenth century or Primitive Methodists in the nineteenth can be related to political or economic change.[29] Between the thirteenth and eighteenth centuries, Western man changed irreversibly from mythic to measurable time,[30] from the year of the Lord (*Anno Domini*) to the calendar year, from the interregnum between the First and Second Coming to the timetable of human history, marked by the clock, the calendar, the rise and fall of civilizations. As Frye remarks, post-lapsarian human creativity "has in it the quality of *re*-creation, of salvaging something with a human meaning out of the alienation of nature." The same author speaks of "a second or participating apocalypse," in the believer's mind after reading Revelation, "a making of all things new."[31] Both internal application and its concomitant, transforming activism within the world, began with the Franciscans (though the Benedictines before them turned primeval forest into farm)[32] but came to depend upon printing and popular literacy, essential for reading and inwardly applying the Word.

HEAVEN

Undoubtedly, as Frye adds, the three early and medieval Christian images of paradise — the garden, the celestial city, the palace — go back beyond the New Testament and even the Eden myth to the nomadic and urban phases of Israelite culture.[33] But historical relativism came into fashion so recently that we have to unthink it in looking at hymns on Heaven. The images had for poets the absolute authority of revelation. From the paradisal orchard of "Solomon" to the heavenly palace of Fulbert and even the enclosed garden (for the Church) of Watts,[34] the images have a givenness, a literal or symbolic truth derived from their origins in Genesis, the Gospels, or the Song of Songs. Admittedly the apocalyptic images of crowns for the elect and white throne for the Judge predominate in Evangelical hymns. By the time of Wesley and Cowper, however, to take them literally was the exception that had formerly been the rule. St. John the Divine cannot have imagined how his dream-vision would underpin the medieval hierarchy, nor how irrelevant it would appear when thrones had fallen and new class systems evolved.

Beside these three images of order in nature and society, we find those of the eternal light and the bridal feast. Although the first, like the Sun-god image of Christ, appears a survival from Apollo and the Unconquered Sun (*Sol Invictus*), the Church as the Moon reflecting Christ may be traced back to the Song of Songs (6.10). Even the Fourth Evangelist, like the Neoplatonists, ultimately derived his image of Christ as "the light that lighteth every man" from Hellenistic philosophy and thence from pagan myth. The bridal feast, of course, goes back through the utterances of Christ to the Song of Songs. In a secular sense it represents an ordering of the sexual wilderness, in a spiritual sense the light of Christ the Sun shining into our natural darkness through the Church its Moon.

Once the faith had spread from Palestine and Syria, in hymns at least the Apocalyptic overwhelmed the Edenic image of heaven. For better than a thousand years, sacred poets fixed their eyes upon the heavenly city, leaving nature to the underground stream of neo-pagan verse in, for example, the *Carmina burana*.[35] This judgment must be qualified insofar as the city did not exclude parkland (the root meaning of "Paradise") nor cut off access to river or field, so that the iconography of celestial vegetation and eternal spring harmonized with that of city and palace.

Our earliest Latin hymn on Heaven, the "Aeterna Christi munera" of St. Ambrose, combines the palace (or rather court) image with that of spiritual warfare to develop the Christian paradox or reversal, that transforms martyrs into *ecclesiarum principes* ("princes of the churches"), *belli triumphales duces* (triumphal war leaders), and *caelestis aulae milites* (soldiers of the court of heaven).[36] Their faith ensures that Christ's love leads in triumph the Prince of the world. Inasmuch as eucatastrophe (the joyous upturn) reverses natural law, to the sceptic the Christian hope grounded in the Resurrection must appear a fantasy.

Images of heaven in ancient and medieval hymnody never correspond to the Victorian ideal of home, being mainly those of the city, palace, or homeland (*patria*). Whether because hymns in the classical tongues originated in monastic communities, or because the permanent single family home is an ideal of modern times, the heavenly dwelling is always public, salvation always communal. To agree with Ariès that the normal urban pattern was to live as servant or master in a large household appears safer than to infer the reflection in hymns of aristocratic values.[37]

The sense of exile underlines the vast majority of hymns on heaven in all periods. The 1632 revision of "Lucis Creator optime" differs from the original text in that the concentric universe of Platonic tradition has given place to the three-decker universe.[38] In the older text, the soul seeking its prize of eternal life hopes to knock on heaven's innermost part (*intimum*), in the newer at the heavenly gate (*caeleste ... ostium*), but in neither does it belong to earth, being *vitae ... exsul*.

It was from this life that the hermit or band of cowled monks might feel alienated. In Damiani's beautiful "De Gloria Paradisi"[39] the thirsty soul longs for the fount of eternal life, the spirit imprisoned in flesh for its own country. Sadly the poet gazes at the jewelled walls and golden streets, unfading roses, and perpetual health and peace, all forfeited by sin.[40]

The poet of "Urbs beata Jerusalem" intertwines confusingly the images of bridegroom, city, and palace. Christ leads his bride, the Church, through the glittering gate of pearl along the street of pure gold, yet in the portion "Angularis fundamentum" ("Christ is made the sure foundation"), the newly dedicated church itself becomes part of the heavenly city. The note of yearning resounds in both the martyrs' vision of peace (*pacis visio*) and the blows they endured, thereby polishing stones for the city.[41]

In all these poems, the exile bonds only to fellow exiles, to martyrs or, especially, to the heavenly community. In none does he form the personal relationship with Christ that a Franciscan passion poet enjoys. Nor does he speak of friendship even in Heaven, but of the city, its adornments, the Church, and its Bridegroom.

The exile's longing informs in more subtle ways the most famous evocations of heaven, in three hymns culled from a lengthy satire on social and celestial corruption by Bernard of Morlas, and in the supremely beautiful "O quanta qualia" of Abelard.

Until the Anglo-Catholic Neale translated Bernard's lines on heaven from "Hora novissima" they had never been used as hymns. "The World is very evil / The times are waxing late" and "Brief life is here our portion" make lugubrious reading.[42] The former, on striving to attain salvation, interests us chiefly for its assemblage of ancient and oriental with Victorian domestic imagery, heaven being at once a "palace" re-echoing with "festal song and mirth," a "garden breathing spices," and a "home of fadeless splendour" where those exiled here shall "dwell as children." As a funeral hymn "Brief life is still our portion" continues to appear, though its imagery of "short toil, eternal rest" and of roses and lilies (for martyrs and virgins) dates it as faded Victorian. In their original context, both excerpts encouraged medieval Christians to endure the evils of a dark age until the impending Judgment, and so enjoy in the palaces of heaven the eternal light.

The remaining translation from Hora novissima, "Jerusalem the golden," has enjoyed such popularity that in 1974 a Canadian novelist could with confidence use "halls of Zion" as a chapter heading.[43] The Authorized Version being familiar to all prospective singers, Neale turned *patria lactea* ("milky homeland") into "with milk and honey blest" and *regis ibi thronus* into "there is the throne of David." It is not only the sweetly nostalgic tune "Ewing" that continues to endear his hymn to congregations despite his archaisms ("social joys") and latinisms ("conjubilant"). The longing for the "sweet and blessed country" and even the apocalyptic images ("robes of white") are redolent of the "weariness" conjoined with "hope of something better" that in Newman's view have been the lot of Christians in every age and seem likely to endure as long as that faith itself.[44]

"O quanta qualia," composed for use in the convent of Heloïse, reads best in the translation of Helen Waddell. That of Neale, however awkward to sing, conveys the sense better than does that of Ronald Knox, who introduces a note of military triumph more fitting in the early twentieth century than the twelfth.[45]

No translation has reproduced the liquid and inevitable flow of

O quanta qualia	How mighty are the Sabbaths,
sunt illa sabbata	How mighty and how deep,
quae semper celebrat	That the high courts of heaven
superna curia;	To everlasting keep.
quae fessis requies,	What peace unto the weary,
quae merces fortibus,	What pride unto the strong,
cum erit omnia	When God in Whom are all things
Deus in omnibus	Shall be all things to men.

nor any hymnal version the yearning of the rhetorical questions

Quis Rex, quae curia,	But of the courts of heaven
quale palatium	And Him who is the King,
quae pax, quae requies,	The rest and the refreshing,
quod illud gaudium	The joy that is therein,

followed by the simple response *vere Jerusalem / est illa civitas,* that city where the heart attains all it desires. All translations convey the ruling typological metaphor of the exile's return from Babylon to the heavenly Jerusalem whose peace is unfading joy.

Abelard's poem owes its beauty and enduring relevance to his delicate avoidance of both triumphalism and material detail. No harps and crowns, no pearly gates or white robes offend the modern spirit. Abelard passes beyond these to their essence, that in singing the anthems of Sion, the blessed return perennial thanks for divine grace:

Illic, molestiis	There, all vexation ended
finitis omnibus	And from all grieving free,
securi cantica	We sing the song of Zion
Sion cantabimus,	In deep security.
et iuges gratias	And everlasting praises
de donis gratiae	For all Thy gifts of grace
beata referet	Rise from Thy happy people
plebs tibi, Domine.	Lord of our blessedness.

In his "obstinate questionings of outer sense," Wordsworth found cause for thankfulness and "perpetual benediction," while in a Beethoven slow movement Aldous Huxley sensed a like "blessedness."[46] That the one located heaven in his own past and the other in aesthetic experience inspires the belief that to contemplate beatitude Abelard must in some measure have enjoyed it.

That the state of grace, however fleeting in this life, has so often been experienced as foretaste of eternity[47] may cushion us against the shocking realization that in almost every particular Abelard's evocation confirms the Freudian view of Eden and Heaven alike as an imagined regression to the womb. After in his sixth stanza describing this life as an interlude of building minds (*mentes esiere*), Abelard uses for the exile's return the root verb (*regredi*) of our word "regress." Without our needing to read a standard Latin verb in a Freudian sense, the whole text is devoted to a longed-for regression. The heavenly state of timeless peace, though inexpressible, satisfies every need, for God is all-sufficient (*erit omnia Deus in omnibus*). For God substitute the mother — as in the cult of the Virgin — and in Abelard's heaven we have the blissful dependence of the embryo, paralleled in our own time by the longing for the "dateless, timeless peace of childhood" aroused in C.S. Lewis by a reading of Ruskin's autobiography.

We have it but for two features that undermine the entire Freudian case: perpetual thankfulness and life as soul-making. First, thanksgiving, whether individual or collective, involves a conscious realization of the state from which deliverance has come. Likewise, the sense of sacredness, of the numinous, wherein we briefly savour the heavenly state, demands self-consciousness. No embryo can experience being, in Wordsworthian phrase, "laid asleep in body" to "become a living soul."[49] Second, the soul that would experience heaven as a homecoming must enlarge itself in preparation. Man redeemed has two dimensions of awareness unknown either to his embryo or to his primeval forebears, that of himself and that of his imperfect state in this life.

Modern positivist values implicit in, for example, the writings of Freud or the late F.R. Leavis, exalt maturity as the equivalent of redemption and thereby presuppose a psychic growth completed during childhood and adolescence, or thereafter, or not at all. Given their celibacy, shorter life-span, and poorer nutrition, perhaps the majority of medieval clerics never outgrew the idealism, the quest for certainty, and the wish-fulfilling fantasies of adolescence. But the self-consciousness and critical detachment of Abelard and Bernard, not to mention SS. Bernard of Clairvaux, Bonaventura, and Thomas Aquinas, all imply a dimension that includes yet also transcends that of psychological maturity. To cite authors not committed to dogmatic Christianity, Keats groped towards this dimension in his famous letter on life as a "vale of soul-making," Matthew Arnold in his definition of genius as "largeness, freedom, insight and benignity," Wordsworth and Huxley in their accounts of detachment and "blessedness."[50] The young C.S. Lewis, well before his conversion, wrote of detachment from stereotypes and stock attitudes, as seeing life "as Spirit sees" it.[51] I have called its complementary aspects — benignity, thanksgiving, and the sense of a numinous quality in life — "heavenliness." We need not endorse the world-denying asceticism of Thomas à Kempis to perceive as beacons of the heavenly spirit the *Imitatio Christi* and *Jerusalem luminosa,* the latter pared down into a famous Victorian hymn.[52]

The Myth and The Reformation

10

THE FATHER RETURNS

The Supreme God of the sky is the creator of earth and of man.
He is the "fashioner of all things" and the "Father."
He created things visible and invisible
and it is still he who makes the earth fruitful.
Mircea Eliade[1]

Upon reaching the vernacular psalmody of the English Reformation, it is pertinent to enquire what the preceding study of early and medieval hymns can contribute to our understanding of the English hymn proper. Hitherto, I have tried to steer between the limitless ocean of cultural history and the secluded bay of hymnology past which many a critic and historian sails unaware.

The treatment of hymnody as an index to Christian culture confronts us with unacceptable alternatives, a historical determinism that involves selecting data to fit a linear sequence, and a critical empiricism that involves treating every text or known author as a self-contained module. This dilemma, familiar to modern literary scholars, could be evaded by the production of an uncritical history or else a series of unrelated commentaries. Instead, I have tried to chart an evolution of Christian consciousness in hymns on the divine nature and human destiny, together with some alternating currents or impulses.

This evolution has a self-pacing mechanism, to wit the arrest and release of historical consciousness. As Frye has recently demonstrated from biblical motifs, during the ascendancy of the Myth, Christian peoples lived encapsulated within it, conceiving of this life as an interregnum between the Redemption and Judgment. Though peasant and monk alike were governed by the rhythm of seed-time and harvest, they attended less to events in the social order than we who measure our lives by clock and calendar and inhabit a world of competing faiths and cultures. Whether the end of this encapsulation was the cause or the consequence of the explorers' sea voyages is a chicken-or-egg question.[2]

It by no means follows that between the enthronement of Constantine and the secession of Luther the capsule stood still. Our study of the Myth in hymns has recorded an evolution from human passivity as a Heavenly King puts to flight the rebel angel (or serpent or dragon) responsible for man's expulsion from Paradise to a passionate identification with that Redeemer in his lowly birth and cruel death; from awe before the God who has descended for man's redemption to a love of Jesus that alternated with a fear of Christ the Judge so intense as to make death more terrifying than if believed final; from a retelling of the *mythos* or "sacred history" to a defining of the Spirit's operation within the heart, or a connecting of personal misdeeds with the "sins of the world" for which Christ died.

That increasing participation in the spiritual drama was far from being a one-way movement from objective to subjective religion. A long-lost collection of early Christian poems revealed as "enthusiastic" a personal commitment and experience as in any Evangelical hymnal. It also expressed belief in a transcendent yet bisexual deity who seems incompatible with the paternal God of the Old Testament or the semi-divine Mother so adored during the Middle Ages. Again, the strain of naturalism in the hymns of, say, Fortunatus, yielded to mythopoeia, its contrary, only to reassert itself in allegorical guise in Franciscan lyrics and sermons.[3]

Some conflicts have affected hymnody from without, notably that between the iconoclasm of the Byzantine imperial bureaucracy and the popular use of icons. In this instance, learned and popular religion were at one, though they had been at odds when the Church endeavoured to suppress Arian and non-scriptural hymns. Unquestionably the Trinitarian victory made possible the popular devotion of the Middle Ages, whether to Christ the King in "Gloria, laus et honor" or to the Crucified and His Mother in the "Stabat Mater" and countless other Franciscan lyrics.

Before considering the about-face after the Reformation to worship of the loved yet dreaded Father-god of the Old Testament (significantly followed by the reappearance of unitarianism) we should note some oscillations in European history. Each new culture, whether Renaissance, Augustan, Romantic, or Modernist, has arisen from social breakdown or catastrophe, usually multiple: the Black Death, Hundred Years War, and Wars of the Roses; the Thirty Years War and English Civil War; the American and French revolutions; the First World War and Russian Revolution. Each has repudiated the arts and values of its predecessor while endorsing those of an earlier culture, the Renaissance those of Greece and Rome, the Romantic and Victorian those of medieval Christendom, the modern to an extent those of the French Enlightenment and the English empiricism of Bacon and Locke.[4]

This fruitful atavism may be discerned in the Lutheran chorales based upon psalm or prophecy,[5] and the Calvinist (hence Anglican) rejection of hymn-singing in favour of psalmody. As a result, German hymnody had its golden age in the sixteenth and seventeenth centuries, English in the eighteenth and nineteenth. What happened to the Myth in popular devotion during the age of psalmody in England, from the death of Queen Mary (1558) to the first Dissenting hymnal by Isaac Watts (1707) and the licensing of hymns (1822) for use in Anglican services?

Not all biblical scholars, but the vast majority of worshippers in the mid-sixteenth century, believed that King David had under divine inspiration composed the entire Psalter.[6] As late as 1719, this belief remains implicit in the choice of title by the learned Isaac Watts: *The Psalms of David Imitated*. More simply than the Breviary, the Book of Common Prayer could provide for each psalm to be recited monthly during matins or evensong. The most reflective worshippers certainly could have distinguished between psalms of personal and of collective thanksgiving, penitence or lamentation, and divided a psalm into its typical opening formula, body, and conclusion. They doubtless followed typological references to the Exodus better than most of us. To share their view we need to unthink associations many psalms have acquired with Handelian arias and choruses; with English national occasions; or with school services, weddings, or funerals. Above all, we need not associate their substance with the splendid language of Cranmer, for before Elizabeth had disposed of Queen Mary of Scots (1576) her subjects had begun singing the metrical versions of Sternhold and Hopkins. Instead of "I will call upon the Lord, who is worthy to be praised; so shall I be saved from mine enemies. The sorrows of death compassed me: and the overflowings of ungodliness made me afraid" sung in four parts to the now familiar Anglican chant, they would sing line by line after the parish clerk:

> When I sing laud unto the Lord, most worthy to be serv'd,
> Then from my foes I am right sure that I shall be preserv'd.
> The pangs of death did compass me, and bound me everywhere,
> The flowing waves of wickedness did put me in great fear.[7]

That hearing clergyman and clerk read from the Prayer Book could have imprinted Cranmer's phrases upon the parishioners' minds so deeply as those they sang appears unlikely.

Whether psalm-singing reflected or caused a reorientation in popular devotion is another chicken-or-egg question best answered as "both." Though Calvin had identified Yahweh with Christ, clergy and congregations now praised or petitioned "the Lord" more as Father than as Son or Spirit. This had the important consequence that now the Father's judgment was to be feared, and, as psalm after psalm makes plain, in this life also. The Lord would judge the princes of the earth,[8] provide for the needy, the widow, and the orphan[9] and destroy the ungodly.[10] Monks and nuns may well have understood these assurances quite differently, as referring to their voluntary poverty and renunciation. The Levellers and millennialists of Cromwell's time were to understand them in a social or an apocalyptic sense.

Second, as compared with the old carols and passion lyrics, the psalms forged between man and God a quite different bond. The Creator of this world voiced his wrath in the thunder, showed his bounty in the harvest, bid the waves be still and, anachronistically, sent the sun upon its daily course. What this implied was that showers and dew, thunder and sunshine, no longer mystically signified qualities of Christ but had value in their own right. Their Creator and Mover could not be pitied like the Babe and Victim, or loved in the same way. Give us "an heart to love and dread Thee, and diligently to live after Thy commandments," runs a petition in Cranmer's Litany. The phenomena of nature were dignified in the stately rhythms of the Benedicite, recited at Morning Prayer. God, in short, had turned or reverted into a remoter, more peremptory, and masculine figure.

His authority, however, filled Lutheran or Calvinist with reassurance rather than gloom, for the whole network of intermediaries had vanished into the thin air of the Protestant cosmos. Every petitioner enjoyed direct access to the being described in the Psalter as King, Shepherd, and Lord of Hosts. We too readily project back subsequent puritan or evangelical strictures on pleasure, for in its time the Reformation, as C.S. Lewis shows,[11] inspired not gloom but relief. Purgatory was gone, with its indulgences, masses for the dead, pardons, and penances, the whole apparatus for convincing the Catholic that he was never safe. In time, needless to say, anxiety about salvation was to beset the Calvinist also.[12]

Finally, the psalmist offers praise or entreaty to the God of Battles, who taught his adherents to make war.[13] Crusades and heresy hunts attest that this had always been the case, but now the Lord could inspire the meanest foot soldier or sailor before the mast. Psalm 20, for example, was sung not only by Calvinist and Puritan soldiery, but even by the Highlanders at Culloden, in 1745.

At some cost in historical exactitude, I shall illustrate not from Sternhold's doggerel but from a handful of psalm-based hymns that have outlived them. These reveal an accommodation over a century and a half not merely to a reformed religion but to a new model of the cosmos.

The title of our grandest metrical psalm, William Kethe's "All people that on earth do dwell," sung ever since 1561 to "Old Hundredth,"[14] proclaims the universalism implicit in this and other psalms but often overlaid by its counter-theme, the chosen people. The effect of singing "to the Lord with cheerful voice" is implied in "Him serve with mirth" (*joyeusement* in Kethe's French model). The substitution "with fear" in the Scots version of 1650 denotes reverence more than terror, but misses the implication common to most religions that to praise and serve God is the condition of emotional health and joy in life. "Mirth" itself connotes not conviviality but the reverential "gladness" (a word now as rare as "joy") of the Prayer Book version.

Although the biologists have undercut "without our aid He did us make," the advent of republics and crowded cities has not robbed the royal and pastoral metaphors of their force. To this day congregations sing "Approach with joy His *courts*" and "We are His flock, He doth us feed," tacitly adjusting to the language of the old monarchical, pastoral and collective culture. The gravely reassuring tread of the very tune that makes this text indispensable can distract us from the main theme of what is, like many psalms, a reflexive hymn: the duty and joy of worshipping the Creator.

The metaphors of King and Shepherd recur times without number in metrical psalms and religious lyrics of the sixteenth and seventeenth centuries: to express not only collective dependence as here, but individual dependence in versions of the 23rd Psalm or in Herbert's "Teach me, my God and King." Though its best expression, "Ein feste Burg," was not yet available in English, that of God as fortress, refuge or tower[15] recurs so often in the Psalms that its continuance in folk religion can be asserted right through to the mid-Victorian "For all the Saints."[16]

The fifteen-year-old Milton's astonishing paraphrase "Let us with a gladsome mind" (Ps. 136) epitomizes the old world conception of God the Father. Some features of this are implicit in the selection from its twenty-three stanzas in a modern hymn-book. In "of gods He is the God" (st. 2) who "doth the wrathful tyrants quell" (st. 8), Milton extends the Lutheran image of God as defender of the true faith against idolatry. In praising the Creator who "did fill the new-made world with light," cause the "golden-tressed Sun" (st. 8) to run, and the "horned moon" (9) to shine, he endorses the model of God and nature evident in so many psalms. In several long-omitted stanzas he endorses its obverse, likewise present in the Hebrew psalter. With his "thunder-clasping hand" God smote the first-born of Egypt (10), destroyed its army at the Red Sea, and sustained the Israelites with the manna that leads the young poet to acclaim His providence in the still extant line "All living creatures he doth feed" (22). The verses now sung represent God as ruler, creator, and provider but no longer as tribal deity during the Long March of the Israelites. We should not underrate the influence of such motifs upon all who identified the English cause with that of the Israelites and their Catholic foes with heathen idolaters.[17] It was unfortunate that the thanksgiving "Nun danket," sometimes called "the German 'Te Deum'," took two centuries to reach the English hymnbook and heart. Until recently, English hymn-singers preferred the Lord of hosts to the bounteous God of whom Rinkart beseeches "peace ... in Israel for ever."[18]

A fine but rarely sung hymn by John Mason, "How shall I sing that majesty" (1694), may be called the meeting point of old and new world religion. In his

humility before the heavenly choir, being but "dust and ashes," the poet exclaims
"but who am I?". Imploring "a beam" from God, by whose light the angels see,
the poet introduces a major theme of eighteenth-century hymnody, heaven within
the converted heart:

> Enlighten with faith's light my heart,
> Enflame it with love's fire,
> Then shall I sing and bear a part
> With that celestial choir.[19]

He ends by sounding a keynote of romantic religion (though one struck by St.
Augustine):[20]

> Thou art a sea without a shore,
> A sun without a sphere;
> Thy time is now and evermore,
> Thy place is everywhere.

Whether the shoreless ocean be referred to the womb or to the sea voyages of
explorers, the concept of divine infinitude and the question "Who am I?" (instead
of "What is man?") savour more of the romantic or existentialist than the biblical
world view.

The New Version by Tate and Brady would appear the last place to look for
the religion of the future and indeed "As pants the hart for cooling streams" (Ps.
42) expresses a longing for the divine as old as our race itself. Nevertheless,
"Through all the changing scenes of life" (Ps. 34) expounds the confirmation of
faith by experience, an Evangelical leitmotif that doubtless explains the wide
use of this hymn in the nineteenth century. There is no idea in the text that cannot
be found in the psalm. Even

> O make but trial of his love,
> Experience will decide
> How blest are they, and only they,
> Who in His truth confide

is an expansion of "O taste and see that the Lord is good: blessed is the man
that trusteth in him" (Ps. 34:8, *AV*). The diction, not the thought, was new. At
about that time, John Locke replied to his own enquiry as to whence the mind
derived its powers and sources of knowledge: "To this I answer, in one word,
from experience." Doubtless without realizing it, Nahum Tate had recast the
psalm verses in the language of the new empirical philosophy, which since the

foundation of the Royal Society had been in the air as evolution was for two generations before Darwin wrote the *Origin of Species*. Although the Wesleys rarely strayed from the Bible either in their preaching or hymnody, in its verification of scriptural teaching from religious experience Methodism can be viewed as a kind of Christian empiricism.[22]

We must leave psalmody a while to observe an unfavourable aspect of inwardness in a stanza of Bishop Ken's famous morning hymn for Winchester School, "Awake, my soul, and with the sun":

> Let all thy converse be sincere,
> Thy conscience as the noon-day clear;
> Think how all-seeing God thy ways
> And all thy secret thoughts surveys.[23]

The verse hits off the difference between old and new world religion, alluding not merely to the future Judgment but to a present and continuing assessment by a God infiltrated into the heart. Though of Calvinistic and ultimately of scriptural origin, subjective piety may, according to disposition and social environment, prompt in the young either self-assurance or irrepressible anxiety.

To turn from the psychological to the cosmic aspect of new world religion, a psalm version now little used represents Addison's accommodation of the Creator figure to Newtonian cosmology.

> The spacious firmament on high,
> With all the blue ethereal sky,
> And spangled heavens, a shining frame,
> Their great Original proclaim.
> The unwearied sun from day to day
> Does his Creator's pow'r display;
> And publishes to every land
> The work of an Almighty hand.

For the psalmist's beautiful anthropomorphism of the sun as bridegroom coming forth from his chamber,[24] Addison substitutes a metaphor, "publishes," that reflects partly his literary calling but partly voyage literature. A travel book fifty years earlier had described the sun as "publishing" the new year upon reaching the equator. More important, his sun "unwearied" in its "shining frame" belongs to a mechanical universe of inconceivable magnitude and splendour. Not in the sensory but in "reason's" ear do the "radiant orbs" sing "The hand that made us is divine." God manifests Himself in the constellations.

For a striking example of spiritual reorientation, we must again forsake psalmody for the original text of Addison's fines hymn, "When all thy mercies, O my god!", the editorial condensing of which concealed its highly significant structure.[25] Whereas in "Corde natus ex Parentis" the Roman poet recounts human history from the Fall to the Judgment, the Augustan essayist recounts his experience of providence from when he lay "in the silent womb," then "hung upon the breast," through the "slippery paths" of his youth, in sickness and health, sin and sorrow, to his prosperous manhood, and finally vows to adore God in "distant worlds" hereafter. Both poets are "lost in wonder, love and praise" at the workings of Providence, the ancient in the history of mankind, the modern in his own life.

Addison contrasts his pre-conscious and youthful experience, before his "infant heart conceived" whence "these comforts flowed," or when "with heedless steps" he ran, impelled to manhood by an "arm unseen," with his mature awareness of divine favour. Prudentius relates man's experience of creation, fall, and redemption, verifiable from Christian teaching; Addison's is a personal if not uncommon experience to which only he can witness.

As everyone knows, Isaac Watts, challenged by his father to improve on the metrical psalm, developed the first successful English hymnal out of the Psalms. I have delayed discussing his greatest hymns on the Creator in order to relate them to the preceding contrast of old and new world religion. A Freudian could find Watts *père* influential in other ways. A touching story of the child Isaac whipped for speaking constantly in rhyme yet sobbing an apology in couplets recalls Aldous Huxley's speculation on corporal punishment as conducive to belief in a remote and punitive deity.[26] Watts himself records that he felt a "considerable conviction of sin" at fourteen, that he was "taught to trust in Christ" at fifteen, and that Bible-reading had subdued his "sinful appetite" and raised him "from death to life."[27] We may suspect auto-eroticism briefly indulged and renounced, for his tiny frame, large head, and intellectual precocity seem unlikely to have attracted the opposite sex. (His only recorded proposal, in middle life, drew the response, "I wish I could … admire the casket as much as I admire the jewel.")[28] An early poem on "The Hazard of Loving the Creatures" indicates a conscious sexual sublimation:

> 'Tis dangerous to let loose our love
> Beneath th'eternal fair.
>
> Souls whom the tie of friendship binds,
> And partners of our blood,
> Seize a large portion of our minds,
> And leave the less for God.[29]

Whether this sublimation was responsible for his bouts of fever and prostration experienced in times of stress remains uncertain.[30] At all events, Watt's talents as poet, preacher, and divine, allied to the benignity of Sir Thomas and Lady Abney, enabled him to devote his long life to writing, as a permanent house guest. His early poems, *Horae Lyricae*, reveal a regressive personality, conceivably affected by a difficult birth as first child. Death is "that unfathomable sea" where "living waters" play or "fiery billows roar." Jesus, whose name he would carve on the bark of a tree has "all my powers possesst." This "Fairest and only Beloved" is the "Ocean" in whom the "passions of the mind" find "joys and freedom unconfin'd."[31] Remembering that Watts grew up within sight of Southampton Water, we should not make too much of this oceanic imagery that, according to Freud, expresses an unconscious longing for the womb. The preoccupation with storm and thunder, in a poem on the Apocalypse wherein "red lightning" and "hoarse thunder" appal sailors, reminds the poet, however, of the "wild disorder" to come when the "great Archangel / Shakes the creation," suggesting a buried memory of the birth trauma.[32]

In these early poems Watts consistently depicts God the Father as a despot inspiring love and terror. He asserts love of the Father but demonstrates it only of the Son. The terror constantly appears in images of sun, lightning, frost, fire, drought, famine, plague, and earthquake, summed up as "flashes of a wrathful eye."[33] The supreme God dwells beyond the heavens, "conceal'd in radiant flame."[34] Whereas in "Lead, kindly Light" Newman longs to be led out of darkness, the young Watts confesses himself dazzled and appalled. To adapt a recent theory on the near-death experiences as a reliving of the birth trauma, among four kinds of birth imagery that of contraction predominates in *Horae Lyricae* over those of stasis, journey, and emergence.[35]

This and the admixture of love and terror felt by most children of Puritan fathers can account for the origin but not the substance of the Wattsian psalm-cum-hymn on the Creator. The same is true of his sexual sublimation and images of Christ. We must look to the circumstances of Independent congregations in the early eighteenth century for an explanation of his endeavour in philosophy, theology, and hymnody alike to accommodate the Calvinist doctrine and ethic to the sensibility of a more tolerant and sceptical age. Suffice it here to illustrate accommodation briefly from "Before Jehovah's awful throne" (Ps. 100) and more extensively from "The Lord Jehovah reigns" (Ps. 148) and the classic "Our God, our help in ages past" (Ps. 90).[36]

In the first lyric three new features deserve attention: "Ye nations" for "all people"; the collective promise that "We'll crowd thy gates" with thankful songs and "earth, with her ten thousand tongues" resound in praise, and the prediction that the truth of God shall endure "firm as a rock" when "rolling years have ceased to move." Here Watts combines the permanence of time and the nation-state with apocalyptic motifs of God as first and last, creator and destroyer, and 10,000 voices chanting praise.[37] But "shall fill thy courts" can refer to worship here or hereafter, and "Wide as the world is thy command" to Christendom newly expanded by exploration or to the promise of the Apocalypse.

To Watt's celebrated endeavour to "sink" his style to the "meanest capacity" of believers in all Protestant churches, we owe the strong, simplistic phrases of "The Lord Jehovah reigns," which appeared frequently in hymnals until the late nineteenth century. These enunciate every image of the Father: His "throne," "garments" of "light and majesty," beams too bright for mortal eye, thunder and wrath in dispensing justice, "wisdom" confounding the powers of hell, and "sovereign will" brooking no denial. The only other being in the hymn, the poet himself, combines Calvinist *angst* ("And will he write his name, / My Father and my Friend?") with love of the divine name and "word." In this stanza, not based on any psalm verse, Watts reconciles God's terrible with His loving countenance, in assertions that carry less conviction than the earlier metaphors of the divine majesty and terror.

With editorial aid, "Our God, our help in ages past" has adapted supremely well to the changing environment not only of Dissent but of English Christianity. Had critics attended to hymns as to secular poems, the post-structuralist thesis that a text evolves new meanings might have developed long before it did.[38] Just when Watts first rendered the opening of Psalm 90 into a tribal lay first of Independents, and eventually of the English people is immaterial. When it came out, five years after Queen Anne's sudden death had ensured the repeal of a Schism Act imposing new disabilities on Dissenters, it was understood to imply that the Almighty, as in "ages past," had intervened to give his true adherents hope for years to come.[39] Read this way, each of the original nine verses makes sense. God has sheltered his saints from the "stormy blast" of persecution. They "have dwelt secure" under the shadow of His "throne" during the Commonwealth; His "arm alone" suffices for their defence now.

The next five stanzas contrast the eternal changelessness of God with the transience and total dependence of human civilisations, including the present that barely tolerates Dissenters:

> Thy Word commands our flesh to dust,
> "Return, ye sons of men";
> All nations rose from Earth at first,
> And turn to earth again.
>
> A thousand ages in thy sight
> Are like an evening gone;
> Short as the watch that ends the night
> Before the rising sun.
>
> The busy tribes of flesh and blood,
> With all their lives and cares,

Are carried downwards by the flood
And lost in following years.

Time, like an ever-rolling stream
Bears all its sons away;
They fly forgotten as a dream
Dies at the opening day.

Like flow'ry fields the nations stand
Pleas'd with the morning light;
The flowers beneath the Mower's hand
Lie withering ere 'tis night.[40]

As personal and absolute ruler, God sentenced men and nations to death after the Fall. The "busy tribes," whether people absorbed in worldly business or the hours and minutes of human time (accurate clocks being of recent invention),[41] roll to destruction on the flood of irreversible change. Those that attend to things of time rather than eternity are forgotten like last night's dream. Their cultures flourish until cut down by "the Mower," death or the divine will. The faithful remnant, however, may securely pray God to shelter them during present troubles and in eternity.

As time and change made the original meaning obsolete, verses were dropped and words altered. John Wesley's change to "O God" (1737)[42] turned the hymn into a prayer apostrophizing a universal rather than sectarian deity. Reduction to the present five stanzas removed not only the idea of death as a divine despot's sentence upon all save His elect, but all reference to the tension between Dissenters and English society at large that naturally eased when the Hanoverian dynasty survived the rebellions of 1715 and 1745.

Isolated by the excision of surrounding stanzas, "Time, like an ever-rolling stream," and especially "They fly forgotten as a dream," seemed, if its originating psalm be disregarded, to make the un-Christian assertion that death closes all. John Wesley tried the following emendation:

Death, like an overflowing Stream,
Sweeps us away; our Life's a Dream:
An empty Tale; a morning flow'r
Cut down and wither'd in an Hour.[43]

Watt's original stanza, as now sung, imparts what Wordsworth calls "an alien tinge of melancholy"[44] characteristic of English folk songs.[45] What gave the hymn a fresh, wider, and ironically different context and meaning was a decision by the founding editors of *Hymns Ancient and Modern* (1861) to set it to an even older tune, "St. Anne." In this setting it became not only an "internationally famous"[46] expression of trust in Providence, but a "second national anthem."[47] As a British tribal lay, it suited perfectly the sombre context of Remembrance Day services all over the Commonwealth (a term originally signifying the Puritan regime), that were designed to ensure that fallen soldiers should *not* "fly forgotten as a dream." The indomitable tune confirmed the unspoken belief that the national institutions — Throne, Parliament, and Church — could endure despite change, vicissitude, and slaughter. Ironically, the omitted stanzas had said precisely the opposite.

Even so, Watts the patriot would have approved the new interpretation, for by naturalizing the Psalms he endorsed the transferences of divine favour from Israel to Britain made in George Wither's hymns[48] and in Milton's famous sentences:

> God is decreeing to begin some new and great period in his church, even to the reforming of Reformation itself; what does he then but reveal himself to his servants, and as his manner is, first to his Englishmen? . . . Methinks I see in my mind a noble and puissant nation rousing herself like a strong man after sleep, and shaking her invincible locks: methinks I see her as an eagle mewing her mighty youth, and kindling her undazzled eyes at the full midday beam; purging and unscaling her long-abused sight at the fountain itself of heavenly radiance.[49]

By making England holy, Cromwell and his fellow Puritans ensured that future generations would find her sacred. As faith in the supernatural faltered, they would find transcendence in the national institutions. Inevitably, the Dissenters were patriotic, for the Pretenders had French and Scottish support, but Watts always transferred the role of chosen people to "Britain, since "England and Scotland" replaced "Israel and Judah."[50] To the Established Church of England, the Act of Union with Scotland brought in a Presbyterian counterweight.

The typology of Britain as a second Israel had its historical origin in the Puritan attempt to found a kingdom ruled by God alone, without temporal or spiritual viceroy.[51] As regards hymnody, the image originated jointly in the attempt to Christianize the Psalms and in the perils of Dissenting congregations represented in Watts's "Hymn of Praise for Three Great Salvations" (1695), composed for the anniversary of the Gunpowder Plot. The "counsels" of the Lord decreed the English Reformation, then in turn saved Protestant England from the Armada of "bloody Rome," from the Gunpowder Plot, and from the tyranny of James II.[52] Although we usually associate patriotic hymnody with the Established Church, it began with the Dissenting churches, which had a vested interest in the Hanoverian succession.

Several hymns by Philip Doddridge, also an Independent theologian, entreat God to love, chasten, and spare "the British Isles" as he had Israel. God's beloved land, exclaims one, "a Rebel to that Love hath proved."[53] Another defines the same special relationship in calling on Britons to prepare humbly to meet God rather than in "mad Rebellion" defy Him.[54] "O God of Bethel" (originally "Israel") lends itself to interpretation in terms of divine care for the Dissenters, or the English nation, or Christians as a whole. It is this capacity to extend or renew meaning that accounts for the survival of our greatest hymns.

To revert to those based on psalms, two of the finest show different kinds of adaptation. "Praise the Lord! ye Heavens adore him," written for singing at Foundling's Hospital services to Haydn's Austria,[55] offers an unusual reverse transference of a tune from patriotic to religious use. The text combines the old objective theology of the Creation with the new physics, in that the cosmos — angels, mankind, sun, and moon — unites in praise and in obedience to immutable "laws," which are at once the Commandments and the laws of motion. This accommodation between religion and science came under strain only with the advent of Darwinism.

Sir Robert Grant's equally heart-stirring "O worship the King" (1833) (Ps. 104) reiterates the psalmodic images of royalty, providence, protection, and "chariots of wrath" forming thunderheads, but intensifies them by enthroning the "Ancient of Days" as an oriental despot "Pavilioned in splendour," with robe and canopy, a being of infinite and unchanging power who takes on a different guise when dispensing (Christian) grace and love, robed in light and overhung by a canopy of "space." As creator of an earth with wonders "untold," that are at once countless and yet undiscovered, whose changelessness is exemplified in the laws of nature, as provider of our sustaining elements of air, light, and water, God embodies the rhythms of nature and the life cycle. Finally, the contrast of our "feeble lays" with the angelic hymns is balanced by the experience of divine providence in "nor find thee to fail."[56] If primarily an expression of Old World religion, this famous hymn accommodates the modern sense of God in nature and of common humanity. Hence even staunch republicans in the United States can sing it without feeling they have left the world they know for one dead beyond recall.

Our last great psalm-based hymn to the Father, Francis Lyte's "Praise, my soul, the King of Heaven" (1834) (Ps. 103) shows yet another kind of plasticity. A stanza often rightly omitted, "Frail as summer's flower we flourish," contrasting transient mortals with God who "endures unchanging on," intrudes the "all flesh is grass" theme, perhaps owing to Lyte's ill health.[57] In general, nevertheless, the poet employs the traditional images of King, Father, and Shepherd. Into their thanksgiving for being "ransomed," "healed," and "forgiven" the singers draw sun, moon, and angels, in the ancient Judaeo-Christian tradition. But since each has his own sense of restoration, his own cause of thanksgiving, each gives his own meaning to the poem. By the same principle, every gathering that sings it, as at a wedding or other celebration, attaches its own cause, so that "Praise my soul," like "Now thank we all our God," becomes a passkey to release whatever collective or private feelings of thankfulness or relief its singers may have.

Over some two and a half centuries, then, the images of the Creator or Father derived mainly from the Hebrew Psalter took forms suiting the circumstances of Protestants in general, Dissenters in particular, the English nation, and ultimately the individual. Each context interlocks with the rest, in that the survival of Calvinist Dissent was bound up with that of the nation and its monarchy, and that of Christianity itself with accommodation to the Newtonian model of the cosmos. This flexibility, the amazing variety of situations to which, for example, "Our God, our help in ages past" could be adapted (in 1983 some debt-ridden Canadian farmers sang it when trying to prevent a foreclosure) made the hymn, still more the hymn book, open to use in furtherance of idolatry or class interest between the time of Watts and the First World War.

11

CHRIST APPLIED

INCARNATE

As this and the previous epigraph suggest, myths and sacred books reveal periodic oscillations between cults of a remote and passive Sky-god and an accessible and dynamic Sun-god. In Judaic and Christian countries the swings have been moderated by the continuing encounter of Yahweh with his Chosen People and by the doctrine of the Trinity. The *mythos* of Christ Incarnate, Crucified, and Risen ensured, moreover, that divine abstractness and concreteness would at once remain in mind, for what the Father had initiated the Son endured. The Puritan movement in England represents a rough parallel with the reversion to the Sky-god, in reaction against the medieval "idolatry" of the Virgin and the bodily symbols of Christ. The High Church and Arminian Wesleys led a Christocentric movement roughly parallel to the swing towards the Sun-god, with historical analogies in the Latin and German communions. The extreme of abstraction being the Unitarian (otherwise Socinian) faith adopted by English Presbyterians, Coleridge wittily notes: "Socinianism, Moonlight; Methodism, a Stove. O for some sun to unite heat and Light."[2] The tendency of Calvinist and Unitarian theologians to reduce the faith to abstractions gives support to Nietzsche's view of Christianity as an "Apollonian" religion. Methodism, as Coleridge implies, represented its Dionysian polarity. (Roman Catholicism, to judge from its hymnody, has room for both.) The one produces creeds, codes of behaviour, and veneration of a remote Creator, the other visual or verbal images, and personal love of the Son. Again the contrast must be tempered, for the Calvinist Watts produced one of our warmest passion lyrics, the Arminian Charles Wesley one of our grandest tableaux of the Last Judgement. Like the sophisticated hymnists they were, they kept in balance both sides of the Christian paradox that the Divine Word was rocked in a cradle and nailed to a cross.

Today, images of the Nativity abound where the doctrine of the Incarnation has been forgotten or never known. In Tokyo, as in the West, stars glitter over shopping streets; it was once my pleasure to hear Hindu students burst spontaneously into carol singing, joined by Fijians, black Africans, and even a Jew from South Africa. Our carols, with their age-old tunes and imagery of shepherds, wizards, and seraphim, seem to have been sung since time immemorial. In fact, as Routley and others tell us, an astonishing proportion were composed during the Victorian refurbishing of medieval ritual and folk lyrics in the wake of the Oxford Movement. True carols appeared in denominational hymnals only in the twentieth century. Since the Pickwickians and their hosts could not have sung "Away in a manger," "O little town of Bethlehem," "It came upon the midnight clear," or "Good King Wenceslas," the Christmas party at Dingley Dell must have been less sentimental than is commonly supposed.[3]

That company could have sung some nativity hymns that must concern us here. The medieval carol, as Routley explains, faded out with the festivities that gave it meaning. During the Commonwealth, the Christmas holiday itself was forbidden. Christmas songs survived but tended towards endearment or narration. In the seventeenth century, even nativity hymns leant more towards narration than paradox. Only "Behold the great Creator makes / Himself a house of clay" (1659), composed by an Anglican priest on the eve of the Restoration, reflects upon the divine mystery of Incarnation, in the "eternal Word / Like a weak infant cries."[4] By exhorting all hearts to celebrate the birth, Thomas Pestel set the tone for Watts, Byrom, and others in the following century, but in his time narration prevailed, as in "The first Nowell" and "While shepherds watched."

The latter, one of six authorized hymns in Tate and Brady's New Version (1696), so closely followed St. Luke's narrative as to find a place in the rigorously scriptural *Scots Paraphrases* (1781).[5] Apart from its shapely tune, its charm resides in naïvely objective reportage, devoid of sentimentalism. In what it says and what it omits, "While shepherds watched" is redolent of old world Protestantism. "The Angel of the Lord came down" implies the transcendent deity, three-decker universe, and celestial hierarchy from which "glory shone around." The contrast between the numinous apparition and humble men filled with dread can still move us. The paradox of the deity "meanly wrapped" is not dwelt upon; "to human view displayed" suffices to inform these unlettered rustics who, like the sentries in *Hamlet*,[6] can yet perceive the numinous. The poet neither enquires how the child is to fulfil the pledge of goodwill nor concludes that war and grief are at an end. The religious consensus allows him to leave the future to the preacher and keep to his wondrous tale.

A parallel, *"Les anges dans nos campagnes,"* much altered as "Shepherds in the fields abiding," embroiders the narrative only with a question and response on the meaning of the angel's song. "It is no fable" is the Victorian translator's assurance.

Watts involves the singers of "Joy to the world" (still a favourite in North America) by exhorting every heart to "prepare him room." So does Byrom those of "Christians awake": "Rise to adore the Mystery of Love / With hosts of Angels."[7]

The real impetus towards participation, however, came from German hymns. Though not translated until the nineteenth century, *"Brich an O schönes Morgenlicht"* ("Break forth, O beauteous heavenly Light") (1641), immortalized by Bach, exemplifies a collective human viewpoint from which the poet apostrophizes the festal day, shepherds, and incarnate Christ.[8] Even earlier, Luther adopted the *persona* of Christ in the stanza of *"Vom Himmel hoch"* ("From heaven on high to earth I come"). In another famous for its tender setting by Bach, he responds in his own person, praying the Infant Jesus to abide in the "quiet chamber" of the heart.[9]

Charles Wesley's "Hark, the herald angels sing," while adhering to a collective viewpoint, carries internalization much further.[10] Even his original opening, "Hark, how all the welkin rings!," brings the event into present time and involves the congregation. He attends far more even than Watts to the theology of Incarnation. If God be "reconciled" and grant "second birth," the "sons of earth" have been alienated. God pledges "light and life" to "all," not an elect, hence all are sinners in need of rebirth. The heavenly hierarchies are enjoyed, not contemplated, for the poet speaks from the Angel's viewpoint. Like Tate and Brady, Wesley brings out his implication by links and contrasts, but also by a kind of reversal. In one stanza Christ emerges from the womb to dwell "in his wings," combining thus the powers of man and the "Sun of righteousness" *(Malachi 4:2)*. In the opening verse, the Angel, using "joyful" as an inversion, calls on "ye nations" to rise as from their knees; in the third, with a like inversion, he describes the divine descent, "Mild he lays his glory by." By implication, man can rise reborn because God has descended to be born.

In lines hymnal editors have long omitted, Wesley relates the Redemption to the Fall before internalizing the Incarnation more explicitly:

> Come, Desire of nations, come,
> Fix in us thy humble home,
> Rise, the Woman's conquering seed,
> Bruise in us the serpent's head . . .
>
> Adam's likeness, Lord, efface,
> Stamp thy image in its place . . .
>
> Let us thee, tho' lost, regain,

> Thee, the Life, the inner Man:
> O! to all thyself impart,
> Form'd in each believing heart.

By their deletions, the editors produced a more singable text. If this omission of the last couplet appears philistine, they sensed, no doubt, that few singers were ready for this profound relocation of the biblical event within the individual consciousness.

The American and English singers of "O little town of Bethlehem", some century-and-a-half later, were far readier to sing "Be born in us today". By their time, both carol-singing and revelation via the imagination had established themselves as, alas, sentimental moralizing had driven out numinous awe. The editors did well to delete this unspeakable stanza:

> Where children pure and happy
> Pray to the blessed Child,
> Where misery cries out to thee,
> Son of the mother mild;
> Where charity stands watching
> And faith holds wide the door,
> The dark night wakes, the glory breaks,
> And Christmas comes once more.[11]

The unevenness of the text normally sung indicates the prevailing wind. Muddle and empty rhetoric mar the narrative stanzas. The birth takes place in a modern town of "dark streets," below "silent" stars, but the "morning stars" (of Job. 38.7) are to acclaim it as they did the Creation. What does the poet mean by the apostrophized town's "dreamless sleep" or the "hopes and fears of all the years" that meet there? In the meditative stanza on the silence with which God "imparts to human hearts / The blessings of his heaven" the tone may be sentimental ("The dear Christ"), but the meaning is clear. The concluding stanza focuses entirely on the birth within the hearts of the present-day singers, who "hear the Christmas angels" tell their "glad tidings." Its final plea, "O come to us, abide with us, / Our Lord, Immanuel" is sung with such fervour as to discourage attention to the relocation of the coming of "God with us" from an entry into the human race at a historical time and place to an infinite series of entries into the hearts of individual singers. The English folk-melody "Forest Green", with its perfect balance of rising lines and elaborate cadences, seems more an appropriate expression of this shift from narrative to application. The North American tune "St. Louis" suits only the sentimentalism and the archness of, for example, angels watching over mortals in "wondering love," as mothers over their infants.

Though also blessed with an apt tune, descending and rising figures for the divine descent and human response, "Joy to the world," happily preserved in North America, satisfies by virtue of its single stance and aim.

At first sight a like singleness of purpose appears in "Adeste Fideles" ("O come all ye faithful") ascribed to the English Catholic Wade. His stanzas (written soon after "Hark! how all the welkin rings") simply instruct the faithful to come rejoicing and behold "God of God, / Light of Light," and the angels to sing "Gloria / In excelsis Deo." Wade's final stanza begins, as literally rendered:

Ergo qui natus	Therefore thou who art born
die hodierna	This day
Jesu tibi sit gloria	Jesu, be glory.

This the Victorian translators rendered as "Yea, Lord, we greet thee." The poem Wade wrote was objective and doctrinal, in the tradition of Latin hymnody. About the end of the eighteenth century, Abbé Borderies inserted three stanzas, those on the Shepherds; the Godhead "in flesh appearing," and the human response. The last of these begins literally:

Pro nobis egenum	For us [born] needy
et foeno cubantem,	and laid in the hay
piis foveamus amplexibus:	let us love with holy embraces

then asks which of us would not love in return for being so loved. The translators again intensified the emotion by inserting "dearly" and "with awe and love." In the mid-nineteenth-century addition, on the gifts of the Magi, original and translation are at one: *Jesu infanti / corda praebeamus* (literally "To the Infant Jesus, / Let us offer our hearts"). Wade's original poem differs little in substance from any medieval hymn on the Incarnation. During the nineteenth century, on both sides of the Cloth Curtain, imaginative participation and response come to the fore.[12]

The Incarnation Applied governs the structure of Doddridge's great Advent hymn, "Hark the glad sound! the Saviour comes." On the one hand, he combines the common exhortation "Let every heart prepare a throne" with the ancient image of the liberator before whom "gates of brass" and "iron fetters" yield; on the other, he acclaims the social blessings of the Messiah's teaching in a summary of the proclamation in the Synagogue:

> He comes the broken heart to bind,
> The bleeding soul to cure,
> And with the treasures of his grace
> To enrich the humble poor.[13]

Clearly the Saviour ministers to both material and spiritual needs, hence to believers of all ranks. In contemporary Latin Advent hymns (considered as English Victorian) such as "Veni, veni Emmanuel" and "Instantis adventum Dei," the liberator motif bears its age-old message of deliverance from Satan.[14]

It is important to realize that in the hymnody of both Old and New Dissent (the latter term being loosely applied to Methodism), traditional objective methology continues side by side with psychological and even social application. The eighteenth century witnessed a transition, never total, in all facets of the Myth before the Oxford Movement brought back ancient and medieval hymns and doctrines. Advent hymns by Wesley and his contemporary Robert Robinson run the whole gamut from the sublimely impersonal to the intimately subjective.

The former's "Lo, He comes, with clouds descending" depicts the Last Judgment with no less objectivity than the "Dies irae":

> Every eye shall now behold him
> Robed in dreadful majesty;
> Those who set at nought and sold him,
> Pierced and nailed him to the tree,
>   Deeply wailing
> Shall the true Messiah see.[15]

The vindictiveness of these lines results from somewhat ambiguously phrased details not present in the originating text "They shall look upon him whom they pierced" (John 19.37, after Zach. 12.10). Though only one person "sold" Jesus, the subject pronoun "Those" appears to make this a collective act of the Jews and Roman soldiers.

Wesley's still popular "Come, thou long-expected Jesus" internalizes the Advent, yet still in a collective sense. Christ who will free "us" from "fears and sins" is at once the "Dear desire of every nation" and "Joy of every longing heart." A single phrase, "Israel's strength and consolation," suffices to invoke the prophetic tradition concerning the Messiah.[16]

A splendid and still current Scottish paraphrase of Isaiah 9.2-7, "The race that long in darkness pined," widens the collective application.[17] After following his original on the Light shining upon "people that walked in darkness" and "dwell in the land of the shadow of death," Morison inserts "To hail thy rise, thou better Sun, / The gathering nations come." As a Presbyterian he modulates from the Chosen People, through the Gathered Church of the elect in every nation, to the nations themselves.[18] During the eighteenth century, alongside the objective and internalizing strains, there ran a current of universalism visible in the Gospels and the source of an immense outpouring of missionaries during the nineteenth.

Robinson's "Come, thou fount of every blessing" (1758)[19] points the new direction by being cast in the singular, for Christ has sought "me" to bind "my" wandering heart to Himself. A touch of legal imagery and the formal structure redeem the lyric from egocentric emotionalism. As "debtor" for grace, the poet bids Christ "seal" his heart to prevent further wandering. His response to the Saviour's quest for him is preceded by the invocation "Tune my heart to sing thy grace."

CRUCIFIED

John Wesley, of course, had found his vocation in a lifelong mission to the British lower classes that was tantamount to reliving the Incarnation. The condescension, in its best sense, of the Wesleys to the outcast and the poor, resulted, however, in a preaching and hymnodic tradition centred on the Atonement, and has important implications for the whole notion of class conditioning in the hymn-book, to be explored in the next volume of this study. The endeavour by hymnists, very few of whom had been labourers or waifs and strays, to fix attention upon salvation through the blood of Christ as the only hope of the poor could seem intended to preserve the wealth and power of the employing classes.

In the flood of passion hymns during the eighteenth and nineteenth centuries, some erotic items have delighted Marxist and Freudian critics.[20] Undeniably, Moravian odes to the Wounds,[21] or harrowing narratives of the Scourging in both Catholic and Protestant hymnals, evince womb-regressive and sado-masochistic tendencies. Critics who pounce gleefully on these are less apt to note John Wesley's excision of erotic imagery in his translations of German chorales, or his omission of "Jesu, Lover of my soul" from his great *Collection* (1780). Nor have any demonstrated that Culy's masterpiece on the "precious side-hole's cavity" or the Moravian plea

> Hungry and thirsty, lo! I come
> O let me in thy Wounds find room;
> There let me find a shelt'ring place
> To hide and screen me from disgrace,[22]

or the thirty-four undignified stanzas on the same in "The Saviour's blood and righteousness / My Fin'ry is and my Wedding Dress," ever became widely known in England. We may therefore pass over such erotica in favour of passion hymns by Watts, the Wesleys, Toplady, and Cowper that we know to have been widely read and sung.

The finest English hymn on the Passion, "When I survey the wondrous Cross," was published among Watts's "Spiritual Songs" for the Lord's Supper. About to receive the Sacrament, the poet meditates upon the love that turned that instrument of judicial torture and death into the channel of divine compassion. Watts derives his vision from an act of willed imagination rather than the relic that prompted Fortunatus to compose the "Vexilla regis."[23] The Augustan poet beautifully transposes the blood and water of the Roman hymn into the moral abstractions of sorrow and love, for to meditate is to infer meaning from a mental image. But first, he draws the singer into his act of imagination by supplying such detail and putting such rhetorical questions as may call forth a like emotion:

> See from his head, his hands, his feet
> Sorrow and love flow mingled down;
> Did e'er such love and sorrow meet?
> Or thorns compose so rich a crown?

where Fortunatus lets the images speak for themselves. Once drawn in, the singer also renounces whatever "vain things" most "charm" (enchant or delude) him. In the tune "Rockingham," the accents of "Whereon the Prince of Glory died" fall no more happily than those of the original line "Where the young Prince . . ." but the revision, accepted by Watts, removes an identification of Christ with the young that was perhaps an effect of self-projection, since at the time of writing Watts was about the same age.

The omission of the following stanza by the preacher Whitefield has been deplored by Routley and, with reserve, by Davie:

> His dying crimson like a robe
> Spreads o'er his body on the tree,
> Then am I dead to all the globe,
> And all the globe is dead to me.[24]

Whitefield may have wished to remove the blood-image, but most editors since have surely thought the entrancement of the last two lines a state the majority of singers could not share.

Although Watts here echoes St. Paul,[25] in "The Heart given away" he says of his passion for Christ:

> I feel my warmest passions dead
> To all that earth can boast:
> This soul of mine was never made
> For vanity and dust.[26]

The touch of genius that transmutes an obsession into a response all can share lies in the magnificent concluding hyperbole:

> Were the whole realm of nature mine,

> That were an offering far too small;
> Love so amazing, so divine
> Demands my soul, my life, my all.

A modern singer pledges his reciprocal offering (*My* life, *my* all) without troubling himself with the Calvinist assumption that no response could pay off his debt, or realizing that he offers a commitment once required only of those taking monastic vows.

The "Vexilla regis" called for no individual response, Christ having died for the whole race. In the "Stabat mater," the poet as Everyman begs the Virgin to respond for him, that the love of Christ may be implanted in his heart. By evoking in each singer a vision of the Crucifixion, "When I survey" demands of each a personal and reciprocal response. Once part of the general repertoire, it made nonsense of the Calvinist poet's belief that only the elect could be saved.

Even the most explicit love image of Watts, "Scarce shall I feel Death's cold embrace / If Christ be in my arms,"[27] does not approach the eroticism of some Moravian hymns. It is in John Wesley's naturalizing of these and other hymns that we see where his yet unrealized union of Christian myth and experience was to take him.[28] The future direction both of his pietism and his life stands revealed in adaptations that remained for a century among the best-loved Methodist hymns. A good example occurs in "O Jesu, source of calm repose." Where the German stanza runs:

> Groszer Sieges-Held! tod sünd, höll und welt,
> alle krafft des groszen drachen
> hast du woll'n zu schanden machen
> durch das löse-geld deines bluts,
> > o Held!

> Great hero of victory! Death, sin, hell, and the world
> and the strength of the great dragon
> you wanted to put to shame
> through the ransom of your blood,
> > O hero![29]

Wesley's version goes:

> The world, sin, death oppose in vain;
> Thou, by Thy dying, death hast slain,
> My great Deliverer, and my God!
> In vain does the old dragon rage,
> In vain all hell its powers engage;
> None can withstand Thy conquering blood.[30]

Wesley transposes the fight to a continuing present tense, emphasizes the Devil's antiquity rather than his power, subsumes the hero motif under "conquering blood," and eliminates the ransom theory of the Atonement. Above all, by writing from a first person viewpoint he applies the Myth individually rather than narrating it collectively. The Myth internalized and the Blood Applied were to become the hallmarks of Methodist theology.

A further mark of Wesley's optimistic temperament was his substitution in the first stanza of "those whom death's sad fetters bound" for those chosen (*auser-köhren*) who live yet are lost (*verlohren*).

Finally, he tones down the baroque intensity of *deinen scepter will ich küssen* (Thy sceptre will I kiss) to "To Thy dread sceptre will I bow" with, incidentally, "duteous reverence" rather than sitting like Mary at the feet of Christ (*sitzen dir zu füszen*). He also excises two stanzas on the German poet's wish to burn with love for and recreate himself within Christ. The Wesleys invariably follow St. Paul in praying, conversely, for Christ to reform Himself within the soul. Nothing better exposes the incompatibility of baroque imagery with Wesley's sober English temperament than his refashioning of Freylinghausen's conclusion:

> Einen helden-muth, der da gut und blut
> gern um deinet willen lasse,
> und des fleisches lüste hasse,
> gib mir, höchstes gut! durch dein theures blut.

> The courage of a hero who will give
> body and soul for You
> and who will hate the passions of the flesh,
> give to me, highest treasure! by Your precious blood.

into

> A patient, a victorious mind
> That, life and all things cast behind,
> Springs forth obedient to Thy call,
> A heart that no desire can move,
> But still to adore, believe, and love,
> Give me, my Lord, my Life, my all.

Though by a High Churchman, this stanza bears the imprint of Watts.

It is easy to exaggerate the eroticism of the Moravians, notably Zinzendorf. The exuberant imagery of the baroque culture never took root in English verse except in Crashaw's. Germans, like English soldiers of a later time, were addicted to improvising verse after verse with but the slenderest thread of meaning. Like the Welsh, they sang in harmony as if by nature. Many Moravian hymns amounted, therefore, to harmonic litanies built upon the emotional associations of images rather than upon passages of scripture. By condensing and toning down, Wesley tried to give a structure of ideas to such interminable lyrics by Zinzendorf as *Rein der bräutgam meiner seelen* ("Jesu, to Thee my heart I bow").[31] Here he condenses nine stanzas on Christ the Bridegroom into a single one ending "Be Thou my Lord, my Life, my Love." In the next section (stanzas 10-12) he tones down *Liebe, deine glut entzünde / meine kalt-gewordne brust* (Love, your passion set on fire / My breast, which has grown cold) into the decorous Augustanese of: "All heaven Thou fill'st with pure desire; / O shine upon my frozen breast; / With sacred warmth my heart inspire."[32] By the time he had excised the figures of the soul in need of milk and wine from the divine breast but corrupted by the drink of harlots, and of the Bridegroom's kisses, Wesley had turned the seventeen verses of Zinzendorf into six of his own, of which only the third in "I see Thy garments roll'd in blood, / Thy streaming head, Thy hands, Thy side" retains the concreteness and verve of the original. But Wesley's version could be sung by an English congregation that Zinzendorf's would have reduced to embarrassed silence.

Even the twenty-four stanzas to which Wesley reduced the thirty-three of "Christi blut und gerechtigkeit" ("Jesu, Thy blood and righteousness")[33] have been so further condensed — to eleven in Wesley's own *Collection* — that very little of Zinzendorf's text has percolated into later English hymnals. Originally Wesley transposed collective mythic encounter into personal experience by, for example, omitting the figure of the Devil lamenting his loss of souls. At almost every point decorum prevails: lust becomes "pride, desire, wrath"; the soul's refusal of temptation "Swift to my sure resort I flee." For his *Collection* Wesley, or his brother, pared down this sprawling and exuberant lyric wherein the Moravian poet runs naked from the Devil and plunges into the bottomless sea of the Saviour's blood[34] into an impeccable version of scriptural typology: the Christian expecting at the last day to wear the "blood and righteousness" of the "unspotted Lamb" as his (bridal) robe of salvation, his assertion of faith in the redemption that began with the choosing of Abraham, his call upon God to redeem likewise the living and the dead. An English clergyman and Oxford don to boot could never have given out the German hymn as written. Wesley took over, however, Zinzendorf's simplification of the Christian faith into a single "grand topic . . . the person and propitiation of our Saviour, Jesus Christ."[35]

Christocentric religion had run its quiet course throughout the seventeenth century in the meditative lyrics of George Herbert or the superb passion lyric "My song is love unknown" (1664) by another Anglican priest, Samuel Crossman, significantly published in a book of meditations.[36] Both Herbert and Crossman depict Christ as Lover. In Crossman's poem the hosannas to the King, immediately followed by shouts of "Crucify," sharply contrast the fickleness of the herd with the fidelity of the individual who responds to "my Saviour's love" by vowing to spend his days in "sweet praise." Narration, being subordinate to meaning, is quite free of the bloody stripes that offend the eye in not a few hymns of Charles Wesley and the Evangelicals, as in the most garish ecclesiastical art. For all its beauty, "My song is love unknown" implies no act of identification with or accusation by the Figure on the Cross. Christ remains distinct from both the poet and the "loveless," to whom He exemplified love by leaving his heavenly home for their sake. With its theology of the Crucifixion as paradigm of love rather than atonement for sin, this poem could have been written by Abelard.

The theologies of love and atoning blood meet in "Behold the Saviour of mankind" by Samuel Wesley, father of John and Charles.[37] Even here, however, the initial emphasis falls on the "vast" love that inclined Christ "to bleed and die for thee," the "ransom" being paid in the third stanza. Wesley senior eschews detail of suffering for the typology of earthquake and sundered temple. In his diary for 1738, Charles records singing his father's hymn "at the execution of a black servant for robbing his master" after telling him of "One who came down from heaven to save lost sinners," of the "sufferings . . . sorrows, agony and death" of the "Son of God." The weeping black, says Wesley, cried "Was it all for me?" and mounted the scaffold a believer.[38] The realization by this pitiable victim of the Bloody Code followed by a bare two months that of Charles himself, who with his yet unconverted brother sang the first hymn to convey the Methodist doctrine of the Blood applied:

> And can it be, that I should gain
> An interest in the Savior's blood!
> Died he for me? — who caused his pain!
> For me? — who him to death pursu'd.
> Amazing Love! how can it be
> That thou, my God, shouldst die for me!
>
> 'Tis mystery all! The immortal dies!
> Who can explore his strange design?

The initial "and" signals a still unfolding experience, ironically made explicit by the very legal metaphor that has rendered these lines unsingable. "Interest" has two terms: the death, and the benefit accruing to the criminal by his victim's will. The climatic line "That thou . . . ," which anticipates the negro's outburst of wondering joy, brings to a head the inward realization of the Fall and Incarnation that spurred the Wesleys to visit the condemned in loathsome cells: the conviction of being criminals themselves, accountable in some way for the Crucifixion.

Some better-known lines of "And can it be" uncannily foreshadow the very prison where Charles Wesley taught the thief to associate his impending death with that of Christ:

> Long my imprison'd Spirit lay
> Fast bound in sin and nature's night:
> Thine eye diffused a quick'ning ray:
> I woke; the dungeon flam'd with light;
> My chains fell off, my heart was free,
> I rose, went forth, and followed thee.

Here Wesley uses the miraculous deliverance of St. Peter[39] as a metaphor of the inward realization that was the essence of the Methodist conversion:

> Still the atoning Blood is near,
> That quench'd the wrath of hostile heav'n;
> I feel the life his wounds impart;
> I feel my Saviour in my heart.[40]

In his more famous lines "O for a thousand tongues to sing / My dear Redeemer's praise,"[41] Wesley gives form to the surge of joyous vitality that impelled his brother and himself to deliver their message in cells, in market-places, in the face of mobs, or in cottages to dying women who sang verses from the hymns as they expired.[42]

In the long poem "Glory to God, and praise and love" that includes "O for a thousand tongues," Wesley describes the "glad day" of his conversion as that on which "the glorious Sun / Of Righteousness arose" and his second life "began." The new life growing within the convert would reach its culmination in the life to come. Here the believer could "anticipate" heaven in the knowledge of his forgiveness, and own "that love is heaven."

Apart from misreading of the Wesleyan hymns, a further cause of the "Crosstianity" to be reviled by Bernard Shaw was that, as it fell out, Charles Wesley's magnificent hymns on the Incarnation, "Hark! the herald angels" or "Christ, whose glory fills the skies" (a modern Canticle to the Sun) fitted particular seasons or times of day, whereas those on the Cross or on heaven were sung throughout the year. John contributed to this by omitting seasonal hymns from his *Collection* to avoid any implication that the Methodists had become a separate church.[43] Many have seen the Methodist realization as foreshadowing the Romantic cult of inwardness, of truth "proved on our pulses."[44] Fewer have noted the extension of the Christian paradox from the Incarnation to the Crucifixion — from the Infinite confined in a crib to the death of the Immortal.

Even their most fervent admirers cannot acquit the poet Charles and the editor John of a fixation on the Cross and Blood. In "Where shall my wond'ring soul begin," Charles urges his "guilty brethren" in best Moravian fashion to take refuge in the "bleeding Heart" and "open side," whence flowed the "purple Current."[45] In the same section of his brother's *Collection*, at least nine out of seventeen hymns define the "Goodness of God" as wholly or mainly consisting in the suffering on the Cross. Some, like "Ye that pass by, behold the Man" call attention to the torn back bound to the "bloody pillar;"[46] a few, like "I thirst, thou wounded Lamb of God / To wash me in thy cleansing blood,"[47] voice a morbid longing to "dwell within thy wounds" that can only be called escapist. Even in his most moving evocations of divine love, Wesley has in mind a God who descended in order to die, who calls "weary sinners" home to their true and only rest. This fascination gripped even more strongly the Wesleyan editors of the 1830 *Collection*, for at least twelve of the nineteen texts in this section are almost totally concerned with the Passion.[48]

In their cruciolatry, Methodists and Evangelicals were not alone, witness the Catholic cults of the Sacred Heart and the Precious Blood, and especially the petitions of the prayer "Anima Christi," "Water from the side of Christ, wash me" and "Within Thy wounds, hide me."[49] To seek social causes of this fixation on both sides of the Cloth Curtain would take us beyond the sphere of hymnology.

For English hymnody there could be no going back. Hymnists of the Oxford and Catholic revivals would picture again the Via Dolorosa, thieves, nails, and spears, but the Christ who delivered the race without reference to its members belongs to an older time. The passion hymns that survive from the eighteenth century are those conveying a personal application of the Blood. Notwithstanding the initial conversion of Joseph Hart by Moravians, his objective accounts of the Passion and Atonement for his Independent congregation have long since gathered dust as Calvinist museum pieces.[50]

Should some latter-day Calvinist leap to his feet crying "Rock of Ages!," his example proves my case. That long-beloved lyric derives such emotional force as it still has from the Blood Applied, the "Rock . . . cleft for me." As suggested in the introduction to this book, Toplady's rejoinder to the Arminian doctrine of the Wesleys has changed its meaning. What Toplady wished to subvert may be appreciated from some phrases in "On this glad day the glorious sun." As Wesley relized the Atonement, the "legal strife" of old-fashioned Anglicanism gave place to a second and "real" life. John Wesley entitled an important collection *Hymns for Real Christians*. The total dependence upon God, as child upon parent, that Toplady's hymn continued to instil after its doctrinal purpose had been forgotten and which has since Freud become suspect as neurotic, was what Toplady had in common with the Wesleys.

Even more common was the self-abasement of "Foul, I to the fountain fly; / Wash me, Saviour, or I die." Watts and Wesley regard themselves as "worms of earth;" Newton is amazed that Christ would die to "save a wretch like me"; Cowper calls himself "vile" as the Thieves upon Calvary. Self-abasement of a different kind from the rhetorical prostration of Calvinist hymnists before God the Father[51] resulted from the sense of personal responsibility for the Passion. In Newton's "My Saviour hanging on the tree," the look that will haunt him till his dying day "seem'd to charge me with His death."[52] The "second look" of forgiveness brought a relief proportional to the tension aroused by the first.

Those without the ex-slaver Newton's cause of guilt needed the external pressure of Methodist or Evangelical "shock-and-relief" preaching and the various forms of follow-up.[53] One such means, the meditative hymn "Sweet the moments, rich in blessing, / Which before the Cross I spend" (1770) furnishes an instructive contrast with some medieval devotions described by Bennett. After claiming "Life, and health, and peace" as fruits of the Passion, the joint authors exclaim:

> Truly blessed is this station
> Low before his Cross to lie,
> While I see divine compassion
> Floating in his languid eye.[54]

Whatever the sense of "floating," the metaphorical self-prostration contrasts with the physical prostration in the Catholic Good Friday rite inasmuch as the religion of the Word seeks to stimulate imagination by metaphor, the religion of the Image by ritual.

Once as ubiquitous as "Rock of Ages," Cowper's "There is a Fountain filled with blood" repels today for reasons other than personal application or the consequent self-abasement. A revision by Nathaniel Micklem intended to make the hymn singable suggests that one reason lies in accidental association, another in the poet's overheated conscience. With traditional typology, Cowper applies to Christ a text of Zachariah. In Micklem's revision,

> There springs a fountain, where for sin
> Immanuel was slain;
> And sinners who are washed therein
> Are cleansed from every stain.[55]

Cowper's fountain is "drawn from Emmanuel's veins," his sinners 'plunged beneath that flood.'' Discern as we may the traditional connotations of the fountain symbol (grace, new life) and admit as we must the dramatic impact of Cowper's phrases, most of us would be too repelled by either the apparent image of the blood-filled bowl or the intended one of blood-letting (acceptable when medicine was still "leech craft"), and by the melodrama of "guilty stains," to sing this hymn so beloved of our forebears. Our inability to imagine the Good Thief rejoicing as the blood spurts from Christ, or think ourselves "as vile as he," our hesitation over "washed all my sins away," doubtless betray want of conviction. We surely do not err in finding Cowper's lines on the "blood-bought free rewards" and "golden harp for me" mawkish and egocentric. Even his final stanza, on the harp "strung and tuned" for eternity and formed by "power Divine"

to sound no other name but "Jesus" may, for all its resonance, induce in the non-
Evangelical a kind of claustrophobia. Cowper sounds more himself when he
avows his devotion in direct statement:

> E'er since by faith I saw the stream
> Thy flowing Wounds supply,
> Redeeming love has been my theme,
> And shall be till I die.
>
> Then in a nobler, sweeter song,
> I'll sing Thy power to save,
> When this poor lisping, stammering tongue
> Lies silent in the grave.

But here he writes more as lyric poet than as Calvinist-evangelical hymnist.

The secular and sacred poet work in perfect harmony in Cowper's "Hark, my
soul, it is the Lord," a dramatic monologue within a framework of commentary,
yet also a well-used Evangelical hymn. The poet as Everyconvert puts himself
in the presence of Christ, who as Good Samaritan "delivered thee when bound,"
who as Good Shepherd "sought thee wandering, set thee right," and who, better
than a mother her child, "will remember thee." Only then does Christ make his
central affirmation "Mine is an unchanging love . . . free and faithful, strong as
death," his promise "Thou shalt see my glory soon" and his demand "Say, poor
sinner, lov'st thou me?" Finally, the poet returns to his limited viewpoint, of one
whose "love is weak and faint," to offer his response and petition: "Yet I love
thee and adore, / O for grace to love thee more!" Even Watts never so triumphantly
succeeded in suiting his diction to the average level of comprehension. In point
of fact, the Anglican Cowper was writing for villagers far poorer and less literate
than the Dissenters in London for whom Watts wrote. The usual tune, "St. Bees,"
matches well the stark, reiterative rhythms of this superb hymn.

Though not in any normal sense a passion hymn, "Hark, my soul" has a place
in this context because it represents both the distinctively eighteenth-century
Protestant response of the lay worshipper to the divine love and what may be
called the Abelardian as distinct from the Anselmian view of the Atonement. In
other words, it represents the Incarnation, life, and death of Christ as an effect
and example of unconditional love. In the liberal theology of the following
century this view, paradoxically expressed here by a strict Calvinist, was to drive
out the ransom theory.

RISEN

The last peak of hymnody on the Risen Christ occurred between the mid-eighteenth and mid-nineteenth centuries, from the dawn of the Wesleyan revival to the Victorian flood of translations. "Finita iam sunt proelia," rendered as "The strife is o'er, the battle done," repeats the well-worn trope of the Victor snapping the chains of hell, with an application in the concluding appeal:

> Lord, by the stripes which wounded thee
> From death's dread sting thy servants free,
> That we may live, and sing to thee
> Alleluia.[56]

Another famous Latin hymn translated in the eighteenth century but originating in the fourteenth, "Christus surrexit hodie" ("Jesus Christ is risen today")[57] blends the vertical cosmos, the old trope of the Fall Reversed ("suffer to redeem our loss"), and the scriptural teaching that Christ came to save sinners. By reason of its surging tune, it remains popular despite its outworn cosmology.

It naturally invites comparison with Wesley's "Christ the Lord is risen today." For several stanzas the eighteenth-century master narrates the Resurrection in the ancient way, inviting the heavens and earth to hail the "Sun" who "sets in blood no more," the "glorious King" who has "burst the gates of hell" and "open'd Paradise." The Augustan abstraction. "Love's redeeming work is done" heralds another variant of Christ the Victor in "Fought the fight, the battle won." Wesley's real difference from any medieval poet lies in his application. The medieval hymnist who wrote the lines

> Soar we now, where Christ hath led
> Following our exalted Head;
> Made like him, like him we rise,
> Ours the cross, the grave, the skies

might well have been put to trial, if not for these, then for "Everlasting life is this: / Thee to know, thy power to prove . . ."[58] The former might have seemed the epitome of Pride (*Superbia*), the latter surely a new fangled heresy of personal experience as essential to salvation.

In view of the influence upon the Wesleys of German hymns, we need not wonder that Gellert appears to echo them in "Jesus lebt" (1757) ("Jesus lives, thy terrors now") by equating purity of heart with living to Jesus alone.[59] The Lutheran philosopher-poet, nevertheless, employs the collective "we" and neither applies the Resurrection psychologically nor argues from religious experience. Salvation remains to be won by faith alone.

In the eighteenth century, hymnists distinguished the Resurrection from the Ascension more sharply than their successors. Perhaps the very improbability of the Ascension, once Newton and Kepler had disposed of the vertical cosmos, challenged hymnists from Wesley to Christopher Wordsworth to write better on that topic than did any of their time on the Resurrection. Apart from the excellence of their settings and editing, what common elements have the Ascension hymns of the Methodist, the Evangelicals Perronet and Kelly, the Catholic Matthew Bridges, and the Anglo-Catholic Christopher Wordsworth?

The first is a response to the scientific challenge that can be inferred from the third stanza of Perronet's "All hail! the power of Jesu's name" (1780): "Crown him, ye morning stars of light / Who fixed this floating ball." Despite the impression of crudeness given by one setting that requires repeated cries of "Crown him!,"[60] this hymn makes a considerable concession to the astronomers. Matthew Bridges, in "Crown him with many crowns" (1851), more successfully blends post-Newtonian cosmology with apocalyptic vision:

> Creator of the rolling spheres,
> Ineffably sublime.
> Glassed in a sea of light,
> Where everlasting waves
> Reflect his throne . . .[61]

As if familiar with Handel's chorus, poets of the Ascension make liberal use of the psalm verse "Lift up your heads, O ye gates" (Ps. 24.7). Handel's direction *Pomposo* explains Wesley's now odd-sounding introduction to his paraphrase:

> There the pompous triumph waits:
> "Lift your heads, eternal gates;
> Wide unfold the radiant scene;
> Take the King of Glory in!"[62]

Wesley's next stanza, beginning "Circled round with angel powers, / Their triumphant Lord, and ours," and a similar one by Perronet, "Let high-born seraphs tune the lyre / And . . . fall / Before his face who tunes their choir," are now generally omitted. Apart from an awkward repetition in the latter, we may attribute this to the modern tendency to downplay the heavenly hierarchy. Yet Wesley's unimaginable image of the Redeemer lifting his hands on high to show "the prints of love" remains in use. He gets away with an amazing mixture of literalism and inwardness, for though Christ be "parted from our sight . . . above yon azure height," the hymnist begs Him grant "our hearts" to "thither rise" following him "beyond the skies . . . on the wings of love" to become "partners of" His "endless reign" and find our "heaven of heavens" in Him.

No other poet treats the Ascension so audaciously. Perronet follows an ancient convention by treating it as the Fall Reversed in fulfilment of a prophecy. The Catholic Bridges (converted in 1848) also views Christ in typological vein as "fruit of the mystic Rose" in Isaiah and the Song of Songs who, His wounds "in beauty glorified," reigns in Paradise restored.

While all three poets view the Risen Christ as ruler of mankind, Wesley gives universalism a mere nod in "Still he calls mankind his own" before imagining "his gracious lips" blessing "His church below"; Perronet ends by exhorting "every tribe and every tongue" to "shout in universal song"; and only the mid-Victorian Bridges hails Christ as "Lord of peace" wielding power "from pole to pole, that wars may cease." Is it fanciful to attribute this to Wesley and Perronet having lived in a time of almost continuous war and Bridges during the Pax Britannica?

Lesser hymns on the Risen Christ, even by poets of Old Dissent, tend towards egoism. Anne Steele's "And did the holy and the just" (1760)[63] is exceptional in being couched in the third person, for the "sovereign of the skies" first sank "that worthless man might rise." Her fellow Baptist Samuel Stennett, in another expression of wonder at the Redeemer's love, conforms more to the current fashion by writing "Majestic sweetness sits enthroned" (1787)[64] entirely in the first person singular: "He makes me triumph over death, / And saves me from the grave." Both lyrics end with a resolve to give the "heart" in response. Samuel Medley's "I know that my Redeemer lives" (1775) begins with the "sweet joy" of this objective truth, but its conclusion is only preserved from bathos by the leitmotif of divine constancy that has resounded all through:

> He lives my mansion to prepare,
> And he will bring me safely there;
> He lives, all glory to his name,
> Jesus, unchangeably the same.[65]

This theme, which underlies also Cowper's "Hark! my soul, it is the Lord" and "God moves in a mysterious way," suggests that during the early and mid-eighteenth century poets were concerned to adapt the Christian Myth to the Newtonian cosmos, but later they became intent upon finding stability and transcendence amid political and economic revolutions. Likewise the finest Ascension hymn in English, Kelly's "The head that once was crowned with thorns," and other early nineteenth-century lyrics seem to embody a conservative reaction to the upheavals of that troubled era.

IMAGES

Medieval adoration of Jesus as source and object of every human longing culminated in the "Jesu dulcis memoria" of Bernard of Morlas; that of Him as incarnating the love of God to mankind in poetry and prose by Abelard, and the hymn "O amor quam ecstaticus" by Thomas à Kempis.[66] After the Reformation, in England, at least, the figure of Jesus was emptied of emotional content. Thus in Milton's *Paradise Regained* or Bunyan's *Pilgrim's Progress*, the sacerdotal and admonitory roles of Christ predominate, virtually to the exclusion of the beloved human Jesus. Bunyan knows him as Emmanuel, or "God with" Christian in his pilgrimage through the wilderness of this world. In the great pilgrimage hymn based on the Exodus, "Guide me, O thou great Jehovah" (1742) the poet transfers that role to the Father. The paternal and authoritarian Jehovah-Christ figure of the Puritans gives way to a Jesus who in eighteenth-century hymns appears mainly as a masculine but sometimes as a feminine love object. This psychoanalytic view fails, however, to account for those images best comprehended in mythic, natural, or social terms: the Light that lights every man, the Sun that knows not his going down, the heavenly King and Friend of the poor and unloved.[67] Nor can it account for the sequence of images in hymn texts between the times of Watts and of Montgomery. Above all, it fails to explain the historical tendency that has been the focus of this chapter, the enrichment of the biblical and theological figures of Christ by one traceable to the Pauline epistles, but verified in the believer's experience by being formed within the heart.

Bunyan's allegory of Christian called to become a pilgrim from the City of Destruction implies a radically pessimistic view of this world. Not coincidentally, it was written after the collapse of the Puritan Commonwealth, as St. Augustine's *City of God* after the sack of Rome. *Pilgrim's Progress* remained for generations a sacred text for Dissenters of the servant class. It was primarily in Dissenting hymns, however, that during the next century and a half Christ came to be represented as capable of transforming this world into His kingdom, to the benefit of the poor and ignorant. At the same time, in Wesleyan and Evangelical hymns, He reigned within and transformed the heart and conscience. To prefer hymns at either end of the scale from world-denying pietism to reforming activism would be critically indefensible, for there are classics in each kind: "How sweet the name of Jesus sounds"; "Christ, whose glory fills the skies," and "Jesus shall reign where'er the sun" or "Hail to the Lord's Anointed." Nor, since Watts and Montgomery wrote the last two lyrics, can we place the images in linear sequence: what happened was the entry of a new element without loss of the old. Indeed, the medieval figure of Christ as Judge appeared as late as 1812 in "Great God! what do I see and hear,"[68] and even, if its symbols of morning sun and Judgment be combined, in the courtroom scene of Dickens's *Great Expectations* (1860).[69] For convenience, the images will be grouped as mythic, psychological, and social.

The nearest modern equivalent to "Jesu dulcis memoria" came from the unlikely pen of John Newton. "How sweet the name of Jesus sounds" does not, despite its title, quite catch the sense of piercing sweetness, of almost painful joy recorded by the medieval poet, by George Herbert, and in our time by C.S. Lewis.[70] Nevertheless, the objective assertions of its opening and subjective application of its conclusion list almost every function and image of Christ. Within eight lines, Newton describes how devotion consoles and heals the "wounded spirit," calms the "troubled breast," and, in traditional terms offers refreshment ("manna") and rest. That his topic is, at this point, devotion is signified by his address to the "dear name" as "shield," "hiding-place," "rock" on which to build, and unfailing "treasury" of grace. Only after a pivotal verse long since omitted does Newton address Jesus himself:

> By thee [the name] my pray'rs acceptance gain,
> Although with sin defiled;
> Satan accuses me in vain,
> And I own'd a child.

The naïve figure in the third line, ambiguous reference in the second (is poet or prayer "defiled"?), and obsolete sense of "own'd" (acknowledged) in the fourth make unsingable the very lines that explain the ensuing joyous outburst:

> Jesus! my Shepherd, Husband, Friend
> My Prophet, Priest and King,
> My Lord, my life, my way, my end,
> Accept the praise I bring.

These encapsulate almost every image of Christ developed between the Reformation and the poet's own time. Even the odd-sounding "husband" might be defended as bringing together the ancient figure of the Bridegroom and the idea of Christ as "husbandman" nurturing the soul. In the concluding stanzas, "when I see thee as thou art / I'll praise thee as I ought" and "may the music of thy name / Refresh my soul in death" make clear, with the echoing finality of an eighteenth-century musical cadence, the whole movement from first hearing the Name through the Redeemer's intercession and nurture to final union at death.

A traditional image missing from Newton's poem fills the whole of the famous morning hymn "Christ, whose glory fills the skies" (1740).[71] Writing quite soon after his own conversion (1738), Wesley sheds light upon the convert's dependence in his second stanza, "Dark and cheerless is the morn." His intention, clearly, is to trace out the old analogy between the rising sun and the "Sun of Righteousness," the Christian soul's "true" and "only light." With the fervour of a recent convert he believes that the "radiancy divine," having dispelled unbelief, sorrow, and the "gloom" of sin, will shine "more and more" within until the "perfect day" of heaven. But before his final petition, "Visit then this soul of mine," he admits his need of continual reassurance:

> Joyless is the day's return,
> Till thy mercy's beams I see;
> Till they inward light impart,
> Glad my eyes and warm my heart.

This compulsive need and concomitant obsession, natural enough in Newton as a guilt-ridden ex-slave trader, or in the redeemed alcoholics or gaolbirds who testified at Salvation Army gatherings, tends in our society to cut the Evangelical off from the rest. The generations that have sung this stirring lyric and tune at school have surely greeted the return of morning and new life, admitting only general dependence upon the source thereof.

The images listed by Newton appear separately in various eighteenth-century lyrics: the King, a little unpleasantly, in "Rejoice, the Lord is King"; the Shepherd, in Cowper's "Jesus, where'er thy people meet" (in Calvinist vein Shepherd "of thy chosen few"); the spiritual healer in Newton's now forgotten "Physician of my sin-sick soul";[72] the Friend or Bridegroom in numberless discarded texts like "He dies! the Friend of sinners dies,"[73] but more importantly in "Jesu, Lover of my soul," to be considered shortly, and the famous "Love divine, all loves excelling."

"Love divine" epitomizes the Wesleyan transference of imagery from the mythic to the psychological field. Its trellis work of scriptural allusions should caution us against any inference of heresy or innovation. The new creation by Christ in the final verse was derived from St. Paul, the final obeisance of casting crowns before him in heaven from the Apocalypse. But Wesley's original ideas form the substance of the first: "Fix in us thy humble dwelling . . . / Visit us with thy salvation, / enter every trembling heart." In these lines he transposes the whole scene of the Nativity into the human heart, while retaining the essence of the Incarnation as the effect of divine compassion, "pure, unbounded love." He thus gives new meaning to the ensuing "new creation," which becomes the nurturing and regeneration touched on "How sweet the name." Yet without the intervening stanza on Christ dwelling in human "temples" (not to mention one omitted from the *Collection* as heretical) "Love divine" can be read on the mythic plane as being about the historical Incarnation leading to the recreation of human-kind.[74]

This is but the most important of Wesley's psychological applications. In some early verses against war he internalizes the Second Coming by asking Christ to plant "the kingdom" of His 'love / In every heart of man,'' so that war being renounced, He may restore "our long-lost paradise." Elsewhere he implicitly defines the "real Christian" as one who inwardly enacts the Gospel scenes: "Touch me and make the Leper clean, / Purge my iniquity . . . / Behold for me the victim bleeds."[75] In no case does he substitute the internalized for the historical visitation, for he seeks to apply, not supersede, traditional beliefs. Not until after

Darwin and Freud did an interior loss of innocence replace the historical Fall, nor self-knowledge replace the knowledge of God as our chief end.

The hypnotic "Jesus, Lover of my soul," so long a theme song of the afflicted, raises important issues for hymnologist and singer alike. It embodies a figure more like a mother than a lover, with a "bosom" upon which the soul "hangs" to shelter from the "storm of life." As always, an apparently obscure clause, "*while* the *nearer* waters *roll*," leads us to the heart of the poem, for it implies further waters undisturbed and beyond time. Where shall the soul find timeless stasis, shelter, sustenance, and all-sufficient love ("all I want")? In heaven, certainly, but "bosom" and "waters" recall an earlier Eden, where the embryo was fed from the "fountain of life."

Elsewhere, Wesley's many allusions to "Eden lost"[76] and his oceanic images — Christ's love as "boundless . . . bottomless sea," "unexhausted abyss," and "ocean of mercy"wherein our "thoughts are drowned"[77] — point to a more than conventional analogy between the first and the "second birth." From these and the repeated figures of taking refuge in the "cleft" of Christ's wounded side, we must conclude that a regressive eroticism supplied much of his creative energy. Long after his conversion, he found his "carnal mind" difficult to subdue, yet married only in his mid-forties and was haunted into his old age by an incessant hunger for "perfect Love."[78] Such a feeling (doubtless occasional) of unfulfilment in wedded love point, like his brother's flirtations and disastrous marriage,[79] to a failure to outgrow attachment to a dominant mother.

But in what way need this concern the singers, who in their singing of "Jesus, Lover of my soul" cling to the final support of the afflicted? They care only that the poem enables them to voice their shared emotion. Subjective eroticism and guilt feelings in so many eighteenth-century hymns concern mainly the social historian. In this Protestant hymn, nevertheless, the maternal deity stands out as exceptional, for with Mary substituted for Jesus it could find a place in any Catholic collection. The bisexual God of the earliest Christian hymnal,[80] divided later into the figures of Jesus and Mary, reappears in the Christ of Wesley, usually to express the poet's own need. In the hymns of Victorian authors steeped in the Scriptures, the feminine image of Christ was to prove a stumbling-block to former Sunday school pupils.

The honour of inaugurating the "social gospel" should probably be divided between Watts and Doddridge, the former mainly for a charity school sermon,[81] the latter for "Hark! the glad sound" and "Jesus, my lord, how rich thy grace." Despite its quaint argument, the second text repays close reading. Unable to repay his debt to Jesus, Doddridge, an even milder Calvinist than Watts, asks what in his "poverty" he can give to the owner of "all the worlds." He answers that Christ has "brethren" and "partners" of grace, namely the poor:

> In them thou may'st be clothed, and fed,

> And visited, and cheered,
> And in their accents of distress
> My Saviour's voice is heard.
>
> Thy face with rev'rence and with love
> I in thy poor would see;
> O let me rather beg his bread
> Than hold it back from thee.[82]

In the light of this paraphrase of 'inasmuch as ye have done this" we must read literally as well as metaphorically the corresponding line in "Hark! the glad sound," on Christ enriching the "humble poor." In stanzas now omitted, the poet prays Christ to wipe away "thickest films of vice," pour "celestial day" on "blind eyeballs," bind broken hearts, and cure the "bleeding soul."[83]

As Doddridge sees in Christ the reformer both of self and society, so did the Radical journalist Montgomery. A single stanza of "Hail to the Lord's Anointed!" (1819) suffices to make the point:

> He comes in succour speedy
> To those who suffer wrong;
> To help the poor and needy,
> And bid the weak be strong;
> To give them songs for sighing,
> Their darkness turn to light,
> Whose souls condemned and dying
> Were precious in his sight.

After a stanza on Christ judging the poor "with justice, mercy, truth," Montgomery presents another scriptural image of Christ, as fertilizer:

> He shall come down like showers
> Upon the fruitful earth,
> And love, joy, hope like flowers
> Spring in his path to birth.[84]

Not surprisingly, this Evangelical champion of slaves based his great hymn on the very psalm (72) Watts had used for "Jesus shall reign where'er the sun."[85]

In that missionary hymn, Watts enriches the mythological with the literal sense
of liberation. Christ frees from sin and Satan but also from "chains" of idolatry rather than poverty or absolutism. Social reforms and education were means to the missioner's end, the spread of the faith. This becomes clear from Watt's

his anticipation that "barbarous nations" will "submit and bow and own their Lord." Nevertheless where Jesus reigns charity abounds, for "all the sons of want are blest." Watts's text as a whole warrants no further social inference, for the following stanza limits the "healing power" of Christ to remission of death and the "curse" of exile.[86]

The pietist image of Christ, as in Cowper's beautiful lyric "Jesus, where'er thy people meet,"[87] predominated during the Evangelical revival. In his amplification of "where two or three are gathered together," this far sterner Calvinist than Watts or Doddridge limits the church's mission to teaching its members to desire and envisage heaven. Let Christ "come quickly down" and "make a thousand hearts his own."

The figure of Christ the King, though predominantly mythic, had in the mid-eighteenth century a social relevance not to be overlooked. "Rejoice, the Lord is King,"[88] in the assured power of its Handelian setting, clearly teaches that "our Jesus" will extend His reign "Till all his foes submit" in a missionary or apocalyptic rather than political sense. If its triumphalism jars upon us, Wesley's celebration of the Risen Christ cannot be extended beyond the confines of the Myth. In the Wesleyan image of Christ the King, however, there is usually an underthought or resonance of Christ as confirming the monarchical order. Methodism, though less dependent upon the Hanoverian dynasty than Old Dissent, enjoyed royal patronage. One of Charles Wesley's rare patriotic hymns orders God to give the King the "necks" of his enemies (probably the Pretenders),[89] and John staunchly supported the royal sovereignty in America. For both Wesleyan and Old Dissenter, the way to spread the Kingdom was by inner and moral transformation, reading of the Word, and philanthropy. The day of the "social gospel" as political activism had scarcely dawned.

12

HOW THE END OF THINGS APPEARED

When rising from the bed of death,
O how shall I appear?
Addison, 1712

Great God! what do I see and hear?
I see the end of things appear.
Collyer, 1812

Appearances notwithstanding, in the century between these verses there began a shift of focus from the collective Judgment at the end of time to the individual, or "particular," Judgment in the moment of death. Once the millennial resurgence of Collyer's time had died away, more and more texts implied an instant passage of the soul to the 'heavenly home'' formerly reserved for saints and martyrs.[1] Catholic theologians endorsed the teaching of Aquinas that in the moment of death an irreversible particular judgment consigns the soul to Heaven, Purgatory, or Hell, while the body sleeps until reunited with the soul at the general Last Judgment, when all deeds become known. Luther envisaged death as his "slumber,"[2] but by the late seventeenth century the Gallican De Santeuil could use sleep and trumpet blast as metaphors when calling the slothful to spread the faith.[3] In eighteenth-century hymns, images of the general and particular judgments, and even of judgment within the souls of the living, continue side by side.

Watts and Doddridge, as good Calvinists, reserve the judgment for the end of time. Like any Renaissance poet, Watts dwells upon decaying corpses but, with a paradoxical twist to an old motif, insists that "worms" will "refine" these "vile bodies" till the Redeemer bid them "rise and shine" (a scriptural injunction now used to awaken soldiers).[4] In his equally impressive "And will the Judge descend?" Doddridge imagines the dead arising under "all discerning eyes" to hear a "dread sentence" that will spread "black despair" through that "guilty throng."[5] He thus recalls or perhaps alludes to the Bloody Assize or those eighteenth-century courts where felons were despatched to the gallows en masse.

The earlier poet is the less consistent, for his stanza on the "busy tribes of flesh and blood" in "Our God, our help in ages past" implies permanent oblivion for the ungodly, verging on the mortalist heresy, while in his long popular "Why do we mourn departing friends?" (1707)[6] he predicts quaintly that though their souls already rest in the "arms" of Jesus, their "flesh" shall "fly" thither at the "great rising-day." Watt's co-laureate, Charles Wesley, appears even less consistent, if we compare his famous tableau of the Second Coming, "Lo! He comes, with clouds descending" (1758) with two successive meditations on death in his collection for children.[7] In "And am I born to die?" the narrator's "trembling spirit" flies into unknown regions where "all things are forgot," yet as soon as it leaves earth "Eternal happiness or woe" must be its portion. Nevertheless the narrator, wakened by the Last Trump, will rise to behold the Judge and "flaming skies." As anxiously as Addison, Wesley broods on whether angels or devils will bear him away before he proclaims Christ as the Way to "shun the dreadful wrath severe." His Miltonic construction of noun flanked with adjectives oddly suits his Janus-eyed stance with respect to ancient and modern images of the Judgment. In his sequel, "And am I only born to die?" he defines the Christian way during the "kind reprieve" of this life: "My sole concern, my single care, / To watch, and tremble, and prepare / Against the fatal day!" With the Judge even now "at the door," and "all mankind" fated to stand before the "inexorable throne," nothing deserves a thought but how to escape the "death / That never, never dies" and secure a "mansion in the skies." The concluding prayer for Christ to "write the pardon" on his heart that he may "depart in peace" implies an assurance incompatible with either the particular or general Judgment as hitherto conceived.

Similarly, the wailing of the lost upon beholding the "true Messiah," in "Lo, he comes" implies that those who acknowledged Christ in this life sleep assured of being awakened to bliss. Nevertheless, in "Come, let us join our friends above,"[8] Wesley presents believers and saints above as "one communion," with the former constantly passing over to join the latter.

For all his strong convictions, Newton oscillates between two views of death. Within his small groups of "Funeral Hymns" (*Olney Hymns* II, 72-79), one headed "Day of Judgment" (No. 77) announces the swift approach of the Judge "our nature wearing" to summon the dead who "rise from earth and sea," though the first (72) has proclaimed the instant passage: "We scarce can say, They're gone / Before the willing spirit takes / Her Mansion near the throne." Conversely, in "Alarm" (III, 2) the sinner hears his "awful doom" in the moment of death, as his sins crowd round to cry out for vengeance. As in late medieval and Renaissance iconography, the dying man's life unfolds, but in the "blood-crimson" hue imparted by the doctrine of Total Depravity. The collective resurrection at the Last Day belongs to the older culture, the instant and therefore solitary passage to the modern culture and its individual consciousness.

In accordance with the Ariès principle that cultures unload obsolescent artefacts upon their young,[9] the Wesleys assigned hymns on judgment and hell to children and Addison's fearsome evocation appeared in a Methodist collection for Sunday schools in 1816.[10] No doctrinal difference can be discerned between Addison's anxiety lest he be dragged by devils to the left or borne by angels to the right and Collyer's more objective vision of the righteous "surrounding" God, before whom fearful sinners stand "unprepared." At least in native English texts, the transition from Long Sleep to Instant Passage had, however, occurred by the mid-nineteenth century, which saw the publication of hymns used at funerals.

A vestige of the old belief remains in the enigmatic second stanza of Sarah Adams's "Nearer, my God, to thee" (1841), used but not designed for funerals:

> Though like the wanderer,
> The sun gone down,
> Darkness be over me,
> My rest a stone . . .[11]

The author, previously "nearer" in her dreams, finally imagines herself "cleaving the skies" on "joyous wing," having "forgot" sun, moon, and stars, as if spiritualized like Shelley's Skylark.

Again, Bonar's "A few more years shall roll" (1844) begins in the old way, with the dead "asleep within the tomb" and the author beseeching Christ to prepare him for 'that great day.'' Thereafter the time gap closes verse by verse. After a few more sunsets, we shall be where "suns are not" and where "tempests cease"; after "a few more toils" and tears "we shall weep no more," after a few more Sabbaths reach the "endless rest" of the final Sabbath, but finally, in "a little while," Christ shall come again.[12] The inconsistency between middle and end appears to reflect a disparity between a notional old and a real new belief. Sculptors and painters represented the soul as instantaneously passing on a clear century before sacred poets, who doubtless felt more bound to conform to the words of Scripture and the Creeds.[13] Though surviving in translations stemming from the Oxford Movement, in native English lyrics the old belief had become confined to hymnals for millenarian sects like the Primitive Methodists that spread among the poor in the hard times after 1815.[14]

Several hymns published between 1867 and 1881 assert or imply some form of instant passage. "Now the labourer's task is o'er," declares Ellerton in 1871; "now the battle-day is past" and "now" the voyager lands on the "further shore" where his "work of life" will be tried by a "juster Judge" than here.[15]

Unconsciously, no doubt, Neale projected the mid-Victorian idea of death as safe conduct to instant bliss into his translation "Safe home, safe home in port!"[16] At any rate, he represents the Byzantine poet Joseph as anticipating a collective arrival, lambs safely penned and exiles home with, apparently, no intervening sleep or final judgment.

Although the oft-reprinted "Ten thousand times ten thousand" of Dean Henry Alford echoes the Revelation in its "ransom'd saints" singing hallelujahs to "a thousand harps," it likewise allows for no intervening sleep. "Sever'd friendships" are taken up, orphans no longer "fatherless," and its final call for the Second Coming reads as if Christ will release the living.[17]

An American and an English lyric much in use before the First World War represent an idea of death that has rarely attracted poets of distinction. Fanny Crosby's "Safe in the arms of Jesus" (1868) has slightly the more to recommend it. The blind gospel hymnist, imagining herself on the "gentle breast" of Christ, endures patiently the "night" of his life till morning break on the "golden shore."[18] No critical reader can miss the eroticism of "Safe in the arms . . . by his love o'ershadow'd," or the life-denying passivity enjoined primarily by women in this and other consolation hymns of New (and old) England.

"Safely, safely gathered in" (1886), sinks to a yet lower level, for in her pitiful effusion Mrs. Henrietta Dobree congratulates a dead child on being free from sorrow and temptation, and egregriously hails as the child's "truest gain" that God has "saved from weary strife" this "fresh young life" that awaits us above, "Resting in the Saviour's love."[19]

In Alford's still popular "Come, ye thankful people come" (1844, rev. 1861) the harvest metaphor represents perhaps the final appearance of the Last Judgment in English hymnody.[20] If not every singer enjoys thinking of the "tares" cast "in the fire," Alford at least regards the saved as "free from sorrow, free from sin" without denying the value of life. In no English hymn still in common use is hell any more explicitly described. Watts and Newton, however, mingle the imagery of Revelation and *Paradise Lost*, Watts in the "darkness, fire and chains" of his children's hymn contrasting heaven and hell,[21] Newton in his pictures of Satan in the "burning lake" and vast dungeon. But the latter inspires more conviction in recording the sinner's prospect of "everlasting woe."[22] On hell itself, his doggerel provokes laughter where Milton's epic inspired awe. What "rage and despair," he avers,

> Fill Satan's dark dwelling,
> The prison beneath;
> What weeping and yelling,
> And gnashing of teeth.[23]

Cowper carries less than his usual conviction when berating the multitudes that sink with despairing groans from "pleasure into endless woe."[24] Outside the Gothic novel, it is difficult to think of convincing literary accounts of hell between *Paradise Lost* and the very different image in C.L. Lewis's *The Great Divorce*.[25] For all the apocalyptic imagery in ephemeral Baptist or Primitive Methodist effusions, poets have, on the whole, left hell to the preacher and the children's hymnist.[26]

Heaven and its expectation proved more stimulating. The two need to be distinguished, for both in England and North America the paradigms of the heaven-bound life came from the Exodus and *Pilgrim's Progress*. These mythological and literary origins go far to explain the artistic superiority of the negro spiritual to the manufactured "gospel song"[27] and of "Guide me, O thou great Jehovah" to its many rivals. In this classic of early Evangelicalism, the poet traces out his future course in typological detail through the barren land of this life, across the "Jordan" and to "Canaan." Since its heart-stirring tune "Cwm Rhondda" dates only from 1905, memories of Welsh choirs cannot account for its appeal ever since 1771. The secret lies in the detail that enables the poet to accommodate old mythology with new inwardness. Every biblical image corresponds to a personal experience: manna to the Eucharist; crystal fountain to healing grace; pillar of cloud to the Gospel that leads the convert forward; Jordan to death and Canaan to heaven. Above all, the controlling metaphor of life as a pilgrimage through the desert epitomized the experiences of miners and mill hands. The substitution of "Redeemer" for "Jehovah" (in high Anglican hymnals) would have spoiled the effect, for it was the Father who led them as the Israelites through the wilderness of the industrial world.[28] The heartening tramp of "Cwm Rhondda" perfectly matches this quintessential folksong of those who could not choose their path in life.

By comparison, Charles Wesley's "How happy is the pilgrim's lot"[29] somewhat artificially adapts the pilgrim motif to the lot of the "real Christian" who sets his heart on things above. In very truth John and his preachers had "lighten'd" themselves of their possessions to pursue "things eternal," owned "no foot of land" or "cottage" in this "wilderness" and thus lived as wayfarers, but the poem remains important as illustrating how the Wesleys employed a medieval and puritan archetype. In no way does it prove the Marxist case by proffering illusory benefits to the involuntarily poor.

As regards heaven itself, hymns since the time of Watts manifest an accelerating decline in poetic quality *pari passu* with increasing secularization, reflexiveness, and, needless to say, wish-fulfilment. No adult and committed Christian can be mistaken for the personae of all too many hymns on heaven that were imposed upon children who eventually threw out their faith with their school-books.

To begin with "Jerusalem, my happy home," the original twenty-six quatrains ascribed to a priest condemned about 1593 explore every image of heaven save, understandably, those of palace and court.[30] "F.B.P." imagines a "happy harbour" of saints, a city with gates of pearl and golden streets, a paradise of "vineyards and orchards" and, chiefly, the Church Triumphant wherein "our Lady sings Magnificat," SS. Ambrose and Augustine the "Te Deum." For the most part, however, his poem consists of negations. Saints know not sorrow, toil, sickness, or the fear of death. Jerusalem knows no mist of terror or darkness of confinement, for "God himself gives light." The poet views heaven and the life he knows as mutually exclusive: there flourish not "lust," "lucre," or "envy," neither "hunger, heat no cold"; here in our "banishment," every "sweet is mixed with bitter gall," each "pleasure is but pain."

Seventeenth-century poets not subscribing to the millenarian view of the Commonwealth continued to locate "Jerusalem" entirely within the next life.[31] In the early eighteenth century, Watts depicted heaven partly in real, partly in mythological terms. In "A Prospect of Heaven makes Death easy," the "land of pure delight" combines the paradisal exclusion of death, night, pain, winter, and decay with the "Sweet fields beyond the swelling floor" visible both to the Iraelites across the Jordan and to the poet across Southampton Water. Unlike the life we know, the paradisal state knows no contraries. As in "Jerusalem, my happy home" and "Guide me, O thou great Jehovah," this life and our impending death correspond to the Exodus and the Jordan.[32]

By the end of the century, Blake aspires to recreate Jerusalem entirely within "England's green and pleasant land," cleaning up the "dark satanic mills" not only of armament works in London but of scientific rationalism and sexual puritanism.[33] By treating the "mills" literally instead of symbolically, singers of Parry's setting have, in effect, turned Blake's lyric into a hymn of the social gospel. The social activism of "And did those feet in ancient time," so interpreted, would surely have been dismissed by Bernard or even Abelard as heresy and delusion.

As late as the Second World War, servicemen were singing the late Victorian sacred song "The Holy City" in their communal bathrooms.[34] Unlike St. John the Divine, its author dreams not of the accoutrements of the City, nor of the Lamb and Whore of Babylon, but of the heavenly vision itself. Whatever his intent, so far had the Apocalypse faded from the common awareness that the servicemen were singing a daydream. Their singing of this among the erotic daydreams of popular songs may, like that of "Abide with me" in the Cup Final ritual, represent a fumbling after lost transcendence.

The text of "Abide with me" reveals another intrusion of subjective and secular material. This prayer of a dying priest is in one sense more Christian than Watts's "A Prospect of Heaven" since Lyte draws upon not the Exodus but the Walk to Emmaus. Some inferior stanzas now omitted extend the New Testament allusion by calling upon Christ to remain with the poet as with the disciples.

> Come not in terrors, as the King of kings;
> But kind and good, with healing in thy wings,
> Tears for all woes, a heart for every plea,
> Come, Friend of sinners, and abide with me.

Forgivably, Lyte recalls how Christ "smiled" on his "early youth" and, despite rebellion and wandering, has "not left me, oft as I left Thee." This leads into the familiar conclusion ("I need Thy presence . . ."), which is closer to the

Neoplatonism of Shelley's *Adonais* than the orthodox doctrines concerning Death, Judgment, and Heaven: "Speak through the gloom, and point me to the skies: / Heaven's morning breaks, and earth's vain shadows flee."[35] The *Weltschmerz* of "Jerusalem, my happy home" applied specifically to the Deadly Sins and the afflictions of martyrdom. That of "Abide with me" applied to the human condition, especially of the dying poet, and appealed to a mixture in the Victorians of faith, sentimentalism, and an Evangelical death wish.

Except for the omitted verse of "Abide with me," none of these lyrics illustrates poetic decline, for even "The Holy City" compares favourably with most Victorian love ballads. Of seventy-five texts on heaven taken from hymnals between the early eighteenth and mid-twentieth centuries, the one-third based on scriptural teaching show nothing like so consistent a decline as the remainder that embody a wish for death, escape, or consolation, or that treat heaven as "home" or abode of children.[36]

Some scriptural hymns of a transcendent and objective character fall into this chronological order: "Ye holy angels bright" (1672, rewritten 1838); "How bright those glorious spirits shine" (1707); "The Son of God goes forth to war" (pub. 1827); "Palms of glory, raiment bright" (1829); "Bright the vision that delighted" (1837).[37] Though by no means the most inspired poems of Montgomery and Heber, "Palms of glory" and "The Son of God" lapsed into disuse more by reason of a mawkish tune and a reaction against battle imagery than their poetic shortcomings. To these, images from Revelation and Acts impart substance and structure. Similarly, because Isaiah (6.1-3) gives a solid core to "Bright the vision," Bishop Mant, though no Isaac Watts, is far from disgraced. The decline sets in when lesser poets than Blake leave their Bibles behind.

To speak of Wesley in this connection savours of blasphemy. "Come, let us join our friends above" (1759), in its original form, represents a half-way stage between the total transcendence of the medieval heaven and the anthropomorphism of that envisaged by many post-Romantic hymnists. While largely devoted to the familiar typology of the Exodus, it departs from the Scriptures in its assurance: "Come let us join our friends above / That have obtained the prize;" in its domestic image "One family we dwell in him"; above all, in its long-suppressed conclusion on meeting above "our old companions in distress":

> And we are to the margin come,
> And we expect to die:
> His militant embodied host,
> With wishful looks we stand,
> And long to see that happy coast,
> And reach the heavenly land.

there to meet "Our old companions in distress."[38] The Victorian editor whose version ("Let saints on earth . . .") we now sing made the text more objective, less over confident yet also less consolatory. Numbers of Wesleyan hymns conclude in a generalized expectation such as "closely walk with Thee to heaven."[39]

Another kind of wish-fulfilment is apt to stick in the throat in the case of J.M. Neale's beautiful refashioning of "Jerusalem luminosa" by Thomas à Kempis. "Light's abode, celestial Salem" combines the ancient motifs of the heavenly palace and Christ the undying Sun with the Pauline injunction to bear the burdens of this life for the sake of joy to come. The lines now most obtrusive in their wish-fulfilment:

> O how glorious and resplendent,
> Fragile body, shalt thou be,
> When endued with so much beauty,
> Full of health, and strong, and free,

faithfully render, however, the Latin poet's restatement of the "resurrection of the body" as set forth by St. Paul.[40] The ruling image of celestial light fits perfectly both the rebirth conveyed in a twentieth-century lyric as a "leap" and "explosion into light"[41] and these "out-of-body" experiences reported by victims of heart attacks.[42] In both original and translated passages, Neale voices a wish not for death but for eternal life.

Faber's "Hark! hark, my soul! Angelic songs are swelling" (1854) expresses a cluster of wishes.[43] In contrast to its cheerful opening, on songs swelling over "green fields" and "wave-beat" shores, its refrain has the angels sing to "pilgrims" in the "night" of this life, wherein "weary souls" trudge "home." At death, the daylight implicit in the opening must "dawn" as the heart enters heaven, its "true home." This text fulfils every wish save that for coherence.

Though free of this enervated muddle, the once popular American gospel hymn, "Shall we gather at the river" (1870) reiterates ad nauseam the River Jordan image of death, envisaged as perpetual holiday:

> On the margin of the river
> Washing up its silver spray,
> We will walk and worship ever,
> All the happy golden day.
>
> Ere we reach the shining river,
> Lay we every burden down;
> Grace our spirits will deliver,
> And provide a robe and crown.[44]

Doubtless because grace would deliver its singers not just from work but from their humdrum surroundings, this feeble lyric became a folk-song of the Moody and Sankey revival.

Many forgotten lyrics expressed longings for death and rebirth. It was, however, in escapist and consolatory hymns that the myth of the Last Things most fully transformed itself into the likeness of the time. Just when escapism reached its peak may be judged from the following sequence. In 1760, heaven is "Far from these narrow scenes of night."[45] In 1803, "For weary [Baptist] saints, a rest remains."[46] In 1819, Montgomery exclaimed, 'O where shall rest [i.e., stability] be found?''[47] In 1843, a now unknown Scots hymnist named Young dreamed of "a happy land / Far, far away;"[48] in 1845 S. Lyth affirmed that "There is a better world, they say."[49] Adding to these one of the same year on "A home in heaven, what a joyful thought," to the "poor man" who after toiling in his "weary lot" is driven from his "home on earth,"[50] we observe world-weariness apparently deepest during the disturbances of the Hungry Forties.

The last, however, turns out to have been written in the United States, where "home" had quite different connotations. In a text apparently composed there in 1843, the hymnist dreams of reunion with loved ones in "a land mine eye hath seen."[51] In her essay on "consolation literature" in New England, Ann Douglas finds the overriding theme of liberal clergy and women writers to be the social consolation of reunion with loved ones. Hymns by Fanny Crosby or Lydia Sigourney, like contemporary novels and prayer manuals, visualized heaven as an extension of domestic bliss.[52] A nation of migrants might naturally envisage paradise as a permanent family home.

In England, though a few lyrics like "There is a bright and happy home" (1885)[53] specify a dwelling free of domestic strife, the majority treat the "Heavenly Home" in some broader sense, as a final relief from alienation. While Christian moralists have always accounted involuntary poverty among the evils of a fallen world, they have not, like Marx, traced our sense of exile to the alienation of the exploited. In its graceless way, this much reprinted lyric from early in the century conveys the essence of both Catholic and Puritan teaching

> I'm but a stranger here, —
> Heaven is my home;
> Earth is a desert drear, —
> Heaven is my home:
> Danger and sorrow stands
> Round me on every hand,
> Heaven is my fatherland,
> Heaven is my home.[54]

The alienation of its short-lived author, like that of the consumptive Lyte, is traceable to ill health; that of Kelly, in "We've no abiding city here"[55] to official

disapproval of his evangelical extremism; that of the martyr "F.B.P." to persecution; that of the monk Joseph of the Studios to renunciation of family and goods.
Even allowing for the frequency of escapist lyrics in hard times, it is impossible
to trace all forms of alienation to a single cause.

Nor can images rooted in antiquity be traced to our current preoccupations.
Susan Tamke has stigmatized as "commercial" the apocalyptic motifs of pearly
gates and golden streets that Victorian hymns share with earlier lyrics.[56] Since
most Victorian hymnists believed Revelation as inerrant as the Gospels, this
judgment cannot stand. For "commercial" imagery we must look to non-biblical
metaphors of law and commerce in hymns by Watts and Wesley.[57] The poor and
deprived could find their overcompensations more easily in hymns on Providence
("Poor and needy though I be / I have a rich, almighty Friend")[58] than in those
on heaven.

By the late Victorian era, the common hymns on heaven came from three
sources: ancient and medieval texts in translation; idealized projections of family
life notably in American gospels and spirituals; and adaptations for children of
the apocalyptic imagery. In addition to translations, surviving older hymns like
a condensed version of "Jerusalem, my happy home" embodied the traditional
imagery, as with variations did "For all the saints" (1863).[59] In the latter, which
lives on more by its splendid tune than its words, two modern subthemes are
discernible: the natural day "blown up" (as photographers say) to include the
whole of time, to enable saints to march in as "golden evening brightens in the
west"; and a triumphal march of "warriors." The subject is this triumphal entry
rather than heaven itself. Despite the archaisms, "countless host" ("a multitude
whom no man could number") suggests a modern army. In consequence, Bishop
How's hymn has proved adaptable to national occasions he could not have
foreseen.

Such domestic idylls as "I have a dear and happy home"[60] were limited to
elementary school hymnals, but in the seventies a number of imports from North
America represented heaven as the exile's "homeland." In a relatively prosperous
era, it was doubtless their memorable tunes that spread beyond the Salvation
Army citadel or dockside settlement, "Swing low, sweet chariot" and "We're
going home tomorrow,"[61] those folk-songs of slaves and migrants. As will be
shown in the ensuing volume, it was to children of industrial cities that compilers
sold heaven as consolation for the drudgery that lay before them. They consoled
adults chiefly for sickness, bereavement or, if female, for enforced passivity.

The consecration of childhood was the cardinal heresy of the Victorian age
as the cult of adolescence has been that of ours. It was inextricably bound up
with the cult of domestic life. After Wordsworth had idealized childhood and the
cottage, Dickens and Hans Christian Andersen sanctified the deprived child and
the lower class family. No doubt, like the collectors of tales and folk-songs, they
expressed a common nostalgia for the pre-industrial past. From *As You Like It*

and Cowper's *The Task* we see that life in the past has always appeared simpler and purer. Nor did all children's hymns on heaven come from the Victorians. John Cennick's "Children of the heavenly King," one of the most persistent, originated in 1742; Jane Taylor's many children's hymns that mention heaven in 1804; and even the ubiquitous "Around the throne of God in heaven / Thousands of children stand," as early as the 1830's;[62] Cennick, however, adhered to his scriptural texts by inviting singers of all ages to travel home as "children" of God. Even as "little flock," they remain within the terms of Christ's address to the Apostles. It was his Victorian revisers who appropriated the "kingdom" and "seat" to children, for whom to this day his hymn is assigned.

The first of three Victorian hymns found in almost every children's collection came from the pen of Jemima Luke, a rector's daughter from Somerset who, after composing "I think when I read that sweet story of old" (1841), married a Congregational minister, thereby becoming a spiritual descendant of Watts.[63] A paraphrase of "Suffer little children to come unto me," this Sunday school lyric remains of significance by virtue of its unintentional treatment of the Gospel as a folk tale and Heaven as the preserve of children. The child who seeks Jesus will find him in a "beautiful place" prepared "For all that are washed and forgiven. / And many dear children are gathering there, / For of such is the kingdom of heaven." The hymnist imputes to the child a longing for all that "never heard of the heavenly home" to find it where "dear little children of every clime" flock to the arms of Jesus.

To a lesser extent the second example, Anne Shepherd's "Around the throne of God in heaven," Victorian by virtue of having entered the hymn-book around 1850 via a missioner's translation, conveys a like impression of heaven as the abode of children. The thousands dressed in "flowing robes of spotless white," being "bathed in that pure, redeeming flood" of the Saviour's blood, distinctly remind us of children bathed and ready for bed ("Behold them white and clean"). This hymn turns up in so many collections, including one for council schools in 1905, [64] that its influence must also have spread far and wide.

A still current example, Plymouth Brother Albert Midlane's "There's a Friend for little children"[65] assures each "little pilgrim" the heaven is a "rest" and "home" for "little children," who by 1859 (the year of the *Origin of Species*) seem to have appropriated from adults the crowns, alleluias, harps, robes, and palms of the Apocalypse. The three-decker universe of the refrain, "Above the bright blue sky," lingered on in Sunday school hymns long after adults had come to ignore it as a dead metaphor. Some responsibility for the widespread disbelief in the afterlife during this century rests with Victorian hymn-writers for failing to provide metaphors children would not outgrow. A mere allusion to "pearly gates" or "harps" has often disposed of the whole notion of heaven. Ironically, such phrases came from Sunday school hymns not sung within living memory.[66] Outside church and seminary, few adults can have heard the Last Things discussed at an adult level.

Modern Hymns: The Mutations of God

13

THE MUTATIONS OF GOD: THE FATHER

Man makes God in his own image
Ludwig Feuerbach

in the Father's loved abode
Our souls arrive in peace
Doddridge [1]

Luther and Calvin recharged the Christian faith from that of the Primitive Church and its worship from the Psalms, as the Franciscans had drawn new energy from the Gospels. Since Calvin, in particular, had based his liturgy upon the vernacular psalter, his followers directed their devotional energies to God as Creator and Father, conceiving of the Son in somewhat legalistic terms. As English Calvinism began its long decline, Watts produced the first successful English hymn-book from Psalms reinterpreted in a Christian sense. Not surprisingly, as attention reverted to the Son, the use of Watts's finest hymns on the Father's power and majesty slowly declined, while that of "When I survey the wondrous Cross" never ceased to grow.

A further cause of change lay in the need to adapt Christian folk-song to the new model of the cosmos. The immense but predictable Newtonian cosmos could inspire hymnists as the more radically reoriented worlds of industrialism and of Darwinism could not. A good illustration is the double reference, in "Praise the Lord! ye Heavens adore Him," of "laws which never shall be broken" to the Commandments and the laws of motion.

Watts and Doddridge had needed to modify independent worship after the failure of the Commonwealth and accustom their community to dependence upon the Hanoverian succession. The strain of monarchical imagery in hymns by Watts and the Wesleys was undoubtedly inspired by this and the Jacobite uprisings.[2] The immediate occasion of "Our God, our help in ages past," it has been suggested, was the dynastic change that removed a threat to the Dissenters.

To the enclosures of common lands and the Industrial Revolution, the harshest uprooting since the Norman invasion, the church and its hymnody have never truly adjusted. That uprooting, so pathetically described in Goldsmith's *The Deserted Village*, must have given Wesley's lines on possessing "no foot of land" or "cottage in the wilderness" a deeper meaning for former peasants than for the poet, as no doubt it did "pilgrim through this barren land" in "Guide me, O thou great Jehovah." In the immensity of the Newtonian cosmos, sacred poets found new evidence of the divine majesty; in the industrial landscape they found none. Their helplessness can be gauged from the irrelevance of even the best English hymn on work, "Forth in thy name, O Lord, I go": how dared Wesley call the twelve-hour shift of a miner or mill hand an "easy yoke"?

Watts did more than found the English hymn. He began its relatively swift transition from unflinching eschatology to sentimental education. This denotes a historical shift of "real assent" from a transcendent deity to one immanent in nature and society. As that shift accelerated, his hymns that evoked a fiercely patriarchal God dropped out of use, while others took on new meanings. Their characteristic pattern of statement, amplification, and response[3] to the divine initiative enabled many to survive the decay of Calvinism by compelling singers to attend to a whole text, not merely its opening. His influence can be judged from the subtitle, "Supplement to the Hymns of Dr. Watts," appended even to Victorian hymnals.[4]

The demise of that archetypal despot of the Old Testament ridiculed by Blake as "Nobodaddy" was accompanied by changes in the notions of Providence and Nature. The Old Dissenters (Baptist, Independent, Presbyterian) who believed themselves most dependent on Providence endorsed the most absolute form of predestination. Consequently, their hymns extolled the divine power and lamented human helplessness. Examples by Watts abound, but as if by design the Baptist collection of Ash and Evans (1769) has no fewer than sixteen successive first lines referring to God as "great."[5] A few of its earlier titles convey this sense of divine transcendence and human helplessness:

> Before Jehovah's awful throne (26)
> Begin the high celestial strain (54)
> Begin, ye Saints, some heavenly theme (82)
> Behold how Sinners disagree (220)
> Behold the lofty Sky (77)
> Behold the Wretch whose Lust and Wine (217)
> Behold what wonderous (*sic*) Grace (170)
> Benign Creator, bounteous Lord (36)

Even this collection makes concessions to the Christocentric teaching of the Wesleys in, for example, "Christ the Lord is risen today" (104).

A few years later George Burder, future editor of Watts, issued as a "Supplement" a *Collection . . . by Various Authors* (1784), revealing a marked change of atmosphere. Directed against the Unitarians, this includes praise of Watts's "incomparable works" for their "evangelical truth" and "experimental religion."[6]

The Independents — Watts, Doddridge, or Burder himself — would designate hymns to accompany sermons. In one for funerals, Doddridge bids the bereaved "kiss the rod of Jehovah," man being "beset with snares . . . in life's uncertain path." To be fair, in another he urges Providence to heal the "bleeding hearts" of bereaved children and supply guardians to care for them.

But from the greatest providence-hymn in English, Cowper's "God moves in a mysterious way," the attentive reader can infer a prophecy. From several metaphors emerges a composite image of an obscured sun: the storm, the dread clouds that will break with blessings, the frowning providence hiding the smiling face, and the divine intent to make plain work that "blind" unbelief scans in vain. God as the beclouded sun, to emerge only in His own good time, fits not only the poet's recovery from depression but that sense of God's withdrawal from the world attested in the following century by authors from Nietzsche to the Catholic Hopkins.[7]

Of course we cannot read one of the "great literary classics"[8] of the Calvinist or any other tradition as denying the providence its author set out to affirm. The metaphors but amplify objective assertion by scriptural allusion. "He plants his footsteps in the sea, / And rides upon the storm" illustrates the mysterious operation of divine power directly from Christ walking on water and indirectly from the psalm verse "Thy way is in the sea, and thy path is in the great water, and thy footsteps are not known" (Ps. 77.19). More subtly, Cowper illustrates the providence in Nature from images of the four elements: the Creator's inscrutable workmanship from "unfathomable mines" not of colliers but, to judge from "treasures up his bright designs," of smiths or gnomes; His mercy from the clouds pregnant ("big") therewith; and, by implication, from the sun (the source of fire). He follows these elemental metaphors with an analogy between the expected blessings and a sweet flower opening from a bitter bud that also harks back to classical and Judaeo-Christian parallels between the natural and the divine. Being no less compatible with the modern tendency to discern God in Nature, these images show once more how flexibility is the essence of a great hymn.

Its series of paradoxes, no less than its steadfast tune, has endeared to generations of worshippers this supreme expression of the age-old view of fate as providence. Between the reverent agnosticism of "God is his own interpreter / And he will make it plain" and that of Tennyson's "There lives more faith in honest doubt . . . than in half the creeds," the tide of certitude had ebbed considerably.[9] To ask for more assurance than Cowper supplies is to expect more than poets, as distinct from mystics, can give. That this has been among the four or five most printed hymns indicates how it has enabled English-speaking Christians to express their conviction that not faith but unbelief is "blind," even if they can no longer trace every happening to a special providence.[10]

We should be cautious about dating the demise of predestination. Two hymns by Joseph Irons published in 1816 remained in use throughout the nineteenth century: "I sing the gracious, fix'd decree . . . The Lord's predestinating love" (148) and "How safe are all the chosen race / Preserv'd in Christ their head" (175).[11] "Light in Darkness" — the heading of "God moves in a mysterious way" — forms the central symbol of two hymns known to all Victorian church-goers and schoolchildren: "Bright the vision that delighted" and "Lead, kindly Light" (1833). The former and more explicitly scriptural falls into three parts: an account of Isaiah's vision of angels in the Temple, a verse linking their songs with those sung at Bethlehem, and a claim that the Church still repeats them. The Object of this noble encomium on the timelessness of the divine vision remains in obscurity and rightly so. From the text of "Lead, kindly Light," it would be difficult to infer either its title, "The Pillar of the Cloud," or its Object, for not only Israelites but desert scenes are missing, "moor and fen . . . crag and torrent" being features of an English wilderness especially familiar to readers of Milton and Wordsworth.[12] To most readers, moreover, "Light" would suggest the Holy Spirit rather than the Father.

From the contemporaneity of this exquisite lyric, never intended as a hymn and now rarely sung, with "O worship the King" and "Holy, holy, holy! Lord God Almighty," certain inferences can be made. Newman and Grant in some degree accommodate Judaeo-Christian myth to the current awareness of Nature. Grant, whose adaptation of Psalm 104 was noted earlier, is content to summarize the Psalmist's protracted and magnificent description of the created world. Two passages where he goes beyond it would out of context appear to portray within (rather than beyond) Creation the God "whose robe is the light, whose canopy space." This and the stanza on the "bountiful care" that "breathes in the air . . . shines in the light . . . streams from the hills" and "distils" in dew and rain could have come from the young Wordsworth's notebook.[13]

Heber's paean to the Trinity, as befits its liturgical purpose, remains within the framework of Revelation, and "All thy works shall praise thy name . . ." could have come from any early Christian poet between St. John the Divine and Prudentius. What is significant here is the undivided Trinity, surprisingly rare since the Reformation. Nowhere does the poet hint at the Lamb, the Ancient of Days, or the fire of the Spirit. Even more than in "Lead, Kindly Light," and certainly more than in Revelation, they are fused into one. Heber so obviously paraphrases Scripture that only the least instructed could read into "man / Thy glory may not see" an allusion to the sun. Indeed, he paraphrases too literally, for the "Casting down" of "golden crowns around the glassy sea"[14] can neither be imagined nor explained, while "though the darkness hide thee" can only be reconciled with "early in the morning" if God's invisibility results, as in Cowper's hymn, not from the divine nature but from our blindness. The darkness of fallen man obscures God and renders the celestial hierarchies visible only to the eye of faith, that is to imagination. The God who "wert and art and evermore shalt be" is the Alpha and Omega of Revelation, of "Corde natus ex Parentis," and of the age-old "Gloria patri" repeated after every psalm and canticle. "All Thy works shall praise Thy name," however, leaves an unintended opening to the nineteenth-century doctrine of emergent evolution. Though verbally and musically among the most powerful and inspiring productions of old-world Christianity, "Holy, holy, holy!" can to this extent accommodate the Romantic and Victorian "religion of Nature."

In reacting against gory and egocentric hymns by composing more objective verses to accompany the Anglican Sunday services, Heber conformed to the spirit of his age beyond merely imitating its nature imagery. Two famous Anglican hymns of his time and one of a later that apparently address God the Father actually address the Trinity. Few singers remember more of "Father of Heaven, whose love profound" (1805)[15] than its well-worn refrain on sinners bending before the Throne. Its stanzas address each Person in turn and finally the Trinity. The same is true of that anthem for all whose relatives go down to the sea in ships, "Eternal Father, strong to save" (1861). Furthermore, in "Lead us, heavenly Father, lead us" (1821),[16] which in turn apostrophizes Father, Son, and Spirit, the "desert" refers not to the Exodus but directly to the Saviour's forty-day fast and obliquely to his Passion. Viewed as metaphor, the desert combines with the "tempestuous sea" through which we are led by the Father to render this world meaningless, for the Spirit is to infuse love and "heavenly joy" into our hearts, not into the world. Except for its typology and trinitarianism, this could have come from an existentialist poet. Evangelicals and existentialists alike, in the turmoil of war and economic collapse, find the world without meaning; it is their belief in prospective union with the divine that differentiates the former.

In the happier times that followed the Hungry Forties, Anglican and Congregational preachers, in particular, emphasized that the Incarnation conferred meaning and value upon the natural order. The lifelong effect of the earlier stereotype of life as journey through the desert may be observed in a powerful section of James Thomson's *City of Dreadful Night* (1874). An orator recounts his life story as a trek without hope or fear until he reached a seashore, representing death, where his soul "grew mad with fear" and longing for a woman who clearly symbolizes the poet's mother. Before dying in his childhood, she had taken him to Irvingite services that combined Calvinist doctrine with Catholic ritual. Subsequently his father had taken him to meetings of an evangelical sect. Deprived of faith and love, the atheist poet symbolically retraces his steps to seek primal innocence.[17]

As the Victorian religious consensus — the tacit acceptance of Protestant ethics and observances — broke up, the transcendent Creator and Father Almighty faded from the manuscript-books of hymnists, who, moreover, failed to find a common symbol of life to replace the soul's Exodus or pilgrimage through the wilderness of this world, yet the accumulation from the past ensured the continuance of Father and pilgrimage in hymnals. So categorical a statement requires justification. This, after all, was the day of *paterfamilias*, of "Nearer, my God, to Thee," "Immortal, invisible, God only wise," and "Eternal Father, strong to save."

During the reaction after the French Revolutionary wars, Anglican hymnists gave hymnody a nudge in a neo-orthodox, trinitarian direction. As reflexive hymns, nevertheless, "Father of Heaven" and "Holy, holy, holy" concern present acts of worship, while "Lead us, heavenly father" symbolically depicts the lower class life James Edmeston must have observed in his native Wapping.[18] In each text, human life and worship assumed a greater importance than in objective hymns of the late Roman empire.

The hanging judge whose all-seeing eye discerned each sinful thought and act was relegated to the children's hymnal, whence he whispered to the conscience until the 1860's. So, in the end, was the Provider of earth and its creatures, of food, clothing, and above all of the Bible, as in the Sunday school hymn "How dearly God must love us" (1841).[19] The complex of images concerning the Creator in mid-Victorian hymns for adults was prefigured in romantic poetry and paralleled in early Victorian novels. The subject of "Nearer, my God, to Thee" is not God but the soul that dreams of him, for in imagination the poet climbs the ladder as in Jacob's dream in the hope of praising God in the daylight beyond death. Her present depression she depicts in her metaphors of the wanderer, the dark and the stone; her yearning she expresses in her reiterated "I would" and her Shelleyan self-image as a bird or angel cleaving the sky "on joyful wing." Thus like Emily Brontë she narrates a Neoplatonic dream of liberation from the flesh.[20] Significantly, her hymn has appealed to the dying and bereaved.

The neurotic torpor discernible in the invalid Linton Heathcliff forms a counterpoint to the wonder of F. W. Faber's overrated hymn "My God, how wonderful thou art" (1849).[21] Even images from impeccable sources in Jewish ritual and Revelation, the eternal sun and "mercy-seat" surrounded by adoring "spirits," lack vitality owing to the plethora of adjectives: "wonderful," "bright," "beautiful," and especially "prostrate." The "rapture" of lying "prostrate" before the throne to "gaze and gaze" on the Father is a somewhat ignoble consummation. It is, however, Faber's self-absorption that deserves the name of neurosis:

> O how I fear thee, living God,
> With deepest, tenderest fears!
> And worship thee with trembling hope
> And penitential tears.

Aspiring to produce for Catholics an equivalent of the *Olney Hymns*, he echoes Newton in projecting an image of man as a "sinful child" more beloved of God than of its father or mother, but without the vitality evident in Newton's "Froward" child whom God must make "teachable."[22] The popularity of "My God, how wonderful thou art" is a sad comment on late Victorian spirituality, somewhat answered by that of Horatio Bonar's "Fill thou my life, O Lord my God" (1866), on finding God in work.

At the opposite extreme from Faber, the Unitarian author of "Father, hear the prayer we offer" reflects American transcendentalism in both its optimism and its muddle. Mrs. L.M. Willis "contradicted" the 23rd Psalm, a sin Routley could not forgive, by representing in "green pastures" not heaven ahead but childish dependence behind.[23] In her spell against nostalgic regression, the young smite "living fountains" from the rocks along their 'steep and rugged pathway.'' By means of typology inverted and so accommodated to "healthy-minded religion," the author depicts this life as the ascent of a mountain path, as in subtler ways did Wordsworth and his devotee Matthew Arnold.[24]

William Whiting, no sailor but a master at Winchester, clearly intended to put typology to practical use in his prayer for "those in peril on the sea." Despite his muddled metaphors, the Father's arm binding the "restless waves" on which the Son walks and the Spirit broods, and the "angry tumult" of chaos into which the Spirit breathed "peace" as well as "life," Whiting urges his "triune God of love and power" — a figure memorably employed by Browning — to 'shield" sailors, his "brethren" from shipwreck, fire, and foe, that "glad hymns of praise" might resound "from land and sea" rather than in heaven. In no way does this imply disbelief, only imaginative reorientation.[25]

The textual history of two further odes says much about the Creator's mid-Victorian mutation. W. Chalmers Smith reputedly composed "Immortal, invisible, God only wise" (1867) after a mystical experience on the shore near Aberdeen. It combines biblical terminology of the "Ancient of Days" with language naturalistic to the verge of pantheism. As life-giver hidden by "the splendour of light," God resembles the sun, and we human beings the leaves that flourish and wither. The original ending tells us most:

> *But of all thy rich graces this grace, Lord, impart —
> *Take the veil from our faces, the veil from our heart.
>
> All laud we would render, O help us to see
> 'Tis only the splendour of light hideth thee.
> *And so let thy glory, Almighty, impart,
> *Through Christ in thy story, Christ in thy heart.

Until Percy Dearmer wisely formed the present concluding verse by dropping the starred lines,[26] singers presumably gathered that, its veil torn away, God's glory would reach them in the form of Christ implanted in their hearts by his "story," the Gospel. In trying to expound a mystical intuition in biblical and natural terms, Smith employed a term used of folk tale or fiction. Although the same unconscious implication will be observed in the next chapter in mid-Victorian carols, the modern interest in etymology increases the possibility of an author's being aware of the Old English meaning of gospel, "good story."

The original text of "God the All-terrible! King, Who ordainest" (1842), composed for a Russian air, has vanished beyond recall. Two altered versions exist, one by John Ellerton (1870), the other a cento from this and its original.[27] Though never widely sung, they are important in that the original text represented the last appearance of the "Thunder-God," on whose decline that of Ellerton (published during the Franco-Prussian war) supplied its own comment. In H.F. Chorley's original the "King" ordained "great winds" as His clarion and lightning as His sword. Because the English editor adopted an alteration made during the American Civil War, "God the Omnipotent, / Mighty Avenger," the original substance of the second stanza remains uncertain. The third,

> God the All-merciful! earth hath forsaken
> Thy way of blessedness, slighted Thy word;
> Bid not Thy wrath in its terrors awaken;
> Give us peace in our time, O Lord.

was omitted by Ellerton, who no longer expected, as had Newton during the American Revolution, that God would pour out the vials of His wrath on sinful man.[28] In both extant versions the hymn continues by proclaiming that man had defied God the "All-righteous," who by the "fire" of His "chastening" would restore earth to "freedom and truth" and whose children would eventually sing "Peace to the nations and praise to the Lord." In other words, God now reveals His will in the consequence of human action instead of in special acts of vengeance.

This demythologizing of the Old Testament deity underlies the only distinguished late Victorian hymn on God the Father, Kipling's "Recessional," to be considered in my later book in connection with imperialist idolatry. Suffice it here to note the melting away of armies and navies as the natural effect of arrogance and neglect of God, not of His intervention.

Between Kipling's hymn for the Diamond Jubilee and the recent resurgence of hymnody that has given us "Lord of the dance," no English hymn in praise of God the Father has established itself, for "All creatures of our God and King" (1910) was a free version of the Franciscan Canticle to the Sun.[29] Before "ecology" had entered the common vocabulary, this joyous paean and its shapely tune appealed to the romantic delight in Nature that had somehow survived the shock of Darwinism. But on the heavenly Father no new hymn has taken root.

Lest we loose wild tongues on a supposed "Disappearance of God," we should note how mid-Victorian translators recharged sacred verse not only from Latin and German texts, but from their own storehouse of ideas. In "Be Thou my guardian and my guide" (1842), the tractarian Isaac Williams prays for divine aid against the world, the flesh, and the devil like any hymnist since Augustine.[30] In rendering the Ambrosian hymns Neale reintroduced their noble and austere Creator of the sun and stars.[31] In translating "Nun danket," Catherine Winkworth produced a thanksgiving hymn fully equal to "Our God, our help in ages past."

Not uncommonly translators projected into their texts the values of their own time. A good example is the altered translation by Winkworth of Neander's "Lobe den Herren", that appeared in hymnals around the turn of the century. In adapting Psalms 103 and 150, the German poet praises God as King of honour and exhorts the congregation to awaken psaltery and harp. The final English version suppressed both this German Renaissance motif of "honour" and the musical imagery, while praising God as "health and salvation" and so restoring the health motif of Psalm 103.3 that Neander had omitted.[32] After this display of muscular Christianity tinged with philistinism, it weakens Neander's logic by separating the desire granted in what God has ordained from the requested sustaining of worshippers, and so imports a nineteenth-century flavour of feminine resignation. Finally, where Neander praises God for blessing the singer's station in life, the translator hopes (with warrant from Ps. 90.17) that He may "prosper thy *work* and defend thee," as if to endorse the Victorian work ethic. Though "Praise to the Lord, the Almighty, the King of creation" has become a classic only in this century; its language and ethos are Victorian.

Equally so is George MacDonald's translation of a Lutheran psalm paraphrase, "Happy who in God's fear doth stay," in counting among the divine blessings a healthy family.[33] Dean Stanley's imitation of "Let us with a gladsome mind" exalts the family and throne among the blessings of English life.[34]

This slight evidence points towards a hypothesis so critical as to need testing from a wider field: that being "of human composure"[35] hymns represent God according to the temper of their age. In the late eighteenth century a plethora of guilt-haunted hymns suggested a contemporary cause such as the slave trade or the American Revolution. Then and in the early nineteenth century a deluge of metaphors on hunger, thirst, poverty, and disease mirrored times of severe winters, enclosures, and social turmoil, of self-defence by the rich and desperation for the poor.[36] Even the fair number of regressively erotic hymns, German or English, may have had some less tangible cause in child-rearing customs, parental mortality, the displacement of rural families or, more likely, a new consciousness of childhood as a distinct stage in life.[37] For whatever cause, hymns current in the time of Blake depict a threatening Jehovah and many in the late Victorian era a kindlier, almost brotherly figure.[38]

Conversely, the longings of an age find expression in its art forms, as witness a recent spate of television serials on Victorian upper class life. It is reasonable to suppose that any collective art form, such as balladry or hymnody, reflects contemporary experience and aspirations. This falls far short of the Marxist claim that man makes God in his own image. In no way does it preclude revelation or continuing tradition, for in addition to a psalm adapted by Watts or Montgomery, the worshipper recites one translated in the sixteenth century, and hears portions of the Authorized Version. If Anglican, he also recites a creed formulated before the fall of Rome.

Nevertheless, the hypothesis is radical enough to need substantiation from a range of texts on other *topoi* and to challenge the whole basis and enterprise of hymnody. When we have discounted economic or social circumstance, class conditioning, and the superego, what validity or transcendent meaning remains in the Christian or any other religion? In the light of modern scholarship, science, and psychology, must all wither away after lingering awhile, like the mythologies of Greece and Rome, in secular music, art, and literature?

In an appendix to this volume the hypothesis that hymns depict the deity in the likeness of their times will be tested by a survey of images of God in sample texts between the sixteenth and early twentieth centuries. The wider question, whether or not we can find evidence in hymns of God's "eternal changeless-ness,"[39] must be set aside pending conclusions in the succeeding volume as to what hymns were sung by worshippers of a given age, class, and denomination, and for what purpose.

For the present, evidence from the best-known lyrics and psalm versions produced during some sixteen centuries appears to warrant the following inferences:

1. Although the ancient and medieval church worshipped the Creator primarily in its psalms, a few Latin hymns portray Him as a hidden source of light who spoke in the thunder. In later medieval hymns His roles as Judge and Consoler were exercised respectively by Christ and the Virgin.

2. Members of Lutheran and Reformed churches worshipped God as their Creator, Father, and Shepherd, as did the Israelites and early Christians. About the end of the seventeenth century, after Anglicans and Puritans had in turn failed to establish a theocracy, hymnists began, like Donne and Herbert before them, to discern God more in personal than collective experience.

3. During the eighteenth century, as authors consciously or otherwise accommodated their faith to discovery and social change, God became less despotic and mankind less helpless. At the same time, God extended His suzerainty from the churches to the nation.

4. Save for the pietist (Wesleyan or Calvinist), God's bounty and providence

in everyday events became matters of faith rather than common sense. During the nineteenth century, His will revealed itself in consequence of human action rather than in special "judgments."

5. As hymn writers perceived God more in nature and society, so (like St. Ambrose of old) they directed praise to the Trinity. Of God the Father no consistent image appears in hymns of the middle and late nineteenth century.

14

THE MUTATIONS OF GOD: THE MESSIAH

Ring out the feud of rich and poor,
Ring in redress to all mankind.
Ring in the Christ that is to be.
Tennyson, IN MEMORIAM. cvi:11-12.32

Hitherto, clarity and critical focus have required me to make a somewhat artificial division between hymns on Christ Expected, Incarnate, Crucified, and Risen. Owing to the familiarity of many nineteenth-century texts, and the increasing importance of the spirit of the age consequent upon the growth of historical consciousness, this division will now be abandoned in favour of a grouping of texts by period.

While eighteenth-century poets produced classic hymns on all four *topoi*, those who flourished during the nameless "time of troubles" between the loss of the American colonies and the accession of Queen Victoria composed hymns on the Passion of an excellence not attained, save by Watts, since the age of St. Francis. The flood of carols (rather than Nativity hymns) reached its high-water mark half-way through Victoria's reign but continued far into the twentieth century. On the figure of Christ in general, poets from Doddridge in the eighteenth century to Montgomery in the early nineteenth and Kaan in the late twentieth took increasing note of His teaching as a stimulus to social reform.

Was there then a trade-off between the Myth and the Message, as earlier between the Myth and Nature? To speak of Christ as the "Medium" would distort the theology of the Incarnation, which holds Him to be also the Author. Further, since Wesleyans and Evangelicals campaigned so vigorously against the slave trade, among other abuses, what relationship existed between the Message and the internalized Myth? Some texts from both sides of the Cloth Curtain then dividing Catholics from Protestants enable us to view these relationships in more concrete terms.

EIGHTEENTH CENTURY

From the Gallican Advent hymn "Veni, veni Emmanuel" (1710), J.M. Neale and the editors of *Hymns Ancient and Modern* (1868) fashioned one of the few liturgical hymns from Latin beloved by all sorts and conditions of worshippers. Beside its numinous tune, its typological allusions to Mount Sinai and to Christ as "Rod of Jesse" and "Key of David" opening the way to heaven impart to His coming an old-world air of *mysterium tremendum et fascinans*.[1] Those Latin words not translated show how medieval this eighteenth-century text is. Since Emmanuel shall be born (*nascetur*) (not "come") to Israel to rescue us from the claw of the enemy (*ex hostis tuos ungula*), the Latin presents the Myth more concretely than "from Satan's tyranny" would suggest. Further, Christ will lead us from the cave, or abyss, of the lower world instead of giving "victory o'er the grave."[2] Thus the Latin poem depicts a more desperate plight than does the most commonly used English version, and therefore expresses a more intense longing for the Saviour. Though it includes one reference to hell, the Victorian version otherwise substitutes for the fear of hell that of natural death, specifying "death's dark shadows" for the ambiguous *dirasque noctis tenebras*.[3] Finally, in rendering *legem dedisti vertice / in maiestate gloriae* as "In ancient times didst give the Law / In cloud and majesty and awe," the translation muffles the whirlwind of the mountain top and introduces a historical distancing foreign to its original. To the Latin poet, the drama of history has as third act deliverance from Satan by God-with-us, the first being the Fall and the second the instruction of the chosen people in the divine Law.

Amazingly enough, "Veni, veni Emmanuel" was composed during the childhood of Philip Doddridge (1702-51), whose "Hark the glad sound" has such a modern ring, with its hosannas to the Prince of Peace come to "enrich the humble poor." Yet its most "mythological" stanza has survived:

> He comes the prisoners to release
> In Satan's bondage held;
> The gates of brass before him burst,
> The iron fetters yield.

while that of most social import has for aesthetic reasons dropped out:

> He comes from thickest films of vice
> To purge the mental ray,
> And on the eyeballs of the blind
> To pour celestial day.[4]

However imperfectly, this compassionate Dissenter brings together the coming

of Christ, His inspiration by the Spirit, and His prophecy in the Synagogue, and
so treats the Incarnation as the central event of man's historical, inner, and social
life. In so doing, he announces almost every theme of Nativity hymns since his
time.

English society was far from ready to hear that Christ had come to turn it
upside down. Even Doddridge spoke but of mending hearts and enriching the·
"humble" poor with grace. The age of "God rest you merry, gentlemen" expected
not social revolution but "comfort and joy."[5] Only in the late twentieth century
has the radical strain prevailed over the conservative. The former is typified by
Montgomery's "Hail to the Lord's Anointed" (1822, rev. 1853), the latter by that
paradigm of royal bounty to the poor, "Good King Wenceslas."

The middle and lower classes, though ready to hear the Wesleyan message of
Christ incarnate in the heart, have preferred the old-world and mythological
"Jesus Christ is risen today" to Wesley's "Christ the Lord is risen today." Other
poems of the Revival apportioned to the individual not merely the fruits of the
Passion ("cleft for me") but the guilt, as when Newton fancies that the Victim's
look "seem'd to charge me with his death."[6] Their authors tended to apply the
Atonement to the individual, the Incarnation and Resurrection to the human race.
They viewed the Crucifixion in the new mode of individual consciousness and
internal application, the Resurrection in the old, collective mode, as deliverance
of the race from Satan. Their texts on the Incarnation and Resurrection presuppose
a static and hierarchical society, in need of divine charity. Yet on both sides of
the Curtain, the human race must no longer remain passive, as in Roman times,
but must invite Christ to enter and cleanse each breast — as in "Jordanis oras
praevia" ("On Jordan's bank the Baptist's cry") — or at least welcome His offer
of peace, as in "Instantis adventum Dei" ("The advent of our God").[8] The practice
of auricular confession implicit in "Jordanis oras" must have surprised its Anglo-
Catholic adaptors far less than their insertion of a "home" for the divine "Guest"
would have surprised the author of "Instantis adventum" or, *a fortiori*, their
alteration of Chandler's translation "fill the world with love divine" to "restore
/ Earth's own true loveliness." Here the editors of *Hymns Ancient and Modern*
projected backward the domestic and natural idylls of their time.

ROMANTIC

Between the fall of Napoleon and the accession of Victoria several splendid
texts on Christ Crucified and Ascended seem to belie my earlier contention that
internalizing of the Christ myth was irreversible. Those of Heber and Milman
represent a reaction by Anglican poets of scholarship and talent against the
blood-spattered lyrics pumped out in the wake of the revival, yet two of the
finest came from the Evangelical extremist Kelly. Milman's "Ride on, ride on

in majesty," with Kelly's "We sing the praise of him who died" and "The head that once was crowned with thorns" form a triptych on the Triumphal Entry, Crucifixion, and Ascension fit to stand alongside the masterpieces of Theodulf, Abelard, and Fulbert. On docrinal as well as poetic grounds, to compare Kelly's with those of Fortunatus and Aquinas would be absurd, for their plainness of utterance, in contrast to the symbolic richness of "Vexilla regis," "Pange lingue," or "Lauda, Sion salvatorem," bespeaks not just a lesser gift but a difference of spirit and aim. Kelly wrote not for learned monastic communities but for the populace. Milman, Newdigate prizeman and Professor of Poetry at Oxford, employed a far greater range and density of image. Blending lucidity and highly conscious art, his "Ride on, ride on in majesty" yields to no hymn in English in its appeal to the whole range of human intelligence and sensitivity.

At first glance, all three appear hammered on "an age-old anvil."[9] In "We sing the praise," Kelly reaffirms the vertical universe and celestial hierarchy by calling the Cross the sinner's refuge "below" and "angels' theme . . . above";[10] in "The head that once was crowned," the "mighty Victor" adorned with "royal diadem" is acclaimed "King of kings," "Lord of lords," and "eternal Light" as in Revelation or the Fourth Gospel.[11] Even in "Ride on, ride on," the angelic "squadrons" that behold an "approaching sacrifice," like that in Keats's "Ode on a Grecian Urn," still look "down."

Both poets show a more highly developed sense of paradox than any of their precursors save Abelard and Wesley. But whereas Abelard and Wesley wonder at the death of the Immortal in "We sing the praise," Kelly infers from an inscription, "God is love," a hope for the race whose guilt his (imagined) Cross has taken away. He develops the paradox by discerning in this death of a loving God a hope for the coward it emboldens and for the dying whose bed it "gilds" with light. Despite this foreshadowing of Pre-Raphaelite portraiture, we might ascribe Kelly's objectivity to his use of an eighteenth-century text, until in his other hymn he explores the Paradox with the same incisiveness and economy:

> The cross he bore is life and health,
> Though shame and death to him;
> His people's hope, his people's wealth,
> Their everlasting theme.

Kelly set the tone for Anglican poets by combining the vertical universe, (understood metaphorically) and collective devotion of former times, with a treatment more imaginative than literal, a doctrine more implied than stated.

Milman, again, describes not the historical but an imagined Entry, hailed by "*all* the tribes" of Israel, or indeed Christendom. Content at first to contrast that multitude with the "humble beast," he loses no opportunity for paradox, whether in his twice-used oxymoron "lowly pomp" or his final antithesis "Bow thy meek head to mortal pain, / Then take, O God, thy power, and reign."[12] From "and reign," he draws not a social but a purely eschatalogical inference. Primarily he directs a ritual enacted in a cosmic amphitheatre before "winged squadrons of the sky." Aided by his feeling for paradox and pageantry, he thus recreates the simple narrative in a form reminiscent of a Keatsian ode.

The same author's "Bound upon the accursed tree" depicts every detail of Christ's suffering as in a baroque painting, while its Shakespearesque refrain, "our suppliant knees we bow," denotes worship rather than "interest" in Wesley's sense.[13] But the very form of this dramatic litany implies the participation of singers, for each stanza opens with "Bound upon the accursed tree" and applies the question "Who is he?" to a different act of the drama: "Faint and bleeding" to the scourging and crucifixion, "Dread and awful" to the sixth hour, and so on. In all but one verse, lines echoing as in

> By the eyes so pale and dim,
> Streaming blood and writhing limb,
> By the flesh with scourges torn,
> By the crown of twisted thorn,

invite the response "'tis thou," preceded each time by a different appellation of Christ.

In some more direct way, each surviving Passion hymn of the period requires the participation of narrator or singer. Though even the least have merit, their flaws together anticipate every feature of the long poetic decline during the latter half of the century. In "Bound upon the accursed tree" Milman at least overpaints the Object. In "Go to dark Gethsemane," Montgomery's imperatives insist too much, for "Shun not suffering, shame or loss" and "Trust in Christ, and learn to die" are instructions that, taken literally, profit none but thieves and undertakers. In Heber's otherwise moving "Bread of the world, in mercy broken," it is the worshipper who over-insists upon his tears and grief. For a parallel to this un-English emotionalism, we must turn to the lyrics of the Catholic revival (focused, to be fair, upon their objects of adoration) or to the pages of Mrs. Radcliffe.[14]

Heber and Milman can be described as Romantic poets, a term but superficially applicable to the Congregationalist Josiah Conder, whose "Bread of Heaven, on Thee I feed" (1824)[15] shows the Evangelical aptitude for paradox at its best, for the Sacrament brings life out of death, healing out of wounds. The equal of Heber's in concise utterance, Conder's text has more of scriptural substance and cogency, and less of passionate declamation. His metaphors apply in both a biblical and horticultural sense, for vines do in fact bleed and the soul "rooted" in and "grafted" on Christ resembles a fruit tree transplanted to better soil.

The unevenness of two American hymns results from the dissonance between their scriptural and, in a pejorative sense, their Romantic motifs. That Ray Palmer composed "My faith looks up to thee" (1830) with "tender emotion" but "little effort" no doubt explains his blend of fluency, egoism, and nostalgia.[16] Like Watts, he contemplates an imagined figure upon the Cross. Like every "real Christian" he prays for inner strength and deliverance from guilt. In seeking guidance through "life's dark maze," he simply varies the Puritan voyage through the wilderness; in praying Christ to "wipe sorrow's tears away" he echoes the dreamer of Revelation. It is his own dream that ruins his poem. His self-indulgence in "may thy love to me / Pure, warm and changeless be" is incompatible with his self-dedication in "let me from this day / Be wholly thine." His adjectives here betray desire for a love quite other than the "living fire" of God's love, a return to infantile dependence. As if knowingly indebted, like so many nineteenth-century children, to a mother who had nearly "died for" him at his birth, he longs not to "stray" from the universal parent, but be borne "safe above" from "life's transient dream." His nostalgia runs beneath a Christian surface, in that he likens death to the "sullen stream" forded by Bunyan's Christian. Like "Rock of Ages," this egocentric hymn owes much to a hypnotic tune.

If Charles Everest could not rival Heber, Milman, or Kelly in poetic skill, his " 'Take up thy Cross,' the Saviour said" (1883)[17] remains deservedly popular on account of its simple reiterative framework and what Victorians loved to call "manliness." In strength and directness its second stanza rivals the best of Kelly:

> Take up thy cross; let not its weight
> Fill thy weak spirit with alarm;
> His strength shall bear thy spirit up,
> And brace thy heart, and nerve thine arm.

In the next two verses, the slow march tune disguises defects of logic and language. The cross challenges not the singer's courage but his "foolish pride," as if he would mount Calvary once assured of not looking a fool. Nor is it clear how the cross enabled its Victim to brave "sin's wild deluge." Only its fine conclusion, traditionally associating cross and crown, retrieves this poem from disaster. Everest, like Palmer, stumbles once he strays from scripture or tradition.

As will be seen later, a characteristic of Victorian hymnists was their sense of historical distance from the Gospel events. In the case of Sir John Bowring, colonial administrator and author of "In the Cross of Christ I glory" (1825), the distance was also geographical. In Macao he observed a "great metal cross" over a ruined Roman Catholic church built centuries earlier which therefore "towered" over "wrecks of time." To judge from the "light of sacred story" that gathers over it, Bowring views the Cross as enhancing rather than informing his life. In times of "woe and disappointment" it "glows with peace and joy," while in happier times its "radiance" adds lustre to his "sun of bliss." All this explains why his Cross bears no Figure, but Bowring lacks the spiritual depth and precision of language to rise above sentimental recollection.[18]

VICTORIAN

First of all, Victorian poets and translators, like their medieval forebears, naturalized the Gospel settings. The more thoroughly they transposed the Nativity to an English winter landscape, the better the result. In that most exquisite of Victorian carols, "In the bleak mid-winter," not only does earth freeze "hard as iron" and water "like a stone," but the snowfall acquires a mythological dimension ("snow had fallen, snow on snow ... long ago") as if in Lewis's Narnia.[19] By contrast, the naturalizing of Caswall's "See amid the winter's snow" is superficial, having no relevance to its theme.[20]

Alternatively, poets naturalized in a social sense. Rather than fashion children after Christ, Cecil Frances Alexander refashioned Christ as a Victorian model of mild obedience, "our childhood's pattern." There was, however, an important sense in which Victorian carolists, like their fathers, did *not* naturalize the Christian social ethic. In domesticating Christ "with the poor and mean and lowly," Mrs. Alexander no more offered an opiate to the underprivileged than had the saintly Heber in reflecting, about 1811, that the "prayers of the poor" pleased God more than the gifts of gold.[21] A constant benefactor of the poor in her husband's diocese,[22] she followed Heber, Pusey, Keble, and Neale in upholding the Anglican conservative tradition of noblesse oblige. Freely as the Apostles had they received, and so freely gave.

Some Anglo-Catholic poets naturalized Christmas backwards. In "Good King Wenceslas" Neale adapted a Bohemian St. Stephen's day legend to the English Boxing Day custom of giving to the poor.[23] Again, in "Good Christian men, rejoice,"[24] he has Christ open the "heavenly door"[25] to admit mankind to His everlasting "hall," in allusion to the domicile of medieval lords and Victorian gentry.

The radical tradition presently in the ascendant came via Dissenting authors, among whom Montgomery roundly declared that Christ had come to "break oppression," set captives free and "rule in equity."[26] The radical tradition is in a sense the older, for it goes back to the prophets and the Psalmist, Montgomery's source being the verse: "He shall judge the poor of the people, he shall save the children of the needy, and shall break in pieces the oppressor" (Ps. 72:4). Only two years after Mrs. Alexander, the American E.H. Sears gave the radical tradition its modern tinge of sceptical humanism, reflecting sadly that "Beneath the angel stain" had rolled "two thousand years of wrong." Like the prophet Micah,[27] nevertheless, he sees the days "hastening on" to the promised age of peace.

Second, most Victorian hymns about Christ involve a personal response. This may not go beyond observing the liturgical calendar, as when Mrs. Alexander's "He is risen"[28] (one of the few Victorian Easter hymns still in use) calls its Anglican singers to raise hearts and voices in relief that "Lent's long shadows are departed" and the Passion ended. At a deeper level, J.S.B. Monsell turns from the Risen Christ to the "trembling hearts" assured that "death or hell" shall never "enthral" them.[29] On both sides of the Cloth Curtain hymnists employ the Evangelical tropes of the Blood Applied and Christ in the heart with mediocre results. The Catholic convert Faber, with the *Olney Hymns* and "Stabat mater" as his models, urges his flock to "come and mourn" with him at the side of Mary. After contemplating the crucified body organ by organ, he cries in Franciscan style,

> O break, O break, hard heart of mine;
> Thy weak self-love and guilty pride
> His Pilate and his Judas were:
> Jesus, our Love, is crucified.[30]

Let the broken heart implore mercy, for it is "love's cradle." By this ambiguity, Faber associates the heartbroken devotee with the heartbroken Christ, as a prelude to Love's final victory. On the Protestant side, texts in this kind have sunk to the sub-literary milieu of the Gospel hall compilation.

The Victorian carol and hymn most perfect in their kinds exemplify two different forms of response. Christina Rossetti's carol relates the Nativity to the Second Coming in this masterpiece of compression:

> Our God, heaven cannot hold him, In the bleak mid-winter
> Nor earth sustain; A stable place sufficed
> Heaven and earth shall flee away The Lord God almighty,
> When he comes to reign: Jesus Christ.

Rarely has the paradox of Incarnation been more succinctly or more sharply enunciated. With the same laconic profundity, the poet answers the question "What shall I give him / Poor as I am?" in three words, "Give my heart," as from all accounts she did.

As a Sunday school Passion hymn, Mrs. Alexander's "There is a green hill far away" (1848)[31] stands as far above its rivals as "Vexilla regis" or "When I survey the wondrous Cross." Nothing could attest this better than that adult congregations sing it not from nostalgia but in full seriousness. Mrs. Alexander directs our gaze not even to an imagined figure but to a fertile hill outside an unnamed city "far away." (Fortunatus ascribed fertility to the Tree itself.) Her use of the past tense in narrating the Passion but the present in exhorting her child singers further distances the event. By coincidence, long afterwards her study window looked out on just such a hill outside Londonderry.

Mrs. Alexander dwells not on the suffering but on its redemptive purpose. She presents Christ as archetype of virtue, alone "good enough" to unlock Heaven's gate. Her hymn demands the responses of love, trust, and imitation, not of Christ's death but of His "work." Ultimately she exhorts children to behave well in this life, with heaven as a distant prospect ("at last"). Sparing infant sensibilities as Watts never did, she represents the Crucifixion at a great distance. This her finest hymn cultivates the feelings of children about the idea, rather than the mental image, of the suffering Christ. It invites children to feel and resolve, rather than behold and worship. While she recited the same creeds as Fortunatus and would never have descended to writing "Tell me the old, old story," her Passion hymn bears in embryo Tennyson's "Christ that is to be" or Renan's heroic teacher, and gives the sacrifice a natural setting resembling that of Keats's "Ode on a Grecian Urn."

Here Mrs. Alexander draws moral implications without descending to the manipulative sentimentality of "Once in royal David's city" and of some ephemeral school hymns to be noticed in the ensuing volume. Nor does her distancing of the Crucifixion run to the maudlin extremes of "Tell me the old, old story" or "There's an old rugged Cross."[32]

On both sides of the religious divide, learned clerical poets composed panegyrics on the Crucified and Risen Christ until the mid-sixties. For poems on the wonder and mystery of the Incarnation, however, we must turn to women poets, Christina Rossetti or to Mrs. Alexander, whose famous lines tug at our heart-strings not merely because of their melody so beautifully sung by the King's College choir, but by the seeming artlessness with which they evoke child-like wonder at the ancient paradox:

> He came down to earth from heaven,
> Who was God and Lord of all;
> And his shelter was a stable,
> And his cradle was a stall;
> With the poor and mean and lowly
> Lived on earth our Saviour holy.

How sensitively the tune follows the pattern of narrative and application.

In later stanzas of "Once in royal David's city" and still more throughout "See amid the winter's snow," objective and consistent devotion is corrupted by the Victorian cult of childhood. Caswall's image "the Lamb," his archaism "built the starry skies," and his paradox of the Almighty in the manger have nearly two millennia of sacred verse behind them, nor does he depart from theological tradition in his final address to the Child. It is his tone that is wrong. The divine descent indeed manifests "tender love," but the Babe's face "so meek and mild" belongs to the saccharine school of ecclesiastical art. In calling for that face to teach humility, Caswall joins the crowd of Victorian hymnists intent upon the consecration of arrested development.

About 1868, the Scotswoman Elizabeth Clephane composed the last lyric of note to employ the Puritan image of this world as a wilderness. It opens impressively:

> Beneath the cross of Jesus
> I fain would take my stand —
> The shadow of a mighty Rock
> Within a weary land;
> A home within a wilderness,
> A rest upon the way,
> From the burning of the noontide heat
> And the burden of the day.[33]

Like so many before her, she falters upon leaving the safe highway of scriptural myth and parable.

> O safe and happy shelter!
> O refuge tired and sweet!
> O trysting-place where heaven's love
> And heaven's justice meet.

Returning to the highway, she likens the Cross to Jacob's ladder but, alas, once more sets free her invention to dream of an open grave beyond the Cross, two arms outstretched between "us" and it to "guard the way / From that eternal grave" like a "watchman." From this even her tears over Christ's "redeeming love" and her own "worthlessness" come as a relief. Until the recent crop of new hymns, this was the last in the line of English passion hymns.

It is more fitting to end this survey of Victorian hymns on the Myth with two of more consistent quality, one Anglican, the other Roman Catholic.

Bishop Wordsworth was more a typological than a nature poet, for his image in "Alleluya! Alleluya! / Hearts to heaven and voices raise": "Then the golden ears of harvest / Will their heads before him wave," refers to the "holy harvest" of the saved at the Second Coming. The very "rain and dew" he associates with the Resurrection as metaphors for grace.[34] His stately and somewhat Miltonic poem "See the Conqueror mounts in triumph" (1862) marks the close of the epoch that had begun with the earliest Greek and Latin hymns on Christ the Victor.[35] The slightest comparison with the Golden Kanon of St. John Damascene will show how in even this objective text of a scholar deeply influenced by Orthodox hymnody the focus has shifted over a millenium from Christ to the congregation. Wordsworth follows iconographic tradition in raising the Prophets to heaven, but brings together *topoi* often treated separately, the Ascension, the coming of the Holy Spirit, the martyrdom of Stephen, and the Second Coming. His claim that the Ascended Christ "has raised our human nature on the clouds to God's right hand" so "we sit in heavenly places" and in Christ's Ascension "behold our own," though acceptable to "Solomon" the Odist, might conceivably have struck the Byzantine poet as a blasphemy. Again, the final prayer to be lifted up on "wings of faith and love" so that "our youth renewed like eagles," we might rise with Christ at the Second Coming might well have appeared the ecstasy of presumption.

Bishop Wordsworth's "Lord of battles" and his strain of poetic diction — gates being "portals" and a welcoming fanfare a "trump of jubilee" — would have earned a rebuke from his illustrious uncle and seem unlikely to endear it to the modern congregation. It bears reading, however, as the only text to treat the Ascension as Wesley treated the Passion, by proceeding from an objective to an internalized event.

Newman wrote "Praise to the Holiest in the height" to be sung by the Fifth Choir of Angelicals in his *Dream of Gerontius* (1865). As a hymn, it became a favourite in all English-speaking countries save the United States.[36] About to glimpse the Risen Christ before entering Purgatory, Gerontius is reminded of the Redemption, now seen from the far side of death: the "words most wonderful" of commandment, prophecy, and Gospel; the "loving wisdom" of the divine Incarnation and self-sacrifice whereby as "Second Adam" Christ rescued man from the "sin and shame" of the Fall, recounted earlier by the Fourth Choir. His "double agony," mentioned by the Third Choir, signifies the physical pain combined with the spiritual anguish of desertion by the disciples and apparently by God. A semi-colon after "for man should undergo" indicates that the sense continues into the next stanza:

> And in the garden secretly,
> And on the cross on high
> Should teach His brethren and inspire
> To suffer and to die.

Christ, therefore, set His disciples (including Gerontius) the supreme example of self-giving love.

On the verge of old age (signified in the hero's name), Newman composed the *Dream* rapidly upon an impulse, a sure sign of the unconscious at its work of reassurance in what was, like each of his other imaginative compositions, a rite of passage. Six years after Darwin's *Origin of Species,* he composed verses of comparable grandeur and substance to the "Pange lingua" of thirteen centuries earlier. "When all was sin and shame," for example, should be read more as an existential statement about the condition of fallen man than as a historical assertion, for to Newman, as to Fortunatus, the Myth and history were one.[37]

SUMMARY

To pull together this study of some indicative hymn texts, the best from the eighteenth and early nineteenth centuries concern the Crucifixion, the best Victorian hymns the Infant and the Risen Christ. During the nineteenth century those that internalize the Passion decline in quality. Even the earlier masterpieces by Milman and Kelly, if as objective and paradoxical by intent, differ from their ancient or medieval precursors in their metaphorical treatment of the vertical cosmos, their conscious dramatization and historical distancing of the event, and their implicit participation and response.

Victorian poets tended to set the Nativity in the English winter landscape, and to project into it the Victorian ideals of nature, family, and especially childhood. Alternatively, they drew from the event or festivities a radical or else responsibly conservative social ethic. Montgomery had hailed Christ as inaugurating a reign of justice for the poor with more assurance and less of anguished entreaty than did Sears. The conservative view of the Incarnate Christ as setting a pattern for the privileged to succour the unprivileged best appears in hymns inspired by the Oxford movement. While virtually all Victorian texts require some personal response to Christ, this may take other forms than remedial action, from a simple commitment of the heart to an imitation in obedience and self-denial. Even the most learned clerical poets, Bishop Wordsworth or J.H. Newman, envisage an emulation of the Saviour's death and rising quite foreign to their late Roman or Byzantine counterparts.

These inferences are borne out by a much larger number of hymns listed by Routley as occurring in at least twelve major collections since 1900,[38] and therefore durable. The following tables show relative numbers composed and set in the early nineteenth century, the early, middle, and late Victorian eras, and the twentieth century.

	to 1836	1837-49	1850-69	1870-99	1900-
Nativity	4	3	12	6	8[39]
Passion/Rising	15	5	20	17	9[40]

Of the latter group, difficult to subdivide as texts often refer to the whole sequence of events, the proportions during the Victorian era are:

	1837-49	1850-69	1900-
Palm Sunday	1	0	
Passion Week	(5)	5 (3 U.S.A.)	7[41]
Passion Applied	(5)		
Easter and Ascension	8	4	1[42]
Eucharistic	1	6	3[43]

All Passion hymns in the last two columns save Archbishop MacLagan's "It is finished, blessed Jesus" (1865)[44] apply the event to the lives of an individual or a group. While some Victorian eucharistic hymns treat of the effects of grace in subsequent life,[45] those of the early nineteenth century, by Heber or Conder, were confined to the devotional or personal life. Late Victorian hymnists no longer represented the Passion in detail; even for the American "hot-gospellers" mere allusion to the Cross and Blood sufficed. By that time, the Resurrection and Ascension inspired few hymns with survival value. The Nativity, however, has inspired poets throughout the present century.

TWENTIETH CENTURY

Twentieth-century hymnody falls into three periods: in the first, Percy Dearmer and Vaughan Williams compiled the *English Hymnal* (1906); in the second, Dearmer turned in *Songs of Praise* (1925) from Anglo-Catholicism to a modernism tempered with orthodoxy in the enlargement by G.W. Briggs (1932) and a critical fastidiousness evident both in the two versions of *Songs of Praise* and the numerous hymnals compiled by Briggs for secular schools;[46] the third continues. For literary reasons, both editors imported into the hymnal lyrics by Herbert and Donne and traditional carols, many of which were included in the *Oxford Book of Carols* (1928). Although during the third period, which began in the late sixties, editors and authors have far outstripped their predecessors in productivity, the time is not ripe for critical assessment, and in any case present-day hymnody lies outside the scope of this book. Some recent Nativity lyrics, however, represent the culmination of the radical trend and the eclipse by default of the conservative. Being responsible for the social reforms of Wilberforce and Shaftesbury, this aristocratic conservatism has no connection with that of latter-day fundamentalists in the United States.

Two eucharistic hymns introduced in the *English Hymnal,* the finest and most durable product of the Anglican liturgical movement, reveal another fact of the conservative tradition. "Strengthen for service, Lord, the hands" (329) unites a newly revised translation of an ancient Indian liturgical hymn with a Reformation chorale tune "Ach Gott und Herr" ("God and Lord").[47] In the spirit of the

Byzantine Resurrection Kanon, communicants leave the natural for the spiritual world:

> The feet that tread thy holy courts
> From light do thou not banish;
> The bodies by thy Body fed
> With thy new life replenish.

They sing of a moral rather than social transfiguration, for if their hands be "strengthened for service," their ears become dead to "clamour," their tongues free from deceit, their eyes fixed upon the divine love and "blessed hope."

In "Wherefore, O Father, we thy humble servants" (335), by W.H.H. Jervois, a member of the hymnal committee whose education at Rugby and Oxford typifies the upper class background of many Anglo-Catholic clergy,[48] worshippers who offer the "Sacrifice immortal" as "humble servants," thereby intercede as "children" for all God's "people, living and departed." At the altar, they enter the transcendent world of grace.

In the same strain, "Ye watchers and ye holy ones," the last English hymn on the Risen Christ to attain wide use, calls upon the celestial hierarchies, saints, patriarchs, and prophets, whose aureoled faces surround the high altars of the many huge and never-filled High Anglican churches erected in city centres and industrial suburbs during the late nineteenth and early twentieth centuries, to join in repeated alleluias. One of the most inspiring tunes in modern hymnody rises to a climax before descending through the alleluias into one of the most beautiful codas. Nevertheless, this is a hymn for the initiate. The worshipper who can identify the Blessed Virgin in the second verse must know his Catholic theology better than most in the twentieth century.

> O higher than the Cherubim,
> More glorious than the seraphim,
> Lead their praises, Alelluia!
> Thou bearer of the eternal Word,
> Most gracious, magnify the Lord,
> Alleluia, &c.

Surprisingly enough, this text by Althelstan Riley, translator of Latin hymns and co-editor of the *English Hymnal,* has attained its widest use in the United States.[49]

Both the aristocratic connections of Gabriel Gillett, as alumnus of Westminster School and Keble College, Oxford and former chaplain to the Anglo-Catholic Viscount Halifax, and the purport of his Passion hymn "It is finished! Christ hath known" (118)[50] typify the conservative tradition. He pleads for Christ, who has made human joys, sorrows, and needs His own, to lead worshippers in His way of self-sacrifice upon the "Tree of Healing." His conclusion, were it more felicitously put, could come from the pen of Prudentius or Fortunatus:

> It is finished! Christ our King
> Wins the victor's crown of glory;
> Sun and stars recite his story,
> Floods and fields his triumph sing.
> Lord, whose praise the world is telling,
> Lord, to whom all power is given,
> By thy death, hell's armies quelling,
> Bring thy Saints to reign in heaven.

The transfiguration of Nature by Myth, however right and inevitable in a late Roman poet, appears forced in one writing a generation after Darwin and Mendel. In his previous stanza, Gillett welds an Abelardian with an ascetic view of the Passion, for "love" revealed in the divine suffering is to "purge our passions, scourge our vice." As in the slaying of Christ "on the altar of creation," his theology and poetic tone are medieval. In the spirit of Keble's lectures at Oxford, Gillett expounds the medieval analogy between Nature and the Christian mysteries.[51]

With the exception of G.R. Woodward's carol "This joyful Eastertide" (1894), which alludes to the Crucified bursting "his three-day prison" and the general rising after flesh has slept "a season," late Victorian texts consider the Resurrection in general terms only. In Dearmer's own "A brighter dawn is breaking," Christ defies death to give "life abundant," light and "kindness" to the world, "resurrection" to sinners, "healing and revelation" to the sick and doubtful.[52]

Paul Fussell's recent study of literature associated with the First World War[53] confirms an opinion formed from the poems of Wilfred Owen and Siegfried Sassoon (together with Benjamin Britten's *War Requiem*) that soldier poets ironically applied the sacrifice upon the Cross to that of their own generation, so making it a catalyst of doubt. Except in Eliot's *Murder in the Cathedral* and in recent hymnals, modern lyrics of consequence have come from secular poets. A single example must suffice to illustrate this ironic scepticism. On a broken wayside crucifix, Owen writes:

> One ever hangs where shelled roads part.
> In this war He too lost a limb,
> But His disciples hide apart;
> And now the Soldiers bear with Him.

That the formerly Anglo-Catholic poet once served in a parish with a view to ordination intensifies the acerbity of:

> Near Golgotha strolls many a priest,
> And in their faces there is pride
> That they were flesh-marked by the Beast
> By whom the gentle Christ's denied.[54]

It is otherwise with lyrics on the Nativity, for the sceptical undertone resulting from biblical criticism and the headlong rush from a pastoral to an industrial society has prompted some of our finest modern carols. Despite its archaic title, "All poor men and humble,"[55] an expanded translation from Welsh, addresses a specified human rather than an angelic audience as in "Angels from the realms of glory." Even the most orthodox hymnists have avoided the sentimental distancing of the Nativity, as in a fairy-tale, that mars "Once in royal David's city" or "Silent night," either by reverting to the ancient paradox, as in the Canadian carol "Gentle Mary laid her child" (1930),

> There he lay, the undefiled,
> To the world a stranger.
> Such a babe in such a place,
> Can he be the Saviour?[56]

or by naturalizing the event entire, not merely the climate. This can limit circulation of a carol, for Canadian city-dwellers nourished on their national myth of the untamed wilderness can sing with a straighter face than Europeans a seventeenth-century account of the Nativity for Amerindians that in its English version describes God as "Gitchi Manitou" lying in a "robe of rabbit skin" in the "forest free."[57] The same is true of the conscious antithesis between the Palestinian and the prairie environment in "No crowded eastern street," by which the birth takes place in a "sturdy farm house" with "stable, shed and . . . barn," beneath "no bright celestial choir" but the light of stars and passing aircraft.[58] Within their native habitat, such carols convey mystery and wonder without sentimentality.

The sceptical undertone first evident in "It came upon the midnight clear" has kept alive the Nativity. In his frankly naturalistic Epiphany carol "Catch the bird of heaven," the Quaker Sydney Carter[59] treats institutional religion as incompatible with the elusive "bird" whom "Bell and book and candle" can no longer hold. In advising the seeker to "keep on travelling," he implies that religion, like science, is a matter for perpetual discovery. In his better-known "Every star shall sing a carol"[60] he adorns his speculation on whether incarnations take place on other planets with a relativistic refrain "God above, man below; / Holy is the name I know."

The converse of this sceptical humanism is the stark reality underlying the social radicalism of Fred Kaan's Nativity hymns. "Tomorrow Christ is coming" presents a "world full of darkness" that also finds no room for Christ, in which those "symbols of existence" the "stable, cross and tomb" await the unknown child born every minute.[61] Kaan broods on the "nameless millions" for whom the star of Christmas "will never shine." His eucharistic hymn "Down to earth, as a dove" offers hope that God can defeat "darkest night" by sending Christ to "feed / hungry men."[62] Although in a liturgical context this assurance loses some of its startling impact, it is worlds away from the sprightly confidence of "On Christmas night all Christians sing" which Vaughan Williams collected and set half a century before.[63]

Over the past century or so the Incarnation has acted at first as a means of conditioning children to remain so, or conversely as an expression of nostalgia for a pre-industrial way of life, but of late became the vehicle of an explicit and radical criticism of society and even the Church. In this tendency we may discern the influence of Marxism, the gravest threat to the continuance of institutional Christianity. Because it lends itself both to nostalgia and social activism, the Nativity continues to inspire authors and congregations. The Passion, by contrast, has inspired poets outside the Church, or within it learned and allusive poets such as Eliot or David Jones,[64] more than popular hymnists. While this book cannot take account of the latest Passion hymns, the best anthologized during this century come from non-European sources, the negro spiritual "Were you there when they crucified my Lord?"[65] or the Chinese lyric translated as "My heart looks in faith / to the Lamb divine,"[66] whose poet, like a latter-day Wesley, treats of divinely inspired faith, hope, and love. Most English hymns on Christ during the twentieth century feature other *topoi* than the holy mysteries of His birth, crucifixion, rising, and Second Coming.

15

THE MUTATIONS OF GOD: THE HOLY SPIRIT

The orthodox Christian view is to accept both elements of the paradox of
law and love. The gnostic position is always revulsion against both elements
. . . Wesley believed law and love were one, paradoxically related in time,
but eternally one. Blake visualized no final judgment to be pronounced by
any power outside man. . . . saw no sweetness in commandment or statute,
no love in any discipline imposed from without.[1]

Earlier in this book, three great medieval hymns were seen to embody a "testament" or witness of the Holy Spirit working in the Christian community and
soul. The most collective and dogmatic, "Venì Creator Spiritus," attracted distinguished translators from the sixteenth to the eighteenth centuries; the most
psychologically penetrating, "Veni sancte Spiritus," drew the most popular translations in the nineteenth (the great age of the English novel), while the most
fervent and subjective, "Discendi amor santo," translated in 1867 as "Come
down, O love divine," attained universal popularity when set by Vaughan Williams
in the early twentieth.[2] Most hymns on the Spirit followed this evolution from
collective to individual utterance until the First World War, since which the very
few known to me have returned to collective concern of a different kind. The
difference, amounting to a reorientation of human life, gives a new direction to
this charting of the Christian myth in Christian folk poetry.

Why, in view of the modern tendency to perceive God in nature and in the
psyche, do so few poets of distinction address God as Spirit? The stature of those
who do steadily declines, from Dryden to Wesley, then from Keble, Newman,
and Neale to hymnists otherwise unknown, while outside the Church, novelists
and playwrights, such as Samuel Butler, Aldous Huxley, or Bernard Shaw, can
pay tribute to their nameless or unconscious source of inspiration. Few among
the secularized masses know what the Whitsun holiday is about, let alone what
powers or functions the Christian religion ascribes to the Spirit. Even fewer
could explain the origin of the term "pentecostal." Some have a vague idea that
the spirit operates in the rites of confirmation or ordination, or in the process of
ecclesiastical decision-making. Others may sometimes feel guided in making

personal decisions or in creative endeavours. No doubt most of the clergy address a prayer to the Spirit before preaching and some, as did the Wesleys, before reading the Scriptures.[3]

Parallel to if not responsible for the increasing vagueness about the Spirit was the tendency of hymnists to employ the biblical symbols — wind, tongues of flame, dove, or guiding light — in a less and less literal sense.

Over three centuries hymnists have ascribed to the Spirit the functions of creation or renewal, of cleansing or healing, of enlightenment — intellectual or psychological — and of inspiring love or unity. From time immemorial they have envisaged it as acting through the Church and its ritual. In denouncing John Wesley's claim to be inspired by the Spirit as "a very horrid thing," Bishop Butler struck out bravely against the tide that had set towards individual inspiration. No doubt he would have found the poet Wordsworth's claim to be "a dedicated spirit"[4] equally embarrassing. By the late nineteenth century, mediums were addressing their own "spirit guides" at seances.

The scriptural passages on the Spirit permit either a symbolic or purely moralistic treatment, the former being more congenial to poets. Writing a century apart, the Independent Simon Browne and John Keble, soon to instigate the Oxford Movement, combine both approaches. Using the first person singular, Browne entreats the "heavenly Dove" to direct "every thought and step" as "Guardian and guide." He seeks guidance not in decisions but in doctrine and discipline, praying the Spirit to "display" the "light of truth," make him "know and choose" its way to Christ and thus to "Heav'n," his "final rest in God." A little incongruously, he begs the Dove implant "holy fear" in his heart to ensure his continuing devotion. As a Calvinist, Browne intends "gracious" in his opening invocation "Come, gracious Spirit, heavenly Dove"[5] (1720) to signify precisely that grace, the divine initiative prerequisite to knowledge and fear of God, operates in the person of the Spirit, as when it descended in likeness of a dove at the Saviour's baptism.

As a High Churchman, Keble in 1827 took an Arminian and Catholic view. "When God of old came down from Heav'n, / In power and wrath" "fires ... rush'd" upon Sinai and a "trump, that Angels quake to hear" sounded from the cloud. When the Spirit descended for "the second time," it hovered over the baptized Christ as a dove, then spoke to the disciples at Pentecost as a "rushing, mighty wind." That wind now fills not only the Church but the "sinful world" around, except for "stubborn hearts." By his punctuation and phrasing:

> Come Lord, come Wisdom, Love and Power,
> Open our ears to hear;
> Let us not miss the accepted hour;
> Save, Lord, by love or fear.[6]

Keble clearly denotes fear and love as alternative means of bringing souls to God, and "Wisdom" and "Power" (an allusion to the final praise of Christ in Revelation 19.1) as allowing more for human judgment and initiative than in Browne's hymn. The universalist idea of the Spirit filling the world could have been imbibed either from Anglican theology or from the Wordsworth of the "Intimations" Ode and the *Excursion*. Though too churchy for present-day taste and too subtly allusive for its tune "Winchester" (more familiar in "While Shepherds watched their flocks by night"), Keble's poem reveals a significant shift even in one as much a zealot as Browne.

In petitioning the Spirit to kindle "sacred love" within his "cold" human heart, Browne employs a conventional metaphor. Charles Wesley, a truer poet, extends and amplifies the fire symbol:

> O Thou who camest from above,
> The pure celestial fire to impart,
> Kindle a flame of sacred love
> On the mean altar of my heart.
> There let it for thy glory burn
> With inextinguishable blaze. ...[7]

As if blazing a trail for Blake, Wesley builds his whole lyric around the one symbol, vowing that the inner fire shall rise "trembling" as prayer and praise and seeking aid to "guard the holy fire." Less by design of the Wesleys than of their editors in 1830, the nine hymns on the Spirit in the revised *Collection* (Nos. 649-57) apply the symbols of Creation and Pentecost in a more collective sense.[8] These deal with the Spirit's role in the Creation, the life of Christ and the regeneration of "our earth" (649, 650), with the promise of Christ to send this "Guide infallible," and with the Pentecostal manifestation (655, cf. 658). One hymn designated for Pentecost, "Come, Holy Spirit, raise our songs" (653), implies a charismatic reliving of that episode, for after proclaiming the "apostolic promise" of "Pentecostal powers" given to present disciples, Wesley calls on God to "fix in us the Guest divine," come as "a mighty rushing wind" (653). A little later, he proclaims that the "heavenly Teacher" will inscribe in "our heart" the sayings of Jesus and distribute His "legacy" of "unutterable peace" (655). In some Wesleyan hymns, as Rattenbury comments, Christ and the Spirit are indistinguishable. In an accompanying text by another hand, the "Eternal Spirit" is bidden to enter and repair its "meanest home," the "heart of man" (657). While Wesley does anticipate Blake and Wordsworth in symbolism and democratic spirit, the insistence, in this hymn, upon all souls as "ruin'd" (not merely those of Byronic heroes) places it theologically in the tents of old-world Christianity.

Even Wesley innovates poetically and psychologically, not doctrinally, for he extends the symbolism by converting the fire into a solar symbol (usually associated with Christ) in "Light of life, seraphic fire," a plea for the Spirit to "shine" in each "drooping" heart, scatter its "guilty gloom," and appear in its "human temples." Wesley might have endorsed the plea of the Independent minister Joseph Hart for the Spirit to cheer "our desponding hearts,"[9] "convince us" of sin and so lead us to Christ but does not himself invert the biblical order of events.

The text, and especially the variants of "Spirit of mercy, truth and love,"[10] exemplify a developing doctrine of the Spirit. Justly praised by Routley for its "brevity and sobriety of diction," this appeared in the 1774 hymnal for the Foundling Hospital, the London orphanage founded by Evangelicals in response to the "social passion of the Wesleys."[11] Beyond the moral influences specified in the first line, the Spirit will "from age to age convey / The wonders of this sacred day" and ensure the singing of God's "eternal praises" in "every clime" and "tongue." Let this "unfailing comfort" and "heavenly guide" prevail over its "favoured church," that mankind may still its "blessings prove." Here the Spirit ensures a historical continuity of Christian worship and ethic. The editors of *Hymns Ancient and Modern* replaced "eternal praises," the phrase linking human with celestial worship, by the Miltonic sun image "surpassing glory";[12] and "favoured church" by "Holy Church," presumably to substitute a Catholic for a Calvinist implication. Critics of the public school system might see sinister implications in the substitution at Rugby School (1843) of "Spirit of *power,* truth and love" for the original first line.[13]

The parallel between human and angelic praise so heedlessly obliterated by the *Hymns Ancient and Modern* editors was common to Protestant and Catholic, as can be seen from the doxology of "O Holy Spirit, Lord of grace," an early Victorian translation of "O fons amoris, Spiritus" (1736).[14] While there is nothing new in the fire from heaven inflaming the "inmost heart" of "saints" below, the parallel between mankind and the Godhead in the prayer for the Spirit to bind those saints in "mutual love," as it does the Father and Son, might have startled earlier English hymnists. As implied by the word "saints," human concord interests the translator as a reflection of the divine. In our time that view has been inverted, but before considering the modern viewpoint we must turn to some texts that illustrate subjective and specifically Victorian elements in hymns on the Spirit.

"Come, Holy Spirit, come" (1800),[15] a Baptist "Veni, sancte Spiritus," is subjective in a purely verbal sense, for the Spirit is to melt "this frozen heart" and subdue "this stubborn will," so as to "form me anew," and cause "beams of mercy" to shine on "this poor-benighted soul" with "energy divine." As the last phrase reminds us, Beddome was a contemporary of Blake. Self-concern obtrudes in an English and an American hymn "Come, Holy Spirit, calm my mind"[16] (1807) and "Come, Holy Ghost, my soul inspire" (1824),[17] the latter a quintessentially Evangelical petition for the Spirit to "Bear witness that I'm born again."

Neither a collective viewpoint nor objective tone could prevail against the *zeitgeist* and the demands of the hymn medium. Andrew Reed's "Come, Great Spirit" (1817),[18] despite the currently fashionable Amerindian phrase in its opening line, and its impeccably biblical images of the "light," "fire," "dove," and "wind," presumably fell out of use by reason of its Calvinistic pessimism and moral rigidity, exemplified in "make a lost world thy home," "reveal / Our emptiness and woe" and "lead us in the paths of life / Where all the righteous go." Even the fame of Montgomery could not preserve some gouty lines in his "Spirit of the living God" (1823, 1825),[19] "Be darkness at thy coming, light: / Confusion, order in thy path," or a stiffly worded petition for the Spirit to descend in its "plenitude of grace" upon "our apostate race."

From an age of great hymns on the Passion, therefore, only one on the Spirit has remained in common use. The glutinous tune and Victorian death-bed diction of the opening lines may blind us to the scriptural images and collective viewpoint of Harriet Auber's famous "Our blest Redeemer, ere he breathed / His tender, last farewell" (1829).[20] As a whole, this text blends literal belief in the original "tongues of living flame" with intuitive awareness of heaven, and trust in the inner voice of conscience. Its concluding lines, "O make our hearts thy dwelling-place / And worthier thee" could have come from Wesley's pen. Perhaps, after all, the tune has preserved the text by fitting its rhythms and tone so exactly, but some credit must go to the hymnist for also applying the symbols in a collective sense. Yet there breathes over this almost great hymn a spirit of Victorian motherhood, in its addition of "subdue" to "teaching" and "convince," and especially, its welcome into a "humble heart" for the "gracious, willing guest" whose "gentle voice ... checks each fault."

Hymnists of the Victorian age proper were by no means immune to emanations from secular novels and educational writings. In the very year of Dickens's *Bleak House*, G. Rawson, a Congregationalist, develops in "Come to our poor nature's night" (1853) an image of the Spirit visiting the Lost Child of that novel or of *Oliver Twist*. He urges the "blessed inward light" to "cleanse" the singers who are "sick," "faint," and "lost" till so "restored," for "orphan are our souls and poor." As if alluding to some inarticulate Oliver or Jo, Rawson follows his list of gifts (faith, joy, love, peace, self-discipline, and knowledge of Christ), by praying the Spirit with "voiceless groaning" to plead our "unutterable need" and bear us to our "high abode."[21] Indeed, the lost inheritance and upper class status attained by so many hero figures of novelists from Richardson to Dickens and the Brontës has the finality of heaven, and sometimes follows a final assembly of characters parallel to the Last Judgment.[22]

A late Victorian hymn for elementary and Sunday schools, "Holy Spirit, hear us" (1880),[23] consisting mainly of petitions for children to be taught what they "ought to say" and have their "little deeds of toil" and each "lowly mind" modelled after Christ ("gentle, pure and kind"), concludes in a plea for help to conquer "what is wrong" and to choose the right that would seem more appropriate for the young gentlemen of Rugby or Harrow. An American hymn, "Holy Spirit, truth divine" (1864),[24] evinces not only the Sunday school rhetoric and moral posturing so cruelly caricatured by Mark Twain, but a sense of paradox more essentially Christian. After urging the Spirit to "Dawn upon this soul of mine," and "Glow within my heart" so that he might "strongly love / Bravely bear and nobly strive," Longfellow (the well-known poet's brother) resolves, "Perish self in thy pure fire," that though "firmly bound" by "law divine," he may live "for ever free."

At first sight, the one great Victorian hymn to the Spirit, Edwin Hatch's "Breathe on me, Breath of God" (1878),[25] appears equally self-centred. Closer reading shows a drive towards self-abnegation characteristic of Pauline mysticism. One filled "with life anew" seeks to love and act as the Spirit wills, attain what Kierkegaard defined as "Purity of Heart" and so with the Spirit "will one will."[26] Only then can the "earthly part," the body and understanding, glow with the Spirit's "fire divine." The virtual absence of imagery and overly simple tune can blind us to the depth of meaning in this paraphrase of St. Paul on dying to self to live unto God.[27] Too bald to compare with "When I survey the wondrous Cross," this is nevertheless the profoundest native English hymn on the Holy Spirit, challenged only by "Our blest Redeemer" and Bishop Wordsworth's paraphrase of the Ode to Charity, "Gracious Spirit, Holy Ghost."[28]

Lest the reader point in exasperation to "Lead, kindly Light," let me concede Newman's superiority (indeed Christopher Wordsworth's), as a poet, yet repeat that his "kindly light" was the pillar of cloud that had led the Israelites, and would, metaphorically speaking, lead him beyond his perplexities and regrets. On the principle that this hymn could change its focus like "Our God, our help in ages past," Mahatma Gandhi properly read it as a prayer to God in the capacity of guide or teacher, but we have no evidence that Victorian singers applied it with any precision to the Holy Spirit. Its themes of light in darkness and nostalgia for lost innocence sufficiently account for its popularity.

By far the clearest appeals for guidance came in hymns sung at Anglican Confirmation services, of which Matthew Bridges' "My God, accept my heart this day" (1848) is perhaps the pick. Some lyrics composed by parents of the boy and girl concerned tend to embarrass the critical adult by egocentric and over-simple avowals. Bridges, however, composed his at the time of his reception into the Roman Catholic church, in his late forties.[29] Though in the first person singular, it moves from a conventional and self-centred resolve "That I from thee no more may stray" and a posture before the Cross, "Behold, I prostrate fall," to an application "Let every sin be crucified" that culminates in a self-denial as total and mature as that of Hatch, but more felicitously expressed:

Let every thought, and work, and word

To Thee be ever given;
Then life shall be thy service, Lord,
And death the gate of heaven.

At the opposite extreme, "O Jesus, I have promised" (1866), composed by J.E. Bode for the confirmation of his children but wisely assigned in the *English Hymnal* to "Mission Services," employs some variant of the first person singular in twenty-six of its forty lines, sometimes two or three times.[30] It addresses to Christ petitions that "Our blest Redeemer" had addressed to the Spirit, another indication of theological blurring in the nineteenth century. As "Guide," Christ is to speak "In accents clear and still" above "murmurs of self-will," a clear allusion to the "still, small voice."

A text intended for use at mission services, Baker's "O Holy Ghost, Thy people bless" (1874), explores the meanings of the Creation story.[31] Seeking to "grow in holiness" as children of light, the congregation sings: "Life-giving Spirit, o'er us move / As on the formless deep" to give life and order, light and love where now is "death or sleep." Once this wind blows from heaven, "garden-spices shall spring forth." Whether the vegetation image come from Genesis or *Paradise Lost* is immaterial; what matters is the meaning we attach to the oceanic metaphor. As a High Churchman of his time, the instigator of *Hymns Ancient and Modern,* Baker doubtless believed the Creation story literally true. Here, however, he applies it primarily to the multitude that is without form or spiritual awareness until awakened and informed by the preaching of the good news, for he writes in the first person plural. Only secondarily does his image refer to the individual soul. Fifty years later, in the time of Jung, the formless deep could be seen as the collective unconscious, to which the myth gives form and meaning, while the disciple of Freud would no doubt discern in the restored paradise garden a regression to infancy. As an Anglo-Catholic, Baker offers what may be the last old-world literal image of the Creation and combines it with a collective application devoid of that neurotic self-concern so prevalent in Evangelical mission hymns.

Considering the difficulty with which the modern mind entertains any but an immanent deity — as witness Nietzsche, Shaw, Hardy, or Lawrence — it is astonishing that so few lyrics to the Holy Spirit have appeared in this century. In 1890 George Matheson, better known for "O Love, that wilt not let me go," published an ecumenical hymn, "Gather us in, thou Love that fillest all."[32] Though ahead of its time, and awkwardly allusive in "rend each man's temple's veil," this call for the Spirit to "gather our rival faiths" within its fold might have been expected to start a new wave of lyrics on the "common soul" in "diverse forms" of religion.

In 1920, the theologian F.C. Burkitt published "Our Lord, his Passion ended" among three hymns for Whitsuntide. Reducing the fire symbol to a simile, "like a flame of fire," and distancing the Pentecostal event in saying that the Spirit abides, "though centuries go gliding," he addressed the Spirit as "Lord of every nation." His universalism, so timely in view of the recent blood-bath, could not atone for lame verse and a difficult tune.

After that, poets fell silent on the Spirit until in 1951 George Brandon, in "O God, whose mighty wisdom moves," described an old-fashioned quest for the path leading through scriptural truths to God.[33] Not until 1968 did any hymnist invoke the Spirit in the cause surely uppermost in the hearts of all who in our time pretend to enlightenment.

Since A.M. Jones's "Spirit of Light," published first in Africa collection, only became generally available in 1973, and I have not heard it sung, any judgment must be provisional.[34] Beginning with a familiar idiom from the Prayer Book ("lighten thou our darkness") and traditional symbols employed as verb metaphors ("Guide thou our ways," "fire thou this world of thine"), the text finally voices a concern that in our time must override these Evangelical calls for individual salvation through the blood of Jesus that so often fall on deaf ears:

> Chasten thou the pride of race
> marring our common life.
> Kindle our love, that loving
> all may true brotherhood find ...
>
> breathe o'er this world of thine;
> teach us all to know and do
> all that will make men free.
> Thy kingdom come, on earth as
> in thy blest heaven above,
> come, Spirit, come.

Admittedly prosy in rhythm and old-fashioned in diction, this text at last says what poems by Christians, Hindus, Buddhists, Jews, Sikhs, and even Muslims and Marxists should have proclaimed ever since the First World War. It raises, however, a question that hangs over the future of the Christian or any religion: can ancient images and expectations — the fire, the dove, the still, small voice and mighty wind, the kingdom that awaits the righteous yet must spread on earth — inspire poets and musicians to compose the only songs post-atomic man can afford to sing, those that envision universal brotherhood and unconditional love? Conversely, the doctrine of the Spirit as guide into all truth needs cutting loose from the impossible pretence that any human assembly, sacred or secular, be it the college of cardinals or the Politburo, can claim a monopoly of truth or infallible judgment in making decisions or appointments. The Spirit of God can guide only the spirit of man. It does not operate by machinery.

16

THE MUTATIONS OF GOD:
CONVERGENCE AND CLEAVAGE

To-day I arise
Invoking the Blessed Trinity,
Confessing the Blessed Unity. ...
"ST. PATRICK'S BREASTPLATE"[1]

Although my analysis so far might have seemed inclined towards tritheism, hymnographers often focus on a single Person — Watts on the Father, Wesley on the Son. No poet or era has produced a whole crop of hymns on the Spirit. The Victorians, who came nearest, composed none to compare with those they translated. Emphasis on the Father or Son appears determined more by chronology than denomination. In the eighteenth century, not only the churches of Old (i.e., Calvinist) Dissent — Baptist, Independent — but the Unitarian denomination, which absorbed English Presbyterians with their psalmody, produced primarily patrocentric hymns. The Wesleys, the Anglican Evangelicals, and in the following century Baptists and Catholic converts and even Baptists poured out Christocentric hymns. Finally, the Anglicans, of whatever shade, who were responsible for most Victorian hymns of quality addressed the Trinity, "God," or "The Lord," or quite often each Person in turn. While that elusive entity the *zeitgeist* guides us along the full-flowing river of Victorian hymnody, we can mistake tributaries or eddies for the main course and so judge the beliefs of society in general by those of poets and novelists, or by theories and scholarly activities — Natural Selection or German New Testament criticism — that the majority at best knew hazily and at second-hand. By facing forward, moreover, we may forget the sheer volume of hymnody that still flowed from behind, the proportion in any hymnal that conveys the spirit and understanding of earlier writers and their times.

With all these provisos, texts produced between the fall of Napoleon and the outbreak of the First World War reveal an erosion of precise distinctions between the Persons of the Trinity, somewhat counteracted by High Church and Catholic hymnists, who strove to combat the growing scepticism concerning the biblical accounts of the Creation, the Resurrection, and the Last Judgment.

In a still familiar mission hymn, "Thou whose almighty Word" (1813), the Evangelical John Marriott, no missionary but an absentee rector residing in Devon,[2] distinguishes precisely between the Persons. Whether the "word" of his first line should be uncapitalized so as to refer simply to the divine fiat, or be capitalized and refer to the Son — a quibble best left to theologians — "Let there be light" alludes in successive stanzas to the Creation, the redemptive mission and miracles of Christ, and the Spirit that moved upon the face of the waters. Each time Marriott applies this refrain in the theologically requisite sense, first as a call to mission, second as a transmission of healing to the "sick in mind" and "inly blind," third as a bearing of the "lamp of grace" to "earth's darkest place." Most remarkably, after allegorizing the Persons as "Wisdom, Love" and "Might,"[3] he concludes with an image evidently prompted by English voyages yet virtually identical to that universal flood of faith envisaged by the Odist in the ecstatic dawn of Christianity:

> Boundless as ocean's tide,
> Rolling in fullest pride,
> Through the earth, far and wide
> Let there be light.

For what other reasons British missionaries penetrated every continent during the nineteenth century is for the historian to say. Here we need remark only the precision and confidence of doctrine and allusion.

For liturgical reasons Bishop Heber does not distinguish between the Persons, but his opening, "Holy! holy! holy!," a quotation from the angelic hymn in Revelation[4] (itself an allusion to Isaiah 6.2-3) shows that he has in mind the Redemption and Beautific Vision in which the distinction between Creator, Redeemer, and Sanctifier has no further meaning.

These two hymns, in their imaginative content, frame the mission of Christ and His disciples by describing the Creation and final Vision. With equal assurance and precision, Bishop Mant's "Bright the vision that delighted" (1837), relates the text in Isaiah and the angelic chorus to the present adoration. By "Earth is with its fulness stored," he also, perhaps, alludes to the success of missionaries. In 1870 the Broad Church hymnist John Ellerton can rejoice that the "voice of praise dies ne'er away," but in retrospect his title "The day Thou gavest, Lord, has ended" reads like an ironic prediction of the decline of his church and nation during the twentieth century.

Of the nineteenth, as Horton Davies remarks, hymns were a "spiritual barometer" recording its "stormy weather ... grateful lulls" and the "falling of the gentle rains of mysticism on the aridities of doubt, and the rarer sunshine of Revelation."[5] In the same memorable passage, he associates hymns by Newman ("Lead, kindly Light"), Lyte ("Abide with me"), Faber, Palgrave, and Jean Ingelow, representing the spectrum of belief from Roman Catholic to (liberal) Congregational, as sounding "unmistakable modern notes of a faith won through conflict and a wistful longing for fuller light." For various reasons, virtually all his examples came into use in the mid-Victorian era. "Lead, kindly Light" (1833) had to wait until 1861 for a singable tune. "Through the night of doubt and sorrow," its Danish text by ironic coincidence composed in the year of the *Origin of Species* (1859), was translated in 1867 by the author of the triumphal "Onward, Christian soldiers."[6] "Abide with me" (1847) appeared in 1850 (but acquired its best-known tune in 1861),[7] and Faber's hymns in 1854.[8] Even the exultant hymn "Eternal Light" by the famous Congregational minister Thomas Binney, composed in 1826, came into circulation only in 1855.[9]

Like Newman, the author of "Through the night of doubt and sorrow" applies the typology of the Exodus, but collectively and without nostalgia. Orthodox in transposing the Promised Land to the "far eternal shore," he shows himself almost humanist in focusing upon the "ransomed people" who stride forward clasping hands in brotherhood. This sense of common struggle, as compared with the individualistic use of the same biblical archetype in "Guide me, O thou great Jehovah" and even "Lead, kindly Light," is only one indication of sociological change between the onset of the Industrial Revolution that was to fragment ancient communities and dissever town from country, class from class, and family from clan,[10] and the middle nineteenth century when the theories of utilitarians, together with the endeavours of Christian leaders to implement the Gospel in the social sphere, were again beginning to induce collective modes of thinking and feeling. Ingemann and Baring-Gould take the principle of Christ Applied far beyond Wesley in urging "pilgrim brothers" to journey with the Cross as "aid," and "fight its battle" until the "great awakening." Thanks to Routley's provision of parallel Danish and English texts, we can observe that Baring-Gould omits allusions to Golgotha from the lines on the Cross and to Paradise from the concluding line, which he renders anticlimactically as the "end of toil and gloom." Having also omitted the name "Jesu Christ" from the previous stanza, he to this extent strengthens the pelagian flavour of militant activism, characteristic of his ruling class ethos, by transposing the text from the mythic to the humanist key.

In his "Eternal Light," Binney translates theology into the language of physics by representing the Deity in a strain of solar imagery more explicit and consistent than that of "Abide with me."[11]

> Eternal Light! Eternal Light!
> How pure the soul must be,

> When, placed within thy searching sight,
> It shrinks not, but with calm delight
> Can live, and look on thee.

Though a "spirit" round the Throne can bear this "burning bliss," man in his natural darkness can bear it only if aided by "A Holy Spirit's energies, / An Advocate with God." Thus opaquely these lines denote the Son who with the Spirit prepares us "sons of ignorance and night" to dwell in "eternal light" through "eternal love."

For all Mrs. Alexander's assertive orthodoxy, in her rapidly composed version of "St. Patrick's Breastplate" (1889), she naturalizes her Old Irish text no less than Baring-Gould his modern Danish, but in a different way. In adapting the legend of St. Patrick daring a pagan king to extinguish the Holy Saturday fire, she turns a magic spell into a hymn for the baptisms that by ancient custom were performed on that day. As compared with a more literal translation by the Celtic Scholar R.A.S. Macalister (1927),[12] her version further specifies the Incarnation, Baptism, and Resurrection of Christ. In Tractarian vogue she describes saints as "virgin souls," but above all depicts concretely the "star-lit heaven," sun, "whiteness" of the moon, lightning flash, wind and "salt sea" round "old eternal rocks," whereas Macalister alludes in general terms to the elements as joining in the Saint's adoration along with seraphs, prophets and saints above. Mrs. Alexander, in other words, particularizes and separates the natural elements that the Old Irish poet had integrated with the supernatural events.

Elsewhere she translates the images and personal acts of God into moral terms, for where Macalister says,

> To-day I arise
> With God my steersman, stay and guide,
> To guard, to counsel, to hear, to bide
> His way before, his hosts beside.

she writes,

> The wisdom of my God to teach,
> His hand to guide, his shield to ward;
> The word of God to give me speech,
> His heavenly host to be my guard.

As in a manner she fragments the figure of God, so she depersonalizes and explains the "demon crew" and the Saint's "lusts," in: "Against the demon snares of sin, / The vice that gives temptation force, / The natural lusts that war within" and later expounds "Satan's spells and wiles" as "false words of heresy," "knowledge that defiles," and "the heart's idolatry." In no way does she excise the magical elements, but presents them in the language of historical romance, as the "wizard's evil craft," the "death-wound," and "poisoned shaft." After expanding an invocation of Christ she replaces the conclusion (quoted as an epigraph to this chapter) by formally naming the three Persons and asserting that salvation is of Christ. She asserts the truth of the Myth, yet in some measure undercuts her assertion by representing its figures in the language of morality and romance. Like Newman's "Firmly I believe and truly,"[13] "St. Patrick's Breastplate," magnificent as it is, has won the love of High Church devotees and hymnologists, rather than of churchgoers at large.

Some twenty years later, W.H. Draper, composer of several patriotic hymns to be noticed in the subsequent book, fashioned from the "Canticle to the Sun" of St. Francis the much-loved "All creatures of our God and King." While everyone knows St. Francis to have revered beasts, birds, and the elements as fellow creatures, Matthew Arnold's more literal translation shows him to have addressed his Canticle to God, praised separately for each element.[14] Fundamentally, his Canticle is held together by a characteristically medieval anthropocentrism. The sun exists to give light and signify God to man, wind and weather to support life of all kinds, our humble, clean "sister water" to serve us, "brother fire" to give light in darkness, "mother earth" to sustain us with her fruit.

Draper's "All creatures …," usually sung without its stanzas on "mother earth," on the forgiving and sorrowful who praise God, and on death that leads home the "child of God,"[15] lacks this coherence inherent in the medieval world picture. As sung, it calls upon sun, moon, wind, clouds, and water to praise God but fails to link them with human life and worship. Even if sung, its stanza (No. 4) on the "blessings" unfolded by earth never directly acknowledges our dependence. By contrast, the Canticle of the Sun goes beyond its source, the Benedicite, in binding God, man and the cosmos together in an order both anthropocentric and grounded in the Myth, as in Arnold's rendering of its conclusion:

> Blessed are they who peaceably shall endure:
> For thou O most Highest shalt give them a crown.
> Praised be my Lord for our sister the death of the body:
> Blessed are they who are found walking by thy most holy will.
> Praise ye and bless ye the Lord and give thanks unto him:
> And serve him with great humility.

For all its invigorating tune, "Lasst uns er freuen," Draper's version makes a nowadays artificial appeal to the elements to participate in our chorus of praise while failing to unify them as did the respective lyrics by St. Francis, Prudentius, and Fortunatus. Like Mrs. Alexander's translation, it exemplifies a propensity to find value in the natural elements in separation from the Myth and the medieval cosmos.

A further characteristic of nineteenth-century nature hymns can be illustrated from a brief comparison of the American text "Lord of all being, throned afar"[16] (1859) with the now very popular "Beim frühen Morgenlicht" ("When morning gilds the skies"), translated about the same time.[17] In successive stanzas, the Unitarian Oliver Wendell Holmes develops the solar image of God, whose "glory flames from sun and star," whose "smile withdrawn" is "midnight," whose light and warmth are truth and love, whose rainbow signifies mercy, and whom the poet finds everywhere save in "clouds of sin." By contrast, the German Catholic's worship of Christ absorbs his life and permeates his whole environment.

Many English hymnists of the latter nineteenth century who were by no means Unitarian chose to represent God without distinction of Persons, as "Lord" or even "Father." Their congregations, of course, went on singing "Abide with me," with its suppressed solar image of Christ, and the more explicit "Sun of my soul, thou Saviour dear," once universally popular and now in total eclipse. In the latter, Keble blends this ancient image of the Son with a modern concern for the social implications of His teaching, in "Watch by the sick; enrich the poor." The editors having trimmed away the opening "'Tis gone, that bright and orbed gaze," with other lyric verses,[18] those sung as a hymn inevitably had that flavour of wistful reverie noted by Horton Davies. But late Victorians also sang in school "Lord, behold us with thy blessing," at night "The day thou gavest, Lord, is ended," in time of grief "The Lord's my Shepherd, I'll not want," in time of joy "The King of love my Shepherd is" or "Praise, my soul, the King of heaven," in harvest-time "We plough the fields and scatter," in time of stress "Be thou my guardian and my guide," and increasingly in time of conflict "Mine eyes have seen the glory of the coming of the Lord." The popularity of these texts is significant in view of the appearance, about the turn of the century, of Kipling's "Recessional," Scott Holland's "Judge eternal, throned in splendour" (1902), and Chesterton's "O God of earth and altar" (1906),[19] in all of which a God not distinguished by Person confronts the pride and social injustice of Britain, as of ancient Israel. Even Chesterton's text, the most disputable in this sense, does not extend the distinction between Creator and eucharistic Victim beyond the first line. Though these are but the most explicit in a long line of "radical" hymns, to which Horton Davies adduces American parallels,[20] their appearance when hymnists were disposed to find God in Nature points to a convergence of the triune into a single deity. The plethora of nature lyrics that cluttered up late Victorian children's hymnals, of which "All things bright and beautiful" and "Summer suns are glowing" are the pick, was a further symptom of an increasingly generalized awareness of God.[21] As Lord of a "far-flung battle-line," God more resembles the figure of Israel's Shepherd and Defender than that of Christ Crucified.

The texts by Holland and Chesterton came not from heretics but from deeply orthodox Anglicans. Yet these and the nature hymns suggest that the God revered as directing evolution[22] and the life-cycle transcended the human figure of Jesus (no longer Christ enthroned as Judge) who is still carolled to at Christmas and mourned on Good Friday. In consequence of a century-long decline in the doctrinal substance and precision of hymns, the God who presided over the natural world, society, and the national destiny became less and less identifiable with Jesus the hero figure of youth, whose wayside crucifixes struck a sympathetic chord in the hearts of soldier poets like Wilfred Owen.[23] Almighty as He remained within the context of church or public school chapel, Christ diminished into a more human yet more limited figure, loved yet no longer approached in fear and trembling.

At the outset of this voyage across the ocean of Christian history, snatches of song reached us in an unknown tongue,[24] soon to be drowned by the swelling chant of psalm and hymn in Latin and Greek. Nearer our own coast, we hear no sound but the chanting of psalms, more often in limping verse then in the stately prose rhythms of Cranmer. As our shoreline grows more distinct, we strain to follow the surging chorales occasionally wafted from the opposite coast. After the ship veers inshore, English hymns ring out, often in raucous refrain. More and more of these we recognize yet find alien in their abject and penitential tone, their insistence that our home port lies not here but beyond a river across which a blood-stained pilot must ferry us at his own expense. Having rounded a headland lit with flashes from musket and cannon, our ship glides into a bay lined with smoky towns whence echoes song after song we remember from our schooldays. If sometimes quaintly put, the substance of many rendered from the ancient tongues recalls the opening of Cranmer's Litany, so rarely heard today:

> O God the Father of Heaven, have mercy upon us miserable sinners.
> O God the Son, Redeemer of the word, have mercy upon us miserable sinners . . .
> By the mystery of thy holy Incarnation; by thy holy Nativity and Circumcision; by thy Baptism, Fasting and Temptation. . . .
> By thine Agony and bloody Sweat; by thy Cross and Passion; by thy glorious Resurrection and Ascension; and by the coming of the holy Ghost,
> Good Lord, deliver us.[25]

Others, composed in our own tongue, tell of our home across the river.

As the ship slows, we must strain to pick out the ethereal plainchant of Latin and the four-part harmony of English hymns from the deep-voiced refrains of field slaves, the marching songs of soldiers, and the unctuous trebles of children. No longer can we discern the Persons or events listed in the Litany, for most choruses describe a nocturnal journey, the churches or, above all, the Landlord who owns them, indeed all these towns and surrounding villages. Ignoring the gunfire and fumes that drift on the chill wind from the next two headlands, from the ship we must soon desert, we listen to three songs with sweetly mournful tunes that speak of our elusive Landlord and hopeful yet uncertain prospect.

From a stadium in the largest town, unpractised male voices sing "Abide with me," but to what purpose? Why sing "In life, in death, O lord" before a soccer match? Do the singers blindly follow some folk ritual, or do they grope after some lost transcendence and certitude their world cannot give?

From a church or school sounds a purer, if thinner chorus:

> Lord, thy Word abideth,
> And our footsteps guideth;
> Who its truth believeth
> Light and joy receiveth.[26]

Agog for news of the Landlord and our future path, we listen intently but in vain, for the song speaks only of his Word's effect, "succour to the dying" or "comfort to the living." Yet the singers seem to understand its "message of salvation," presumably because they hear Bible readings.

Though not always to the same tune, there resounds from church or home the plea "Lead, kindly Light." Do the singers understand the purpose of their journey? The title given out clearly refers to that journey through the desert to a promised land, described in the Bible. Have they this in mind, or the aforesaid river crossing, or does each need light for his own journey out of this smoky town, or to some fulfilment or higher status within it? No doubt some wander backward in a circle while intending to march forward.

Such popular hymns no longer spelt out the unambiguous message of "Guide me, O thou great Jehovah," or "Rock of Ages." What has without prejudice to its truth been called the "Myth" of Creation, Christ Incarnate, Crucified, and Risen and the descent of the Holy Spirit, whether objectively narrated or applied to the inner and social life, had ceased to form the major theme in most new hymns possessing both poetic quality and wide appeal. Firmly as the older texts remained entrenched in the hymnals and in popular consciousness, they had been joined by Victorian lyrics portraying God in simpler, more general terms, and the spiritual life in the secular images of home, harvest, work, or conquest. With exceptions, "For all the saints," or "Praise to the Holiest," those relating some portion of the Myth would, like the carols, enshrine the Victorian cult of childhood and home, or describe like spirituals that journey to a Promised Land so meaningful to slaves, or like the gospel hymns of Sankey and Bliss (a spiritual equivalent to the tabloid press) that vicarious suffering which could alone deliver the semi-literate poor or lower middle class from the sweatshops and offices of Chicago, or from the river towns visited by Huckleberry Finn. The Myth entire, Fall, Last Judgment, and hellfire included, thus retreated to the margins of hymnody, while in England at least, obsessive concern with the Atonement became limited to the fringe that worshipped in Salvation Army citadels or Primitive Methodist chapels. A more central role in the formation of social harmony has recently been claimed for the gospel hymn in the United States.[27]

Whether one holds this decentralization of the Myth to portend the demise of the Christian religion or its true implementation depends upon one's belief and commitment. The Unitarian James Martineau was cited at the beginning of this book as holding that a "Christian mythology" had intruded upon the "faith of Christendom," which presumably was the continuing encounter with God recorded by prophets and poets in all ages. An even more radical theologian of our own day, John Hick, considers that the idea of divine incarnation as an "essentially poetic expression of the Christian's devotion to his Lord"; that when turned into a doctrine, so that a metaphorical son of God became a metaphysical God the Son, "poisoned the relationships between Christians . . . Jews . . . and Muslims" and led to a "Christian imperialism" in colonial territories. As a metaphor, "incarnational language" expresses a discipleship to Jesus as the "Lord" whom we follow and "Saviour" who "has initiated our eventual transformation into perfect children of God."[28] At the opposite extreme, Karl Barth says that only Christianity has the "authority and commission" as the "one true religion" to "invite and challenge" all non-Christians to "start on the Christian way."[29] Less abrasively, C.S. Lewis describes the Myth as historically true and warranted to outlive all its liberal perversions. Northrop Frye, who, however, finds myth "inseparable from things to be done or specified actions," and so the cause or result of events in time, regards the Myth as having for two millenia encapsulated and conditioned the peoples of Christendom.[30] Marx condemned it and all forms of religion as an opiate that by proffering a false hope and consolation distracted the masses from the organized betterment of their lot.

No hymnologist, as such, can confirm or refute a theologian's case, be it conservative or liberal. Whether by charting an evolution of the Myth in Christian hymns of many centuries I have confirmed the view of Frye depends upon the soundness of his contention that the Gospels contain the only evidence of the sayings, deeds, or even existence of Jesus. Theologians have always agreed with St. Augustine that "as the Old Testament is manifested in the New, so the New Testament is latent in the Old." The question of extra-biblical testimony, like Frye's philosophical presumption that the outer world of natural and historical events can be separated from the inner world of religious experience, is beyond my scope.

Even the considerable evidence in this study of Christian hymnody for the anthropological or psychoanalytic postulates of an Eliade or Freud neither confirms nor refutes the Christian Creeds,[31] for Christian poets naturally reflect their own compulsions or the orientation of their surrounding culture toward a remote or familiar, a male or female object of worship, unless by ecclesiastical authority confined to the admitted corrective of scriptural paraphrase.

Hymnology can, I believe, shed light in three ways upon the future of Christianity and its relations with Marxism. Denominational and school hymnals, supplemented by the findings of social historians, can show to what degree hymns inculcated forms of class conditioning, especially if the hymnologist can determine which items in a collection were most used. Second, hymnology can show whether, as conservative theologians contend, idolatries rush to fill the spiritual vacuum in a society that abandons orthodox devotion. Contrariwise, the internalization of the Myth in the hymns of Wesley may represent not a decline but an upward evolution of Christian consciousness, a sallying forth of the Christian ethic from the monastery or Puritan family to transform the world of the unlettered masses into the Kingdom of God. To the Evangelicals who secured the abolition of slavery and played their part in improving domestic and working class life, the Myth proved less a distraction than an incentive. The pessimist, on the other hand, regards the decline of objective religion as denoting an emptying of spiritual content and energy from modern society. The Victorian poet James Thomson spoke of his "proud, strong age, fast losing all / Earth has of heaven."[32] Eliot's *Waste Land* suggests a further deterioration in the quality of life.

To investigate these hypotheses, we must desert the mainstream of "classic" hymns for the long discarded hymnals of denominations and schools, buttressing their evidence with surveys, by computer and "by hand," designed to yield not certainty, but something more than conjecture, as to the hymns most used at given times and in given segments of society. To what extent English society made God in its own image must form the subject of a further volume.

It is no mean tribute to the innumerable poets who over almost two millenia have expressed in song the central beliefs of the Christian faith, that their accumulated handiwork, though of "mere human composure," has at different times inspired believers of every tribe, rank, and avocation, playing a major part in the Lutheran, Methodist and Evangelical, Abolitionist, and Ecumenical movements, and in no small measure keeping alive during the nineteenth and early twentieth centuries beliefs that scientists, scholars, and even theologians were on every side forsaking.

APPENDIX

As funds did not permit computer programming, forty texts addressed to God as Father or Son were analyzed according to percentage of lines containing images or figures of speech in the following classes:

1. *God*: (a) royalty, (b) rank (e.g., "Lord"), (c) power, (d) terror, awe, (e) providence, benignity, (f) order (vs. chaos), (g) abstraction (e.g., Creator). (A category (h) "healer" did not give sufficient data.)
2. *Pastoral care*: (a) of Father, (b) of Son.
3. *Nature*, in mythic sense (paradise, garden, pasture).
4. *Love*.
5. *Light*: (a) vs. dark, (b) Sun, (c) Fire, flame.
6. *Blood*: (a) suffering, (b) death of Christ.
7. *Water* (river, flood, etc.).
8. *Military*: (a) applied to God (e.g., rod, sword), (b i) to worshipper generally, (b ii) to missionary.
9. *Nature*, literally: (a) agriculture, (b) forest, (c) mountain, rock, (d) seasons, (e) sun, moon, etc.
10. *Existence* (birth, death, etc.).
11. *Childhood*: (a) divine, (b) human, e.g., littleness, helplessness.

Hymns to God the Spirit were not included, as insufficient were composed in some periods to provide data. A score of 5% (one image in twenty lines) was deemed significant and recorded.

Periods were: A. Pre-1700; B. 1700-1730; C. 1730-60; D. 1760-90; E. 1790-1830; F. 1830-60; G. 1860-1920 (a division of last period impracticable owing to small numbers of relevant texts 1860-90).

In the accompanying tables, brief titles indicate the following hymns:

A. All people that on earth do dwell.
    How shall I sing that majesty . . .
    Awake, my soul, and with the sun . . .
    As pants the hart for cooling streams
    My song is love unknown.

B. When all thy mercies, O my God.
    Our God, our help in ages past.
    The Lord Jehovah reigns
    When I survey the wondrous Cross . . .

C. O God of Bethel, by whose hand
    Guide me, O thou great Jehovah
    Lo he comes with clouds descending
    Jesu, Lover of my soul
    Christ, whose glory fills the skies
    Love Divine, all loves excelling
    Rejoice, the Lord is King

D. Amazing Grace
    God moves in a mysterious way
    Hark, my soul! it is the Lord
    There is a fountain filled with blood
    How sweet the Name of Jesus sounds

E. Holy! holy! holy! Lord God Almighty
    New every morning is the love
    Father of Heaven, whose love profound
    Thou whose almighty Word
    Lead us, heavenly Father, lead us
    The Head that once was crowned with thorns
    Ride on! ride on in majesty

F. O worship the King
    Praise, my soul, the King of Heaven
    Abide with me
    Lead, Kindly Light
    'Take up thy cross!' the Saviour said
    There is a green hill far away

G. Eternal Father, strong to save
  All creatures of our God and King
  God of our fathers, known of old
  O God of earth and altar
  Judge Eternal, throned in splendour

The exaggeration due to recording only scores of 5% and up throws into relief a tendency indicated by figures in Table 1, as summarized in Table 2.

The figures in Table 2 result from dividing the totals in each column containing more than one figure by the number of figures entered. The starred (*) figures indicate a column with three or more figures. The inference warranted by the starred averages is that the awareness of God's sovereignty, power, powerfulness, and providential order reached a peak during the decade or so that followed the end of the Napoleonic Wars. To judge from this small sample, the awareness of God varied inversely with the economic fortunes of the nation, so that the images of divine providence declined in texts written during the prosperous late Victorian and Edwardian eras. A full computer search of a larger sample would furnish more reliable data.

TABLE 1

TITLE	1						2			3	4		5			6		7	8		9					10		11	
	a	b	c	d	e	f	g	a	b		a	b	a	b	c	a	b	a	b(i)	b(ii)	a	b	c	d	e	a	b	a	b
A																													
All people	18	6	6	-	6	6	-																						
How shall	12										12		9	9				9											
Awake my	12									6	9		6					8	8										
As pants the							7			6																			
My song	10				8											5		10											
B																													
When all			6		6	31				8																			15
Our God our					29								16					8							8				
The Lord	16		8		12	12										20	25	5											
When I survey	10	5	5		15																								
Behold the					18		6			6			6			31	25												
C																													
O God of																													
Bethel			5		20			15										11	11							5		5	
Guide me	5	25	5	10				16								12	10	12											
Lo! he comes							-																						
Jesu, Lover					18																								
Christ, whose			5							6			28	28	-			8											
Love Divine	8	8		8	8			16																					
Rejoice	8	28																											9

D											
Amazing											
Grace											
God moves	16		29								
Hark my soul	8		25	16							
There is a		10		7		14	21				7
How sweet		14	25	21							
E											
Holy! holy!	12 12 31		18	12		6					
New every			25								
Father of all	6 25 25		31	18		35	12				
Thou whose	-	10	10 10	10			7				
Lead us		5		16 5	6		5	5			5
The Head that	33		44 5	16	5	8	12 5	5			
Ride on	40 5	5	12				25	15			
F											
O worship	-	10 10 14		-		6	6	6			
Praise my soul	- 10		13								
Abide with me	12 -	- 25	-	6		9 9	6	6			
Lead, kindly	-	5 - 16			27	11 11			- - 5 - 5	
Take up thy											
Cross	- - 8	- 8	-	-			28 20			12	
...Green hill	5 -	- 5	-	-			25		- - 5 - 5		
G											
Eternal Father	- - 25	- 16 12		8			12	12			
All creatures				13						13	10
God of our	16 -	- 6 6	-							12	
O God of earth		8 12									
Judge Eternal	16 27	- 5 11 11				5	5 5		- 5 - -		

TABLE 2

TITLE	1							2		3	4	5		6			7	8			9					10	11
	a	b	c	d	e	f	g	a	b			a	b	c	a	b		a	b(i)	b(ii)	a	b	c	d	e	a	b
A (to 1700)	13*	-	-	-	7*	-	-					10.5	7.5														
B (1700-30)		10.5	6.33*	9	21*					1	1			25.5	25												
C (1730-60)	7*	16.5*	5*		11.2*					17							11.5	9.5									
D (1760-90)	12	12			23.75*	14				8																9.5	
E (1790-1830)	9	23*	14.2*		28*	14*					16.33*			7.33	18.5			10									
F (1830-60)	8.5	6.5			16.2*						8.66*		10			26.5		6			-	-	5	-	-		-10.5
G (1860-1920)	16		6.33*	11.25*	11.5	10.5												8.5									

ABBREVIATIONS

Unless the page is given, all figures in references to hymn collections indicate the hymn number.

AH   Guido Maria Dreves, *et al.*, *Analectica Hymnica Medii Aevi* (Leipzig: Altenburg, 1886-1922, 55 vols.). Reference indicates volume and hymn number.

AM   *Hymns Ancient and Modern*. (London: Clowes). Date follow‑ ing refers to the edition.

AMR   *Hymns Ancient and Modern Revised* (Rev. ed., 1950)

AV   *Authorized Version* (King James Bible)

BCP   *Book of Common Prayer*

Breviary   *The Hours of Divine Office* (Collegeville, Minn.: Liturgical Press, 1963)

Class and Idol   Lionel Adey, *Class and Idol in the English Hymn* (sequel to this volume, projected title)

Coll. P.   John Wesley, *A Collection of Hymns for the Use of People Called Methodists*, Vol. 7 in *Works of John Wesley*, ed. Franz Hildebrandt and Oliver A. Breckerlegge (Oxford: Clarendon Press, 1983)

Coll. P. (1830)   *A Collection of Hymns for ... People Called Methodists, with a Supplement* (London: Wesleyan Conference Office, 1830)

EH   *English Hymnal* (London: Oxford University Press, 1906)

HG   Erik Routley, *An English-Speaking Hymnal Guide* (College‑ ville, Minn.: Liturgical Press, 1979). Figure following *HG* re‑ fers to number of entry.

HSBI	Hymn Society of Great Britain and Ireland *Bulletin*
Julian	John Julian (ed.), *A Dictionary of Hymnology* (2nd ed., 1907, rpt, New York: Dover Publications, 1957). i or ii refers to column on page, e.g., 365 i, page 365, left column.
OH	John Newton, William Cowper, *Olney Hymns* (Olney, 1779); edition used, Edinburgh: Ritchie, 1854
PCH	Erik Routley, *A Panorama of Christian Hymnody* (Collegeville, Minn.: Liturgical Press, 1979)
PMLA	*Publications of Modern Language Association*
Ps.	Psalm
Watts, *Hymns*	Isaac Watts, *Hymns and Spiritual Songs* (London, 1707, 1709, 3 vols.)
Watts, *Psalms*	Isaac Watts, *Psalms of David Imitated* (London, 1719)
Watts, *Works*	*Works of the Reverend and Learned Isaac Watts, D.D.*, ed. George Burder (London: J. Barfield, 1810, 6 vols.)

NOTES

NOTES TO PREFACE

1. Matthew Arnold, "The Study of Poetry" (introduction to T.H. Ward, *The English Poets* (1880)) reprinted in *Essays in Criticism*, 2nd series (London: Macmillan, 1888), pp. 2-3.
2. Joan Brothers, *Religious Institutions* (London: Longmans, 1971), p. 34; Owen Chadwick, in *The Victorian Church* (London: A. & C. Black, 1966), Vol. I, pp. 363-68, gives totals as Anglican 5,292,551; Roman Catholic 383,630, and Nonconformist 4,536,264, a total attendance of 10,212,415, from which census compilers deducted 3,000,000 as presumed children. See also Horton Davies, *Worship and Theology in England* (Princeton: Princeton University Press, 1961-75), Vol. IV, pp. 71-72.

NOTES TO CHAPTER ONE

1. Anna Laetitia Waring, "Father, I know that all my life" (1850). See Julian 367 ii.
2. L.E. Elliott-Binns, *Religion in the Victorian Era* (London: Lutterworth Press, 1946), p. 374.
3. R.W. Dale (comp.), *The English Hymn Book* (London: Hamilton, Adams, 1874), preface, cited by Elliott-Binns, *loc. cit.;* John Mason Neale, article in *Christian Re-*

membrancer (1849), cited in J.V. Higginson, "John Mason Neale and Nineteenth-century Hymnody," *The Hymn* 16 (1965): 101-17.
4. David Martin, *A Sociology of English Religion* (London: SCM Press, 1966), p. 88; also Erik Routley, *Hymns and Human Life* (London: Murray, 2nd ed., 1959), pp. 288-89.
5. Jonathan Gathorne-Hardy, *The Public-School Phenomenon, 597-1977* (Harmondsworth: Penguin, 1979), p. 144: "the splendid hymns of the Church of England, collected together in *Hymns Ancient and Modern*," e.g., "Jesus, Lover of my soul," "God moves in a mysterious way," and "Rock of Ages."
6. For Pauline references, see epigraph to Chapter 2. On distinction between three kinds, see Egon Wellesz, *A History of Byzantine Music and Hymnography* (Oxford: Clarendon, 1961), pp. 33 and 41, where St. Augustine is cited for spiritual songs as wordless expressions of joy, e.g., Alleluia.
   After writing, I saw a similar but fuller explanation of "myth" in Martha Winburn England and John Sparrow, *Hymns Unbidden: Donne, Herbert, Blake, Emily Dickinson and the Hymnographers* (New York: New York Public Library, 1966), p. 44 n2: "narrative sequence, *mythos,* as contrasted with image, symbol, doctrine . . . to emphasize . . . the classic Christian interpre-

tation of the Bible as essentially one story.
. . ."

7. Northrop Frye, *The Great Code: The Bible and Literature* (New York: Harcourt, Brace, Jovanovich, 1982), pp. 32, 39-40, 42.

8. C.S. Lewis, *God in the Dock: Essays on Theology and Ethics,* ed. Walter Hooper (Grand Rapids, MI.: Eerdmans, 1970), pp. 67-68.

9. *PCH* 155, with translation by R.F. Davis (1905), after Neale. For versions and hymnal reprints, see *HG* 843.

10. See Wellesz, p. 147.

11. Originally 14 Odes. Texts and translations in Wellesz, pp. 208-13, 223-28, listed on pp. 37-38 as:
   (i) Song of Moses at Red Sea (Exodus 15.1-19)
   (ii) — before death (Deuteronomy 32.1-43)
   (iii) Prayer of Hannah (1 Sam. 2.1-10)
   (iv) — Isaiah (Isa. 26.9-19)
   (v) — Jonah (Jon. 2.3-10)
   (vi) — Habbakuk (Hab. 3.2-19)
   (vii) — Hezekiah (Isa. 38.10-20)
   (viii) — Manasses (Apocrypha)
   (ix) — Azariah (Daniel 3.26-45)
   (x) Song of Three Children (Dan. 3.52-88), in Apocrypha
   (xi) — Mary (Luke 1.46-55)
   (xii) — Simeon (Lk. 2.29-32)
   (xiii) — Zacharias (Lk. 2.29-32)
   (xiv) Morning Hymn, "Doxa en hypistois Theo" Δόξα ἐν ὑπίστοις Θεῷ

12. Ruth Ellis Messenger, *Ethical Teachings in the Latin Hymns of Medieval England* (New York: Columbia University Press, 1930), *passim.*

13. *Coll. P.,* preface.

14. James Martineau (ed.), *Hymns of Praise and Prayer* (London: Longmans, 1874), preface, pp. vi-viii, cites main incidents of Exodus and "courts of Zion" as "emblems of the pilgrimage of man and providence of God"; the baptism, temptations, transfiguration, sea miracles, crucifixion, and ascension of Christ as "notwithstanding inequalities in their historical accuracy" painting the "crises" and "victory" of the inward life. Compilers of *Essex Hall Hymnal* (London: British & Foreign Unitarian Association, 1891, rev. 1902) say in preface that Martineau went too far.

15. Arnold, *op. cit.,* prefatory self-quotation: "Our religion has materialized itself in the . . . supposed fact . . . has attached its emotion to the fact, and now the fact is

failing it. But for poetry the idea is the fact. . . . Poetry attaches its emotion to the idea. The strongest part of our religion today is its unconscious poetry."

16. E.g., Dickens, *Oliver Twist, Bleak House;* Emily Brontë, *Wuthering Heights.* Appropriate hymns to be discussed in *Class and Idol,* Chapters 3, 4, 8, 9.

17. *Class and Idol,* Chapters 1 and 3.

18. Earliest known citation by St. Basil (4th century), but as already well known. Believed used in catacombs, but "Probably safe to say . . . known in 2nd century" (*HG* 869).

19. St. Augustine, *Ennaratio in Ps. 72:* "Hymni laudes sunt Dei, cum cantico; hymni cantus sunt continentes laudem Dei. Si sit laus, et non sit Dei, non est hymnus: si sit laus, et Dei laus, et non cantetur, non est hymnus. Oportet ergo ut, si sit hymnus, habeat haec tria: et laudem, et Dei, et canticum." Section 1, *Corpus Christianorum Series Latina* (Tournai, 1956), Vol. XXXIX, p. 986. Cf. commentary on Ps. 148, where author repeats definition, adding: "Accipiant sancti eius hymnum, dicant sancti eius hymnum; quia hoc est quod accepturi sunt in fine, hymnum sempiternum" (Section 17, Vol. XI, pp. 2176-77).

   Since first writing this chapter I have seen Geoffrey Wainwright's excellent discussion of this definition in *Doxology: The Praise of God in Worship, Doctrine and Life* (London: Epworth Press, 1980), pp. 198-200, in which all hymns not addressed to God (in either the second or third person) are regarded as "idolatrous." I mainly concur, but would except those concerning the singer's devotion to God.

20. Listed fully in *Class and Idol,* Chapter 5, but (briefly) about 1. Father, 2. Son, 3. Spirit, 4. devotion, 5. mission, 6. spiritual warfare, 7. pilgrimage, 8. death, 9. heaven, 10. worship and the Church, 11. morning and evening, 12. nature or the seasons, 13. the Christian ethic, 14. the Bible, 15. the nation.

21. William James, *The Varieties of Religious Experience,* Gifford Lectures, 1901-2 (New York: Random House, n.d.), pp. 159-60, 477-78.

22. Alan Wilkinson, *The Church of England and the First World War* (London: SPCK, 1978), pp. 153, 218-19.

23. Augustus M. Toplady, in *Gospel Magazine*

(October 1775), in article on "Life's Journey," with maxim "Make these words of the Apostle your motto: 'Perplexed, but not in despair; cast down, but not destroyed'" (*HG* 623). Reprinted in issue of March 1776, at end of article "Questions and Answers Relative to the National Debt," a calculus of sins in financial terms given in *HG*, pp. 113-14. On legend of composition in cave at Blagdon, Somerset, see E.J. Fasham, "Rock of Ages," *HSBI* IV (1957): 76-82. All hymnals have "demands" for "commands" (*PCH* 80).

24. On light in darkness, see Davies, *Worship and Theology*, IV, 206-7.

25. "The Church and Garden of Christ," quoted and discussed in Donald Davie, *A Gathered Church: The Literature of the English Dissenting Interest, 1700-1930* (London: Routledge & Kegan Paul, 1978), pp. 28-30. "Jesus shall reign . . ." after Ps. 72, Part II, in Watts, *Psalms*. As Dr. Hobbs notes, this verse describes in present tense the "happy state of the present kingdom of Christ."

26. On "Dies irae, dies illa," attributed to Thomas of Celano, *c*. 1270, see *HG* 846; on Joseph Addison, "When rising. . . ." (1712), see Julian 17 ii; "Hora novissima," attributed to Bernard of Morlaix, note in *HG* 851 and parallel text *PCH* 162; "There's a beautiful land" discussed in *Class and Idol*, Chapter 9; James Montgomery, "Palms of glory, raiment bright" (1829, for Sunday school, Julian 878 i); on S.J. Stone, "The Church's one foundation," see *HG* 685; "Come, let us join our cheerful songs" in Watts, *Hymns*, I, 62; on "Saviour, again to thy dear name we raise" and "The day thou gavest, Lord, is ended" by John Ellerton, latter originally in *A Liturgy for Missionary Meetings* (1870), see *HG* 627, 688. On imperial theme of latter see Susan Tamke, *Make a Joyful Noise unto the Lord: Hymns as a Reflection of Victorian Social Attitudes* (Columbus: Ohio University Press, 1978), pp. 131-32. Latterly it has been popular at ecumenical services, as referring to universal spread of the faith.

27. Anne Steele, "Father of mercies, in thy Word" (1760), "Lord, thy Word abideth" and Sir Henry W. Baker (1861), rpts. listed in *HG* 185, 436.

28. C.S. Lewis, *Surprised by Joy* (London: Geoffrey Blès, 1955), p. 206, after Samuel

Alexander, *Space, Time and Deity* (2 vols. London: Macmillan, 1920, rpt. New York: Dover, 1966) Vol. I, p. 12 ff.

29. See E.P. Thompson, *The Making of the English Working Class* (New York: Pantheon Books, 1964), pp. 359-60 and Chapter 11, *passim*.

30. In Davie's account, "a lay, *le chant de la tribu*" (*Gathered Church*, p. 21). Adjudged by Oxford dons "a perfect hymn," according to H.A.L. Jefferson, *Hymns in Christian Worship* (London, 1950), p. 221 (cited in Tamke, pp. 20-21). Earliest use I have found under title "National Hymns" is in *Scottish National Hymnal for the Young* (Edinburgh, 1910), 186.

31. Told me by a member of Hymn Society of Great Britain and Ireland in 1979. Mrs. Alexander's father, Major Humphreys, came from Norfolk (see William Alexander, introduction to *Poems of Cecil Frances Alexander* (London: Macmillan, 1896)).

32. Romans 13.1 and "A Catechism . . . to be learned of every person, before he be confirmed," in *BCP* (1662).

33. "Forth in thy name": *Hymns & Sacred Poems* (1749) under "Believers before Work" (Julian 382-83; *Coll. P.* 315); "When wilt thou save . . ." in Ebenezer Elliott, *More Prose and Verse* (1850). On his Calvinism and Chartism, see *HG* 812. On complex history of "Great God . . . ," see Julian 454-55.

34. Horton Davies, Vol. III, p. 303 cites F.D. Maurice's *Kingdom of Christ* on prayers of early Fathers being more concerned with "nature and plans of God" than those of modern authors, preoccupied with self-analysis and world of nature.

NOTES TO CHAPTER TWO

1. C.F.D. Moule, *The Birth of the New Testament* (London: A. & C. Black, 2nd ed., 1966), pp. 26-27. Wainwright, *Doxology*, p. 211: "*psalmos* can bear a . . . more general meaning . . . improvised or ecstatic or . . . specially composed songs . . . as . . . 1 Cor. 14:26." R.P. Martin, in "New Testament Hymns: Background and Development," *Expository Times* 94 (1983): 132-36, cites M. Hengel for the understanding of *psalmos* in its Jewish sense, hymns

being excluded from hellenistic synagogues as heretical.
2. Wellesz, pp. 33-36. J.A. Smith, "The Ancient Synagogue, the Early Church and Singing," *Music and Letters* 65 (1984): 1-16.
3. Also: "Benedicite," part of "Song of Three Children" (Dan. 3), in use among early Christians; "Benedictus" (Lk. 1.68-79); "Magnificat" (1.46-54); "Nunc Dimittis" (2.29-32); otherwise Psalms 95 ("Venite"), 98 ("Cantate Domino"), 67 ("Deus misereatur"), 100 (Jubilate), and the "Te Deum." See Martin, "New Testament Hymns."
4. Wellesz, p. 40, regards proscription as total in Eastern churches from the Council of Laodicea (A.D. 361), but Wainwright, p. 200, limits it to "for some time after the middle . . . third century an attempt . . . to suppress all 'modern compositions' and limit singing to the biblical canticles."
5. Wellesz, p. 41.
6. See Frye, pp. 79, 95, 135-38, but cf. Christ's self-description in John 10.11-16, with Matt. 9.36, Mk. 6.34 and O.T. analogues, e.g., Numbers 27.17, 2 Chron. 18.16, Isa. 40.11, Ezek. 34.12, 23.
7. In "Lead us . . ." "we have no help but thee" differs from Ps. 3.2 (*BCP* and *AV*) in which many say "no help" for speaker "in God." Cf. also Herbert, "The God of love my Shepherd is"; Scottish Psalter, "The Lord's my Shepherd: I'll not want"; Addison, "The Lord my Pasture shall prepare"; Baker, "The King of love my Shepherd is."
8. Charles Wesley, *Hymns and Spiritual Songs Intended for the Use of Real Christians of All Denominations* 1753 (London: Strahan, 1753, 1762 ed.), 453 (a selection from *Hymns and Sacred Poems* (1739, 1740, 1742) issued first anon., then as by John Wesley, then by John and Charles Wesley).
9. Singing of Ps. 124 in Routley, *Hymns and Human Life,* pp. 383-84. Wainwright, pp. 211-12, lists for Lauds Ps. 148-50; for Vespers, 141; Compline, 4, 91, 134; in Mass, psalm verses for Introit, Gradual, Offertory, and Communion (Ps. 34:8); Baptism, Ps. 32, 51; Matrimony, Ps. 19, 21, 45, 128; Burial, Ps. 42, 116; also psalmodic "proof-texts" on Messiah.
10. See J.A.W. Bennett, *Poetry of the Passion* (Oxford: Clarendon, 1982), pp. 67-69, 71-72.

11. E.g., "The Church's one foundation" and "We are a garden wall'd around." Bridal imagery for Church often transmitted via St. Paul, e.g., Ephesians 5.22-27.
12. Discussed in Chapter 6, below.
13. See Chapter 13.
14. See Chapter 11.
15. See Chapter 9.
16. See Chapters 6 (end), 9, 13.
17. F.J.E. Raby, in *A History of Christian-Latin Poetry* (Oxford: Clarendon, 2nd ed., 1953), p. 30, thinks this "more probably liturgical or confessional" than a hymn. Martin, p. 134, considers it, with Phil. 2.6-11 and Col. 1.15-20, to represent Paul's use of a "pre-formed liturgical passage."
18. "At the Name of Jesus," in *The Name . . . and other Poems for the Sick and Lonely* (1861, 1870); see *HG* 58. On Phil. 2.5-11 see G.W.H. Lampe, "Modern Issues in Biblical Studies," *Expository Times* 71 (1970): 359-63; also Wainwright, p. 205.
19. Moule, p. 25.
20. Directly, in "Magnificat": "He hath filled the hungry . . . the rich he hath sent empty away"; indirectly in Ps. 116.6, "The Lord preserveth the simple"; Ps. 127.4-6, re children as "heritage and gift"; both in *BCP* (1662, 1928) "Thanksgiving after Childbirth, commonly called " 'The Churching of Women.'"
21. Moule, pp. 24-27, cites verses from Epistles as conjectural examples of hymns. On both, see Lampe, *op. cit.* On possible stanza forms in Col. 1.15-20 see Martin, *op. cit.* and W. McCown, "The Hymnic Structure of Colossians 1:15-20," *Evangelical Quarterly* 51 (1979): 156-62.
22. Julian Jaynes; *The Origin of Consciousness in the Breakdown of the Bicameral Mind* (Boston: Houghton Mifflin, 1976), Book II, Chapter 4; III, Chapter 3, *passim.*
23. See A. Owen Barfield, *Poetic Diction* (1928, 3rd ed., Middletown, CT: Wesleyan University, 1973), pp. 93-96, 139-40. Wainwright, p. 194.

NOTES TO CHAPTER THREE

1. *The Odes of Solomon,* trans. James Hamilton Charlesworth (Oxford: Clarendon, 1973), translator's preface.
2. Ms. *C* (Pistis Sophia), BL Mss. Add., 5114

(Book 4, A.D. 200-250) includes Odes 1; 5:6-11; 6:8-18; 22; 25. Ms. *H,* John Rylands Library, Codex Syrianus 9, included Odes 2 (missing); 3 (start missing) to verse 31b (Ms. 15th century or later). Ms. *N,* BL Add. 14538 (10th-13th centuries), has Odes 17:7b to 42, 20, each Ode ending "Hallelujah," distinguishing them from *Psalms of Solomon* bound in Ms. *G.* in Bibliothèque Bodmer, Cologny-Genève, which has Ode 11 only (Charlesworth's introduction, pp. 3-5).

3. Harris's translation in J.B. Platt (ed.), *The Forgotten Books of Eden* (New York: Bell, 1980), pp. 120-39. He announced discovery in "An Early Christian Hymn Book," *Contemporary Review* XCV (1909): 420-21, cited in Charlesworth, p. 4. Raby, p. 31, thinks Odes 2nd-3rd century.

4. Charlesworth in "The Odes of Solomon-Not Gnostic," *Catholic Biblical Quarterly* XXXI, 3 (1969): 357-69, adduces nine features not characteristic of Gnostic literature, adding: "in the Odes knowledge is *not* the gnostic idea of salvation through a comprehension of the soul's heavenly origin, subsequent imprisonment in the world of matter and possible ascension into its native abode. In the Odes, knowledge is always of Christ, the Most High and the Lord . . . in Gnosticism . . . it is essentially self-knowledge."

5. Cf. Frye, p. 147.

6. Charlesworth notes that intertestamental texts say Sheol has no door or exit (Ode 42.12 n17).

7. Cf. Jewish exaltation of natural above manmade, as suggested by Mr. D. Peters, in response to my paper on Odes at North-West Conference on Christianity and Literature, Seattle, 1982.

8. A literal war, according to 9 n6. Albert Schweitzer, *Out of My Life and Thought* (New York: Holt, 1933), p. 276.

9. Cf. Galatians 3.28.

10. Odes 4 through 7, 14, 16, 18, 26, 29, 40.

11. Odes, 3, 9, 13, 19, 20, 23, 24, 30, 32-34, 38, 39.

12. Odes 5, 11, 12, 14, 15, 21, 27, 32, 35, 37 and most introductory verses.

13. Odes 1 (B.V. Mary), 8, 10, 17, 22, 28, 31, 36, 41, 42 (all Christ).

14. 5 n14 and Isa. 11.10.

15. Rudolf Magnus, *Goethe as Scientist,* trans. Heinz Norden (New York: Collier, 1961),

pp. 172-73. Dualism in sense of absolute opposition.

16. 4 n7 explains "seal" as denoting baptism and sign of the Cross.

17. John 16.33.

18. My phrase, not allusion by Odist to Unconquered Sun (*sol invictis*).

19. Matthew 28.18.

20. 4 n18 cites Bernard for administration of milk and honey in early baptismal rites.

21. Cf. S.T. Coleridge, "Aeolian Harp."

22. Charlesworth, in a letter. For discussion of *yd,* see his article in *Catholic Biblical Quarterly.*

23. Exod. 33.21-22: "thou shalt stand upon a rock," "I will put thee in a cleft of rock"; Deut. 32.4: "He is the Rock"; 32.15: "the Rock of his salvation"; 1 Sam. 2.2: "is there any rock like our God" (cf. 2 Sam. 22.32), Ps. 18.31; 2 Sam. 22.2 "The Lord is my rock" (cf. Ps. 31.2); Ps. 18.2: "The Lord is my rock and my fortress"; Ps. 62.2.6: "He only is my rock and my salvation." Ps. 71.3: "Thou art my rock and my fortress." Ps. 92: "he is my rock, and there is no unrighteousness in him." Isa. 32.2: "a man shall be . . . as the shadow of a great rock in a weary land"; Lk. 6.48: "founded upon a rock." 1 Cor. 10.4: "And did all drink . . . of that spiritual Rock that followed them: and that Rock was Christ" (alluding to Israelites and pillar of cloud). Cf. "Rock of Ages" and, in "For all the saints," "Thou wast their Rock."

24. Ps. 36.9: "For with thee is the fountain of life." Proverbs 13.14: "The law of the wise is a fountain of life." (Cf. 14.27: "The fear is . . ."). Song 4.12: "A garden enclosed is . . . my spouse; a spring shut up, a fountain sealed." 15: "A fountain of gardens, a well of living waters" (cf. Jeremiah 2.13, 17.13 (of "the Lord")). Cf. hymns: "O fons amoris"; "There is a fountain filled with blood"; "Father, hear the prayer we offer. . . . would smite the living fountains / From the rocks along our way."

25. Exod. 5.5: "rest from their burdens"; 16.23 "of thy holy Sabbath" (cf 31.15); 33.14: "and I will give thee rest." Joshua 3.13:

"shall rest in the waters of Jordan." Ps. 38.3: "rest in my bones"; 116.7: "return unto thy rest, O my soul"; 132.14: "This is my rock for ever." Isa. 14.3: "shall give thee rest from thy sorrow." Zeph. 3.17: "He will rest in his love." Rev. 14.13: "that they may rest from their labours."

26. Charlesworth (3 n.7) lists some twenty references to rest, fifteen in sense of certitude. Cf. Catholic term *refrigerium* and "lovely quiet / Of a strong heart at peace" (D.H. Lawrence, "Ship of Death," ll. 24-25). In 26 n2, Charlesworth cites Bernard's suggested title "Odes of Rest."

27. 2 Cor. 12.2.

28. "Shall we gather at the river." Also in *Hymns for the Chapel of Harrow School* (London, 1855), an item alludes to "dark river of death." (Discussed in *Class and Idol*, Chapter 11.) Cf. Wesley, "Come, let us join our friends above" ("Let saints on earth in concert sing").

29. Walter Drum, "Psalms of Solomon" in *Catholic Encyclopædia* (New York: Appleton, 1912).

30. Coleridge, *Biographia Literaria*, Chapter 3.

31. Title of "There is a land of pure delight," Watts, *Hymns*, II, 66.

32. Philippe Ariès, *The Hour of Our Death*, trans. Helen Weaver (New York: Knopf, 1981), p. 152, citing *L'Évocation de l'audelà*, remarks of Visigothic texts on fires of hell: "Now we are beginning to encounter those terrible images that will pervade the liturgy of funerals until our own time."

33. P. Lønning, in *The Sources and Depth of Faith in Kierkegaard*, Vol. II of *Bibliotheca Kierkegaardiana* (Copenhagen: C.S. Rietzels Boghandel A / S, 1978), p. 169, cites remark that "Christianity does away with the fear of death by establishing the fear of Judgment"; allusion to modern man untraced.

34. In 22 n18, pun is said to apply in Syriac. Cf. Odes 11.5 and 22.12. "Catholic orthodoxy" my anachronism.

35. 19.6. On feminine aspects of God in biblical and patristic authors see Caroline Walker Bynum, *Jesus as Mother: Studies in the Spirituality of the High Middle Ages* (Berkeley, Los Angeles: University of California Press, 1982), pp. 125-128.

36. Wellesz, p. 146: "The singing of hymns . . . an adequate expression of the enthusiastic mood of the early Christians. . . . To the outside world . . . was the most notable aspect of their meetings." He cites Pliny to Emperor Trajan on songs to Christ at dawn "quasi deo dicere secum invicem."

37. Wellesz, p. 34, mentions antiphonal singing of early Christians. "Oratorio" in sense of recitative and aria only.

38. Quotations from Bonnie Kittel, *Hymns of Qumran* (Chico, CA: Scholars Press, 1981), pp. 35, 58, 59, 125, but opinions my own.

NOTES TO CHAPTER FOUR

1. Owen Chadwick, *The Reformation* (Harmondsworth: Penguin, 1972), p. 361.

2. See Steven Runciman, "The Greek Church and the Peoples of Eastern Europe," in Geoffrey Barraclough (ed.), *The Christian World: A Social and Cultural History of Christianity* (London: Thames & Hudson, 1981), pp. 109-22, esp. 112, on Eusebian idea of Christian Emperor which "every Byzantine passionately believed."

3. "Born a Jew": Wellesz, p. 183. Eric Werner, in *The Sacred Bridge: the Interdependence of Liturgy and Music in the Synagogue and Church* . . . (New York: Columbia University Press, 1959), p. 226, adds "converted Jew," also that Andrew of Crete "possible Jew by descent."

4. Wellesz. p. 52.

5. Werner, p. 574-75: "A mighty bridge of the spirit . . . linked the Near East with the European continent. . . . During the first millennium of Christianity an unending host of profound ideas has crossed it. Sciences, religions, arts and all the elements of civilization went first to the West and have returned again."

6. See Werner, p. 181, for comparison of *midrash* to Christian hymns based on Old Testament types; p. 184 for *Kontakion* as "versified *midrash*," further defined on pp. 218-19.

7. *Kontakia of Romanos*, trans. Marjorie Carpenter (Columbia: University of Missouri

Press, 1970), Vol. I: *On the Person of Christ*,
p. 162, Strophe 7 (Sun); p. 212, Strophe 14
(nudity of Christ). (N.B.: in this poem Pilate
is not whitewashed as in the Gospels.)
8. *Kontakia*, p. 214, Strophe 20 (Jonah). In
Strophe 14, p. 212, pillar of cloud becomes
pillar where Christ scourged. "Tear up written decree": p. 163, Strophe (in entry into
Jerusalem). Cf. Malachi 4.2, Matt. 12.39-
40.
9. Ode 3, text and translation in Wellesz, pp.
208-9.
10. Werner, pp. 139-41.
11. Actually eight, as Deut. 32 omitted (see
Werner, p. 227).
12. Wellesz, p. 199.
13. Cf. Werner, p. 140, on hymns as "earthly
symbols of heavenly hymns," as suggested
by St. Augustine.
14. High screen (Iconostas) came into fashion
in late Byzantine era as icons on panels more
accessible to congregational devotion than
if on walls (Runciman, p. 113).
15. Wellesz, p. 148. On angelic hierarchies in
Romanos, see Wellesz, p. 188.
16. Runciman, p. 120ff.
17. Runciman, p. 109-10, explains Hellenistic
doctrine of Eusebius (a friend of Constantine) as that the Emperor, though God's
"earthly representative" was interpreter, not
maker, of the law, whereof transcendent
source was God.
18. Runciman, p. 166.
19. Runciman, p. 112, cf. Wellesz, p. 199.
20. Cf. Wellesz, p. 168, on Iconoclastic movement as, in view of ecclesiastics, an "intrusion of Imperial ambition into the domain
of the Church"; Runciman, pp. 110-11 on
Patriarchate as "to some extent" the "Ministry of Religion," 116 on Cranmer's use of
Eastern liturgy in compiling *BCP*, and 119
on tsarist Russia as "heir of Byzantium."
21. See Wellesz, p. 172, re Ethiopian accompan-
iment of singing by handclaps and rhythmic
steps.
22. Runciman, pp. 111-12.
23. Wellesz, p. 169.
24. Cited in Wellesz, p. 95.
25. E.g., Richard Baxter, *Christian Directory* (1673)
on "mischiefs . . . throughout the earth . . .
caused by the disorders . . . of families," cited
in Levin L. Schücking, *The Puritan Family*,
trans. Brian Battershaw (New York: Schocken,
1970), p. 56; *ibid.*, p. 58 on family spiritual
songs; Joseph Benson, introducing his *Collec-

tion of Hymns for the Use of Methodist Sunday
Schools* (1808, 2nd ed. London, 1816) writes
of hymns as keeping children from singing "vain
and foolish songs."
26. Ode 8, Strophe, translated in J.M. Neale,
Hymns of the Eastern Church (London:
Hayes, 1862, rpt. New York: AMS Press,
1971), p. 153.

NOTES TO CHAPTER FIVE

1. Cited in Gillian Widdicombe, "Tidings of
Comfort and Joy," *Observer*, 18 December
1983, p. 23. On early hymns and Arianism
see Routley, *Hymns and Human Life*, pp.
20-21; Raby, pp. 30-32.
2. Translations of "Phos hilaron" (pre-Arian) by
Keble, Bridges, and E[rik] R[outley] in *PCH*
177, mention Trinity during middle stanza,
main emphasis being on Christ.
3. A.S. Walpole, in editor's introduction to his
Early Latin Hymns (1922, Hildesheim:
Georg Olms, 1966 ed.), pp. xi-xvi, distinguishes an Old (6th-century) and a New (9th-
century) Benedictine Hymnl. Raby, pp. 36-
40, contends that there was only one Hymnal.
4. Werner, p. 129.
5. Werner, p. 135, affirms that psalm texts remained in popular use in Eastern Church.
6. Cf. Raby, p. 365: "[It is] almost true . . .
that in the later Middle Ages, the central
object of the popular cult was . . . the Virgin
Mary, exalted to the rank of Queen of Heaven
. . . and invested with all those human and
tender attributes in which the early Church
had first clothed the figure of the Saviour."
7. *AH* XX 3; Walpole 5; parallel text *PCH*
137. Re attribution, see Raby, p. 33.
8. *AH* L 69; Walpole 36; celebrates sun growing
higher daily and lists spring flowers (ll. 1-
22). Better known for "Salve, festa dies" (ll.
25-50) still in use and given entirely to Redemption. Selection from both parts in trans.
by J. Ellerton, in *Congregational Church
Hymnal* (1884), p. 152, but version by
"M.F.B."in *EH* 624 alludes generally in single stanza to ll. 1-22 before passing to
mythos. Full text of 110 lines appeared in
Fortunatus, *Opera poetica*, ed. F. Leo (Ber-
lin, 1889) but by 10th century, centos in use
focused on Resurrection. Julian (1139 i) adds
citation from Schaff (1870) on original

"sweet poem" as depicting "the whole [of] Nature, born anew in the Spring" which "welcomes the risen Saviour."

9. Walpole 3; Breviary III, pp. 280-81; *EH* 52, *AMR* 2. Raby, p. 34, confirms Walpole's attribution to St. Ambrose.

10. Friedrich Nietzsche, *Birth of Tragedy* (1872), trans. Francis Golffing (New York: Doubleday, 1956), Chapter 1, *passim*.

11. Walpole 17; Breviary I. p. 96; *PCH* 141, *EH* 261, authorship uncertain (Walpole).

12. Walpole 18 (authorship uncertain); *PCH* 142; *EH* 261.

13. Walpole 22; Breviary III, pp. 474-75; *EH* 55, my translation.

14. Re "godly books" see A.P. Davis, *Isaac Watts: His Life and Works* (London: Independent Press, 1943), pp. 75-78.

15. Walpole 74. Source probably Ps. 19: 5-6 (sun), 11-13 (sins).

16. Breviary III, p. 541.

17. George B. Tennyson, *Victorian Devotional Poetry* (Cambridge, MA: Harvard University Press, 1981), pp. 52-56 (Keble), 207ff. (Hopkins); Franco Marucci, *I fogli della sibilla: retorica e medievalismo in Gerard Manley Hopkins* (Messina, Florence: G. d'Anna, 1980), *passim*.

18. Walpole attributes his No. 63 to Alcuin; Routley, in *PCH* 144, following Julian, 809 i, to St. Gregory. On Dearmer's assignation to morning, see *PCH*, p. 56.

19. E.g., "Magnae Deus potentiae," Breviary III, p. 510, stanza 2:

Demersa lymphis imprimens,
Subvecta caelis erigens:
Ut, stirpe ab una prodita,
Diversa repleant loca.

(Cf. raising of some creatures and immersion of others with election of souls.)

20. Walpole 81; Breviary III, p. 213; *PCH* 140; *EH* 254; *AMR* 1.

21. Breviary III, p. 256; *PCH* 143. Walpole, introd. p. xvi, notes that his No. 61, "Christe qui lux es et dies," survived "many centuries" until replaced by "Te lucis," No. 83.

22. E.g., Ps. 8, 19, 46, 78, 95, 98, 100, 104, 121, 135, 146-48, with "Benedicite."

NOTES TO CHAPTER SIX

1. According to Walpole 84; Breviary I, pp. 124-5; (Creator . . .) *EH* 1; *AMR* 45.

2. Cf. Walpole 86 and *AH* XXVII, p. 65 with Breviary I 1078, "En clara vox redarguit").

3. "Jordanis . . .," C. Coffin, *Paris Breviary* (1736). On translations see Julian 606. "On Jordan's bank the Baptist's cry." *EH* 9, *AMR* 50; see *HG* 580. "Veni . . ." text and Neale's version, *PCH* 172; T.A. Lacey's translation (significantly different), *EH* 8; post-Reformation antiphons ("7 Great O's") explained by Frank Colquhoun in *Hymns that Live* (London: Hodder and Stoughton, 1980), pp. 17-24, who, following Neale, considers antiphons early medieval and hymn originally 12th-century. I accept date 1710, in *HG* 502 and Julian 172.

4. *PCH* 551, there dated 2nd century. No. 298 in *Hymnal of Protestant Episcopal Church 1940* (New York: Church Hymnal Corporation, 1940), where source given as Epistle to Diognetus (A.D. 150) but not original title.

5. 8th century, trans. G. Moultrie, "Behold the Bridegroom cometh . . .," *EH* 3. Cf. "Verbum supernum prodiens," Walpole 85, *EH* 2, variously dated 5th to 11th centuries (Julian 1217 ii).

6. Discussed in Chapter 5.

7. *AH* XXVII, 1. Re martyrology in Prudentius and Mozarabic hymns see Raby, pp. 47, 50-54, esp. grave as centre of spiritual power.

8. Walpole 84 ("Conditor . . ."), stanzas 1-3 ascribed to "New Hymnal" (550-900). Breviary I, p. 124 ("Creator . . ."), *EH* 1 stanza 3 (Neale trans.) ascribed to 7th century, *HG* 842 to "7th or perhaps 6th." Translations listed in *HG* and Julian 257-58.

9. Trans. G. Moultrie, "close paraphrase of the ancient opening prayer of Eucharist in Liturgy of St. James" (*HG* 388). French carol tune "Picardy" first used in *EH* 318; otherwise as in David Perry, *Hymns and Tunes Indexed* (London: Hymn Society and Royal School of Church Music, 1980), p. 193.

10. Raby, pp. 47ff., 45.

11. Differences of spelling and lining in Walpole 23; this text and translation by R.F. Davis (1905) from *PCH* 155. Cf. *PCH* 613, based on Neale's (1852). On *Cathemerinon*, the source, see Raby, pp. 45-50.

12. Erik Routley, *The English Carol* (London: Jenkins, 1958), p. 76.

13. Full text: Walpole 31, *AH* L 53. For other

full reprints, and on uses of A-G portion for Christmas and H-L, N and S for Epiphany, see Julian 4-5. Early use of A-G in England *Latin Hymns of the Anglo-Saxon Church* (Durham: Andrews, 1851), p. 50-51. (parallel text Latin/Old English).

14. On reversal see Eric S. Rabkin, *The Fantastic in Literature* (Princeton: Princeton University Press, 1976), pp. 4-5, 45ff., 73ff., etc. "Classical," i.e., accepting Creeds but not scriptural inerrancy. Raymond E. Brown, *The Birth of the Messiah: A Commentary on the Infancy Narratives in Matthew and Luke* (London: Chapman, 1977), pp. 29-32, 284-85.

15. Walpole 6, my translation. Ascribed by St. Augustine to Ambrose (Raby, p. 33). For "without seed of man" see *AH* XX, 93, stanza 2: "Sine viri semine"; 140, st.4: "Non ex virili semine"; XXVII, 9, st. 1: "conceptu sine semine"; L, 212, st. 2b: "sine viro gravida"; XX, 8, st. 5: "Ex viro facta femina / Sine mixtura seminis"; Fortunatus, "Quem terra, pontus, aethera" (Walpole, 39 ". . . sidera"); Breviary I, 976-77, st. 5: Fecunda sancto Spiritu.

16. St. Germanos (634-734), on "wonder-working image of Edessa" (Julian 418-19); trans. Neale, *PCH* 186, under Routley's heading, "The Divine Paradox."

17. *AH* L, 99.

18. *Nativity 12th cent.* Of 19 MSS, 18 French; *12 / 13th* 4 English MSS *13th*: 92 MSS, 8 Fr., 22 Eng., 9 German, 1 Spanish, 48 Irish, rest unassigned; *13/14th* 1 Eng. MS; *14th* 32 MSS: 11 Ger., 1 Eng., 3 Irish, rest unassigned; *14/15th*: 10 MSS, 9 Ger., 1 Eng.; *15th* 17 MSS, 6 Ger., 2 Irish, rest unassigned.
B.V. Mary 11-12th cent. 13 MSS: 3 Fr., 4 Eng., 1 Ger., 1 Ir., rest unknown. *12/13th*: 2 Eng., 1 Ir.; *13th* 15 MSS: 6 Eng., 5 Ger., 1 Fr., 2 Ir., 1 unknown. *14th*: 15 MSS: 1 Eng., 1 Fr., 4 Ger., 1 Ir., rest unknown. *14/15th* 12 MSS: 2 Ger., 1 Ir., rest unknown; *15th*: 15 MSS, mainly unknown: *16th* 8 MSS, 5 Ger.

19. *AH* XX, 6.

20. Raby, p. 110.

21. E.g., *AH*, 108: "Omnes gentes, psallite." Latin hymn lines in macaronic carols listed by R.L. Greene, in *Early English Carols* (2nd ed., Oxford: Clarendon, 1977), introduction, pp. lxxxvi-viii. Renewal theme in refrain "Adam novo nato" to *AH* XX, 93-94;

141 "Nova vobis / Gaudio"; 154 "Novum dedit florem"; *AH* XLVIII, 251(2) st. 2b: "Nova fit in caelis gloria / Nova sint in terris gaudia." Cf. C. Rossetti, "In the bleak mid-winter . . . long ago"; "Tell me the old, old story" (C. Hankey); "I love to hear the story / How once the King . . ." (E. Miller, *AM* (1889), 330), etc.

22. *AH* L, 136.
23. *Ibid.*, 121.
24. *Ibid.*, 249.
25. *Ibid.*, 272.
26. *Ibid.*, 273.
27. *AH* XLVIII, 140-43.
28. See Raby, pp. 345-57, but judgment mine, based on sequences for "Nativitas Domini" and "Pascha," esp. (on renewal) "Quo noscente ligitur," "Res est novus," and "Mundi renovatio," in *Liturgical Poetry of Adam of St. Victor.*, ed., annot. by D.S. Wrangham (London: Kegan Paul, 3 vols., 1881).
29. *AH* XLVIII, 472 ("Apparuit . . .").
30. On *PCH* 167 ("O amor quam ecstaticus"), a partial version, see *HG* 545.
31. Greene, p. xxxviii; Routley, *English Carol*, pp. 108-15.
32. Greene, p. xcviii.
33. *Ibid.*, No. 3.
34. *Ibid*, 2.
35. *Ibid.*, 52 (cf. No. 41, 15th century).
36. *Ibid.*, 11.
37. *Ibid.*, 13.
38. Birth, poverty: Greene, 23, 26, 32, 34, 35, 41, 45, 48, 50, 58, 75, 77-81, 89, 91. Shepherds: 44, 51, 74 (Ryman), 75-79, 81 (Ryman).
39. No. 184.
40. Nos. 172, 177, 202, 217 (flower, Jesse); 173-76, 191-92 (rose); 182, 192, 194 (visions of Moses). For analysis of Latin typological figures see Raby, pp. 359-75.
41. E.g., Chastity: 181, 216, 221; Maternal: 204, 209-210, 216, 227. Queen: 179, 185 (Empress), 186, 191-99; Lady 180, 183-85, 188.
42. Routley, *English Carol*, p. 20ff. (intrusion of sacred); cf. Greene, xxiiff.
43. Routley, *English Carol*, pp. 79-80.
44. Greene, 11.
45. *Ibid.*, 16: "Man, be glad in halle and bour."
46. *Ibid.*, 25: "The sunne of grace."
47. *Ibid.*, 19, 20, 34, and duty of gratitude in Nos. 49, 55.
48. "Jesus refulsit": Walpole 90; *Latin Hymns of Anglo-Saxon England*, p. 48: "A patre uni-

genitus": Walpole, 89; *Latin Hymns* p. 53.
49. Walpole 8.
50. *AH* XXVII, 9.
51. *PCH* 154 (parallel text); *HG* 870; *EH* 40.
52. *PCH* 321; *EH* 39; *AMR* 79.
53. See Colquhoun, pp. 61-65, and for allu-
    sions to Rev., see Chapter 2, p. 17.

NOTES TO CHAPTER SEVEN

1. A parishioner's recollection, apparently
   based on "The Incarnate Son" (*Parochial and
   Plain Sermons*, VI, No. 6): "Now I bid you
   consider that that Face, so ruthlessly smitten,
   was the Face of God himself . . . ," in John
   Henry Newman, *Sermons and Discourses,
   1839-57*, ed. C.F. Harrold (London:
   Longmans, 1949), Vol. I, p. 214.
2. Account in Raby, pp. 86-94.
3. Bennett, *Poetry of the Passion*, p. 15.
4. Wellesz, p. 163.
5. Cf. Bennett, p. 27, on "medieval devotion
   . . . associated with the name of St.
   Bonaventure . . . that focused not on the
   warrior-prince but on his sufferings and
   wounds." Examples in Raby, pp. 419-24.
6. T.S. Eliot, *Murder in the Cathedral* (3rd
   ed., London: Faber, 1937), pp. 76-77, 86-
   87; cf. *Cathemerinon* ix, 87, cited in Raby,
   p. 49.
7. Account and list of translations in Julian
   1219-22. Cf. Bennett, p. 10.
8. Illustrated in Ludwig Freidlander, *Sittengeschichte Roms* (Vienna: Phaedon-Verlag,
   1934), p. 444. Reference owed to Professor
   Herbert Huxley.
9. Walpole 34; my translation. Biblical reference suggested by Dr. Hobbs.
10. See Bennett, p. 198.
11. *PCH*, p. 57. Reason for omission stated to
    me by editor, the late Dr. Anthony Petti.
12. "Abroad the Regal Banners fly," in *Primer*
    (Antwerp, 1685), line used by Neale.
13. Bennett, p. 81 ("most martial . . ."), p. 7
    ("triumphalism").
14. *AM* (1861), 84. Breviary, III, p. 1534 (Exal-
    tation of the Cross). Full text in Walpole
    34; Raby, pp. 89-90 and (ed.), *Oxford Book
    of Medieval Latin Verse* (London: Oxford
    University, 1959), No. 55.
15. *Book of Common Praise* (Toronto: Oxford
    University Press, rev. ed., 1938), No. 128,
    dated there as 1933, apparently mentioned

in *HG* 882 as prepared for *Clarendon Hymn
Book* (Charterhouse School, 1936) and first
to use "Vexilla regis," st. 2 (omitted from
Breviary): "confixa clavis viscera . . ."
Version by J.W. Grant, in *The Hymn Book*
(Toronto: Anglican and United Churches
of Canada, 1971), No. 445.
16. Comparison to marching song, and transla-
    tion, in Raby, pp. 90-91. On reversal of
    Fall, cf. Galatians 3.13, in Vulgate "Chris-
    tus nos redemit de maledicto legis, factus
    pro nobis maledictum: *quia scriptum est:
    Maledictus omnis qui pendet in ligno*" (my
    italics).
17. In Prudentius, *Psychomachia*, according to
    Raby, p. 61, but attributed by Bennett, p.
    47, to St. Bernard, apparently in ignorance
    of earlier source.
18. Bennett, p. 208 n9.
19. *AH* L, 214.
20. *AH* L, 223.
21. *AH* L, 289. On Reginald, see Raby, p. 333.
22. *AH* L, 290.
23. Bennett, p. 77, cf. p. 44.
24. Walpole 36, called by Raby, p. 93, "once-
    famous," but still used in Anglican and
    Roman churches (*EH* 624, 628, 630, 634).
25. Walpole 111, with my literal translation,
    cf. Latin and version by Neale in *PCH* 148.
26. *AH* L, 82, stanza 4. "Olympus" scribal
    error for "Olympi."
27. Omitted in *PCH* 157, Breviary.
28. Phrases in concluding stanza of Walpole
    111, except *ab omni* . . . , in two further
    stanzas of *PCH* 148. Since Walpole regards
    hymn as "of great antiquity" (p. 356), stan-
    zas evidently added, possibly in *Sarum Bre-
    viary*. On subdivision, alterations, and
    translations, see Julian 94-96, and *HG* 837.
29. Walpole 37, *AH* L 70, apparently based on
    Romans 6.3-11.
30. All excerpts from translation of Neale, *A
    History of the Holy Eastern Church*, Vol. I,
    pp. 880-85, used by Wellesz, pp. 206-14,
    with proviso that it showed "great freedom"
    but "drew on the language of the Au-
    thorized Version . . . as John Damascene
    . . . on that of the Greek New Testament"
    so that reader can see scriptural basis of
    poet's language (Wellesz, p. 206 n6).
31. See Wellesz, pp. 40, 147-48, 158.
32. *OH* I, 79, st. 2:

    The dying Thief rejoiced to see
    That Fountain in his day;

And there have I, as vile as he,
Washed all my sins away.

On Montgomery's alteration, see Julian
1160 ii.

33. Chant recorded in *History of Music in
Sound*, Vol. II, "Early Music to 1300," ed.
Don Anselm Hughes, sung by Brompton
Oratory Choir. Cf. "Ellacombe," *EH* 137.

34. *Class and Idol*, Chapters 4, 6, 9, 10.

35. Bennett, p. 3.

36. Raby, p. 175.

37. Text from *PCH* 159; Raby, p. 174-75.

38. *PCH* 180.

39. "Come ye faithful, raise the strain,"*PCH*
178, *EH* 131, *AMR* 133. See Julian 87.

40. See Wellesz, p. 199, and pp. 31, 33
above.

41. *PCH* 151, cf. Fortunatus, "Tempora florigero" (Walpole 36), of which Walpole says
(pp. 181-82) "an extract from the longest
. . . of . . . poetical epistles . . . to Felix
bishop of Nantes . . . In it he dwells with
much poetical force and with deep religious
feeling upon the beauty of spring . . . come
in her gayest attire to greet her risen Lord."
He compares it with other poems on spring
(*ibid.*, Nos. 6, 8, 9) in which Fortunatus
gives "a brilliant view of the external aspect
of things" and "endows nature with a soul,
much as a modern poet might."

42. *AH* L, 102 (esp. stanza 2).

43. *Ibid.*, p. 172, cited in Raby, pp. 194-95.
For other nature poems of Sedulius Scottus,
see Helen Waddell, *Medieval Latin Lyrics*
(4th ed., London: Constable, 1933), pp.
118-25.

44. *PCH* 146, of which Routley remarks (p.
57): "Here at last we have real New Testament imagery, real competition with the
Psalter." Julian, 11 ii, gives earlier MSS
as 8-9th century. "Ad regias Agui dapes,"
Breviary II, p. 1236, etc.

45. Golden Kanon, Odes 5, 6 (Wellesz, pp.
210-11).

46. *AH* L, 141, source of attribution.

47. *AH* XLVIII, 55.

48. *AH* L, 215, trans. Neale (revised in *AM*,
1861) *EH* 122, Campbell in *EH* 139. Other
trans. listed in Julian 224 ii.

49. *AM* (1889) 125; *AMR* 128.

50. *The Hymn Book*, 463 (Campbell).

51. *New Catholic Hymnal* (London: Faber,
1971) 213, trans. Petti, based on Campbell:
"Sing, choirs . . ."

52. David Lyle Jeffrey, *The Early English Lyric
and Franciscan Spirituality* (Lincoln: University of Nebraska Press, 1975).

53. Geoffrey Chaucer, *Troilus and Criseyde*, III,
Proem; Prologue to *Canterbury Tales*, 1-18;
William Langland, *The Vision of . . . Piers
the Plowman*, Prologue.

54. Chaucer, *Canterbury Tales*, A 3187-3854,
"Miller's Tale."

55. Chaucer, *TC* V, 1823-48.

56. *TC* III, 1261. Spoken by Troilus, who mis-
takes sexual for divine love.

57. *PCH* 1 B, also a cento translated in *EH*
130, with plainsong tune.

58. Bennett, pp. 35-36, 42, 55-56, 86.

59. *AH* XLVIII. 168-71. In 169-70, Red Sea,
David vs. Goliath and Samson vs. Philis-
tines applied to Resurrection, to which,
however, springtime applied in 171 (*Veris
grati tempore*).

60. 15th century text *PCH* 168, *O filii et filiae*,
re visit of women to Sepulchre and demon-
stration to St. Thomas.

61. *PCH* 164 and Breviary II, p. 1450.

62. *PCH*, p. 58.

63. Raby, p. 409.

64. *Lòc. cit.*

65. I owe Empson reference, so far untraced,
to the late G.S. Fraser. "Word made flesh,
by word he maketh / Very bread his flesh
to be; / Man in wine Christ's blood par-
taketh, / And if senses fail to see, / Faith
alone the true heart waketh / To behold the
mystery" (Neale, *PCH* 164).

66. *AH* XLVIII, 154; hymn cycle Nos. 152-67.
Trans. "Alone to sacrifice" by Waddell, *op.
cit.*, p. 167. *PCH* 549 and *Hymnal 1940*,
No. 68, have translation by F.B. Tucker
(1938): "Alone thou goest forth, O Lord,"
on which see *HC* 34.

67. See Raby, pp. 428 (on da Todi), 433 (on
poem, "with *Dies Irae* the supreme achievement of Franciscan, indeed of religious
verse, of later Middle Ages)," 439 (use by
Flagellants). In Roman Missal, for Seven
Sorrows of B.V. Mary, since 18th century.
Text used, *PCH* 166.

68. Verse translation by A.G. Petti, in *New
Catholic Hymnal*, 18. On Deposition of
hymns and manuscript illuminations, see
Bennett, p. 36. Devotions at Stations of
Cross "became fairly general by the fif-
teenth century" according to *New Catholic
Encyclopedia*, Vol. 14: "Way of the Cross,"

but article does not mention singing of
"Stabat mater" during rite.
69. *AH* L, 381. The converse, quasi-sensory ex-
periencing of the divine, illustrated from
medieval spiritual writings in Bynum, p.
79ff.
70. Bennett, p. 120ff., esp. p. 125.
71. *AH* XLVIII, 467, stanza 3. "O amor": *PCH*
167 with translation of B. Webb (1852),
also *AMR* 187.
72. "O Nazarene, Lux Bethlem" (Walpole 25),
ll 7-8, "quo fibra cordis expiatur uvidi, /
intemperata quo domantur viscera."
73. Walpole 60.
74. "Christe, qui lux es et dies," Walpole 61,
ll. 9-12: *ne gravis somnus inruat, / nec hostis
nos subripiat; / ne caro illi consentiens / nos
tibi reos statuat*, is at least as specific as
ibid 83, "Te lucis ante terminum" by which
according to Walpole (p. 298) it was replaced.
75. Trans. A.W. Chatfield (1876), *EH* 77.
76. Raby, pp. 315-18, distinguished Pyrenean
Morlas from Breton Morlaix.
77. "Yearning," often used for "romantic longing," physical or metaphysical. In medieval
hymns, longing is clearly for God and
heaven. C.S. Lewis, *Surprised by Joy*, p.
174ff., discussed in Corbin Scott Carnell,
*Bright Shadow of Reality: C.S. Lewis and the
Feeling Intellect* (Grand Rapids: Eerdmans,
1974), pp. 13-15, 21-30.
78. Breviary I, pp. 260, 1261; text *PCH* 163A
as in original, but in hymnals always as
"Jesu, dulcis . . ."; *PCH* 163B, "Jesu, dulcedo cordium." In modern hymnals less sentimental tunes used, e.g., "St. Botolph."
Caswall's version (in PCH) renders *Dans
vera cordis gaudia* as "With sweetness fills
the breast," and *praesentia* as "in thy presence rest," terms common in his time but
foreign to original, cf. "none but his *loved
ones* know."
79. Bennett, pp. 67, 71-72.

NOTES TO CHAPTER EIGHT

1. Translation from B. McGinn, *Concordia
Novi ac Veteris Testamenti*, given in "The
Abbott and the Doctors: Scholastic Reactions to the Radical Eschatology of Joachim
of Fiore," essay in Delno C. West (comp.),

Joachim of Fiore in Christian Thought (New
York: Burt Franklin, 1975), Vol. II, p. 455.
Latin text (p. 467 n22), in full, is:

Primus status seculi initiatus est ab Adam,
fructavit ab Abraham, consumavit in
Christo. Secundus initiatus ab Ocia, fructavit ab Zacharia patre Joannis baptiste ac-
cepturus consumationem in temporibus
istis. Tertius sumens initium a beato Be-
nedicto cepit proferre fructum 22a
generatione ab eodem sancto viro, con-
sumandus et ipse in consumatione seculi.
Et primus quidem in quo claruit ordo con-
iugatorum proprietate mysterii ascribitur
patri. Secundus in quo claruit ordo
clericorum in tribu iuda ascribitur filio. Tertius in quo claruit ordo monachorum ascribitur spiritui sancto.

On interpretations of this passage, see my
note 33 below.
2. Ezekiel 37.2-4, cf. "dry bones" of T.S.
Eliot, *Ash-Wednesday*.
3. Joel 2.5-6, 15-16, 28-29.
4. Barfield, *Poetic Diction*, p. 79ff. I owe information re double sense of *ru'ah* to Professor Henry Summerfield. *Ru'ah ha-
Kodesh* (Holy Spirit) moved upon waters
at Creation (Gen. 1.2). In Khabbalistic tradition *nefesh* means "spirit" as "living" (vs.
dead), *ru'ah* the soul (i.e., psyche), and
neshamah the divine spirit which at death
returns to its native home. (*Encyclopaedia
Judaica*, 10.613ff., 14.364-65.)
5. Walpole 16, *PCH* 140.
6. Walpole 116.
7. Colquhoun, p. 134, identifies the gifts in
"Veni Creator" with the seven spirits before
the throne in Rev. 1.4. Ronald H. Preston,
in *Twentieth Century Bible Commentary* (rev.
ed.), ed. G.H. Davis, A. Richardson, C.L.
Wallis (New York: Harper, 1955), p. 516,
says the spirits "signify divine perfection,"
instancing Isa. 11.24, the basis for the invocation at Confirmation of gifts of "wisdom,
understanding, counsel, spiritual strength,
knowledge, godliness and holy fear"
specified by Colquhoun. In all essentials the
Anglican rite follows that of the medieval
church (see *Concise Oxford Dictionary of the
Christian Church*, ed. E.A. Livingstone,
1977, pp. 124-25). S. MacLean Gilmour, in
*The Interpreter's One-Volume Commentary on
the Bible* (Nashville, TN: Abingdon Press,

1971), p. 949, terms the "sacred number seven" the "symbol of wholeness or perfection," comparing the spirits to the "seven archangels in late Jewish mythology" and the seven spirits in Zorastrian teaching. His tracing of word for "witness" to that for "martyr" seems irrelevant to Rev. 1.4, identical in AV and Vulgate ("septem spiritibus"). The gifts, in *Veni Creator* and *Veni sancte* seem, therefore, moral, as in Isa. 11.2, rather than mystical, a view expounded by Evelyn Underhill in *The Essentials of Mysticism* (New York: E.P. Dutton, 1960), pp. 92-94.

8. Matt. 12.45 (cf. literal seven devils of Mk. 16.9; Lk. 8.2).
9. Messenger, *op. cit.*, *passim*.
10. *AH* XLVIII, 179.
11. Breviary II, pp. 1393-94.
12. *AH* L, 83.
13. *AH* L, 216.
14. *AH* L, 253.
15. *AH* L, 275: "Pater, da per verbum / nobis septiformem spiritum," attributed to Gottschalk (Godalescus).
16. *AH* L, 324: *Sequentia de Sancto Spiritu*, "O ignis spiritus paracliti."
17. E.g., *AH* XLVIII, 180: "Remissionum numerum" 182: "Apostolorum pectora."
18. *HG* 880. Full text in Raby, p. 183. Account by John, Lord de Joinville, in *Chronicles of the Crusades* (London: Bell & Doldry, 1865), p. 383.
19. My literal translation of text in *PCH* 160.
20. Barbara Tuchman, *A Distant Mirror* (New York: Ballantine, 1978), p. 589: "her significance is better known to history than it was to her contemporaries."
21. Raby, p. 158. Dr. Fitch suggests that *amor*, if used in hymns in classical sense of *Eros*, would signify heartfelt rather than willed love (*agape*). Last line usually sung as "ubi caritas et amor . . ."
22. "Come, Holy Ghost, eternal God," given fully in *AM* (1889) 508, partially in Julian 1209 ii.
23. *PCH* 160C, in Watts, *Hymns* II, 34 (1709).
24. *PCH* 160 A, from Robert Bridges (comp.), *Yattendon Hymnal* (1899).
25. *The Hymn Book* (Canada) 246.
26. Wallace Stevens, "Sunday Morning," l. 63.
27. Raby, p. 343-44.
28. For translators see Julian 1214-15, *HG* 881. Text from *PCH* 152, and Raby.
29. Latin text in school hymnals for Harrow (1881), Rugby (1885), Winchester (1910), Eton (1937), Worksop (1938), etc.
30. Galatians 5.22
31. See Julian 1212-15.
32. Information re Joachim of Fiore by M.F. Laughlin in *New Catholic Encyclopedia* (New York: McGraw-Hill, 1967), 7.990-91. For fuller account of works, doctrines, and condemnation of *De unitate seu essentia Trinitatis*, see *Dictionnaire de spiritualité*, Tome VIII (Paris: Beauchesne, 1974), col. 1179-1201.
33. For fuller account of Joachim's numerology, see Marjorie Reeves, *The Figurae of Joachim of Fiore* (Oxford: Clarendon, 1972), pp. 5-19, where two types of concord between the Testaments are noted, "of threes, symbolizing the equality of the three Persons" and "of twos, symbolizing the authority of the Father and the nativity of the Son, and expressed in the two Peoples . . . elected to the faith of the One God." The letter of the two Testaments conveys the "images of Father and Son, but the third dispensation is not a Testament to supersede the others, but a spiritual discernment proceeding from both (*spiritualis intellectus qui utroque procedit*)" (p. 7). Since the third *status* falls within history, "one is led to ask whether it is, after all, a separate stage . . . succeeding the other two." Reeves concludes that it is rather "a state of being emerging at the close of history." The popular view is expressed in Isak Dinesen's *Seven Gothic Tales* (New York: Random House, 1972), p. 5: "Joachim . . . held that . . . the book of the Father is . . . the Old Testament . . . that of the Son . . . the New" but "the testament of the Third person of the Trinity still remained to be written."

The notion of *spiritualis intellectus*, demonstrated but not explained in the "Veni sancte Spiritus," suggests the poet's indebtedness, *malgré lui*, to Joachim, on whose subsequent influence see Marjorie Reeves, *Joachim of Fiore and the Prophetic Future* (London: SPCK, 1976), *passim*. He was thought to have predicted the rise of mendicant orders (notably the Franciscans), the Reformation, and later revolutionary movements. On his apocalyptic theory, see E.R. Daniel, "Apocalyptic Conversion: The Joachite Alternative to the Crusades," in West (comp.), *Joachim . . .*, II, pp. 301-28. Vol. I has bibliographies.

34. Italian and English text in *PCH* 205.

NOTES TO CHAPTER NINE

1. J.R.R. Tolkien, "On Fairy Stories," in C.S. Lewis (ed.), *Essays Presented to Charles Williams* (American ed., Grand Rapids: Eerdmans, 1966), pp. 38-39.
2. Ariès, *Hour of our Death*, pp. 22-26, 31-32, 147-48.
3. Especially George MacDonald, *Golden Key* (New York: Dell, 1967), pp. 54-58, 68; *Princess and the Goblin, Back of North Wind*, in *Back . . . Goblin, Princess and Curdie* (London: Octopus, 1979), pp. 310, 284-87. Baptism in Jordan water in Samuel Butler, *The Way of All Flesh*, Chapter 18.
4. Walpole 29.
5. *Ibid.* 30, and p. 145, where Walpole cites Rambach for belief that text came into use as hymn after Reformation.
6. Raby, pp. 46-47.
7. Walpole 120.
8. Walpole 80: ll. 13-16: *terroris ut cum iudicis / horror supremus ceperit, / laetemur omnes in vicem / pacis repleti munere*, i.e., when terror seizes others, those prepared may rejoice and be rewarded with peace.
9. Raby, pp. 147-48.
10. Walpole 113, noted as of early origin.
11. Neale's translation (*Hymns of the Eastern Church*, pp. 104-5) reprinted in Wellesz, p. 232.
12. Ariès, *Hour*, pp. 38, 47.
13. *AH* XXIII, 78-79.
14. Raby, p. 231-34.
15. *AH* XLVIII, 63-65. Cf. my account with that in Raby, pp. 250-54.
16. Popular medieval view repeated in concluding scene of Christopher Marlowe, *Doctor Faustus* (*c.* 1593); Calvinist view in "Sinners in the hands of an angry God," in *Jonathan Edwards: Representative Selection*, ed. Clarence H. Faust and Thomas H. Johnson (New York: Hill & Wang, 1935), pp. 155-72 *passim*.
17. Viz. seven plagues, Rev. 15.8, 16.1-19 (i: mark of beast (sore) on idolatry; ii: sea, and iii: rivers, etc., of blood; iv: sun scorching blasphemers; v: darkness, pain of unrepentant; vi: Euphrates dried, unclean spirits from mouths of dragon, beast, false prophets; vii: thunder, earthquake, etc.)

Also Lk. 13.28 (weeping, gnashing of teeth); Rev. 10.3, 1 Pet. 5.8 (lions); Isa. 34.13, 35.7 (dragons).
18. James Joyce, *A Portrait of the Artist as a Young Man* (New York: Huebsch, 1916), Chapter 3. On his source, Pinamonti, "Hell opened to Christians to Caution them from Entering it" (Jesuit, 17th century), see Bruce Bradley, *James Joyce's Schooldays* (Dublin: Gill and Macmillan, 1982), pp. 125-28, where a nineteenth-century parallel is adjudged "considerably milder."
19. "Apparebit repentina" (Walpole 120) is an acrostic poem describing Second Coming of Christ as Judge, His praises of righteous and reproaches of sinners (on his left), and despatch to heaven and hell. It is cited by Bede. Text of "Dies irae" from *PCH* 153.
20. Werner, pp. 252-55. Wellesz, p. 183, insists that Theodore's Kanon is modelled on Romanos' Kontakion.
21. Romanos, "Kontakia," p. 379, Strophe 20.
22. Werner, *loc. cit.*
23. Appended lines composed before hymn itself (*HG* 846).
24. "Later medieval liturgies always found a place for" ["Dies" and other Sequences]; "Dies" inspiration of "so many" poets and musicians (*PCH* p. 57; No. 153n). My comment mainly on use in funeral and Flagellant processions.
25. *PCH* 153; *EH* 487.
26. John Henry Newman, *Grammar of Assent* (London: Burns, Oates, 1870, Chapter 4 *passim*.
27. Barfield, *History in English Words* (Grand Rapids: Eerdmans, 1967), p. 170.
28. Routley, in *English Carol*, p. 76, cites Joachim of Fiore for end of "this world" and new age in 1260, based on Rev. 11.3, 12.6.
29. *Class and Idol* Chapter 3.
30. Samuel Macey, *Clocks and the Cosmos: Time in Western Life & Thought* (Hampden, CT: Archon Books, 1980), pp. 17-18.
31. Frye, pp. 137-38.
32. Newman, *The Mission of the Benedictine Order*, originally 1858 (London: Young, 1923), p. 55ff., citing Hallam, Guizot, *et al.*, esp. Soame: "Wherever they came, they converted the wilderness into a cultivated country."
33. Frye, p. 142.
34. On Watts: "We are a garden wall'd around," see Davie, *A Gathered Church"*, pp. 28-31.
35. Waddell, pp. 184-87, 203-79.

36. Walpole 15.
37. Philippe Ariès, *Centuries of Childhood* (L'Enfant et la vie familiale sous L'Ancien Régime), trans. R. Baldick (London: Cape, 1962), pp. 246, 391.
38. Walpole 73; Breviary III, p. 247.
39. Text in *AH* XLVIII, 66 and Raby, p. 254.
40. Cf. Coleridge, Gloss to *Rime of the Ancient Mariner*, IV, 265ff.: "In his loneliness he yearneth towards the journeying Moon and . . . stars . . . the blue sky belongs to them, and is their appointed rest, and their native country."
41. *PCH* 158: *tunsionibus, pressuris / expoliti lapides* . . .
42. *Ibid.* 162; *EH* 495, 371.
43. Margaret Laurence, *The Diviners* (Toronto: McClelland & Stewart, 1974), Chapter 3.
44. Newman, *Grammar of Assent*, pp. 75-76, referring directly to "children" of Nature, but in ensuing discussion to those of Church. Reference owed to Drs. J. Tucker and D.J. DeLaura.
45. Text and translation in Waddell, pp. 163-65, with which cf. trans. by Ronald Knox (1940), in *PCH* 161: "O what high holiday past our declaring, / Safe in his palace God's courtiers are sharing, / Rest after pilgrimage, spoil after fighting! / God, all in all, is their crown and requiting." *New Catholic Hymnal*, No. 191, is translation by Petti, based on that of Neale (*EH* 465), the most widely used.
46. William Wordsworth, "Ode on Intimations of Immortality from Recollections of Early Childhood," ll. 135-36, 143-44. Aldous Huxley, *"Music at Night" and Other Essays* (Harmondsworth: Penguin, 1950), pp. 35-40: "the . . . that is at the heart of things."
47. Underhill, p. 10.
48. C.S. Lewis, *They Stand Together: Letters of C.S. Lewis to Arthur Greeves, 1914-63*, ed. Walter Hooper (London: Collins, 1979), p. 408, citing Ruskin, *Praeterita*.
49. Wordsworth, "Tintern Abbey," ll. 45-46.
50. Arnold, throughout "Study of Poetry," employs terms in various combinations, e.g., adding "shrewdness" in case of Burns.
51. "Summa contra Anthroposophos," unpublished manuscript, passage discussed in Adey, *C.S. Lewis's "Great War" with Owen Barfield* (Victoria: University of Victoria English Literary Studies Monograph No. 14, 1978), p. 53.
52. "Light's abode, celestial Salem," *EH* 431.

NOTES TO CHAPTER TEN

1. Mircea Eliade, *Patterns in Comparative Religion*, trans. Rosemary Sheed (Cleveland, OH: World Publishing Co., 1963), pp. 61-62.
2. Frye, pp. 177ff, 189-98. Davie, *Dissentient Voice* (Notre Dame: Notre Dame University Press, 1982), p. 12: "the discovery of Polynesian cultures by the great Enlightenment navigators . . . finally exploded for thoughtful and responsible people in Western Europe, the assumption that cultural and moral and civic standards had been established . . . at the start of the Christian era, by three mediterranean cultures: Greek, Roman and Hebrew."
3. E.g., in John Pecham's *Philomena* (discussed in Raby, pp. 425-27), in which nightingale typifies soul's longing for heaven.
4. As distinct from English Enlightenment traced by Davie (*op. cit.*) in eighteenth-century poets.
5. E.g., "Ein feste Burg" (Ps. 46).
6. Distinguished by J. Kenneth Kuntz in *The People of Ancient Israel* (New York: Harper & Row, 1974), pp. 435-36, into Davidic (1-41), Elohistic (42-89), and Yahweh Psalms (90-150), but distinction is disputed.
7. Ps. 18 (*BCP*): 3-4, cf. Sternhold text in *PCH* 10, and *AV*: "Sorrows," "floods of ungodly men."
8. Ps. 33.10 ("cast out the counsels of princes"). Point re Calvin owed to Dr. Hobbs.
9. Ps. 72.4, 12; 82.4; 146.9.
10. Ps. 1.5; 63.4.
11. C.S. Lewis, *English Literature in the Sixteenth Century, Excluding Drama* (Oxford: Charendon, 1954), pp. 33-35.
12. E.g., in Walter Scott, *The Heart of Midlothian* (set in early eighteenth century).
13. E.g., Ps. 18.34; 24.8ff.; 144.1.
14. *HG* 20; French and English original texts, *PCH* 7.
15. Ps. 18.2, cf. "tower of David" in R.C. Litany of B.V. Mary.
16. Stanza 2: "Thou wast their Rock, their fortress and their might."
17. Full text in *PCH* 417; Milton *Poetical Works* (Oxford: Oxford University Press, 1904 *et. seq.*), pp. 9-11.
18. Apparently intended as table grace pre-1636, but earliest extant text 1647 (*HG* 492).

19. *PCH* 30. Published 1694, first used as hymn in *EH* 404 (*HG* 300). Julian 1651 ii, misdates publication as 1683.

20. *Confessions*: Book I: 2, 3.

21. Ps. 8.4 (*BCP*): "What is man, that thou art mindful of him, or the son of men, that thou visitest him?"

22. John Locke, *An Essay Concerning Human Understanding*, Book II, Chapter 5 (2 vols., Oxford: Clarendon, 1894), Vol. I, pp. 121-22. On Wesleyan adherence to Bible see Timothy L. Smith, "John Wesley and the Wholeness of Scripture," *Interpretation* XXXIX, 3 (1985): 246-62.

23. For unexplained reason, this verse omitted in *PCH* 29, though according to Julian (pp. 618-19) in both 1695 and 1709 texts. If a later addition, it would underline my distinction between objectivity of old and subjectivity of new-world religion.

24. Ps. 19.5.

25. Full text *PCH* 47. Colquhoun, whose full exposition (pp. 298-305) I had not seen at time of writing, makes the same point re structure, citing *Spectator*, 9 August 1712 on collective human indebtedness. George Wither's "Author's Hymn" (*Hymns*, pp. 298-303, full reference in n48, below) anticipates "When all thy mercies."

26. Albert Edward Bailey, *The Gospel in Hymns: Backgrounds and Interpretations* (New York: Scribners, 1950), pp. 46-48. Routley cites whipping incident in *PCH*, p. 16; text *PCH* 32; Aldous Huxley, *Island* (New York: Harper & Row, 1962), p. 132.

27. Harry Escott, *Isaac Watts: Hymnographer* (London: Independent Press, 1962), p. 115.

28. Bailey, p. 44.

29. Watts, *Works*, IV, p. 449.

30. Davis, *Isaac Watts*, pp. 25, 31, describes symptoms as coincident with consideration of Watts for important pastorate of Mark Lane Chapel, London.

31. "My Thoughts that often mount the sky," "Meditation in a Grove," in *Works*, IV, pp. 450, 451.

32. *Ibid.*, p. 441.

33. *Ibid.*, p. 423.

34. *Ibid.*, p. 424.

35. Carl Sagan, "The Amniotic Universe," in his *Broca's Brain* (New York: Random House, 1979), p. 304-5. (drawing on S. Grof, *Realms of Human Unconsciousness* and *The Human Encounter with Death*). See pp.

307-10 for Sagan's speculation re birth experience as determinant of religious ideas. Application to Watts and to hymns my own.

36. All in Watts, *Psalms*. Original opening stanza of "Before Jehovah's . . .": "Sing to the Lord with joyful voice; / Let every land his name adore; / The British Isles shall send the noise / Across the ocean to the shore."

37. Rev. 1.11; 5.11.

38. See Davie, *Gathered Church*, pp. 19-24, esp. p. 22.

39. Bailey, p. 58, citing Thomas Wright, *Life of Isaac Watts* (1914), p. 118-19.

40. Full text: *Works*, IV, p. 191-92; Davie, *Gathered Church*, pp. 19-20; *PCH* 144 "fly forgotten as a dream / Dies . . . ."

41. On accuracy resulting from invention of balance spring in 1674, see Macey, p. 17. Routley, *HG*, interprets "sons of time" as "probably hours and minutes."

42. Substituted first in Wesley, *Coll.* P. 39 (*HG* 592).

43. First in John Wesley, *Psalms and Hymns* (Charleston, 1737). Other changes include "shadow of thy *wing*" (for "throne") in stanza 2.

44. Wordsworth, *Prelude* (1805), I, 470-71; (1850), 444-45.

45. On songs of British troops, see Esmé Wingfield-Stratford, *A History of British Civilization* (London: Routledge, 1928), Vol. II, p. 1281.

46. *HG* 592.

47. Bailey, p. 56.

48. "We that are Britons enjoy many peculiar privileges and have obtained sundry blessings and deliverances . . . are therefore obliged to a special thankfulness, not only as . . . Christian men, but as Britons also." George Wither, prefatory to hymn "For a Briton," cited in Escott, p. 73. Wither's patriotic hymnody is confined to "St. George's Day" (Song LXXXI); "For Public Deliverances" (LXXXII); "With Israel we may truly say,/ If on our side God had not been, / Our foes had made of us their prey, / And we this light had never seen" (stanza 1, 1-4); "For Peace" (LXXXVII); "For Victory" (LXXXVIII), praising God whose "Almighty arm, / Hast kept us from the spoil and shame / Of those who sought our causeless harm" (st. 1, 1-4), and whose power "made us masters of the field" (st. 2, 2); and "For the King's Day" (XC), texts being otherwise scriptural or liturgical. George Wither, *Hymns and Songs*

of the Church (London: J.R. Smith, 1856, originally 1623), pp. 268-70, 289-90, 291-92, 295-97.

49. Milton, *Areopagitica*, in *Complete Prose Works* (London: Oxford University Press, 1949), Vol. II, p. 553. Cf. pp. 551-52.

50. Bailey, p. 49.

51. Escott, pp. 19-20.

52. *Works*, IV, p. 428.

53. Philip Doddridge, *Hymns Founded upon Various Texts in the Scriptures* (London: Job Orton, 1793 ed., originally 1755), No. 140: "O Righteous God, thou Judge supreme."

54. Doddridge, No. 146.

55. Pasted into various eds. of *Founding Hospital Collection* (1797 *et seq.*) and sometimes headed "Hymn for Ps. 148: Hayden (*sic*)" (*HG* 601).

56. By Sir Robert Grant, published in Bickersteth, *Church Psalmody* (1833). "A good example of the new search for poetic standards which Heber . . . promoted" (*HG* 575).

57. Published in Henry Francis Lyte, *Spirit of the Psalms* (London, 1834). Full text in *PCH* 126. Stanza 4 (originally marked "optional"), ll. 2-3. "Blows the whirlwind it is gone. / But, while mortals rise and perish, God . . ."

NOTES TO CHAPTER ELEVEN

1. Eliade, pp. 110, 124.

2. Cited in John Beer, *Coleridge the Visionary* (London: Chatto, 1959), p. 117.

3. "I care not for Spring," sung in Dicken's *Pickwick Papers*, Chapter 28, treats Christmas as a winter, i.e., secular festival (Oxford: World's Classics ed. 1907), I, p. 470.

4. Rev. Thomas Pestel, "Psalm for Christmas Day," in *Sermons and Devotions New and Old* (1659), first used as hymn *EH* 20 (*HG* 77), text *PCH* 427.

5. *HG* 816.

6. Shakespeare, *Hamlet* 1:1, 128-64.

7. Full text *PCH* 49, where 1819 given for first use as hymn. Fullest hymnal version, 6 stanzas *AMR* 61, omits angelic message to shepherds, and reaction of Joseph and Mary. Usual four stanzas include event and application to present worshippers.

8. On this chorus in the *Christmas Oratorio*, see *HG* 91, and Johann Sebastian Bach, *Bach-*

Werke-Verzeichnis, ed. Wolfgang Schnieder (Leipzig. Breitkopf and Hartel, 1961), p. 367.

9. Text and translation of "Vom himmel" (R. Bainton, 1948) in *PCH* 3.

10. Full text, with scriptural references, *PCH* 59. *Coll. P.* (1830) 602, as "herald angels," has 7 stanzas, including No. 9 ("Adam's likeness . . .") but not 10 ("let us . . ."), thus omitting idea of Christ reborn in each believing heart, another indication of post-Wesleyan conservative reaction among Methodist clergy. On influence of Matthew Henry's scriptural commentary upon Wesleyan inwardness and simplification of life to following Christ, see *Coll. P.*, pp. 472n, 474n.

11. *EH* 15. For more favourable view, see Colquhoun, p. 54ff., esp. p. 59.

12. Latin text *PCH* 175.

13. Original text, in Julian 489 ii, dated 20 December 1735 and headed "Christ's Message, from Lk. 4:18-19," itself a reading of Isa. 61.1-2. Orton's editorial preface indicates that author designed hymn for singing after sermon, as stated by Colquhoun, pp. 32-37, who also points out, p. 36, his "strong social concern" and "deep compassion for the poor."

14. Earliest printed version 1710 (*HG* 502). Lines re liberator: "captivum solve Israel" (2) and "ex hostis tuos ungula" (82). Motif clear in translation of C. Coffin, "Instantis Adventum Dei" (*Paris Breviary*, 1736) by "H.P." (*EH* 11) but suppressed in that of "J. Chandler and Compilers" (*AMR* 48).

15. *Hymns of Intercession* (1758). Variants listed by Julian 681-2, who gives originating text of Cennick, including lines: "All who hate Him must, *ashamed*, / Hear the trump proclaim His day," with Madan's alteration to "must, *confounded*." Wesley's lines specify, but do not limit, application to original betrayal. Not in *Coll. P.* (1780), but No. 66 in 1830 ed.

16. *Hymns for Nativity* (1744), 10. Not in *Coll. P.*, but in collections of Whitefield and Madan (Julian 252-3). Original text, in E.H. Bickersteth (comp.), *Hymnal Companion to Book of Common Prayer* (1878 ed., reprinted London: Longmans, 1919) 470, includes lines quoted.

17. A "new composition" for *Scots Paraphrases* 19 (*HG* 709). Original stanza 2, on slaugh-

ter of Midian's host, usually omitted but is in *PCH* 98.

18. *AM*, alone of leading hymnals, gives "The people that in darkness sat" (*AMR* 80), a title better indicative of wider application. Cf. "Our God, our help in ages past," discussed in Chapters 1 and 10.

19. On variants, misattribution to Countess of Huntington, and text in use, Madan's sts. 1-3 (*Psalms & Hymns*, 1760), see Julian 252.

20. Cited in Thompson, p. 371. For Marxist and Freudian views of Methodism, see Thompson, Chapter 11 *passim*, and Gordon Rattray Taylor, *The Angel-Makers: A Study in Psychological Origins of Religious Change, 1750-1850* (London: Heinemann, 1958; rev. ed. Secker & Warburg, 1973), pp. 130-33, 138-39, 153-56, 186-87.

21. Cited by Thompson and Taylor. For protest against their reductive treatment of hymns, see Davie, *A Gathered Church*, pp. 45-48.

22. Culy's lines cited by Tamke, p. 38, but misattributed to Toplady. "Hungry and thirsty . . ." in *Collection of Hymns from Several Authors with Several translations from the German Hymn Book of the Ancient Moravian Brethren* (London, 1741), p. 10, st. 4. "Saviour's Blood," *ibid.*, p. 35.

23. See Chapter 7, and Chapter 11 n7, above.

24. *HG* 804 says omission "totally indefensible" in view of Watts's title "Crucifixion to the world by the Cross of Christ." Davie, in *Dissentient Voice*, p. 72, says "emasculates the piece quite grievously" by concealing "emblematic motif of the Redeemer's blood."

25. Galatians 6.14.

26. Watts, *Works*, IV, p. 450, st. 4.

27. *Hymns* (1709), I, 19, st. 5, erased by Watts but reprinted in *Works*, IV, p. 157, and cited in John Hoyles, *The Waning of the Renaissance 1640-1740* (The Hague: Martinus Nijhoff, 1971), p. 232, as evidence of Watts's ambivalence, illustrated from hymns in Lionel Adey, "Great-Aunt Tilly's Beautiful 'Ymns: A Victorian Religious Sub-Culture," *Wascana Review* XII, 1 (1977): 21-47, esp. p. 30.

28. Original texts and Wesley's translations in John L. Nuelsen, *John Wesley and the German Hymn*, trans. Theo Parry, Sydney H. Moore, and Arthur Holbrook (Calverley: A.S. Holbrook, 1971, original 1938). On toning down of emotionalism for English

use, Nuelsen, p. 55, cites Wesley's later refusal of erotic hymns as "more suitable in the mouth of a lover than that of a sinner standing in the presence of Almighty God." My German-born assistant, Mrs. M. Abbott, calls the translations so free "that I would not have recognized them . . . successful for the English temperament, but translations they are not." She describes the originals as "a continuation of the old chivalric or . . . folk tradition of amplification of the beauty and details of clothes, body and trappings," thus "pictorial" or "sensuous" rather than erotic. For detailed commentary on style of translations see James Taft Hatfield, "John Wesley's Translations of German Hymns," *PMLA* XI (1896): 171-99.

29. *Coll. P.* 343. Literal translation here by Mrs. Abbott.

30. Nuelsen, pp. 113-14.

31. My comments paraphrase those of Mrs. Abbott.

32. Nuelsen, No. 2, pp. 111-12 (19 stanzas). Wesley also omits metaphors on wicked flame tempting God to follow strange lovers (st. 9), "Shepherd! let me enter the meadow" (st. 11) and "return to me as a child" (st. 12), while retaining theological metaphors of blood-stained garments (11) and Father's rest (12).

33. Nuelsen 28, pp. 153-56; *Coll. P.* 183.

34. Stanza 6 (re Devil), 17 (nakedness), 31 (rendered as "That all who to Thy wounds will flee / May find eternal life in Thee."

35. John Gambold, preface to *Collection of Hymns of the Children of God* (London, 1754), revision of 1741 *Collection*. For fuller discussion see England and Sparrow, pp. 4-16; Ronald Knox, *Enthusiasm: A Chapter in the History of Religion* (Oxford: Clarendon, 1950, 1982 ed.), p. 409.

36. *A Young Man's Meditation . . . Some Few . . . Poems upon Selected Subjects and Scripture* (1664) (Julian, 269 ii). First used in *Anglican Hymn Book* (1868), but "ignored by all mainstream Anglican books until 1950" (*HG* 473). In Congregational (1884) but not Primitive Methodist (1887), Baptist (1900)), or Scottish Church (1898) hymnaries.

37. *PCH* 53, except two stanzas omitted by John Wesley from Charlestown ed., 1737 and *Coll. P.* 22. Julian (130 i) dates before 1709, adding that MS found in garden of Epworth Rectory after fire.

38. Bailey, p. 94.
39. *Hymns and Sacred Poems* (1739), *Coll. P.* 201, *PCH* 58. Cf. Acts 16.25-26.
40. *Ibid.*, st. 5; cf. Ephes. 2.13-14.
41. St. 7ff. of "Glory to God, and praise, and love." Full text *PCH* 60. Nine stanzas (of eighteen) in *Coll. P.* No. 1 include all used in hymn save "He speaks, and listening to his voice" (st. 5 of hymn).
42. John Wesley records in his Journal, 31 October 1766, that a woman died crying "Glory!" after singing "Nature's last agony is o'er"; 21 June 1767, another died "overwhelmed with peace and joy unspeakable" after singing "I the chief of sinners am, / But Jesus died for me." An entry in 1748 records singing of "Lamb of God, whose bleeding Love" by a felon about to be executed. In *Works of John Wesley* (14 vols., London: Methodist Confernce, 1872, rpt., Grand Rapids: Zondervan, 1958-59), Vol. III, pp. 268, 285; II, p. 125.
43. Motive for omission suggested by Dr. Hobbs.
44. John Keats, *Complete Works*, ed. H. Buxton Forman (Glasgow: Gowars & Gray, 1901), Vol. V, pp. 53-55. Cf. Knox, pp. 481-82, 527, 540, and esp. 547: Wesleyans "have succeeded in identifying religion with a real or supposed experience"; J. Ernest Rattenbury, *Evangelical Doctrines of Charles Wesley's Hymns* (London: Epworth Press, 1941), p. 89, on "Blood Applied by the faith I feel"; 95-99 on truth reached not by enquiry but by "spiritual combat"; 175 on Holy Spirit in faith; and esp. 184: "the mystical and imaginative soul leaps over time, turns the past into the present"; George Sampson, "A Century of Divine Songs," in *Proceedings of British Academy* (1953), Vol. XXIX, p. 61 on mystical creative spirit and symbols maintaining contact between spiritual and actual world.
45. *Coll. P.* 29.
46. *Ibid.* 24. Elizabeth Hannon, in "The Influence of *Paradise Lost* upon the Hymns of Charles Wesley" (Unpublished thesis, University of British Columbia, 1985) regards all seventeen hymns in this section as about the death and passion of Christ, and the believer's response.
47. *Coll. P.* 25.
48. Of *Coll. P.* 22-38: Nos. 22-25, 29, 32-35. Of *Coll. P.* (1830), 22-40: Nos. 22-28, 33-36, 39.

49. *Anima Christi* believed 14th century, but cult of Sacred Heart stems from visions of St. Margaret Alacoque, 1673-75, Mass and Office authorized in 1765. Precious Blood celebrated by various orders in 19th century and by whole R.C. Church from 1849, but suppressed in 1969. (See *Concise Oxford Dictionary of Christian Church*.) Bynum, p. 121, quotes Cistercian Guerric (12th century) on Christ as "cleft rock" reviving devotee who takes refuge within Him.
50. "Come, all ye chosen saints of God"; "Now from the Garden to the Cross"; "Much we talk of Jesus' Blood" Nos. 153, 797, 154 in *Gadsby's Hymns* (1814; 1853 Manchester ed.). Julian before list, p. 492 i: many show "passionate love of the Redeemer", i.e., mode, but not theme, obsolescent.
51. E.g., in Baptist collection of Ash and Evans (Bristol, 1769), 16 successive titles in index refer to the Father as "Great."
52. *OH* II, 57, headed "Looking at the Cross," and discussion in Bennett, p. 182-83.
53. On shock and relief technique, see *Class and Idol*, Chapter 1. Follow-up, i.e. Bible classes and mid-week devotional meetings, common to Methodists and Evangelicals.
54. Originally J. Allen: "While my Jesus I'm possessing" (1757); rewritten by W. Shirley for *Countess of Huntingdon's Collection* (1770); three further stanzas by anon. (1854), *HG* 673.
55. *PCH* 91, with rationale and O.T. originating text *ibid.*, p. 38: claim is that Cowper's text now used only in churches not troubled by "antipathetic reaction." Among most frequently reprinted hymns, as indicated in *Class and Idol*, Chapter 5. More favourable criticism in J.R. Watson, "Cowper's Olney Hymns," *Essays and Studies* XXXVIII (1985): 45-65.
56. *Finita, in Symphonia Sirena Selestarum* (Köln, 1695). Usually sung in translation of F. Potts; others listed in *HG* 849. Neale ascribes text to "12th century," but earliest known MS 18th century (Julian 376-77). *AM* (1861), *EH* 625.
57. *HG* 347. Tune "Easter Hymn" associated with text since 1708.
58. *Hymns* . . . (1739), omitted from *Coll. P.* (1780) but No. 629 in *Coll. P.* (1830). Altered by Madan, 1760, esp. by omission of sts. 7-9.
59. Translation by Frances Cox, *Sacred Hymns from the German* (London, 1841) and *EH*

134. On Gellert (1715-69), see Julian 406-7.

60. *Miles Lane* (W. Shrubsole, 1779). Alternative used in Episcopalian churches is *Coronation* (O. Holden, 1793). Both in *Hymnal, 1940*, 355.

61. *PCH* 214, *EH* 381, *AMR* 224.

62. "Hail the day that sees Him rise," *Coll. P.* (1830) 630 (in Supplement); Rattenbury, p. 276, confirms Wesley's love of Handel and, p. 165-66, that Resurrection and Ascension inspired him less than Passion.

63. *Poems* (1760, 1780), i. 175, "The Wonders of Redemption." First used as hymn in John Ash and Caleb Evans, (Baptist) *Collection of Hymns Adapted to Public Worship* (Bristol, 1769), Julian 64 ii. My text from *Parish Hymns* (Philadelphia: Perkins & Reeves, 1843), 94.

64. Published 1787. Text in *Parish Hymns*, 93.

65. Date given is first appearance, but authorship confirmed in Medley's own edition of his *Hymns* (1800), Julian 556 i.

66. *PCH* 167, translation by B. Webb (1852).

67. John 1.9. "Sol Invictus" transformed in R.C. Holy Saturday Lighting of New Fire and in hymns, e.g., "Splendor paternae gloriae" (Cf. "Christ whose glory fills the skies") Cf. R.C. feast of Christ the King, instituted 1925, and medieval hymn "Jesu, Rex admirabilis"; Evangelical Revival hymns, e.g., "Poor, weak and worthless as I am / I have a rich almighty Friend," Newton *OH* I, 30.

68. Expanded by Collyer, 1812, from anon. stanza published 1802. Misattributed to Luther, via Ringwaldt (1596). Many versions listed in Julian 454-55 furnish evidence of apocalyptic temper in early nineteenth century.

69. Dickens, *Great Expectations* (1860), Chapter 56.

70. See Terry G. Sherwood, "Tasting and Telling Sweetness in George Herbert's Poetry," *English Literary Renaissance* XII (1982): 319-40; also C.S. Lewis, *Surprised by Joy*, esp. Chapter 11 *passim*. Full text of "How sweet . . . ," *PCH* 85, called in *ibid.*, p. 38: "as tender as any medieval mystic's devotion." For different view of hymn's structure, see Colquhoun, pp. 201-5, which misses sense of "Husband" as "one who tends."

71. *Coll. P.* 517 is a different text from that commonly sung, calling on Christ, as "Tree of Life" to "rise / In every longing heart." To this image of Fall Reversed are added (st. 4), those of His "people" as His "bride" and "transcripts" of His "holiness."

72. *OH* I, 62.

73. *Coll. P.* (1830), 553. On Madan's alteration (1760) of "He dies . . .," itself based on Watts's "He dies! the Heavenly Lover dies," see Julian 500.

74. Wesley, *Redemption Hymns* (1/47) and *Coll. P.* 374. Source given in *HG* 442 as 2 Cor. 3.18, but in *PCH* as also Ps. 106.4 ("Visit us with thy salvation"), Malachi 3.1 ("suddenly return and never . . ."), 2 Cor. 5.17 ("Finish then thy new creation"), Ephes. 5.27 ("Pure and spotless . . ."); 1 Cor. 13.12 ("till in heaven we see thy face") and Rev. 4.10 ("cast our crowns"). Derivation from Dryden, "Fairest isles, all isles excelling" is a critical commonplace. For omitted verse, objective calling for renewal of power to sin, see *Coll.P.* 17.

75. *Hymns for Real Christians of All Denominations* (1762 ed.), 55.

76. See Rattenbury, p. 260.

77. *Ibid.*, p. 133.

78. *Ibid.*, p. 278-80.

79. See Taylor, *Angel-Makers*, pp. 226-28.

80. See Chapter 3, above, Raby, p. 365, and Bynum, pp. 129-33.

81. To be discussed in *Class and Idol*, Chapter 8.

82. *Hymns*, 188, and *PCH* 51 under title "Relieving Christ in his Poor Saints" (Matt. 25.40).

83. See full text of "Hark . . .," *PCH* 52.

84. Full text (1822) in James Montgomery, *Poetical Works* (4 vols., London: Longmans, Orme, Green, Longmans, 1841), Vol. II, pp. 287-89 (12 stanzas) and *PCH* 108 (rev. 1853) with further scriptural references.

85. Montgomery, *Poetical Works*, "The West Indies," I, pp. 133-79; "Songs on the Abolition of Negro Slavery, in the British Colonies . . .," Nos. 1-5 in IV, pp. 225-34.

86. Full text of Watts, *Psalms*, Ps. 72 (Part 2), in *PCH* 43.

87. *OH* II, 44.

88. *Hymns for our Lord's Resurrection* (1746) (*HG* 612); not in *Coll. P.*

89. No. 453 in both *Hymns . . . for . . . Real Christians . . .* and *Coll. P.*: "Sov'reign of all! whose will ordains," composed in 1744 to rebut slander that Wesleys were agents of Stuart Pretender (Julian 1069 ii).

NOTES TO CHAPTER TWELVE

1. "When rising . . .," last of six weekly hymns in *Spectator*, 1712, "composed during this my sickness." Added to *Scots Paraphrases*, evidence to Julian (17 ii) of popularity.
2. Translations by George MacDonald and Catherine Winkworth in Martin Luther, *Works* (in English), ed. Jaroslav Pelikan (St. Louis: Concordia Publishing House, 1958), Vol. LIII, p. 428, st. 1 of "In Peace and Joy I now depart," ending "As my God hath promised me, / Death is become my slumber."
3. "Supreme quales, arbiter" (1686), *PCH* 170.
4. "And must this body die," Watts, *Hymns*, II, 110.
5. Text from *Hymns of the Protestant Episcopal Church* (Philadelphia: Hooker, 1845), 193. Originally No. 189 in 1755 ed. of *Hymns*, titled "The final Sentence and Misery of the Wicked," and based on Matt. 25.41.
6. Watts, *Hymns*, II, 3, under "Death and Burial for dying Friends."
7. Charles Wesley, *Hymns for Children* (1763), and *Coll. P.* 41-42.
8. Better known as "Let Saints on earth in concert sing" (originally st. 2), in *Funeral Hymns*, 2nd series (1759), then No. 735, i.e., in Supplement of *Coll. P.* (1830).
9. Ariès, *Centuries . . .*, p. 71: "[In 17th century] Childhood was becoming the repository of customs abandoned by adults."
10. *Hymns for . . . Methodist Sunday Schools*, (1816), 209.
11. *PCH* 297, by Sarah F. Adams, based on Genesis 28.
12. Composed for New Year's Day, 1842, published in Horatio Bonar, in *Songs for the Wilderness* (1844), then in *Hymns of Faith and Hope* (1857), titled "A Pilgrim's Song." Text from *Hymnal Companion*, 82.
13. Ariès, *Hour . . .*, esp. plates pp. 428-29, paralleled in secular literature, *ibid.*, pp. 411, 435-46 (re Brontës). On pp. 249, 253 disembodied soul shown in new imagery from 13th century and, p. 285-86, in communion with saints. Duality of body and soul begins in "middle of medieval period" (p. 394) to replace "idea of *homo totus*." Survival or sleep: "Once deprived of the soul, the body was nothing but a handful of dust, which was returned to nature." Cf.

Hamlet, 2.2.308: "quintessence of dust."
14. To be discussed in *Class and Idol* Chapter 3.
15. In *Church Hymns* (1871), full text in *AM* (1889). Inspired by G. Moultrie, "Brother, now thy trials are o'er," in *People's Hymnal* (1867), reproduced as "Now the labourer's toils —," *EH* 358 (*HG* 495). In Moultrie text, angels bear soul to "Fields of Paradise" where "towers of Sion" rise, and at "golden gate" of the "New Jerusalem," martyrs wait to be met on "further shore" by "Friends and dear ones gone before." Traditional images thus combined with those of consolation literature, discussed in Ariès, *Hour . . .*, pp. 450-54.
16. In *Hymns of Eastern Church* but admitted by Neale to contain little of originating text by St. Joseph the Hymnographer (Julian 986 ii). *AM* (1889), 609, not *EH* or *AMR*.
17. Stanzas 1-3, 1866; st. 4, 1870; *AM* (1889), 222, and many late Victorian hymnals, esp. for children. *AMR* 284.
18. Mrs. van Alstyne (1858), but maiden name Crosby conventionally used. "Safe . . ." 1868, published in *Bright Jewels* (1869); her "most popular" (Julian 1204 ii). Further discussed in *Class and Idol*, Chapter 4. On genre, see Ann Douglas, "Heaven Our Home: Consolation-Literature in the United States, 1830-80," in David Stannard (ed.), *Death in America* (Philadelphia: Pennsylvania University Press, 1975), pp. 49-68 (basis of Ariès, *Hour, loc. cit.*).
19. Text from *Baptist Church Hymnal* (London, 1900), 464. Published first in *The Children's Hymn-Book* (London, 1881). Author, identifiable as "E.O.D.," in Julian, 1560 ii, Anglican convert to R.C. faith.
20. Stanza 3, on God taking "his harvest home" purging "All that doth offend, that day [of Judgment]"; and "harvest home" song of "Church Triumphant" when all are "safely gathered" to abide in "God's garner."
21. "There is beyond the sky," No. 11 in Watts, *Divine Songs Attempted in Easy Language for Children* (London, 1715).
22. Milton, *Paradise Lost*, I, 210. Cf. Cowper on "ever-burning lake," *OH* III, 20.
23. *OH* III, 2.
24. *OH* I, 55, st. 5.
25. E.g., William Beckford, *Vathek* (1786); Charles Maturin, *Melmoth the Wanderer* (1820).
26. *Class and Idol*, Chapters 7-9.
27. *Ibid.*, Chapter 4.
28. William Williams (1745), trans. Peter Will-

iams (unrelated), 1771. *Cwm Rhondda* by John Hughes, deacon, Salem Baptist Chapel, Pontypridd, 1905, for Welsh song festival. This information and detailed exposition of source-texts (Exod. 16.4-18; 17.4-6; 13.21; 33.14-16) and New Testament allusions, in Colquhoun, pp. 191-97. "Redeemer" first used 1854 and in *AM* (1889) 196, *EH* 397, etc. Variants listed in Julian 77.

29. Originally, in *Hymns for Those that Seek . . . Have Redemption* (1747), and *Coll. P.*, 66. Thought by Julian (537 ii) "somewhat unreal for general use" though "long . . . most popular with Methodist bodies" and attributed by G.D. Stevenson (*Methodist Hymn Book Notes*, 1883) to John Wesley, whose life hymn fitted the more closely.

30. Routley, *PCH* 410n, ascribes to R.C. priest under death sentence *c.* 1593, in London, and gives source as "Meditations of St. Augustine." His full text alludes to supposed composition of "Te Deum" by SS. Ambrose and Augustine.

31. E.g., Milton, "Lycidas" 84, 172-85; Vaughan, "My soul, there is a country" (*passim*); Crossman, "Jerusalem on high" (*EH* 411, *AM*, 1889, 233, *AMR* 280).

32. Watts, *Works*, IV, p. 428; *Hymns*, II, 66. Bailey, p. 50, tentatively refers vision to Deut. 34.1-4. Routley (*HG* 726) lists suggested scenes but favours Southampton Water.

33. In preface to "Milton" (1804): *Blake: Complete Writings*, ed. Geoffrey Keynes (London: Oxford University Press, 1974), pp. 480-81. On "mills" as armament works, see David V. Erdman, *Blake: Prophet against Empire* (rev. ed., New York: Doubleday, 1969), pp. 395-97. On "mills" and Newtonian cosmology, see Blake, "There is no Natural Religion" (*c.* 1788), Proposition IV, in *Complete Writings*, p. 97.

34. F.E. Weatherly, "Last night as I lay sleeping" tune by Stephen Adams (copyright London: Boosey, 1892). Information by Dr. Bryan Gooch.

35. Cf. "Heaven's morning . . . shadows flee" with *Adonais*, 199-201, 340-41, 352, 460-63. Catalogue of Lyte's library, in Colbeck Collection, University of British Columbia, does not, however, include poems of Shelley.

36. (1) 23 texts based on scriptural passages, e.g., "Bright the vision that delighted"; (2) 15 embody death-wish, e.g., "Shall we gather at the river"; (3) 17 re heaven as escape or consolation, e.g., "Far from these narrow scenes of night" (1760); 19 re heaven as home, e.g., "I'm but a stranger here, / Heaven is my home"; 9 re heaven as especially for children, e.g., "Around the throne of God in heaven." Total number 83, as several texts fit more than one description, e.g., "Abide with me" both (1) and (2).

37. "Ye holy angels," by J.H. Gurney, based on R. Baxter (1672), cf. Ps. 148.2; Rev. 5.11; Heb. 12.1; Lk. 2.13 (*HG* 829). "How bright," Watts, *Hymns*, I, 41 (as "Those glorious Minds, how bright they shine," presently used text revision for *Scots Paraphrases*, No. 66 (1781). (*HG* 297). "Palms of glory," J. Montgomery, cf. Rev. 3.5, 4.4, 5.10, 20.6, etc. Tune of same title by MacLagan.

38. *Coll. P.* (1830), 735, ll. 19-25, not in abridgement by F.H. Murray (1852) used in *AM* (1861) (*HG* 132).

39. End of "Forth in thy name, O Lord, I go." Frank Baker, in *Charles Wesley's Verse: An Introduction* (London: Epworth Press, 1974), p. 15-16, remarks of the hymns that "no matter with what earthly subject they begin, they end in heaven," adding that "a clear belief in an after-life" and "frequent and fervent thoughts about it were common" in Wesley's day, as death "obtruded itself much more upon the attention of adults and children" than now.

40. *AH* XLVIII, 484. On original and analogues, see *HG* 402, Julian 597 ii. Latin is 102 lines in 17 stanzas. Neale's version (*The Hymnal Noted; Joys and Glories of Paradise*) 6, as in *EH* 431. Cf. Neale's close rendering with st. 15: "O quam vere gloriosum / Eris corpus fragile, / Cum fueris tam formosum, / Forte, sanum, agile, / Liberum, voluptuosum, / In aevum durabile." Cf. this with 1 Cor. 15.42-45; Phil. 3.21. Neale otherwise renders sts. 1, 4, 5, 16, 17, omitting accounts of celestial city, climate, music, eternal youth, chastity.

41. "As one who wanders into old workings" in Cecil Day Lewis, *Collected Poems*. (London: Cape with Hogarth Press, 1954), p. 61-62. Poem employs images of emergence from underground to connote social reform.

42. Raymond Moody, *Life after Life* (New York:

Bantam, 1976), *passim*. Cf. Sagan. *op. cit.*
43. F. Faber, *Oratory Hymns* (London, 1854); *AM* 223, *AMR* 354, *EH* 399.
44. R. Lowry (1865). See Julian, 699-700 and *Class and Idol*, Chapter 4. First hymnal reprint apparently *Hymnal Companion* (1878), 444, but revised.
45. Ann Steele, *Poems*, Vol. I, p. 157: "The Promised Land." Abbreviated in collections of Toplady, Ash & Evans (Julian 365 i). In *Hymnal Companion* 231, *Selected Hymns for use of Young Persons* (Quaker, 1903) 18, *Primitive Methodist Hymnal* (London: Dalton, 1887), 1018.
46. David Denham (ed.), *Saints' Melody* (London, 1837), 1005. Not in Julian.
47. Originally for Wesleyan Sunday school. In Cotterill's *Selection* (1819) (Julian 854 ii), then Episcopal Church (USA, 1845) 196 and *Hymnal Companion* 344.
48. A. Young, published Edinburgh, 1843. *Hymnal Companion* 446; *Scottish Free Church Hymn Book*, 1882. On composition see Julian 1161 i.
49. Rev. J. Lyth (Methodist), for infant school. 1845 (Julian 707 i). In *Methodist Scholars' Hymn Book* (1870); *Home and School Hymn Book* of Free Church of Scotland (London, 1892).
50. W. Hunter (1845), born Ireland, emigrated to U.S.A. at 6 (1817). Methodist Episcopal Church minister and Professor of Hebrew (Julian 543 i). In *Methodist Scholar's Hymnbook* and other school books.
51. Text in *College Hymnal* (New York: Biglow & Main, 1897), 365. Julian (1588 i) ascribes to G. Robins, a Boston bookseller. Hymnal reprint has Robins at head and "Charlotte Elliott, 1836" at foot.
52. See n18 above and pp. 62-63 of Stannard, *op. cit.*
53. "There is . . ." by Hester Hawkins, published in *Home Hymn Book* 1885 (Julian 1646 i). Text in (Sunday) *School Hymns* (London: Clarke, 1892), 229.
54. "I'm but . . .," by T.R. Taylor (1807-35), Congregational minister, in last illness (Julian, 562 ii, 1535 ii).
55. Thomas Kelly, *Psalms & Hymns* (1802) (Julian 615 i).
56. Tamke, p. 43, re late Victorian hymns from U.S.A. But cf. texts by Heber, Montgomery, and Neale (trans.) discussed earlier, and Rev. 21 *passim*.
57. E.g., Watts, "When I can read my title

clear," *Hymns*, II, 65; Wesley, "And can it be that I should gain / An int'rest in the Saviour's blood?"
58. Dorothy A. Thrupp, in *Hymns for the Young* (1836), under "Divine Providence" (Julian 1175).
59. On variants and centos, see *HG* 344. "For all . . .," W.W. How, in *Hymns for a Saint's Day.* Originally "Thy Saints." Popular from *AM* (1875) (*HG* 198).
60. To be discussed in *Class and Idol*, Chapter 9.
61. *Ibid.*, Chapter 4.
62. J. Cennick, *Sacred Hymns for Children* (1742), abridged Whitefield, 1753 (Julian 219). Anne Shepherd, n.d., trans. into Bechuana language 1838, thence to (Congregational) *Psalms, Hymns and Passages of Scripture* (London: Partridge & Oakey, 1853). Known as the "Leeds Hymn Book," being compiled by ministers there. Original text in *Methodist Sunday School Hymn Book* (London: Wesleyan Methodist Sunday School Union, 1879), 448 (Julian 82-83).
63. *PCH* 301. *Sunday School Teacher's Magazine, 1841;* first sung Blagdon (Anglican) Church, Somerset (*HG* 322).
64. *Council School Hymn Book* (London: Novello, 1905), 72. For use in other day and Sunday schools, see *Class and Idol*, Chapters 10, 12.
65. Albert Midlane (Plymouth Brethren), in *Good News for Little Ones* (1859). Stanzas rearranged *AM* (1875), 337. (*HG* 728). Full text *PCH* 310.
66. E.g., Frances Havergal, "Golden harps are sounding . . . Pearly gates are opened," in *Children's Hymns* (London: Society for Propagation of Christian Knowledge, 1879), 48; *School Praise* (Presbyterian, London: Nisbet, 1912), 64. Also "A beautiful land by faith I see . . . City of Light . . . gates of pearl" *Leeds Sunday School Union Hymn Book* (Leeds, 1878), 405.

NOTES TO CHAPTER THIRTEEN

1. Popularly attributed to Marx, but not in still-incomplete English translation of Marx and Engels, *Works* (New York: International Publishers, 1975-). The famous passage on religion as "the opium of the people", in the "Introduction" composed

after *Contribution to a Critique of Hegel's Philosophy of Law* (*Works*, Vol. III, pp. 175-77) says that man found "in the fantastic reality of heaven . . . nothing but the semblance of himself" and that "Man makes religion, religion does not make man." In Saul K. Padover, *Karl Marx: An Intimate Biography* (New York: New American Library, 1980), pp. 78-79, this work is dated 1844 and its case against religion traced to Ludwig Feuerbach, *Das Wesen des Christentums* (Leipzig, 1841). As Marx's Critique was translated only in 1926 (Marx-Engels, *Works*, III, p. 593, n. 29), it cannot have been widely known in Victorian England. As my colleague Roger Beehler points out, Feuerbach's work, translated in 1854 as *The Essence of Christianity*, had far more influence. In his *Lectures on the Essence of Religion*, trans. Ralph Mannheim (New York: Harper and Row, 1967), p. 187, Feuerbach says that God "did not . . . make man in His image; on the contrary, man, as I have shown in the *Essence of Christianity*, made God in his image."

2. See esp. Escott, p. 73; Bailey, pp. 49, 55; Charles Wesley, *Hymns for Times of Trouble, for the Year 1745*; passim.

3. Escott, pp. 244-47.

4. On "Supplements," see Louis F. Benson *English Hymn*, pp. 126-29, 144-46, 213-16, 161-68, 180-200. His latest English instance is a Congregational hymnal, 1836.

5. Great God, how infinite art Thou! (4); Great God, Thy Glories shall employ (5); Great God, of Glory and of Grace (156); Great God, of Wonders, all Thy ways (162); Great God, before whose piercing Eye (163); Great God, should Thy severer Eye (227); Great God, the Heavens Thy Name declare (295); Great God, this sacred Day of Thine (308); Great God attend, while Sion sings (316); Great God of Hosts, attend our Prayer (335); Great God of Heaven and Nature rise (336); Great God, Thy Watchful Care bless (344); Great is the Lord, His Power unknown (11); Great is the Lord our God (347), Great King of Kings, eternal God (319); Great Source of Being and of Love (355).

6. George Burder (comp.), *A Collection of Hymns from various Authors, intended as a Supplement to Dr. Watts' "Psalms and Hymns"* (London, 14th ed., 1811), preface.

7. Walter Kaufmann, in *Nietzsche: Philosopher, Psychologist, Anti-Christ* (Princeton: Princeton University Press, 1950), pp. 74-81, shows from various passages that "God is dead" was intended as social, not theological statement, i.e., about current irreligion.

8. *HG* 235.

9. Alfred, Lord Tennyson, *In Memoriam* (1850), xcvi.

10. On this in John Wesley, see Knox, pp. 452-55.

11. See Julian 571, and Joseph Irons, *Zion's Hymns, Intended as a Supplement to Dr. Watt's "Psalms and Hymns," for the Use of the . . . Congregation at Grove Chapel, Camberwell* (3rd ed., London, 1825), originally 1816.

12. *Paradise Lost*, II, 621, 937-50.

13. Cf. Wordsworth *Prelude* (1850), I, 401-15, 464-75; II, 399-413; IV, 323-38.

14. Rev. 15.2.

15. E. Cooper, *Selection of Psalms & Hymns* (Uttoxeter, 1805), based on Litany in *BCP* (*HG* 183).

16. J. Edmeston, *Sacred Lyrics* (1821), for children of a London orphanage (Julian 669). Cf. Matt. 4.1-11.

17. James Thomson ("B.V."), *City of Dreadful Night* (1874), Canto IV, cf. II, XVIII.

18. *HG* 386.

19. Samuel Partridge, *Important Truths in Simple Verse* (1841) (Julian 1585 ii). Text from *School Hymns* 39.

20. Sarah F. Adams (1805-48), in *Hymns and Anthems* (1841), based on Gen. 28. Tune by J.B. Dykes, for *AM* (1861), made lyric popular (*HG* 478). Author in Unitarian congregation of W.J. Fox (Julian 16).

21. Faber, *Jesus and Mary* (1849), familiarized by inclusion in *AM* (1861). Title "The Eternal Father" (Julian 779 ii), "Our Heavenly Father" (*HG* 464). Cf. Lev. 16.23-33; Hebrews 9.5, 24-28; Rev. 1.4; 4.4-5; 5.11, 7.11.

22. Newton's text is *OH* III, 65. Recumbent posture, adopted in Roman feasts and probably at Last Supper, perhaps alluded to by Faber.

23. "The only hymn to win wide currency despite a flat contradiction of the Psalmist" (*HG* 178).

24. *Prelude* (1850) VI, 562-608; XIV, 1-99; Matthew Arnold, "Rugby Chapel," esp. 171-208.

25. W. Whiting (1860) rev. to present form in *AM* (1861) with tune "Melita." Author

(1825-78), 1, Master of Choristers' School, Winchester (*HG* 169). Text in *PCH* 220, *EH* 540, *AMR* 487, etc.

26. Full text *PCH* 342; in *Hymns of Christ and Christian Life* (1867) (*HG* 329). Originating experience a local tradition, related by Mr. P.D. Bell, Department of Religious Education, Aberdeen College of Education.

27. Title line and two stanzas in use from original four by H.F. Chorley (1842). "God the Almighty One, wisely ordaining," by J. Ellerton (1870), referring to Franco-Prussian War, and in *Church Hymns*, including sts. 2 and 4 of present texts. Variants in Julian 440, information *HG* 249.

28. Under "Providence": *OH* II, 64, "On the Commencement of Hostilities in America."

29. Rev. W.H. Draper (1855-1933), translated "Canticle" between 1906 and 1916. First used as hymn in *Public School Hymn Book* (1919), with tune for which lyric written. Original "owes much to the *Benedicite*" (*HG* 13). On Draper's patriotic hymns, see *Class and Idol* Chapter 12.

30. Author served as Keble's curate, 1842-48; influenced by Newman while Fellow of Trinity College, Oxford. In *Hymns on the Catechism* (1842) (*HG* 71). Text used, *EH* 369.

31. E.g., (1) "Deus Creator omnium" (trans. J.D. Chambers), in Appendix to *Hymnal Noted*; (2) "O lux beata Trinitas" (trans. Neale, *op. cit.*); (3) "Splendor paternae gloriae" (trans. Chandler, 1837); (4) "Lucis Creator optime" (trans. Neale, *op. cit.*). 1-3 ascribed to St. Ambrose; 4 to St. Gregory.

32. Parallel texts, *PCH* 199. On Ps. 103.3, "who heals all your diseases," see Artur Weisler, *The Psalms*, trans. H. Hartwell (London: S.C.M. Press, 1962), p. 655. Point re "honour" owed to Dr. M. Hadley.

33. Luther, *Works*, Vol. LIII, p. 293-94, esp. st. 2: "So shall thy wife be in thy house / Like a vine with clusters plenteous, / Thy children sit thy table round, / Like olive plants all fresh and sound."

34. Discussed in *Class and Idol*, Chapter 11.

35. Watts, Preface to *Hymns* (1707), *Works*, IV, p. 255. See Escott, p. 112.

36. Examples to be discuissed in *Class and Idol* Chapters 2 and 3.

37. Ariès, *Centuries* . . ., pp. 46ff., 124ff.

38. *Class and Idol*, Chapters 9-11.

39. In Order for Compline, *BCP* (1928) (London: S.P.C.K., n.d.), p. 733.

NOTES TO CHAPTER FOURTEEN

1. Parallel texts *PCH* 172, dated *HG* 502, where Routley implausibly suggests that order of Antiphons ("7 Great O's") for 16-22 December determined by initials reversed to form *Ero cras* (Tomorrow I shall be there). Latin text uses Nos. 7 ("O Emmanuel, cf. Isa. 7.14); 3 ("O Radix Jesse", cf. 11.1, 5); 5 ("O Oriens," cf. Lk. 1.78); 4 ("O Clavis David," cf. Rev. 3.7); 2 ("O Adonai," cf. Exod. 20.1ff.).

2. *De specu tartari, educ et antro barathri*, which, as Colquhoun notes in his excellent commentary (pp. 17-23), T.E. Lacey (*EH* 8) renders as "nether hell" and "dread caverns of the grave."

3. Lacey: "Dispel the long night's lingering gloom, / And pierce the shadows of the tomb." *Tenebras* can signify "darkness," "lower world," or "ignorance."

4. Doddridge, *Hymns*, 203, MS dated 28 December 1735 (Julian 489). Full text, *PCH* 52.

5. Earliest known text 1770 (*HG* 246).

6. *OH* II, 57, stanza 3.

7. C. Coffin, *Paris Breviary*. and *Hymni Sacri* (1736), trans. J. Chandler, *Hymns of the Primitive Church* (sic), 1837. *EH* 9, *AM* (1875), 50.

8. Coffin, *Paris Breviary*. *HG* 856 lists translators, from Chandler.

9. "No worst, there is none," in *Poems of Gerard Manley Hopkins*, ed. W.H. Gardner & N.H. MacKenzie (4th ed., London: Oxford University Press, 1967), p. 100.

10. *PCH* 104, based on hymn by S. Medley (18th century). In *Hymns . . . not before Published*, 1815 (*HG* 787).

11. Rev. 17.14; John 1 *passim*.

12. In Heber's *Hymns Written and Adapted to the Weekly Church Services of the Year* (London: Murray, 1827), Palm Sunday. Slightly altered in *AM* (1861-89).

13. See Chapter 11, p. 124 above.

14. E.g., Jesus from "opened side" has supplied "thirsty world" with "endless streams of love"; Mary will love orphans "with a Mother's fondling care," in *Hymns for the Year* (London: Burns, Oates, 1867), 32, 178.

15. Original text, *PCH* 134. "I" altered to "we" in Anglican hymnals.

16. Julian 877 i.

17. Original text of Everest, an Episcopalian, in *Visions of Death* (1857), slightly altered for *Salisbury Hymn Book* (1857), *AM*, *EH*. One of only two American hymns in 1861 *AM* (*HG* 676).
18. On missionary, A. Baxter, see *HG* 336.
19. C.S. Lewis, *The Lion, the Witch and the Wardrobe* (London: Blès, 1951), Chapter 2.
20. From *The Masque of Mary* (1858), thence to Bramley & Stainer and 20th-century hymnals (e.g., *Book of Common Praise*, 736). Winter in opening lines only.
21. "Brightest and best of the sons of the morning."
22. "Once in Royal David's city," in *Hymns for Little Children* (1848), on credal clause "conceived of the Holy Ghost and born of the Virgin Mary" (*HG* 583). Account of Mrs. Alexander's benefactions to poor in introduction to *Poems*.
23. From account in J.E. Jones (comp.), *Book of Common Praise*, Annotated Edition (Toronto: Oxford, 1939), pp. 383-85.
24. In *Carols for Christmas* (1853, thence Bramley and Stainer. A "free rendering" of macaronic carol, 15th century (*HG* 254).
25. Cf. "O Saving Victim, opening wide / The gate of heaven to man below," Part 2 of "The heavenly Word proceeding forth," *EH* 330, *Book of Common Praise* 237, combining Neale and Caswall translations of "Verbum supernum prodiens," composed by Aquinas for Corpus Christi (*PCH*, p. 58).
26. Montgomery, "Hail the Lord's Anointed," st. 1. Author Anglican in final years.
27. "It came upon the midnight clear" in *Christian Register* (Boston, 1850), "narrowly predating 'Good King Wenceslas' as the first Christmas hymn in English with a social message" (*HG* 339). Cf. Micah 4.1-3.
28. *EH* 132.
29. "Christ is risen! Alleluia!," *Hymns of Love and Praise*, 1863 (Julian 763 i). Cf. "Jesus lebt" ("Jesus lives! Thy terrors now"), now much better known.
30. *PCH* 212, *EH* 111 are longest available selections (*HG* 501).
31. *Hymns for Little Children*, on credal clause ("suffered under . . . buried"). Mrs. Dorothy Baker, of Hymn Society of Great Britain, described to me view from Bishop's Palace, Derry, of crosses in hilltop cemetery across valley. In 1848, Mrs. Alexander had not met the future Bishop, consecrated in 1867.

32. "Tell me" discussed in *Class and Idol*, Chapter 4.
33. *PCH* 287. Hymnals using text, "composed near the end of her short life" (1830-69) listed in *HG* 82.
34. *EH* 127, *AM* 137, originally "Hallelujah."
35. Comments based on full text, *PCH* 223. Intended for Acension and Pentecost, but divided and abbreviated by compilers, "leaving a torso of . . . one of the profoundest and most scriptural utterances . . . since . . . Wesley" (*HG* 636).
36. First used as hymn in *AM* (1868) and "at once established itself . . . in Britain" but "has never done so in the United States" (*HG* 603). Colquhoun, in the fullest and most sympathetic scriptural exegesis known (pp. 83-90) relates "God's presence and his very self" to Incarnation, not Eucharist.
37. Cf. *Callista*, so discussed in L. Adey, "John Henry Newman," in *Dictionary of Literary Biography: Victorian Novelists* (Detroit: Gale Research, 1983), Vol. XVIII.
38. For list of American (11), British (17), and Canadian (2) hymnals of 20th century, catering for services of all major denominations (including R.C.) and British Broadcasting Corporation, see *HG* iii.
39. (1) *HG* 46, Angels from realms of glory; 96, Brightest and best . . .; 261, Hail to the Lord's Anointed; 652, Songs of praise the angels sang.
    (2) *HG* 500, O come, all ye faithful; 583, Once in Royal David's city; 606, Praise we our God this day.
    (3) *HG* 2, A great and mighty wonder; 55, As with gladness; 317, I love to hear the story; 339, It came upon; 535, O little town . . .; 573, O Word of God incarnate; 635, See, amid the winter's snow; 639, Sing, O sing, this blessed morn; 653, Songs of thankfulness and praise; 739, Thou didst leave thy kingly throne; 788, We three kings . . .; 819, Who is He, in yonder stall.
    (4) *HG* 65, Away in a manger; 75, Behold a little child; 262, Hail to the Lord who comes; 335, In the bleak mid-winter; 341, It is a thing most wonderful; 441, Love came down at Christmas.
    (5) *HG* 21, All poor men and humble; 173, Every star shall sing a carol; 217, Gentle Mary laid her child; 456, Morning has broken; 559, Sing, O sing of

Bethlehem; 579, On Christmas night all Christians sing; 767, Unto us a boy is born, 15th century; 790, We would see Jesus.

40. (1) *HG* 6, According to thy gracious word; 68, Be known to us in breaking bread; 89, Bread of Heaven, on thee I feed; 90, Bread of the world . . .; 224, Go to dark Gethsemane; 336, In the Cross of Christ . . .; 353, Jesus, I my cross have taken; 459, My faith looks up . . .; 619, Ride on . . . in majesty; 656, Spirit Divine, attend our prayers; 695, The Head that once . . .; 701, The Lord is King! Lift up thy voice; 703, The Lord is risen indeed; 756, 'Tis midnight, and on Olive's brow; 787, We sing the praise of him who died.

(2) *HG* 103, Children of Jerusalem; 408, Lord, as to thy dear Cross we flee; 501, O come and mourn . . .; 634, Saviour, when in dust to thee; 725, There is a green hill . . .

(3) *HG* 27, Alleluya! . . . Hearts to Heaven . . .; 28, Alleluia!, sing to Jesus; 42, And now, beloved Lord, thy soul resigning; 85, Blessing and honour and glory and power; 100, By Jesus's grave on either hand; 157, Crown him with many crowns; 201, For the beauty of the earth; 282, Here, O my Lord, I see thee . . .; 349, Jesus, gentlest Saviour; 362, Jesus, my Lord, my God, my All; 364, Jesus, name all names above; 479, Never further than thy cross; 584, Once only . . . once for all; 603, Praise to the Holiest . . .; 633, Saviour, thy dying love; 654, Souls of men, why will ye scatter?; 678, Tell me the old, old story; 689, The eternal (golden) gates . . .; 700, The Lord ascendeth up on high; 752, Thy life was given for me.

(4) *HG* 58A At (In) the Name of Jesus every knee . . .; 82, Beneath the Cross of Jesus; 285, His are the thousand sparkling rills; 293, Hosanna, loud hosanna; 304, I am not worthy, holy Lord; 326, I will sing the wondrous story; 342A, "It is finished!" Blessed Jesus; 354, Jesus, keep me near the Cross; 399, 'Lift up your hearts!': we lift them to the Lord; 415, Lord, enthroned in heavenly splendour; 437, Lord, when thy Kingdom comes remember me;

447, Man of Sorrows! what a name; 551, O my Saviour, lifted from the earth for me; 554, O perfect life of love; 737, This joyful Eastertide; 746, Throned upon the awful tree; 786, We sing the glorious conquest.

(5) *HG* 139, Come, dearest Lord, and deign to be our guest; 342B, "It is finished!," Christ hath known; 396, Lift high the Cross, the love of Christ proclaim; 414, Lord Christ, when first thou cam'st to men; 505, O dearest Lord, thy sacred head; 553, O perfect God, thy love; 665, Strengthen for service, Lord, the hands; 683, The bread of life, for all men broken; 815, Wherefore, O father, we . . .

41. Palm Sunday (2) only: *HG* 103, Passion Week (2): *HG* 78, Behold the Lamb of God; 501, 634, 725; Passion Applied: *HG* 369, Jesus, tender Shepherd; 380, Just as I am; 408; 444, Loving Shepherd of thy sheep; 797, What grace, O Lord, and beauty shone. Both (3): *HG* 42; 479; 633; 654; 752; Both (4) *HG* 82; 326, I will sing the wondrous story; 342A; 437; 447; 554; 746.

42. (3) *HG* 27; 85; 100; 157; 603; 636; 689; 700.

(4) *HG* 58; 293; 551; 737.

43. (2) *HG* 519, "O God unseen but ever near."

(3) *HG* 28; Alleluia, sing to Jesus; 201; 282; 349; 362; 584.

(4) *HG* 304; 399; 415.

44. *EH* 120: on Entombment, Harrowing of Hell, and recognition by Prophets, Thieves, etc.

45. E.g., "For beauty of the earth," original version in Orby Shipley (ed.), *Hymna Eucharistica* (1864), rpt. *PCH* 234, stanzas 3-5 ("joy of ear and eye, — of human love . . . gentle thoughts . . . each perfect gift of Thine"). On eucharistic designation, see *HG* 201.

46. Many for county education authorities were published in 1930's by Oxford University Press.

47. *PCH* 181. Originally Syrian, but from Nestorian rite (India) translated in prose by Neale, versified by C.W. Humphreys and adapted by Dearmer to tune in *EH* 329. Trans. by C.S. Phillips in *AM*, and by Adam Fox in *AMR* 494. See *HG* 665.

48. Information from *HG* 815.

49. *PCH* 266 (*HG* 832).

50. *PCH* 268: "A very sensitive and beautiful

text" (*HG* 342B, source of information).
51. On analogy see G.B. Tennyson, *loc. cit.*
52. *EH* 126.
53. Paul Fussell, *The Great War and Modern Memory* (New York: Oxford, 1979), pp. 118-19.
54. "At a Calvary near the Ancre," in *Collected Poems of Wilfred Owen*, ed. C. Day Lewis (London: Chatto, 1963), p. 82.
55. Anon.: "O Deued Pob Cristion," trans. Katherine Roberts, for *Oxford Book of Carols* (London: Oxford University, 1928), (*HG* 21).
56. Rev. Joseph S. Cook, for *Hymnary* (Toronto: United Church of Canada, 1930), 57. See *HG* 217.
57. Jean de Brébeuf (17th century) trans. J.E. Middleton (20th century), "'Twas in the moon of winter-time": *Hymn Book* (Canada), 412.
58. *Ibid.*, 426.
59. *PCH* 521; critical comment on author *ibid.*, pp. 198-99.
60. *PCH* 522.
61. *Hymn Book* (Canada), 399.
62. *Ibid.*, 425.
63. Collected *c.* 1904 in Sussex and published in *Oxford Book of Carols* (*HG* 579).
64. Adaptations of "Dies irae" in Eliot, *Murder in the Cathedral*, p. 72. *Vexilla regis* painting by Jones, and concluding sequence of *Anathemata* discussed in Bennett, pp. 201-4; religious ideas of poem in Patrick Grant, *Six Modern Authors and Problems of Belief* (London: Macmillan, 1979), pp. 76-83.
65. *PCH* 394. In North American hymnals only (*HG* 792 and, re genre, 223).
66. *PCH* 584. By T.C. Chao, trans. F.W. Price, 1962.

NOTES TO CHAPTER FIFTEEN

1. England, p. 102. Biblical texts and history of doctrines re Holy Spirit discussed in Wainwright, pp. 87-109 where, owing to stress on theology rather than poetic symbolism, a somewhat different selection of hymns from mine.
2. "Down Ampney," for *EH* 152; hymn "popular only after being set . . . by Vaughan Williams" (*HG* 123).
3. Rattenbury, pp. 173-74.
4. Knox, p. 450; Wordsworth, *Prelude* (1850), IV, 337.

5. Simon Browne, *Hymns and Spiritual Songs* (London, 1720), Book I; for original and variants, see Julian 246.
6. Text, *EH* 158. On *AM* selection, see *HG* 801.
7. *Short Hymns* (1762); original text based on Matthew Henry's N.T. commentary, in *Coll. P.* 318 and *EH* 343.
8. Section comprises: 649, "Hail, Holy Ghost, Jehovah, third" (Samuel Wesley, Jr.); 650, "Branch of Jesse's stem, arise" (Charles Wesley); 651, "Sovereign of all the worlds on high" (anon.); 652 "Come, holy Spirit, heavenly Dove" (Simon Browne, 1720); 653 "Come Holy Spirit, raise our songs" (C. Wesley, 1742); 654 "Creator Spirit, by whose aid" (Dryden, 1693); 655 "Jesus, we on the words depend" (C. Wesley, 1746 "word"); 656 "Why should the children of a king / Go mourning . . .?" (Watts, *Hymns*, I, 144); 657 "Eternal Spirit, come / Into thy meanest home" (anon.) None of these appears in *Coll. P.* (1780). As dates indicate, section combines old objective mythology with Methodist emphasis on inner experience, but cf. latter in "Veni sancte Spiritus," etc., discussed in Chapter 8.
9. On Spirit in Wesley, see Rattenbury, p. 180ff. "Light of Life . . ." first in *Hymns and Sacred Poems* II (1749), then *Coll. P.* 387. Cf. water image of Spirit "streaming" grace in No. 650, in n8 above. "Come, Holy Spirit, come," in Joseph Hart, *Hymns Composed on Various Subjects* (London, 1759). On Hart, see Julian 492-93.
10. Anon. See *HG* 658.
11. *PCH* 81, and p. 33.
12. *Paradise Lost*, IV, 32. *AM* (1875), 155.
13. *Psalms and Hymns for Use of Chapel of Rugby School* (Rugby, 1843), p. 23.
14. *Paris Breviary.* "O Holy Spirit, Lord of grace," trans. in Chandler, *op. cit. EH* 453, *AMR* 231. See *HG* 527.
15. Text in *Parish Hymns*, 153. First listed 1800, but by Benjamin Beddome (d. 1795) (Julian, 121-22).
16. *Hymns of . . . Protestant Episcopal Church* (1845), 232, attributed to Burder. Not in Julian.
17. A. Nettleton, in *Village Hymns* (1824), but my text *Hymns . . . Episcopal Church*, 231. Cf. similar title by Mant, *PCH* 206, and Julian 713 ii.
18. *PCH* 131.
19. Full text, *PCH* 109.

20. "St. Cuthbert" (Dykes), in *EH* 157, etc.
21. *Psalms, Hymns . . . Scripture* (1853), 397. Altered in *AM* (1875), 524 (*HG* 543). Cf. Romans 8.26: "the Spirit itself maketh intercessions for us with groans which cannot be uttered" (*AV*).
22. E.g., *Oliver Twist, Martin Chuzzlewit, Nicholas Nickleby, Tom Jones.*
23. William H. Parker, *School Hymn Book*, 1880 (*HG* 290), and *Psalms . . . and Hymns for School and Home* (London, 1882), 64.
24. Stuart Longfellow, *Hymns of the Spirit* (1864), and *AM* (1904), 364. See *HG* 291.
25. *PCH* 253; *HG* 94.
26. Søren Kierkegaard, *Purity of Heart Is to Will One Thing*, trans. Douglas V. Steere (New York: Harper, 1948), *passim*, esp. criticism of "double-minded" condition.
27. Galatians 2.20; Gen. 2.7; Ps. 104.30.
28. *Holy Year* (1862); *EH* 396, *AMR* 233. Abridged to 6 stanzas since *AM* (1868) (*HG* 256).
29. Text, *EH* 341. Set for Confirmation in, e.g., *Worksop College Hymn Book*, 102. See *HG* 461 and 78.
30. *EH* 577.
31. Originally for *London Mission Hymn Book* (London, 1874) then *AM* (1875), 211 (*HG* 526).
32. *PCH* 346.
33. *PCH* 564.
34. *PCH* 592, from *Africa Praise* (1868), and in (Scottish) *Church Hymnary* (1973).

NOTES TO CHAPTER SIXTEEN

1. Mrs. Alexander, for St. Patrick's day, 1889. Text, *PCH* 320A; history of poem and translation, *HG* 626.
2. *PCH*, p. 44 and *HG* 744.
3. Cf. Rev. 5.12, 7.12 and Chapter 3, above.
4. Rev. 4.8, 15.4,
5. Davies, IV, p. 206.
6. Cf. contrast in *PCH*, p. 95, between Baring-Gould leading procession of children singing "rousing" but "superficial" words of "Onward, Christian soldiers" with translation, "beginning tolerably, touching . . . solid scriptural ground, then wilting at the end." In *People's Hymnal*, thence, altered, *AM* (1875) (*HG* 744).
7. *HG* 5. "Eventide," W.H. Monk.
8. Preceded by booklet of 11 hymns for R.C. school, and *Jesus and Mary*, (both 1849).

Oratory Hymns 1854 and *Collected Hymns* 1862. On Faber's wish to produce R.C. equivalent to *OH*, see Julian 361 ii.
9. In *New Congregational Hymn Book* (London: Congregational Union, 1859), See *HG* 171.
10. E.P. Thompson, p. 322: citation: "The rich lose sight of the poor" in division of new cities into districts; 364: Methodist chapel "only community they [the poor] knew"; 379: chapel offered "uprooted and abandoned people of the Industrial Revolution some kind of community"; 407-9: extinction of former recreations; 416-17: disruption of family life.
11. Davies, IV, pp. 226-27: a "sense of the transcendent majesty of God . . . underlies . . . Binney's life-long dedication to . . . bringing back the dimension of reverence into Dissenting worship."
12. *PCH* 320B.
13. Originally in *Dream of Gerontius*, Canto 1, where hero faces first death as oblivion, then as prelude to judgment and damnation. List of reprints in *HG* 196 includes BBC, Church of Scotland (1973), Methodist (1933), otherwise only Anglican and R.C. hymnals, all in U.K.
14. Given in *PCH* 204, with date 1865 and source *Essays in Criticism*, First Series. Trans. follows free verse form of "Benedicite."
15. Full text *AMR* 172, but stanzas 4 ("Mother Earth") and 6 (Sister Death) starred for possible omission.
16. O.W. Holmes, conclusion of *Professor at the Breakfast Table*, 1859 (*HG* 427). Text, *PCH* 375.
17. *AM* (1868), *EH* 512 and *AMR* 223 have variants of Caswall's translation (*c.* 1854), *Hymnal 1940* 367 the less churchy one by Bridges (*Yattendon Hymnal*, 1899). For Caswall's st. 2, on the church bell pealing over "hill and dell" the joyous refrain "May Jesus Christ be praised", Bridges has refrain as "my song of songs" with which "God's holy house of prayer" has none to compare. No stanza by Bridges corresponds with Caswall's on the refrain as "solace" should "sadness fill my mind"; none by Caswall with that of Bridges on the nations finding their "concord" in the praise of Jesus, with which let the whole earth ring "joyous."
18. Keble's original text, in *"Christian Year" "Lyra Innocentium" and Other Poems* (Lon-

don: Oxford University, n.d.), p. 5-6. "Evening," has fourteen stanzas, *PCH* 122 nine, and most hymnals from *AM* (1861) six, e.g., *EH* 274, *AMR* 24 ("Sun of my soul . . ."), sts. 3, 7, 8, 12-14. Themes of omitted vv.: nightfall (1); travel in dark (2); discerning God and Providence in Nature and friends (4-6); last waking thought of rest in Christ (7); prayer for guidance of church and nation (9-11).

19. Respectively *PCH* 256, 265, 269, dated 1897, 1902, 1906, thus alluding to Diamond Jubilee, end of Boer War, and conceivably new Liberal government's social reform program. For occasions see *HG* 241, 378, 613. On Kipling's mixed motives, and allusion to Germans as "lesser breed without the law," see Davie *Dissentient Voice*, pp. 56-64. Chesterton, R.C. only from 1922, composed text for *EH*.

20. Davies (IV, p. 207 n60) notes American texts that "found their way" into English hymnals as expressive of "immanental and social version of the Kingdom of God": W.P. Merrill, "Rise up, O men of God"; Whittier, "Immortal Love, for ever full," "Dear Lord and father of mankind"; S. Johnson, "City of God, how broad and far"; S. Longfellow, "One Holy Church of God appears," "Beneath the shadow of the Cross."

21. My examples of nature hymns for children: "All things which live below the sky," E.J. Brailsford (1841-1921), in *English School Hymn Book* (London: London University, 1939), 7:
"Beauteous scenes on earth appear," R. Robinson (1850), in *A Book of Sacred Song for . . . School Board Schools* (London, 1873), 137:
"Every morning the red sun," C.F. Alexander (1848) in *Birmingham School Board Hymn Book* (Birmingham 1900) and *Hymns and Tunes for Use in Public Elementary Schools* [of West Riding, Yorkshire] (London: Novello, 1908), Nos. 17, 80;
"God who hath made the daisies," E.P. Hood (1852-57), in *Congregational Church Hymnal* (London: Congregational Union, 1884), children's section, 774;
"Great God, the world is full of Thee," H. Bateman (1858), in *School Hymns*, 38;
"Little drops of water," English version by E.C. Brewer, in *PCH* 305 and so exempted from Routley's criticism (p. 124) of

"terrible rubbish . . . fed to Victorian children";
"Suppose the little cowslip," Fanny Van Alstyne (née Crosby), in *Voice of Praise* (London: London Sunday School Union, 1886), 337;
"The morning bright with rosy light," T.O. Summers (1845), *Congregational Sunday School Hymn Book* (London: Congregational Union, 1881), 220.
"There's not a little flower that blows," H. Bateman (*Gospel Hymns Chiefly for Children*, 1850).
Cf. also "The leaves around me falling," in *Voice of Praise*, 372 and "Sunny days of childhood," in *Methodist Free Church School Hymns* (London, 1888), p. 190.

22. According to *Daily Telegraph* reader survey "Do We Believe?," analyzed in George McLeod, *Class and Religion in the Late-Victorian City* (London: Croom Helm, 1874), pp. 229-31.

23. Fussell, *loc. cit.* Gordon S. Wakefield, in "Beliefs in Recent British Hymnody," *The Hymn*, XXII: 1 (January 1971): 13-19, finds that Christ is now less a hero-figure or ideal man and more identified with the outcast and the poor, one who comes incognito.

24. I.e., Syriac, in Chapter 3, above.

25. *BCP*: the Litany.

26. For *AM* (1868), by principal editor, Rev. Sir. H.W. Baker. In subsequent eds. and wide range of hymnals, including R.C. (listed in *HG* 436) with source Ps. 119.89 ("O Lord, Thy word: endureth for ever in heaven").

27. Sandra S. Sizer, *Gospel Hymns and Social Religion: The Rhetoric of Nineteenth-Century Revivalism* (Philadelphia: Temple University Press, 1978), pp. 82ff., 114-15, 134-35, 147ff.

28. John Hick, *God Has Many Names* (Philadelphia: Westminster Press, 1982), pp. 8, 19.

29. Cited *loc. cit.*

30. Frye, p. 42. Cf., however, p. 48, where myth "inseparable from things to be done or specified actions" and so the cause of events in time.

31. Esp. Chapters 5, 10, 11 above.

32. *Suggested by Matthew Arnold's 'Stanzas from the Grande Chartreuse*, Canto I, 64-65, in *Poems and Some Letters of James Thomson*, ed. Anne Ridler (Carbondale: Southern Illinois University Press, 1963),

p. 6. In context, poet refers to loss of faith leading to "Eternal Death," as English "Blinded by our material might, / Absorbed in frantic worldly strife . . . Wealth gorging our imperial marts" (65-66, 68-69, 75).

33. Role of hymns in Lutheran, Wesleyan, and ecumenical movements is memorably discussed by Wainwright (pp. 198-217, 306-7), who, p. 192, cites Maurice Wiles's *Working Papers in Doctrine* on similar role of creeds in the modern crisis of belief.

SELECT BIBLIOGRAPHY

(Limited to works cited first-hand in notes; standard literary works mentioned only if quoted or referred to in detail.)

WORKS OF REFERENCE

Biblia Sacra Vulgatae Editionis. Sixti V. et Clementis VIII. London: Bagster, n.d.
Book of Common Prayer (1662).
Book of Common Prayer:. With the Additions and Deviations Proposed in 1928. London: Society for Promoting Christian Knowledge, n.d.
Concise Oxford Dictionary of the Christian Church. Ed. E.A. Livingstone. Oxford, London, New York: Oxford University Press, 1978.
Dictionary of Hymnology, A. Ed. John Julian. 2nd ed., 1907, rpt. New York, Dover Publications, 1957.
Dictionnaire de spiritualité ascétique et mystique, doctrine et histoire. Ed. Marcel Viller, F. Cavallera, and J. de Guibert. Paris: Beauchesne, 1937.
Encyclopaedia Judaica. Jerusalem, 1971-72.
Holy Bible, The. Authorized version, 1611.
Perry, David. *Hymns and Tunes of Interest by First Lines and Tunes: Compiled from Current English Hymnbooks.* London: Hymn Society of Great Britain and Royal School of Church Music, 1980.
Routley, Erik. *An English-Speaking Hymnal Guide.* Collegeville, MO: Liturgical Press, 1979.

HYMNS AND LITURGICAL VERSE KNOWN BY AUTHOR OR COLLECTOR

Adam of St. Victor. *Liturgical Poetry of Adam of St. Victor.* Ed. with notes by D.S. Wrangham. 3 vols. London: Kegan Paul, 1881.

Analecta Hymnica Medii Aevi. Ed. Guido Maria Dreves et al. 55 vols. Leipzig, 1886-1922.

Ash, John and Caleb Evans. *A Collection of Hymns Adapted to Public Worship.* Bristol, 1769.

Burder, George (comp.). *A Collection of Hymns from Various Authors, Intended as a Supplement to Dr. Watts' "Psalms and Hymns."* 1784. 14 ed. London, 1811.

Chandler, John. *Hymns of the Primitive Church.* London, 1837 (translation of Charles Coffin, *Paris Breviary* (1736) and *Hymni Sacri* (1737).

Cowper, William. *Olney Hymns.* See Newton, John.

Cox, Frances. *Sacred Hymns from the German.* London, 1841.

Dale, R.W., ed. *English Hymn Book.* London: Hamilton, Adams; Birmingham, Hudson, 1874.

Denham, David. *The Saints' Melody.* 1837. Rpt. London, 1870.

Doddridge, Philip. *Hymns Founded upon Various Texts in the Scriptures.* Ed. Job Orton. 1755. Rpt. London, 1793.

Gadsby's Hymns, ed. John Gadsby. Manchester, 1853. Originally *A Selection of Hymns for Public Worship,* ed. William Gadsby. 1814.

Greene, R.L. (ed., introd.). *Early English Carols.* 2nd ed. Oxford: Clarendon, 1977.

Heber, Reginald. *Hymns Written and Adapted to the Weekly Church Services of the Year.* London: John Murray, 1827.

Irons, Joseph. *Zion's Hymns, Intended as a Supplement to Dr. Watts' Psalms and Hymns, for Use of . . . Congregation at Grove Chapel, Camberwell 1816.* 3rd ed. London, 1825.

Keble, John. *The "Christian Year," "Lyra Innocentium," and Other Poems.* London: Oxford University Press, 1914.

Luther, Martin. *Works* (in English). Ed. Jaroslav Pelikan. St. Louis: Concordia Publishing House, 1958, Vol. LIII.

Martineau, James. *Hymns of Praise and Prayer.* London: Longmans, 1874.

Neale, J.M. *The Hymnal Noted.* London, 1854.

Neale, John Mason. *Hymns of the Eastern Church.* London, 1862, rpt. New York: AMS Press, 1971.

Joys and Glories of Paradise. 2nd ed. London, 1866.

Newton, John and William Cowper. *Olney Hymns.* 3 vols., 1779. London, 1843, single volume ed. Edinburgh: Paten and Ritchie, 1854.

Odes of Solomon. Trans. J.R. Harris (1909) in J.B. Platt (ed.), *The Forgotten Books of Eden.*

Odes of Solomon. Trans. James Hamilton Charlesworth. Oxford: Clarendon, 1973.

Kontakia of Romanos. Trans. Marjorie Carpenter. Columbia: University of Missouri Press, 1970.

Routley, Erik, ed. *A Panorama of Christian Hymnody.* Collegeville, MO: Liturgical Press, 1979. Parallel text hymns arranged by period and language, with introductory essays.

Walpole, Arthur Sumner, ed. *Early Latin Hymns.* 1922, 2nd ed. Hildersheim: Georg Olms, 1966. Introduction, Notes, and Concordance.

Watts, Isaac. *Hymns and Spiritual Songs.* London 1707, 1709.

Psalms of David Imitated. London, 1719.

Wesley, Charles and John. *Hymns and Sacred Poems.* London, 1739.

Hymns and Spiritual Songs Intended for the Use of Real Christians of All Denominations. 1753, 1762 ed.
Wesley, Charles. *Hymns for a Time of Trouble for the Year 1745.* London, 1746.
Wesley, John, ed. *A Collection of Hymns for People Called Methodists.* London, 1780.
A Collection of Hymns for the Use of People Called Methodists. 1780, Vol. VII in *Works of John Wesley,* ed. Franz Hildebrandt, Oliver A. Beckerlegge, and James Dale. Oxford: Clarendon, 1983.
A Collection of Hymns for the Use of People Called Methodists. Rev. ed., with Supplement. London: Wesleyan Conference Office [1830].
Psalms and Hymns. Charleston, 1737.
Wither, George. *Hymns and Songs of the Church.* 1623. London: J.R. Smith, 1856.

HYMNALS AND SERVICE-BOOKS

Baptist Church Hymnal: Hymns, Chants and Anthems. London: Psalms and Hymns Trust, 1900.
Book of Common Praise. Rev. ed. Toronto: Oxford University Press, 1938.
Book of Common Praise. Annotated ed. Comp. James Edmund Jones. Toronto: Oxford University Press, 1939.
Book of Sacred Songs for [London] School Board Schools. London, 1873.
Children's Hymns. London Society for Promotion of Christian Knowledge. London, 1876.
Collection of Hymns for the Use of Methodist Sunday Schools. Ed. Joseph Benson. 1808, 2nd ed. London, 1816.
Collection of Hymns from Several Authors with Several Translations from the German Hymn Book of the Ancient Moravian Brethren. London, 1741.
Collection of Hymns of the Children of God, ed. John Gambold. London, 1754.
College Hymnal. New York: Biglow and Main, 1897.
Congregational Church Hymnal. Ed. George Barrett. London: Congregational Union, 1884.
Congregational Sunday-School Hymn Book. London: Congregational Union, 1881.
Council School Hymn Book. London: Novello, 1905.
English Hymnal, The. Ed. Percy Dearmer and Ralph Vaughan-Williams. London: Humphrey Milford and A.R. Mowbray, 1906.
English School Hymn Book. Ed. Alfred H. Body and Desmond MacMahon. London: University of London Press, 1939.
Essex Hall Hymnal. London: British and Foreign Unitarian Association, 1891, rev. 1902.
Eton College Hymn Book. London: Oxford University Press, 1937.
Gospel Hymns, Chiefly for Children. Ed. J.B. Bateman. London, 1850.
Home and School Hymn Book. Edinburgh: Free Church of Scotland, 1892.
Hours of the Divine Office. 3 vols. Collegeville, MO, Liturgical Press, 1963.
Hymn Book, The. Toronto: Anglican and United Churches of Canada, 1971.
Hymn-Book Annotated, The. Toronto: Oxford University Press, 1939.
Hymnal Companion to Book of Common Prayer. Ed. Edward H. Bickersteth. 1870, rev. 1878, rpt. London: Longman, 1919.

Hymnal of the Protestant Episcopal Church, 1940. New York: Church Hymnal Corporation, 1940.

Hymnary, The. Toronto: United Church of Canada, 1930.

Hymns Ancient and Modern. London: Clowes, 1861, 1875, 1889, 1904, 1922.

Hymns Ancient and Modern Revised. London: Clowes, 1950.

Hymns and Tunes for Use in Public Elementary Schools [of West Riding of Yorkshire]. London: Novello, 1908.

Hymns for the Chapel of Harrow School. Ed. Charles J. Vaughan. London, 1855.

Hymns for the Chapel of Harrow School. 3rd ed. Ed. Henry Montagu Butler. London, 1881.

Hymns for the Use of Rugby School. Rugby, 1885.

Hymns for the Year. London: Burns, Oates, 1867.

Hymns of the Protestant Episcopal Church. Philadelphia: Hooker, 1845.

Latin Hymns of the Anglo-Saxon Church. Durham: Andrews, 1851. Parallel Latin and Old English texts.

Leeds Sunday School Union Hymn Book. (Originally 1833) Rev. ed. Leeds, 1878.

Methodist Free Church: School Hymns. London: A Crombie, 1888.

Methodist Scholar's Hymn Book. London, 1870.

Methodist Sunday Schools. 1816. See Benson, Joseph.

Methodist Sunday School Hymn Book. London: Wesleyan Methodist Sunday School Union, 1879.

New Catholic Hymnal. Ed. Anthony Petti and Geoffrey Laycock. London: Faber, 1971.

New Congregational Hymn Book. London: Congregational Union, 1859.

Parish Hymns: A Collection for Public, Private and Social Worship, Selected and Original. Philadelphia: Perkins, Reeves, 1843.

Primitive Methodist Hymnal. Ed. George Booth. London: Edwin Dalton, 1887.

Psalms of Solomon in Platt, *Forgotten Books of Eden.*

Psalms and Hymns for School and Home. London: Haddon, 1882 (Baptist).

Psalms and Hymns for Use of the Chapel of Rugby School. Rugby, 1843.

Psalms, Hymns, and Passages of Scripture for Christian Worship. London: Partridge and Oakey, 1853.

School Hymns. London: Clarke, 1892.

School Praise: A Hymn Book for the Young. London: Nisbet, 1912 (Presbyterian Church of England).

Scottish National Hymnal for the Young. Edinburgh, 1910.

Selected Hymns for the Use of Young Persons. 7th ed. York: W. Sessions, 1903 (Quaker).

Village Hymns for Social Worship. Designed as a supplement to the Psalms and Hymns of Ed. Asahel Nettleton. New York, 1824.

Winchester College Hymn Book. 1910, rev. ed. London: Oxford University Press, 1928.

Worksop College Hymn Book. London: Novello, 1938.

LITERARY WORKS: NON-LITURGICAL

Alexander, Cecil Frances. *Poems of Cecil Frances Alexander.* Ed. William Alexander. London: Macmillan, 1896.

Arnold, Matthew. "Rugby Chapel." 1857.

Augustine, Saint. *Confessions*.

Blake, William, "Milton," 1804, in *Complete Writings*. Ed. Geoffrey Keynes. London: Oxford University Press, 1974.

Butler, Samuel, *The Way of All Flesh*. London, 1903.

Chaucer, Geoffrey. "The Miller's Tale," *Canterbury Tales*. Prologue to *Canterbury Tales*. *Troilus and Criseyde*.

Coleridge, Samuel Taylor. *The Rime of the Ancient Mariner*. London, 1798. Gloss added 1817.

Dickens, Charles. *Great Expectations*. London, 1860. *Pickwick Papers*. 1837. 2 vols. Oxford: World's Classics, 1907 (many rpts.).

Dinesen, Isak. *Seven Gothic Tales*. New York: Random House, 1972.

Eliot, T.S. *Ash-Wednesday*. 1930. *Murder in the Cathedral*. 3rd ed. London: Faber, 1937.

Hopkins, Gerard Manley. "No worst, there is none," in *Poems of Gerard Manley Hopkins*. Ed. W.H. Gardner and Norman H. MacKenzie. 4th ed. London: Oxford University Press, 1967.

Huxley, Aldous, *Island*. New York: Harper and Row, 1962.

Joyce, James. *Portrait of the Artist as a Young Man*. New York: Huebsch, 1916.

Keats, John. *Complete Works*, 5 vols. Ed. H. Buxton Forman. Glasgow: Gowars, Gray, 1901.

Langland, William. *Vision of Piers Plowman*.

Laurence, Margaret. *The Diviners*. Toronto: McClelland and Stewart, 1974.

Lawrence, D.H. "The Ship of Death." *Complete Poems of D.H. Lawrence*. Ed. Vivian de Sola Pinto and Warren Roberts, 2 vols., (London: Heinemann, 1964), Vol. II.

Lewis, Cecil Day. "As one who wanders into old workings," in *Collected Poems*. (London: Cape with Hogarth Press, 1954).

Lewis, C.S. *The Lion, the Witch and the Wardrobe*. London: Blès, 1950.

MacDonald, George. *Back of the North Wind, The Princess and the Goblin, The Princess and the Curdie*. London: Octopus, 1979. *The Golden Key*. 1858 rpt. New York: Dell, 1967.

Marlowe, Christopher. *Tragical History of the Life and Death of Doctor Faustus*. 1588-93 (date disputed).

Milton, John. *Paradise Lost*. 1674. "Lycidas." *Poetical Works*. Oxford: Oxford University, 1904.

Montgomery, James. *Poetical Works*, 4 vols. London: Longmans, Orme, Brown, Green and Longmans, 1841.

Newman, John Henry. *The Dream of Gerontius*. London: Burns, Oates, 1865.

Oxford Book of Medieval Latin Verse. Ed. F.J.E. Raby. London: Oxford University Press, 1959.

Owen, Wilfred. "At a Calvary near the Ancre" in *Collected Poems of Wilfred Owen*. Ed. Cecil Day Lewis. London: Chatto and Windus, 1963.

Shelley, Percy Bysshe. *Adonais*. 1821.

Shakespeare, William. *Hamlet, Prince of Denmark*.

Tennyson, Alfred, Lord. *In Memoriam*. London, 1850.

Thomson, James ("B.V."). *City of Dreadful Night*. London, 1874. *Suggested by Matthew Arnold's "Stanzas from the Grande Chartreuse" in Poems and*

Some Letters of James Thomson. Ed. Anne Ridler. Carbondale: Southern Illinois University Press, 1963.

Waddell, Helen (trans., ed.). *Medieval Latin Lyrics*, 4th ed. London: Constable, 1933. Parallel Latin and English texts.

Watts, Isaac. *Works of the Rev. and Learned Isaac Watts D.D.*, 6 vols. Ed. Geo. Burder. London: J. Barfield, 1810.

Divine Songs . . . Attempted in Easy Language for Children. London, 1715.

Weatherly, F.E. "The Holy City." London: Boosey, 1892. Musical settings by Stephen Adams.

Wordsworth, William. "Ode on Intimations of Immortality from Recollections of Early Childhood." In *Poems of 1807*. London, 1807.

The Prelude, or Growth of a Poet's Mind. 1805, 1850. Parallel text ed., ed. J.C. Maxwell, Harmondsworth: Penguin, 1971.

"Tintern Abbey," in *Lyrical Ballads*, 1798.

BOOKS: CRITICAL, HISTORICAL, OR THEOLOGICAL

Adey, Lionel. *C.S. Lewis's "Great War" with Owen Barfield*, No. 14 in *English Literary Studies* monographs. Victoria: University of Victoria, 1978.

Alexander, Samuel. *Space, Time and Deity.* London: Macmillan, 1920, rpt. New York: Dover, 1964.

Ariès,Philippe. *Centuries of Childhood*, A Social History of Family Life (L'Enfant et la vie familiale sous l'Ancien Régime), trans. R. Baldick. London: Cape, 1962.

The Hour of our Death, trans. Helen Weaver. New York: Knopf, 1981.

Bailey, Albert Edward. *The Gospel in English Hymns: Backgrounds and Interpretations.* New York: Scribners, 1950.

Baker, Frank. *Charles Wesley's Verse: An Introduction.* London: Epworth Press, 1964.

Barfield, Arthur Owen. *History in English Words.* 1926, 3rd ed. Grand Rapids, MI: Eerdmans, 1967.

Poetic Diction. 1928, 3rd ed. Middletown, CT: Wesleyan University Press, 1973.

Beer, John. *Coleridge the Visionary.* London: Chatto and Windus, 1959.

Bennett, J.A.W. *Poetry of the Passion.* Oxford: Clarendon, 1982.

Benson, Louis F. *The English Hymn: Its Development and Use.* 1915, rpt. Richmond, VA: John Knox Press, 1962.

Bradley, Bruce. *James Joyce's Schooldays.* Dublin: Gill and Macmillan, 1982.

Brothers, Joan. *Religious Institutions.* London: Longmans, 1971.

Bynum, Caroline Walker. *Jesus as Mother: Studies in the Spirituality of the High Middle Ages.* Berkeley, Los Angeles: University of California Press, 1982.

Carnell, Corbin Scott. *Bright Shadow of Reality: C.S. Lewis and the Feeling Intellect.* Grand Rapids, MI: Eerdmans, 1974.

Chadwick, Owen. *The Reformation.* Harmondsworth: Penguin, 1972 ed.

The Victorian Church, 2 vols. London: A. & C. Black, 1966.

Coleridge, Samuel Taylor. *Biographia Literaria*, 2 vols. London: 1817.

Colquhoun, Frank. *Hymns that Live: Their Meaning and Message.* London: Hodder and Stoughton, 1980.

Davie, Donald. *Dissentient Voice*. Notre Dame: Notre Dame University Press, 1982.

A Gathered Church: The Literature of the English Dissenting Interest, 1700-1930. London: Routledge and Kegan Paul, 1978.

Davies, Horton. *Worship and Theology in England*, 5 vols. Princeton: Princeton University Press, 1961-75.

Davis, A.P. *Isaac Watts: His Life and Works*. London: Independent Press, 1943.

Eliade, Mircea. *Patterns in Comparative Religion*, trans. Rosemary Sheed. Cleveland: World Publishing Co., 1963.

Elliott-Binns, L.E. *Religion in the Victorian Era*. London: Lutterworth Press, 1946.

England, Martin Winburn and John Sparrow. *Hymns Unbidden: Donne, Herbert, Blake, Emily Dickinson and the Hymnographers*. New York: New York Public Library, 1966.

Erdman, David V. *Blake: Prophet against Empire*. Rev. ed. New York: Doubleday, 1969.

Escott, Harry. *Isaac Watts: Hymnographer. A Study of the Beginnings, Development and Philosophy of the English Hymn*. London: Independent Press, 1962.

Feuerbach, Ludwig. *Lectures on the Essence of Religion*. Trans. Ralph Mannheim. New York: Harper and Row, 1967.

Friedlander, Ludwig. *Sittengeschichte Roms in der Zeit von August bis zum Ausgangs der Antoinine*. 1921 illustrated edition. Vienna: Phaidon-Verlag, 1934.

Frye, Northrop. *The Great Code: The Bible and Literature*. New York: Harcourt, Brace, Jovanovich, 1982.

Fussell, Paul. *The Great War and Modern Memory*. New York: Oxford University Press, 1975.

Gathorne-Hardy, Jonathan. *The Public-School Phenomenon, 597-1977*, 1977, rpt., Harmondsworth: Penguin, 1979 (originally Hodder and Stoughton).

Grant, Patrick. *Six Modern Authors and Problems of Belief*. London: Macmillan, 1979.

Hick, John. *God Has Many Names*. Philadelphia: Westminster Press, 1982.

History of Music in Sound, Vol. II, Early Music to 1300. Ed. Dom Anselm Hughes, London: Oxford University Press, 1953. [His Master's Voice phonodisc, Vol. 2. Ed. Egon Wellesz]

Hoyles, John. *The Waning of the Renaissance, 1640-1740*. The Hague: Martinus Nijhoff, 1971.

Huxley, Aldous. *Island*. New York: Harper and Row, 1962.

"Music at Night" and Other Essays. Harmondsworth: Penguin, 1950.

James, William. *The Varieties of Religous Experience*. Gifford Lectures, 1902, rpt. New York: Random House, n.d.

Jaynes, John. *Origin of Consciousness in the Breakdown of the Bicameral Mind*. Boston: Houghton Mifflin, 1976.

Jeffrey, David Lyle. *The Early English Lyric and Franciscan Spirituality*. Lincoln: University of Nebraska Press, 1975.

Joachim of Fiore. *Concordia Novi ac Veteris Testamenti*. See B. McGinn "The Abbott and the Doctors." In Articles and Essays listed below.

Joinville, Jean de. *Chronicles of the Crusades*. London: Bell and Doldry, 1865.

Kaufmann, Walter. *Nietzsche: Philosopher, Psychologist, Anti-Christ*. Princeton: Princeton University Press, 1950.

Kierkegaard, Søren. *Purity of Heart Is to Will One Thing*, trans. Douglas V. Steere. New York: Harper and Row, 1948.

Kittel, Bonnie, *Hymns of Qumran*. Chico, CA: Scholars Press, 1981.

Knox, Ronald A. *Enthusiasm: A Chapter in the History of Religion*. 1950, 2nd ed., Oxford: Clarendon, 1962.

Kuntz, J. Kenneth. *The People of Ancient Israel: An Introduction to Old Testament Literature, History and Thought*. New York: Harper and Row, 1974.

Lewis, C.S. *English Literature in the Sixteenth Century, Excluding Drama*. Oxford: Clarendon, 1954.

God in the Dock: Essays on Theology and Ethics. Ed. Walter Hooper, Grand Rapids, MI: Eerdmans, 1970.

Surprised by Joy. London: Bles, 1955.

They Stand Together: Letters of C.S. Lewis to Arthur Greeves, 1914-63. Ed. Walter Hooper. London: Collins, 1979.

Locke, John. *An Essay Concerning Human Understanding*, 1690, 2 vols. Oxford: Clarendon, 1894.

Lønning, P. *The Sources and Depth of Faith in Kierkegaard*, Vol. II of *Biblioteca Kierkegaardiana*. Copenhagen: C.S. Rietzels Boghandel A/S. 1978.

McLeod, Hugh. *Class and Religion in the Late-Victorian City*. London: Croom Helm, 1974.

Macey, Samuel A. *Clocks and the Cosmos: Time in Western Life and Thought*. Hamden, CT: Archon Books, 1980.

Magnus, Rudolph. *Goethe as Scientist*, trans. Heinz Norden. New York: Collier, 1961.

Martin, David. *A Sociology of English Religion*. London: SCM Press, 1966.

Marucci, Franco. *Il foglie di Sibilla: retorica e medievalismo in Gerard Manley Hopkins*. Messina, Florence: G. d'Anna, 1980.

Marx, Karl and Friedrich Engles. *Contribution to a Critique of Hegel's Philosophy of Law* in *Works*, Vol. III. New York: International Publishers, 1975.

Messenger, Ruth Ellis. *Ethical Teachings in the Latin Hymns of Medieval England*. New York: Columbia University Press, 1930.

Milton, John. *Aeropagitica*, in *Complete Prose Works*, Vol. II. London: Oxford University Press, 1949.

Moody, Reynold. *Life after Life*. New York: Bantam, 1976.

Moule, C.F.D. *The Birth of the New Testament*, 2nd ed. London: A. & C. Black, 1966.

Newman, John Henry. *An Essay in Aid of the Grammar of Assent*. London: Burns, Oates, 1870.

The Mission of the Benedictine Order. 1858, rpt. London: Young, 1923.

Nietzsche, Friedrich. *The Birth of Tragedy*, trans. Francis Golffing. New York: Doubleday, 1956.

Nuelsen, John L., trans. Theo Parry, Sydney H. Moore, and Arthur Holbrook. *John Wesley and the German Hymn*. German text, 1938. Calverley: A.S. Holbrook, 1971.

Padover, Saul K. *Karl Marx: An Intimate Biography*. New York: New American Library, 1980.

Platt, J.B., ed. *The Forgotten Books of Eden*. World Publishing Co. Originally published 1926. Rpt., New York: Bell, 1980.

Rabkin, Eric S. *The Fantastic in Literature*. Princeton: Princeton University Press, 1976.

Raby, F.J.E. *A History of Christian-Latin Poetry*. 1927, 2nd ed. Oxford: Clarendon, 1953.

Rattenbury, J. Ernest. *The Evangelical Doctrines of Charles Wesley's Hymns*. London: Epworth Press, 1941.

Reeves, Marjorie. *The Figurae of Joachim of Fiore*. Oxford: Clarendon, 1972. *Joachim of Fiore and the Prophetic Future*. London: Society for the Promotion of Christian Knowledge, 1976.

Routley, Erik. *The English Carol*. London: Jenkins, 1958. *Hymns and Human Life*. 2nd ed. London: Murray, 1959.

Schücking, Levin C., trans. Brian Battershaw. *The Puritan Family* (1929). New York: Schocken Books, 1970.

Sizer, Sandra S. *Gospel Hymns and Social Religion: The Rhetoric of Nineteenth-Century Revivalism*. Philadelphia: Temple University Press, 1978.

Stannard, David, ed. *Death in America*. Philadelphia: Pennsylvania University Press, 1975. Essay of Douglas, Ann (*q.v.*).

Tamke, Susan. *Make a Joyful Noise unto the Lord: Hymns as a Reflection of Victorian Social Attitudes*. Columbus: Ohio University Press, 1978.

Taylor, Gordon Rattray. *The Angel-Makers: A Study in the Psychological Origins of Religious Change, 1750-1850*. London: Heinemann 1958, rev. ed. Secker and Warburg, 1973.

Tennyson, George B. *Victorian Devotional Poetry: The Tractarian Mode*. Cambridge: Harvard University Press, 1981.

Thompson, Edward Palmer. *The Making of the English Working Class*. New York: Pantheon Books, and London: Gallancz, 1964.

Tuchman, Barbara. *A Distant Mirror*. New York: Ballantine, 1978.

Underhill, Evelyn. *The Essentials of Mysticism*. New York: E.P. Dutton, 1960.

Wainwright, Geoffrey. *Doxology: The Praise of God in Worship, Doctrine and Life*. London: Epworth Press, 1980.

Weisler, Artur. *The Psalms*, trans. H. Hartwell. London: SCM Press, 1962.

Wellesz, Egon. *History of Byzantine Music and Hymnography*, 2nd ed. Oxford: Clarendon, 1961.

Werner, Eric. *The Sacred Bridge and the Interdependence of Liturgy and Music in the Synagogue and Church*. New York: Columbia University Press, 1959.

Wesley, John. *Works of John Wesley*, 14 vols. London: Methodist Conference, 1872, rpt. Grand Rapids: Zondervan, 1958-59.

West, Delmo C. (comp.). *Joachim of Fiore in Christian Thought*. 2 vols.. New York: Burt Franklin, 1975. (Bibliographies in Vol. I).

Wilkinson, Alan. *The Church of England and the First World War*. London: Society for the Promotion of Christian Knowledge, 1978.

Wingfield-Stratford, Esmé. *A History of British Civilization*. 2 vols. London: Routledge and Kegan Paul, 1928.

ARTICLES AND ESSAYS

Adey, Lionel. "John Henry Newman," in *Dictionary of Literary Biography*, Vol. XVIII (Victorian Novelists before 1885). Detroit: Gale Research, 1983. "Great-Aunt Tilly's Beautiful 'Ymns: A Victorian Religious Sub-Culture." *Wascana Review* XII, 1 (1977): 21-47

Arnold, Matthew. Preface. "The Study of Poetry," in T.H. Ward, *The English Poets*, 4 vols. (London, 1880) and rpt. in Arnold, *Essays in Criticism*, 2nd series (London:

Macmillan, 1888).

Augustine, Saint. "Ennarationes in Psalmos 72, 148" in *Corpus Christianorum Series Latina*. Tournai, 1956. Vols. XXXIX, XL.

Charlesworth, James Hamilton. "*The Odes of Solomon* — Not Gnostic." *Catholic Biblical Quarterly* XXXI, 3 (1969): 357-69.

Daniel, E.R. "Apocalyptic Conversion: The Joachite Alternative to the Crusades." See West (comp.) *Joachim of Fiore in Christian Thought*.

Dictionnaire de spiritualité. Tome VIII: "Joachim de Fiore." Paris, 1974.

Douglas, Ann. "Heaven our Home: Consolation-Literature in the United States, 1830-80" in Stannard, David (ed.). *Death in America (q.v.)*. Philadelphia: Pennsylvania University Press, 1975.

Drum, Walter. "Psalms of Solomon." *Catholic Encyclopedia* XIV. New York: Appleton, 1912.

Edwards, Jonathan. "Sinners in the Hands of an Angry God" (sermon delivered 1741) rpt. in *Jonathan Edwards: A Representative Selection . . .* Ed. Clarence H. Faust and Thomas H. Johnson. New York: Hill and Wong, 1935.

Fasham, E.J. "Rock of Ages." *Hymn Society of Great Britain and Ireland Bulletin* IV. (1957).

Gambold, John. Preface to *A Collection of Hymns of the Children of God*. London, 1754.

Gilmour, S. Maclean. "The Revelation to John" in the Interpreter's *One-Volume Commentary on the Bible*. Ed. Charles M. Layman. Nashville, TN: Abingdon Press, 1971, pp. 945-68.

Hannon, Elizabeth. "The Influence of *Paradise Lost* on the Hymns of Charles Wesley." Unpublished thesis, University of British Columbia, 1985.

Harris, J.R. "An Early Christian Hymn Book" *Contemporary Review,* 1909.

Hatfield, James Taft. "John Wesley's Translations of German Hymns." *Publications of Modern Language Association* XI (1896): 171-99.

Higginson, J.V. "John Mason Neale and Nineteenth-Century Hymnody," *The Hymn* 16 (1965): 101-17.

Lampe, G.W.H. "Modern Issues in Biblical Studies." *Expository Times* 71 (1970): 359-63.

Laughlin, M.F. "Joachim of Fiore," in *New Catholic Encyclopedia*. New York: McGraw-Hill, 1967, Vol. VII.

McCown, W. "The Hymnic Structure of Colossians 1: 15-20" *Evangelical Quarterly* 51 (1979): 156-62.

McGinn, B. "The Abbott and the Doctors: Scholastic Reactions to the Radical Eschatology of Joachim of Fiore." See Delno C. West (comp.), *Joachim of Fiore in Christian Thought*. Translated excerpt from Joachim's *Concordia Novi ac Veteris Testamenti*.

Martin, R.P. "New Testament Hymns: Background and Development." *Expository Times* 94 (1983): 132-36.

Newman, John Henry. *Parochial and Plain Sermons, Vol. VI, No. 6* in *John Henry Newman, Sermons and Discourses, 1839-57,* ed. C.F. Harrold. 2 vols. London: Longmans, 1849, Vol. I.

Preston, Ronald H. "The Book of Revelation of St. John the Divine" in *Twentieth Century Bible Commentary* (rev. ed.) Ed. G.H. Davis, A. Richardson, and C.L. Wallis. New York: Harper, 1955, pp. 513-18.

Runciman, Steven. "The Greek Church and the Peoples of Eastern Europe" in Geoffrey Barrraclough (ed.), *The Christian World: A Social and Cultural History of Christianity.* London: Thames and Hudson, 1981.

Sagan, Carl. "The Amniotic Universe" in *Broca's Brain.* New York: Random House, 1979.

Sampson, George. "A Century of Divine Songs." *Proceedings of the British Academy* *XXIX* (1943).

Sherwood, Terry G. "Tasting and Telling Sweetness In George Herbert's Poetry." *English Literary Renaissance* XII (1982): 319-40.

Smith, J.A. "The Ancient Synagogue, the Early Church and Singing." *Music and Letters* 65 (1984): 1-16.

Smith, Timothy L. "John Wesley and the Wholeness of Scriptures." *Interpretation* XXXIX (1985).

Tolkien, J.R.R. "On Fairy Stories" in *Essays Presented to Charles Williams* (comp.), ed. C.S. Lewis. 1947, rpt. Grand Rapids, MI: Eerdmans, 1966.

Wakefield, Gordon S. "Beliefs in Recent British Hymnody." *The Hymn*: XXII. (January, 1971): 13-19.

Watson, J.R. "Cowper's Olney Hymns." *Essays and Studies* XXXVIII (1985). 45-65.

Widdicombe, Gillian. "Tidings of Comfort and Joy." *The Observer*, 18 December 1983, p. 18.

NAME AND SUBJECT INDEX

INDEX OF HYMNS, CAROLS AND SACRED SONGS

(Further Hymns listed in pp. 230n5, 232-33n39-43)